HISTORICAL DICTIONARIES OF INTERNATIONAL ORGANIZATIONS
Jon Woronoff, Series Editor

Historical Dictionary of Human Rights and Humanitarian Organizations

Second Edition

Robert F. Gorman
Edward S. Mihalkanin

Historical Dictionaries of
International Organizations, No. 26

The Scarecrow Press, Inc.
Lanham, Maryland • Toronto • Plymouth, UK
2007

SCARECROW PRESS, INC.

Published in the United States of America
by Scarecrow Press, Inc.
A wholly owned subsidary of
The Rowman & Littlefield Publishing Group, Inc.
4501 Forbes Boulevard, Suite 200, Lanham, Maryland 20706
www.scarecrowpress.com

Estover Road
Plymouth PL6 7PY
United Kingdom

British Library Cataloguing in Publication Information Available

Library of Congress Cataloging-in-Publication Data

Gorman, Robert F.
  Historical dictionary of human rights and humanitarian organizations / Robert F.
Gorman, Edward S. Mihalkanin. — 2nd ed.
    p. cm. — (Historical dictionaries of international organizations ; no. 26)
  Includes bibliographical references.
  ISBN-13: 978-0-8108-5548-9 (alk. paper)
  ISBN-10: 0-8108-5548-8 (alk. paper)
    1. Human rights—Societies, etc.—Encyclopedias. 2. Humanitarian
assistance—Societies, etc.—Encyclopedias. I. Mihalkanin, Edward S. II. Title.

  JC571.G655 2007
  323.025—dc22

                                                                2006034016

Contents

Editor's Foreword

All too often, international organizations appear remote and abstract to ordinary people. In one area, that is definitely not the case: Those dealing with human rights and humanitarian aid are very close to the lives of every one of us. Certainly, they are most noticeable in extreme cases of violation of human rights or human and natural disasters. But you never know when or where the next crisis or disaster will break out. And for those who are not afflicted, the very existence of an increasingly thick network of such bodies and the heightened awareness they generate contribute to a safer and more stable world community.

Not surprisingly, many of these organizations are grassroots bodies, created by active and concerned individuals in the hope of helping others in need. It is these bodies that usually uncover the violations, publicize the problems, and then prod the larger intergovernmental organizations to act. Many of the initiatives come from ordinary people and not politicians, and much of the progress derives from the base and not the summit. Unfortunately, so much remains to be done that genuine achievements often appear inadequate and fragile in the face of continuing problems. And practice hardly ever lives up to the exalted principles and theories. Still, rather than despair at how much remains to be done, it is healthy on occasion to consider how much has been achieved over a relatively short period.

Historical Dictionary of Human Rights and Humanitarian Organizations is a precious contribution to any such review. It provides information on many (although obviously not all) of the organizations, private and governmental, national and international. These include activists at the grassroots level as well as more established bodies within the United Nations family. Reference is also made to the various goals and activities of these bodies and some individuals who have played outstanding roles. The introduction and certain entries present the goals and principles as well as the documents that enshrine them. The progress made in achieving goals can best be judged by following the course of important events. Further information on all aspects can be found in the books listed in a comprehensive bibliography.

This volume is coauthored by Robert F. Gorman and Edward S. Mihalkanin. Both are professors of political science at Texas State University. Dr. Gorman specializes in refugee questions, having previously worked as a refugee program officer for the U.S. Department of State. He has written *Historical Dictionary of Refugee and Disaster Relief Organizations* in this series, as well as *Mitigating Misery: An Inquiry into the Political and Humanitarian Aspects of U.S. and Global Refugee Policy* and other books and articles. Dr. Mihalkanin specializes in international relations, American foreign relations, and Third World politics, especially of Latin America. He is the author of *American Statesmen: Secretaries of State from John Jay to Colin Powell*.

Jon Woronoff
Series Editor

Preface

In the pages that follow, we sketch out for the user of this book the wide array of intergovernmental and nongovernmental organizations that are engaged in the global network of humanitarian and human rights work. Our efforts have been necessarily limited to those organizations and agencies most actively engaged in these endeavors. Our list of organizations, particularly in the nongovernmental sphere, is surely not exhaustive. We have also attempted to provide the reader with summaries of the chief humanitarian or human rights treaties and agreements, as well as prominent personages who historically advanced the practice, principles, and ideas of human rights and humanitarian aid. Since the 20th century movement toward strengthening human rights can be traced back to the antislavery and women's movements of the 19th century, we have seen fit to include important human rights figures from that period and even somewhat earlier.

Both authors wish to thank their students, with whom they have honed a sense of the importance of human rights over the years as well as a sense of hope concerning the fruitfulness of the enterprise. Ed Mihalkanin wishes to express particular thanks to Orlando Carter and J. P. Hymes for their research assistance.

Acronyms and Abbreviations

ADF	America's Development Foundation
ADRA	Adventist Development and Relief Agency International
AI	Amnesty International
AJWS	American Jewish World Service
AMIS	African Union Mission in Sudan
ANC	African National Congress
APRODEV	Association of Protestant Development Organizations in Europe
APT	Association for the Prevention of Torture
ASEAN	Association of Southeast Asian Nations
AU	African Union
CAP	Consolidated Appeals Process
CARE	Cooperative for Assistance and Relief Everywhere
CAT	Committee against Torture
CATW	Coalition against Trafficking in Women
CCF	Christian Children's Fund
CEC	Conference of European Churches
CEDAW	Committee on the Elimination of Discrimination against Women
CERD	Committee on the Elimination of Racial Discrimination
CERF	Central Emergency Revolving Fund
CESCR	Committee on Economic, Social, and Cultural Rights
CFA	Committee on Food Aid
CHR	Commission on Human Rights
CI	Caritas Internationalis
CIDSE	International Cooperation for Development and Solidarity

CIREFCA	International Conference on Central American Refugees
CLONGD-EU	Liaison Committee of Nongovernmental Development Organizations to the European Union
CMW	Committee on Migrant Workers
COE	Council of Europe
COHRE	Centre for Housing Rights and Evictions
CRC	Committee on the Rights of the Child
CSCE	Conference on Security and Cooperation in Europe
DATA	Debt, AIDS, and Trade in Africa
DHA	Department of Humanitarian Affairs
DRC	Democratic Republic of the Congo
EC	European Communities
ECHO	European Community Humanitarian Office
ECHR	European Court of Human Rights
ECOSOC	Economic and Social Council
ECOWAS	Economic Community of West African States
ENHR	European Network for Housing Research
ERC	Emergency Relief Coordinator
EU	European Union
EUROSTEP	European Solidarity towards Equal Treatment of People
FAO	Food and Agriculture Organization
FEDEFAM	Fighting against Forced Disappearances in Latin America
FFH	Food for the Hungry
FIAN	FoodFirst Information and Action Network
FIDH	Fédération Internationale des Droits de l'Homme/ International Federation of Human Rights
GATT	General Agreement on Tariffs and Trade
GIST	Geographic Information Support Teams
HABITAT	United Nations Conference on Human Settlements
HAI	HelpAge International
HIAS	Hebrew Immigrant Aid Society
HRC	Human Rights Committee
HRF	Human Rights First
HRFT	Human Rights Foundation of Turkey

HRIC	Human Rights in China
IACHR	Inter-American Commission on Human Rights
IACT	Inter-American Court of Human Rights
IADL	International Association of Democratic Lawyers
IASC	Interagency Standing Committee
IAW	International Alliance of Women
IBA	International Bar Association
IBRD	International Bank for Reconstruction and Development
ICAO	International Civil Aviation Organization
ICARA I	First International Conference on Assistance to Refugees in Africa
ICARA II	Second International Conference on Assistance to Refugees in Africa
ICC	International Criminal Court
ICEM	Intergovernmental Committee for European Migration
ICFTU	International Confederation of Free Trade Unions
ICHRP	International Council on Human Rights Policy
ICJ	International Court of Justice
ICM	Intergovernmental Committee for Migration
ICMC	International Catholic Migration Commission
ICRC	International Committee of the Red Cross
ICTR	International Criminal Tribunal for Rwanda
ICTY	International Criminal Tribunal for the Former Yugoslavia
ICVA	International Council of Voluntary Agencies
ICW	International Council of Women
IDA	International Development Association
IFAD	International Fund for Agricultural Development
IFC	International Finance Corporation
IFRC	International Federation of Red Cross and Red Crescent Societies
IGCR	Intergovernmental Committee for Refugees
IIHL	International Institute of Humanitarian Law
ILO	International Labour Organization
IMC	International Medical Corps

IMF	International Monetary Fund
INSARAG	International Search and Rescue Advisory Group
INSTRAW	International Research and Training Institute for the Advancement of Women
IOM	International Organization for Migration
IPU	Inter-Parliamentary Union
IRC	International Rescue Committee
IRO	International Refugee Organization
ISHR	International Society for Human Rights
IWPR	Institute of War and Peace Reporting
LCHR	Lawyers Committee for Human Rights
LICROSS	League of Red Cross and Red Crescent Societies
LWF	Lutheran World Federation
LWR	Lutheran World Relief
MIGA	Multilateral Investment Guarantee Agency
MINUSTAH	United Nations Stabilization Mission in Haiti
MONUA	United Nations Observer Mission in Angola
MONUC	United Nations Organization Mission in the Democratic Republic of the Congo
MOSOP	Movement for the Survival of the Ogoni People
MRG	Minority Rights Group International
MRI	Migrants Rights International
MSF	Médecins sans Frontières/Doctors without Borders
MWL	Muslim World League
NAACP	National Association for the Advancement of Colored People
NATO	North Atlantic Treaty Organization
NGOs	Nongovernmental Organizations
NLD	National League for Democracy
OAS	Organization of American States
OAU	Organization of African Unity
OCCDP	Canadian Catholic Agency for Development and Peace
OCHA	Office for Coordination of Humanitarian Affairs
OECD	Organization for Economic Cooperation and Development
OMCT	World Organization Against Torture
ONUB	United Nations Operation in Burundi

ONUC	United Nations Operation in the Congo
ONUMOZ	United Nations Operation in Mozambique
ONUSAL	United Nations Observer Mission in El Salvador
OSCE	Organization for Security and Cooperation in Europe
OXFAM	Oxford Committee for Famine Relief
PAC	Pan-Africanist Congress
PCIJ	Permanent Court of International Justice
PHR	Physicians for Human Rights
PLO	Palestine Liberation Organization
QIPs	Quick Impact Projects
RUF	Revolutionary United Front
SACC	South African Council of Churches
SADC	Southern Africa Development Community
SAHRDC	South Asia Human Rights Documentation Centre
SARRED	Southern Africa Refugees, Returnees, and Displaced Persons Conference
SASO	South African Students Organization
SAWSO	Salvation Army World Service Office
SCA	Save the Children Alliance
SCF	Save the Children Federation
SHAEF	Supreme Headquarters of the Allied Expeditionary Force
TRC	Truth and Reconciliation Commission
UN	United Nations
UNAMET	United Nations Mission in East Timor
UNAMIC	United Nations Advance Mission in Cambodia
UNAMSIL	United Nations Mission in Sierra Leone
UNAVEM	United Nations Angola Verification Mission
UNCED	United Nations Conference on Environment and Development
UNDAC	United Nations Disaster Assessment and Coordination
UNDP	United Nations Development Programme
UNDRO	United Nations Disaster Relief Organization
UNEP	United Nations Environment Programme
UNESCO	United Nations Educational, Scientific, and Cultural Organization
UNFICYP	United Nations Forces in Cyprus

UNFPA	United Nations Fund for Population Activities
UNHCHR	United Nations High Commissioner for Human Rights
UNHCR	United Nations High Commissioner for Refugees
UNICEF	United Nations Children's Fund
UNIFEM	United Nations Development Fund for Women
UNITA	National Union for the Total Independence of Angola
UNITAF	Unified Task Force
UNITAR	United Nations Institute for Training and Research
UNMIH	United Nations Mission in Haiti
UNMIK	United Nations Interim Administration Mission in Kosovo
UNMIL	United Nations Mission in Liberia
UNMIS	United Nations Mission in Sudan
UNOCA	United Nations Coordinator for Humanitarian and Economic Assistance Programs Relating to Afghanistan
UNOCHA	United Nations Office for Coordination of Humanitarian Affairs
UNOMIL	United Nations Observer Mission in Liberia
UNOMSIL	United Nations Observer Mission in Sierra Leone
UNOSOM	United Nations Operation in Somalia
UNPAAERD	United Nations Program of Action for African Economic Recovery and Development
UNPROFOR	United Nations Protection Force
UNRISD	United Nations Research Institute for Social Development
UNRRA	United Nations Relief and Rehabilitation Administration
UNRWA	United Nations Relief and Works Agency for Palestine
UNSMA	United Nations Special Mission in Afghanistan
UNTAC	United Nations Transitional Authority in Cambodia
UNTAET	United Nations Transitional Administration in East Timor
UNU	United Nations University
UNWCC	United Nations War Crimes Commission

USCRI	U.S. Committee for Refugees and Immigrants
VOICE	Voluntary Organisations in Cooperation in Emergencies
WARC	World Alliance of Reformed Churches
WCC	World Council of Churches
WCIP	World Council of Indigenous Peoples
WCL	World Confederation of Labor
WFP	World Food Programme
WFTU	World Federation of Trade Unions
WHO	World Health Organization
WILPF	Women's International League for Peace and Freedom
WR	World Relief
YMCA	Young Men's Christian Association
YWCA	Young Women's Christian Association

Chronology

1824 Britain begins interdiction of the slave trade.

1863 U.S. President Abraham Lincoln issues the Emancipation Proclamation.

1864 The Red Cross is founded.

1893 New Zealand becomes the first country to recognize women's suffrage.

1899 The first Hague Peace Conference is held to revise laws of war.

1903 Emmeline Pankhurst founds the Woman's Social and Political Union.

1906 Finland becomes the first European country to grant woman's suffrage.

1907 The Hague Convention on the Laws of War is adopted.

1912–1914 Balkan Wars lead to significant refugee flows.

1914–1918 World War I and aftermath displace millions.

1915 Poison gas used for first time during World War I by German forces on the Western Front. Armenia experiences genocide.

1917 Russian revolution precipitates flight of hundreds of thousands, stimulates Red Terror and numerous summary killings.

1918–1921 Red Cross responds to Russian refugee situation.

1919 League of Nations is established. Constitution of the International Labour Organization (ILO) is adopted.

1920 League of Nations and the International Labour Organization (ILO) officially commence. Palmer Raids in the United States lead to arrest and deportation of thousands of immigrants and radicals. League of Woman Voters is established. Nineteenth Amendment to the U.S. Constitution gives women the right to vote.

1921 Armenian/Greek refugee problem begins. Assyro-Chaldean, Assyrian, and Turkish refugee situations emerge with breakup of Ottoman Empire. **September:** League of Nations High Commissioner for Russian Refugees is established. **November:** International Labour Organization (ILO) Right of Association Convention is adopted. Famine assistance begins to Russia.

1922 Nansen passports for stateless persons initiated.

1923 Bulgarian refugee situation erupts.

1925 **June:** Protocol for the Prohibition of the Use in War of Asphyxiating, Poisonous or Other Gases, or of Bacteriological Methods of Warfare is adopted.

1926 Indian women given right to run for elective office. **September:** Convention to Suppress Slave Trade and Slavery signed in Geneva.

1927 International Relief Union is established.

1929 League of Nations replaces High Commissioner for Russian Refugees with Nansen International Office.

1930 Convention on Conflicts of Nationality Laws signed at The Hague. International Labour Organization (ILO) Forced Labor Convention adopted.

1932 La Matanza (massacre) occurs in El Salvador revolt.

1933 Concentration camps go into operation in Nazi Germany.

1934 Stalin-era purges of political opponents commence.

1936 South America's first fascist regime assumes power in Paraguay.

1937 Japan captures Nanjing, exposes population to brutalities. Spanish civil war begins, produces refugees and international concern.

1938 Nansen International Office is terminated. League of Nations High Commissioner for Refugees is established. Autonomous Office of

High Commissioner for Refugees Coming from Germany is established. International Conference on Refugees at Evians-les-Bains is held, leads to creation of Intergovernmental Committee for Refugees (IGCR).

1939 World War II breaks out in Europe, leading to six years of devastation and bloodshed, the brutalities of the Holocaust, the widespread violation of the laws of war, and the introduction of vastly destructive weaponry.

1941 August: Atlantic Charter is adopted.

1942 January: Declaration by the United Nations is adopted. Ethiopia outlaws slavery.

1943 United Nations Relief and Rehabilitation Administration (UNRRA) is formed to deal with persons displaced by war. Food and Agriculture Organization (FAO) is formed. **October:** United Nations War Crimes Commission is established in London, prepares groundwork for Nuremburg Trials.

1945 Charter of the International Military Tribunal (Nuremburg Tribunal) is established to try war crimes, crimes against peace, and crimes against humanity; superior orders defense plea is rejected. International Military Tribunal for the Far East established. **June:** United Nations Charter is signed. **August:** World War II comes to an end with atomic bombings of Hiroshima and Nagasaki; Japanese surrender in the Pacific ending years of carnage. **November:** United Nations Educational, Scientific, and Cultural Organization (UNESCO) is established. **December:** World Bank (International Bank for Reconstruction and Development [IBRD]) and the International Monetary Fund (IMF) are established.

1946 July: World Health Organization (WHO) is established. **October:** London Convention on travel permits for the benefit of refugees is signed. **December:** United Nations International Children's Emergency Fund (UNICEF) is established.

1947 United Nations Relief and Rehabilitation Administration (UNRRA) and Intergovernmental Committee for Refugees (IGCR) functions consolidated into the International Refugee Organization (IRO). Indo-Pakistani partition leads to massive refugee flows.

1948   Israel is established as a Jewish homeland; first Arab/Israeli conflict produces hundreds of thousands of Palestinian refugees. Indian government bans discrimination against Untouchables. **April:** Organization of American States (OAS) Charter is adopted. **May:** Inter-American Charter of Social Guarantees is adopted. Inter-American Convention on the Granting of Political Rights to Women is adopted. American Declaration of the Rights and Duties of Man adopted by the ninth Pan-American Conference. **July:** Revised International Labour Organization (ILO) Night Work (Women) Convention is adopted. **December:** United Nations Relief for Palestinian Refugees (UNRPR) is established. Genocide Convention is adopted. Universal Declaration of Human Rights passed by United Nations General Assembly. Berlin blockade, crisis, and airlift lead to deepening of Cold War; refugees from Eastern Europe seek asylum in the West.

1949   Chinese refugees flee communist victory on mainland, establish the Republic of China on Taiwan. **May:** Council of Europe Statute is adopted. **July:** Revised International Labour Organization (ILO) Migration for Employment Convention is adopted. ILO Protection of Wages Convention is adopted. ILO Right to Organize and Collective Bargaining Convention is adopted. **August:** Geneva Red Cross Conventions Relative to the Treatment of Prisoners of War and to the Protection of Civilian Persons in Time of War are adopted. **December:** Convention for the Suppression of the Traffic in Persons and of the Exploitation of the Prostitution of United Nations Relief and Works Agency for Palestine (UNWRA) replaces United Nations Relief for Palestinian Refugees (UNRPR) to deal with Palestinian refugees.

1950   Korean War breaks out; United Nations intervenes. China occupies Tibet. United Nations Korean Reconstruction Agency is established as a temporary means of coordinating relief and reconstruction in war-torn Korea. **November:** European Convention on Human Rights is adopted, enters into force in 1953. **December:** United Nations High Commissioner for Refugees (UNHCR) is established by the United Nations General Assembly.

1951   **January:** United Nations High Commissioner for Refugees (UNHCR) commences operations, replacing International Refugee Organization (IRO). **June:** International Labour Organization (ILO) Equal Remuneration Convention is adopted. **July:** United Nations Convention

Relating to the Status of Refugees is adopted. **December:** Brussels Conference on Migration establishes the Provisional Intergovernmental Committee for the Movement of Migrants from Europe (PICMME).

1952 March: Protocol I of the European Convention on Human Rights is adopted. **June:** Revised International Labour Organization (ILO) Maternity Protection Convention is adopted. ILO Social Security Convention is concluded. **September:** Universal Copyright Convention (revised with protocols) is adopted. **November:** The Intergovernmental Committee for European Migration (ICEM) is established.

1953 United Nations General Assembly extends United Nations High Commissioner for Refugees (UNHCR) mandate from three to five years. **October:** Protocol Amending the Slavery Convention of 1926 is adopted.

1954 United Nations General Assembly authorizes the United Nations High Commissioner for Refugees (UNHCR) to establish a Program of Permanent Solutions. One million Dien Bien Phu–era refugees resettled in Southeast Asia. Algerian civil war breaks out; over two million are uprooted prior to independence in 1962. **March:** Inter-American Conventions on Diplomatic and Territorial Asylum are adopted. **May:** United Nations Educational, Scientific, and Cultural Organization (UNESCO) Convention for the Protection of Cultural Property in the Event of Armed Conflict is adopted. **September:** Convention Relating to the Status of Stateless Persons is adopted.

1955 Civil war in Sudan leads to flight of thousands of refugees. United Nations High Commissioner for Refugees (UNHCR) receives its first Nobel Peace Prize. **August:** Standard Minimum Rules for the Treatment of Prisoners is adopted. **December:** Supplementary Convention on the Abolition of Slavery, the Slave Trade, and Institutions and Practices Similar to Slavery is adopted.

1956 Hungarian revolt begins, Soviet intervention and refugee flows occur; United Nations High Commissioner for Refugees (UNHCR), Intergovernmental Committee for European Migration (ICEM), and International Committee of the Red Cross (ICRC) respond to humanitarian crisis.

1957 January: Convention on the Nationality of Married Women is adopted. **June:** International Labour Organization (ILO) Abolition of

Forced Labor Convention is adopted. **December:** European Agreement on Regulations Governing the Movement of Persons between Member States of the Council of Europe and the European Convention on Extradition are adopted.

1958 **April:** Convention on the High Seas is adopted. **June:** International Labour Organization (ILO) Discrimination Convention is adopted.

1959 Chinese invasion of Tibet precipitates refugee flows. Inter-American Commission on Human Rights (IACHR) is established. United Nations General Assembly authorizes United Nations High Commissioner for Refugees (UNHCR) to assist Chinese refugees in Hong Kong. **November:** Declaration on the Rights of the Child is adopted. Victory of Fidel Castro forces in Cuba leads to refugee flows. Tutsi refugees flee from persecution in Rwanda.

1960 World Bank divided into three institutions—International Bank for Reconstruction and Development (IBRD), International Development Association (IDA), and International Finance Corporation (IFC)—and begins to focus more on long-term development in developing countries. **December:** United Nations Educational, Scientific, and Cultural Organization (UNESCO) Convention against Discrimination in Education is adopted. Declaration on the Granting of Independence to Colonial Countries and Peoples is adopted. Congo crisis precipitates Western intervention to protect foreign nationals, leads to refugee flows and substantial internal displacement; United Nations Operation in the Congo (ONUC) forces deployed by United Nations.

1961 Berlin Wall is constructed. Adolph Eichmann is tried by Israel for war crimes. Amnesty International is founded. War of independence leads to refugee flows into the Congo. Western governments establish the Organization for Economic Cooperation and Development (OECD) to enhance aid cooperation. The World Food Programme (WFP) is established by joint United Nations General Assembly and Food and Agriculture Organization (FAO) resolutions; commences operations in 1963. **August:** Convention on the Reduction of Statelessness is adopted. **October:** European Social Charter is adopted.

1962 Year of crisis in flight of Chinese refugees to Hong Kong. **June:** International Labour Organization (ILO) Conventions on Social Policy and on Equality of Treatment in Social Security are adopted. **November:** Convention on Consent to Marriage, Minimum Age for Marriage, and Registration of Marriages is adopted. **December:** United Nations Educational, Scientific, and Cultural Organization (UNESCO) Declaration on Permanent Sovereignty over Natural Resources adopted.

1963 Martin Luther King Jr. delivers "I Have a Dream" speech. **May:** Protocols II, III, and IV of the European Convention on Human Rights are adopted. Organization of African Unity (OAU) is formed. **November:** Declaration on the Elimination of All Forms of Racial Discrimination is adopted.

1964 U.S. Civil Rights Act is passed by Congress. **March:** United Nations Forces in Cyprus (UNFICYP) deployed to Cyprus to restore order and promote delivery of relief supplies. **April:** European Code on Social Security and Protocol are adopted. **July:** International Labour Organization (ILO) Employment Policy Convention is adopted. **October:** Cairo Declaration: Program for Peace and International Cooperation adopted.

1965 Indonesian crackdown on communists leads to many deaths. **November:** Inter-American Declaration on Racial Integration in the Americas adopted. **December:** International Convention on the Elimination of All Forms of Racial Discrimination is adopted. Hutu refugees flee from persecution in Burundi.

1966 War for independence in Mozambique leads to refugee flows. **January:** Protocol V of the European Convention on Human Rights is approved. **November:** United Nations Educational, Scientific, and Cultural Organization (UNESCO) Declaration on the Principles of International Cultural Cooperation is adopted. **December:** The International Covenant on Civil and Political Rights and the International Covenant on Economic, Social, and Cultural Rights are adopted by the United Nations General Assembly. Biafran civil war in Nigeria leads to flight or displacement of millions and prolonged humanitarian crisis.

1967 Conference on the Legal, Economic, and Social Aspects of African Refugee Problems is held in Addis Ababa. Association of Southeast Asian Nations (ASEAN) is formed. Tens of thousands of Eritrean refugees flee into Sudan from civil conflict in Ethiopia. **April:** European Convention on the Adoption of Children is adopted. **November:** Declaration on the Elimination of All Forms of Discrimination against Women is adopted. **December:** Declaration on Territorial Asylum is issued.

1968   May: Proclamation of Teheran Human Rights Conference reaffirms principles of the Universal Declaration of Human Rights. **November:** Convention on the Nonapplicability of Statutory Limitations to War Crimes and Crimes against Humanity is adopted.

1969   **United Nations Fund for Population Activities (UNFPA) is established. **May: European Agreement Relating to Persons Participating in Proceedings of the European Commission and Court of Human Rights is adopted. **June:** International Labour Organization (ILO) Medical Care and Sickness Benefits Convention is adopted. **September:** Organization of African Unity (OAU) Convention Governing the Specific Aspects of Refugee Problems in Africa is adopted, incorporates a broader refugee definition. **November:** Inter-American Convention on Human Rights is adopted, enters into force in 1978. **December:** Declaration on Social Progress and Development is adopted.

1970   **Lt. William L. Calley is court-martialed for My Lai massacre. The Moscow Human Rights Committee is founded, excites repression from Soviet government. **May: European Convention on the Repatriation of Minors is adopted. **June:** International Labour Organization (ILO) Conventions on Minimum Wage Fixing and on Holidays with Pay are adopted. **October:** Declaration on the Occasion of the 25th Anniversary of the United Nations is adopted. **December:** Basic Principles for the Protection of Civilian Populations in Armed Conflicts is adopted. Convention for the Suppression of Unlawful Seizure of Aircraft is adopted by the International Civil Aviation Organization (ICAO) at The Hague.

1971   **United Nations Development Programme (UNDP) is established. United Nations Disaster Relief Organization (UNDRO) is established. Ten million Bengali refugees flee to India during the Indo-Pakistani War. **September: Convention for the Suppression of Unlawful Acts against the Safety of Civil Aviation is adopted at Montreal.

1972   **Ethnic violence in Burundi leads to refugee flows. Macias Nguema assumes presidency for life in Equatorial Guinea, commences a reign of terror until his overthrow in 1979. Sahelian drought brings famine emergency to Africa. **June: Declaration of the United Nations

Conference on the Human Environment is proclaimed at Stockholm; United Nations Environment Programme (UNEP) is established. **December:** European Convention on Social Security is adopted.

1973 Military takes over in Chile, Salvador Allende overthrown and killed. Military takes control of Uruguay; repression follows. **June:** International Labour Organization (ILO) Minimum Age Convention is adopted. **November:** International Convention on the Suppression and Punishment of the Crime of Apartheid is adopted. **December:** Convention on the Prevention and Punishment of Crimes Against Internationally Protected Persons, Including Diplomatic Agents is adopted.

1974 Aleksander Solzhenitsyn is expelled from Soviet Union and has citizenship stripped. Cyprus dispute leads to displaced persons crisis; United Nations High Commissioner for Refugees (UNHCR), Red Cross, World Food Programme (WFP), and UN peacekeeping forces respond with aid. Angolan civil war commences upon Portuguese withdrawal; refugee flows result, which last for two decades. **June:** International Labour Organization (ILO) Paid Educational Leave Convention is adopted. **November:** Universal Declaration on the Eradication of Hunger and Malnutrition is adopted. United Nations Educational, Scientific, and Cultural Organization (UNESCO) Recommendation Concerning Education for International Understanding, Cooperation and Peace, and Education Relating to Human Rights and Fundamental Freedoms is adopted. **December:** Declaration on the Protection of Women and Children in Emergency and Armed Conflict is adopted. World Food Council is created by the United Nations General Assembly.

1975 Repression by Indonesian government deepens in East Timor. Western Sahara dispute produces refugee flow into Algeria. Repression in Malawi produces refugees. Khmer Rouge takeover in Cambodia leads to egregious human rights abuses and policies of genocide. Soviet dissident Andrei Sakharov is awarded the Nobel Peace Prize. Indochinese boat people exodus begins. Rhodesian civil war leads to increase in violence and refugee flows. **June:** International Labour Organization (ILO) Conventions on Human Resources Development, Rural Workers' Organizations, and on Migrant Workers are adopted. **July:** Declaration of Mexico on the Equality of Women is proclaimed. **August:** Helsinki Accord: Final Act of the Conference on Security and Cooperation in Europe is concluded. **October:** European Convention on Extradition and the European Agreement on the Legal Status of Children Born Out of Wedlock are adopted. **December:** Declaration on the Protection of All Persons from Being Subjected to Torture and Other Cruel, Inhuman, or Degrading Treatment or Punishment is adopted. Declaration on the Rights of Disabled Persons is adopted.

1976 Lebanese civil war begins; United Nations High Commissioner for Refugees (UNHCR) entrusted with coordination of relief assistance. Military government of Argentina begins the "dirty war" against leftists; thousands killed. Soweto riots break out in South Africa. **June:** Vancouver Declaration on Human Settlements is proclaimed. **July:** Declaration of Abidjan calls for an end to apartheid, racial discrimination, colonialism, injustice, and inequality in Africa and the developing world. Asia's deadliest earthquake kills more than 240,000 in China's Tangshan Province; China's communist government responds to disaster without international assistance. **November:** United Nations Educational, Scientific, and Cultural Organization (UNESCO) Recommendations on the Development of Adult Education and Its Recommendation on Participation by the People at Large in Cultural Life are adopted.

1977 Shaba conflict in Zaïre precipitates flow of 200,000 refugees. Stephen Biko is murdered by his interrogators while in prison in South Africa. International Fund for Agricultural Development (IFAD) is established. Amnesty International is awarded Nobel Peace Prize. Soviet Union cracks down on Helsinki Watch Group. Equatorial Guinea refugees flee into Gabon and Cameroon. **January:** European Convention on the Suppression of Terrorism is adopted. **June:** Geneva Conventions, Protocols I and II, are adopted, call for protection of victims of international armed conflicts and for victims of noninternational armed conflicts. International Labour Organization (ILO) Working Environment Convention is adopted. **August:** Lagos Declaration against Apartheid is adopted. **September:** Declaration on the Rights of Deaf-Blind Persons is adopted. **November:** European Convention on the Legal Status of Migrant Workers is adopted. **December:** International Declaration against Apartheid in Sports is adopted.

1978 June: International Labour Organization (ILO) Labor Relations Convention is adopted. **September:** United Nations Educational, Scientific, and Cultural Organization (UNESCO) Declaration on Race and Racial Prejudice is adopted.

1979   Indochinese boat people crisis reaches its height. Repression and war in Nicaragua causes refugee flows into Honduras, Costa Rica, and Panama; Sandinista victory leads to flight of former government supporters. Civil war in El Salvador begins more than a decade of human rights abuses, forced migration, and displacement. Mariel boat lift of Cuban refugees leads to intensified flow of asylum seekers into the United States. Brutal regime of Idi Amin takes power in Uganda; Ugandan refugees flee into Zaïre and Sudan. Refugees flee from Ethiopia to Somalia. **May:** Arusha Conference convenes to discuss African refugee situation. **July:** International Conference on Refugees and Displaced Persons in Southeast Asia convenes. **December:** Soviet Union invades Afghanistan intensifying refugee flows into Pakistan and Iran; stiff, ultimately successful resistance to intervention commences. United Nations General Assembly adopts the Code of Conduct for Law Enforcement Officials. International Convention against the Taking of Hostages is adopted. Convention on the Elimination of All Forms of Discrimination against Women is adopted.

1980   Guatemalan government undertakes violent campaign against its indigenous Indian population. Solidarity Union leads strikes in Poland, demanding reforms. Chadian civil war leads to refugee flows. Lusaka Declaration establishes the Southern African Development Coordination Conference, later known as the Southern Africa Development Community (SADC). The International Research and Training Institute for the Advancement of Women (INSTRAW) is established. **May:** European Convention on the Custody of Children is adopted.

1981   United Nations High Commissioner for Refugees (UNHCR) receives its second Nobel Peace Prize. **February:** Inter-American Convention on Extradition is adopted. **April:** First International Conference on Assistance to Refugees in Africa is held in Geneva. Convention on Prohibitions or Restrictions on the Use of Certain Conventional Weapons Which May Be Deemed Excessively Injurious or to Have Indiscriminate Effects is adopted with protocols. **June:** International Labour Organization (ILO) Conventions on Collective Bargaining, Occupation Safety and Health, and Workers with Family Responsibilities are adopted. African Charter on Human and Peoples' Rights is adopted. **November:** Declaration on the Elimination of All Forms of Intolerance and of Discrimination Based on Religion or Belief is adopted. **December:** United Nations Declarations on the Inadmissibility of Intervention and Interference in the Internal Affairs of States, and on Prevention of Nuclear Catastrophe are adopted.

1982 Hundreds of Palestinian civilians are killed in raids on refugee camps in West Beirut. Civil war, human rights abuses in Guatemala lead to refugee flows. Canada adopts a new Constitution and Charter of Rights. **January:** European Recommendation Concerning International Cooperation in the Prosecution and Punishment of Terrorism is adopted. **April:** European Declaration on Freedom of Expression and Information. **December:** Declaration on the Participation of Women in Promoting International Peace and Cooperation.

1983 Klaus Barbie faces charges for Nazi war crimes in France. **April:** Protocol VI of the European Convention on Human Rights is adopted. **August:** Declaration of the Second World Conference to Combat Racism and Racial Discrimination is adopted. **September:** Geneva Declaration on Palestine is proclaimed.

1984 Drought and famine spread through much of Africa; United Nations creates the Office for Emergency Operations in Africa to coordinate international assistance. **May:** Convention on International Civil Aircraft is adopted. Inter-American Convention on Conflict of Laws Concerning the Adoption of Minors is adopted. Safeguards Guaranteeing the Protection of the Rights of Those Facing the Death Penalty is adopted. **June:** United Nations General Assembly and Economic and Social Council (ECOSOC) Nairobi Forward-looking Strategies for the Advancement of Women are adopted. **November:** Declaration on the Right of Peoples to Peace is adopted. Protocol VII of the European Convention on Human Rights is adopted. **December:** Convention against Torture and Other Cruel, Inhuman, or Degrading Treatment or Punishment is adopted. Declaration on the Control of Drug Trafficking and Drug Abuse is adopted.

1985 Argentine government leaders are convicted of human rights abuses. Mikhail Gorbachev initiates glasnost (openness) policy in Soviet Union. Civil war in southern Sudan recurs; refugees flee to Ethiopia. Civil conflict in Sri Lanka causes significant refugee flows. Mozambique's civil war intensifies; refugee flows commence. Civil war and famine in Ethiopia precipitate massive refugee and displaced person flows; Ethiopian resettlement of displaced persons attracts international criticism. **March:** Protocol VIII of the European Convention on Human Rights is adopted. **July:** Live Aid concert is organized by Bob Geldof and Midge Ure and held at Wembley Stadium in London, JFK Stadium in Philadelphia, with other performances in Sydney, Australia, and in Moscow, connected by satellite link-ups and TV broadcasts, in an unprecedented humanitarian aid fundraiser that attracted 1.5 billion viewers in 100 countries, raising about $250 million in famine relief. **November:** Declaration of Basic Principles for Victims of Crime and Abuse of Power is adopted. **December:** Inter-American Convention to Prevent and Punish Torture is adopted. International Convention against Apartheid in Sports is adopted. Declaration on the Human Rights of Individuals Who Are Not Nationals of the Country in Which They Live is adopted.

1986 Muslim anti-Russian sentiment leads to riots in Kazakhstan. **December:** Declaration on the Right to Development is adopted.

1987 Jean-Bedel Bokassa, former ruler of the Central African Republic, convicted of human rights abuses. Palestinian *intifada* (uprising) begins in Israeli-occupied territories. **June:** European Convention for the Prevention of Torture and Inhuman or Degrading Treatment or Punishment is adopted. **November:** European Social Charter Protocol is approved.

1988 Fifty thousand Kurdish refugees flee into Iran, escaping Iraqi military actions and use of poison gas. U.S. Congress apologizes to Japanese World War II internees; pays compensation to survivors. Civil war deepens in southern Sudan, tens of thousands starve. **March:** Khartoum Declaration is adopted by the International Conference on the Human Dimension of Africa's Economic Recovery and Development. **August:** Southern Africa Refugees, Returnees, and Displaced Persons Conference (SARRED) is held in Oslo. **November:** American Convention on Human Rights, Additional Protocol with Regard to Economic, Social, and Cultural Rights is adopted. **December:** Body of Principles for the Protection of All Persons under Any Form of Detention or Imprisonment is adopted. Armenian earthquake levels cities, killing tens of thousands and leaving half a million people homeless; United Nations estimates damage at about $14 million, as international aid workers respond.

1989 Mass demonstrations held in Tienanmen Square, Chinese government eventually calls on military to suppress them. Kenyan government represses dissent. Berlin Wall is torn down as Germany moves toward reunification. **April:** United Nations Transitional Authority in Cambodia (UNTAC) operation paves way for repatriation of Namibian refugees and movement toward Namibian independence. **May:** International Conference on Central American Refugees is held in Guatemala to discuss development impacts of refugees and displaced persons. **June:** International Labour Organization (ILO) Indigenous and Tribal Peoples Convention is adopted. **August:** Tallinin Guidelines for Action on Human Resources Development in the Field of Disability are adopted. **November:** International Convention on the Rights of the Child is adopted by the United Nations General Assembly. United Nations Security Council authorizes deployment of force to provide security in Central America and to demobilize and repatriate Contras. **December:** Second Optional Protocol to the International Covenant on Civil and Political Rights, Aiming at Abolition of the Death Penalty is adopted.

1990 Refugee flows from East Germany help to precipitate fall of communism in Europe and the reunification of Germany. Liberian civil war leads to humanitarian emergency; West African states intervene as refugees flee to neighboring states. Nelson Mandela is freed from prison in South Africa, heralding political reforms. **June:** Major earthquake devastates two provinces in northwestern Iran, killing 40,000, injuring 60,000, and leaving more than 105,000 families homeless; large amounts of international aid were made and international disaster teams fielded, but the Iranian government orders the departure of foreign disaster workers after a week. **August:** Persian Gulf Crisis erupts as Iraq invades Kuwait, displaces millions, and later provokes United Nations to authorize use of force to restore Kuwaiti independence. **September:** World Summit for Children is held in New York, adopts the World Declaration on the Survival, Protection, and Development of Children and a Plan of Action. **December:** United Nations General Assembly unanimously adopts the International Convention on the Protection of the Rights of All Migrant Workers and Members of Their Families.

1991 Somali civil war leads to downfall of Siad Barre government; hundreds of thousands of Somali refugees flee insecurity and famine during the next two years. Iraq evicted from Kuwait by United Nations Coalition; International Community steps in to avert Kurdish refugee crisis; Operation Provide Comfort is initiated by United States, United Kingdom, and France; no-fly zones are established to encourage Kurdish repatriation. **July:** United Nations Observer Mission in El Salvador (ONUSAL) begins. **October:** United Nations Advance Mission in Cambodia (UNAMIC) is authorized to prepare Cambodia for successful repatriation and elections.

1992 Dismemberment of Yugoslavia leads to massive refugee flows; United Nations (UN) humanitarian intervention is prompted with United Nations High Commissioner for Refugees (UNHCR) taking lead. **February:** United Nations Protection Force (UNPROFOR) authorized by United Nations Security Council to protect humanitarian relief to needy and displaced in the Balkans. **March:** UN replaces United Nations Advance Mission in Cambodia (UNAMIC) with United Nations Transitional Authority in Cambodia (UNTAC) peacekeeping force to ensure transition to democratic rule in Cambodia. **April:** United Nations Security Council authorizes deployment of United Nations Operation in Somalia (UNOSOM) forces to bring security to emergency relief operations in Somalia; Somali famine worsens. UN establishes the Department of Humanitarian Affairs with aim to improve coordination of UN disaster and humanitarian agencies. **June:** United Nations Conference on Environment and Development is held in Rio de Janeiro, Brazil, adopts Rio Declaration on Environment and Development and Agenda 21. **October:** United Nations Security Council establishes Commission of Experts to examine serious violations of international humanitarian law in the territories of the former Yugoslavia. **December:** United States undertakes Operation Restore Hope in Somalia with UN authorization to reestablish security for delivery of emergency famine aid. United Nations Operation in Mozambique (ONUMOZ) is authorized by United Nations Security Council to oversee peace agreements in Mozambique and ensure security for relief supplies.

1993 Fighting in former Soviet Central Asia prompts international relief work in Armenia, Azerbaijan, Tadjikistan, and Georgia. **January:** Fighting in Togo prompts the flight of 230,000 refugees into neighboring states. **April:** Second United Nations Operation in Somalia (UNOSOM II) takes over in Somalia from U.S.-led operation.

May: United Nations Security Council establishes the International Criminal Tribunal for Yugoslavia. **June:** World Conference on Human Rights is held in Vienna, adopts the Vienna Declaration and Program of Action for Human Rights. **August:** Oslo Accords signed, signaling willingness of Israel and the Palestinian leadership to explore end to violence at the heart of the Middle East conflict. **September:** Successfully completing its mission in Cambodia following election of a democratic government in May, the United Nations Transitional Authority in Cambodia (UNTAC) operation is terminated. **December:** United Nations General Assembly creates the new position of United Nations High Commissioner for Human Rights (UNHCHR). United Nations General Assembly adopts the Declaration on the Elimination of Violence against Women.

1994 Death of Rwandan president sets off months of ethnic violence in Rwanda; Tutsi population decimated by Hutu government policy; Rwandese Patriotic Front, dominated by Tutsi forces, defeats Hutu government, precipitating massive refugee flows into neighboring countries. **May:** World Conference on Natural Disaster Reduction is held in Yokohama, Japan. **July:** United Nations High Commissioner for Refugees (UNHCR) spearheads massive emergency response to head off humanitarian disaster in Rwanda; assistance activities continue throughout the year. United Nations Security Council authorizes the use of "all necessary means" to secure removal of the military government of Haiti. **September:** Restoration of democracy in Haiti, human rights monitoring begins under U.S. military supervision, which paves way for eventual transfer to United Nations Mission in Haiti. International Conference on Population and Development is held in Cairo, Egypt. United Nations General Assembly establishes United Nations Human Rights Verification Mission in Guatemala. **October:** Mozambique holds first successful democratic election. **November:** United Nations Trusteeship Council is terminated, having successfully overseen granting of independence to all 11 trust territories; UN Security Council establishes the International Criminal Tribunal for Rwanda. Taliban forces emerge as a factor in Afghanistan civil war. **December:** United Nations Operation in Mozambique (ONUMOZ) mandate is terminated after successful implementation of security, humanitarian aid, and elections in Mozambique; United Nations Transitional Authority in Cambodia (UNTAC) completes withdrawal from Cambodia ending one of the United Nations's most ambitious and successful multidimensional peace-building operations.

1995   February: Civil war in Chechnya deepens, leading to refugee flows, humanitarian emergency as United Nations Human Rights Commission calls for a cease-fire. **March:** World Summit for Social Development is held in Copenhagen, Denmark. Second United Nations Operation in Somalia (UNOSOM II) forces leave Somalia after failed effort to resolve civil war. **April:** United Nations Observer Mission in El Salvador (ONUSAL) forces leave El Salvador on successful completion of elections. **September:** Fourth World Conference on Women is held in Beijing. **October:** International Conference on Families meets in New York. **November:** World Ministerial Conference on Organized Transnational Crime meets in Naples. Dayton Accords are signed by warring parties in Bosnia, paving the way for deployment of international peacekeeping forces and cessation of human rights abuses.

1996   March: United Nations Department of Humanitarian Affairs (DHA) launches major appeal to provide humanitarian aid to Bosnia in wake of the Dayton Accords. **July:** Rwandan refugees in Burundi begin returning to Rwanda. **August:** Liberian factions agree to peace plan and elections. **September:** Taliban forces in Afghanistan capture Kabul and Jalalabad, provoking flight from cities; begin consolidating power in a five-year reign that involves substantial human rights abuse. **October:** Rebellion in the eastern parts of the Congo leads to reduction of refugee camps, flight and repatriation of Hutu refugees, and to the eventual overthrow of President Mobutu Sese Seko. **November:** Humanitarian situation in eastern Zaire deteriorates. World Food Conference meets in Rome. **December:** United Nations Security Council approves controversial oil-for-food program to meet humanitarian needs in Iraq. Military coup deepens humanitarian crisis in Sierra Leone.

1997 United Nations Security Council deploys the United Nations Verification Mission in Guatemala to supervise the peace agreement reached between the government and its opposition, to disarm and demobilize combatants. **March:** Hutu refugees in the Congo flee into jungle, fearing forced repatriation to Rwanda; United Nations (UN) bodies intensify effort to rescue and assist them. **May:** Military coup in Sierra Leone overthrows elected government. **June:** Civil war in Tajikistan

comes to an end with peace accord. **September:** Liberia holds successful elections, bringing to a temporary close its civil war; UN forces are
withdrawn. **August:** Security Council condemns National Union for the
Total Independence of Angola (UNITA) forces in Angola and invokes
sanctions against the rebel group as the humanitarian situation there deteriorates. **October:** International Conference on Child Labor meets in
Oslo. **December:** United Nations General Assembly adopts the International Convention for the Suppression of Terrorist Bombings.

1998   United Nations Department of Humanitarian Affairs (DHA) is
replaced by newly established United Nations Office for Coordination
of Humanitarian Affairs (UNOCHA), as part of reorganization of the
United Nations Secretariat. Famine intensifies in North Korea, leading
to international appeal to avert widespread starvation. **February:**
Newly formed UNOCHA issues humanitarian aid appeals for Sierra
Leone and Sudan. **April:** A Draft Statute for the International Criminal
Court is produced by the United Nations Preparatory Committee. **June:**
United Nations General Assembly Special Session on Countering the
World Drug Problem convenes. **July:** Security Council authorizes deployment of the United Nations Observer Mission in Sierra Leone;
United Nations Diplomatic Conference in Rome establishes the International Criminal Court. **August:** Resistance to new Laurent Kabila
government in the Democratic Republic of the Congo intensifies as
rebels capture Goma. **September:** Human rights violations and civil
war in Kosovo provoke Security Council decision to demand a cease-
fire, but conflict persists. International Criminal Tribunal for Rwanda
issues first judgment by an international court concerning punishment
of the crime of genocide. **December:** United Nations Security Council
expresses grave concern about violations of human rights in
Afghanistan, authorizing the establishment of a civil affairs unit to promote respect for human rights.

1999   **January:** Operation Life Line Sudan appeals for nearly half a
billion dollars in emergency aid to combat worsening situation in Sudan.
February: United Nations (UN) forces permanently pull out of Angola
as it continues to be embroiled in civil war with widespread human
rights abuses and humanitarian assistance needs. **March:** Ottawa Treaty
on Prohibition of Land Mines enters into force. North Atlantic Treaty
Organization (NATO) begins bombing of Serbia, precipitating a new

wave of ethnic cleansing in Kosovo and the flight of 500,000 Kosovar refugees in a matter of weeks, with the population rising another 300,000 in less than a month; UN emergency assistance bodies scramble to address the crisis. **May–June:** President of Serbia, Slobodan Milosevic, is indicted at The Hague for war crimes. Congo civil war intensifies and spreads even as African countries embroiled in the conflict reach a tentative peace accord. World Food Programme (WFP) calls for aid to 1.7 million internally displaced Angolans. Bombing in Serbia ends, as the Serb government capitulates; Kosovar refugees begin spontaneous and rapid return; United Nations Security Council authorizes deployment of the United Nations Mission in Kosovo. United Nations Security Council establishes the United Nations Advance Mission in East Timor (UNAMET) to organize a popular consultation to determine future status of the territory. **July:** As Kosovar refugee repatriation continues, 200,000 Serbs flee from Kosovo. **August–September:** Popular consultation in East Timor shows overwhelming support for independence, but Indonesian-backed forces reject outcome and begin a campaign of violence in East Timor, prompting humanitarian crisis; Security Council authorizes deployment of an international force led by Australia to stop the fighting. **September:** Organization of African Unity (OAU) adopts Sirte Declaration for establishment of the African Union. **October:** War in Chechnya resumes with large flows of refugees. Security Council establishes the United Nations Transitional Administration in East Timor (UNTAET) to guide progress toward full independence. Security Council establishes the United Nations Mission in Sierra Leone to disarm, demobilize, and reintegrate contending forces. **November:** Security Council establishes the United Nations Observer Mission in the Democratic Republic of the Congo. The African Charter on the Rights and Welfare of the Child enters into force.

2000   April: United Nations Conference on Crime and Justice meets in Vienna. **May:** United Nations (UN) holds its Millennium Forum for nongovernmental organizations (NGOs). Rebel forces in Sierra Leone capture about 500 UN peacekeepers, evoking Security Council condemnation. **June:** United Nations General Assembly holds Special Session on Women 2000: Gender Equality and Peace in New York and a Special Session on Social Development in Geneva. **July:** United Nations Economic and Social Council (ECOSOC) establishes the Permanent Forum on Indigenous Issues. **September:** United Nations Millennium Summit produces the Millennium Declaration in affirmation of human rights and in advancing goals for UN action. Second *intifada* begins, as peace efforts are derailed and a wave of suicide bombing attacks by Palestinians, and Israeli reprisals take hundreds of lives during the ensuing years of conflict.

2001 June: United Nations General Assembly convenes in special session to discuss the HIV/AIDS issue and its relationship to human rights. **July:** United Nations Conference on the Illicit Trade in Small Arms and Light Weapons is held in New York **September:** World Conference against Racism concludes in Durban, South Africa. **11 September:** Terrorist attacks in New York and Washington, DC, kill more than 3,000, and usher in a new era of concerted action against terrorist acts.

2002 January: United Nations (UN) and the government of Sierra Leone agree to establish a special court to prosecute war crimes and crimes against humanity committed during Sierra Leone's civil war. **March:** Operation Iraqi Freedom begins as coalition forces overthrow the Baathist regime, noted for its pervasive human rights abuses; a long period of instability ensues as insurgent elements continue fighting, often with terrorist tactics. **May:** East Timor achieves independence as Timor Leste; United Nations Transitional Administration in East Timor (UNTAET) is terminated and succeeded by the United Nations Mission of Support in East Timor to assist in promoting the stability of the new country. United Nations General Assembly convenes special session in New York on Children. **July:** The African Union officially replaces the Organization of African Unity (OAU) at the Durban Summit. Statute of the International Criminal Court enters into force. **September:** The Quartet (of the UN, the United States, the EU, and the Russian Federation) offer the "road map" for peace in the Middle East, which has been wracked by a Palestinian uprising, suicide bombing attacks, and Israeli government reprisals. **December:** Gbadolite Agreement in Democratic Republic of the Congo (DRC) holds out hope for end to Africa's worst conflict and humanitarian emergency, but the conflict persists in the eastern parts of the DRC, complicated by disagreements among the three rebel groups vying for control, as nearly 2.3 million displaced persons and 350,000 refugees await return to their homes in security.

2003 January: United Nations (UN) launches the Literacy Decade (2003–2012). **April:** UN humanitarian coordinator for Iraq and staff return to Iraq to begin task of reconstruction following coalition intervention and toppling of the Saddam Hussein regime. **May:** UN revokes sanctions against Iraq, as coalition partners work with Iraqis to establish a new government and UN reconstruction efforts intensify with visit by representatives of World Health Organization (WHO), World Food Programme (WFP), United Nations International Children's Emergency Fund (UNICEF), and United Nations Development Programme (UNDP). **August:** United Nations Security Council establishes the United Nations Observer Mission in Georgia to verify compliance of parties to a cease-fire; it later takes on humanitarian assistance and human rights supervision duties. Terrorists bomb UN headquarters in Baghdad, killing Sergio Vierira de Mello, the secretary-general's special representative for Iraq, and 21 others. **September:** United Nations Security Council established the United Nations Mission in Liberia to protect civilians, oversee demobilization of combatants, and provide security for refugee repatriation and humanitarian assistance. **October:** United Nations General Assembly condemns Israeli construction of the security wall in the West Bank; Israel ignores international opposition in favor of protecting its own citizens from suicide bomber attacks. **December:** Devastating earthquake destroys much of the ancient city of Bam, Iran, leaving more than 30,000 dead and 60,000 homeless, prompting large international rescue and rehabilitation effort.

2004 **June:** United Nations Security Council decides to establish a United Nations advance mission in Sudan to address massive human rights abuses and humanitarian needs in Darfur, Sudan; hails the early handover of sovereignty to the interim government in Iraq. **July:** International Court of Justice Advisory Opinion declares Israeli building of Security Fence in the West Bank illegal. **September:** Chechnya civil war is punctuated by terrorist hostage taking at school; hundreds of children are killed or injured as the stand-off ends in violence. **October:** Afghanistan holds historic democratic presidential elections; Hamid Karzai wins in victory for the democratic process. **November:** Death of Yassir Arafat and rise of new Palestinian leadership offers hope of renewed progress toward peace settlement; Israel begins limited pull out from West Bank and Gaza. **December:** Tsunami hits countries along the Indian Ocean littoral, leading to massive international humanitarian and disaster relief response in following months.

2005   January: Historic elections in Iraq usher in new era of democracy. **February:** Pro-Syrian Lebanese Prime Minister Omar Karami resigns amid massive demonstrations in wake of assassination of popular former Prime Minister Rafik Hariri; momentum builds for Syrian troop pullout. **March:** United Nations Security Council establishes the United Nations Mission in Sudan to work with African Union Mission and local parties to implement comprehensive peace settlement and end the genocidal violence in Darfur province. **April:** Syrian military forces pull out of Lebanon, paving way for free elections there for the first time in thirty years. **May:** Violence breaks out in Uzbekistan leaving hundreds dead. **June:** Wave of democratic elections in Middle East continues with anti-Syrian forces winning a parliamentary victory in Lebanon. **August–October:** Hurricane Katrina strikes New Orleans and U.S. Gulf Coast; dikes break in New Orleans, leading to massive and destructive flooding and hundreds of thousands of homeless. About 1,500 people perish as some $75 billion in estimated damage is wrought by the deadliest and most destructive hurricane in U.S. history. **October:** Constitutional elections in Iraq pave the way for election of a new national Parliament. Devastating earthquake strikes northern Pakistan, killing more than 80,000, and prompting a huge international emergency response. **December:** Iraq elects a new Parliament; international monitors declare the elections free and fair, certifying outcome.

2006   January: Election of Hamas to legislative control by Palestinians throws the Palestinian political scene into turmoil; in succeeding months, Western governments cease aid until it renounces terrorism and its policy of seeking the destruction of the state of Israel. First judges elected to new African Court of Human and Peoples' Rights. **February:** Haiti holds fourth set of democratic elections, with Rene Preval winning after controversy over ballot counting. **March:** United Nations General Assembly approves new Human Rights Council to replace Commission on Human Rights. Slobodan Milosevic dies in custody of International Criminal Tribunal for the Former Yugoslavia (ICTY). Former president of Liberia, Charles Taylor, is extradited by Nigeria back to Liberia and to eventual trial for crimes against humanity before the Sierra Leone Special Tribunal. **May:** Tentative peace agreement reached in Sudan's Darfur conflict; Violence breaks out in East Timor.

Introduction

The idea of human rights and humanitarian assistance has ancient roots. The history of these notions and their practice can be traced back primarily into the classical Hebrew, Greek, and Roman worlds, to the earliest days of Christianity, and also to the writings and practice of ancient Chinese thinkers, among others. Indeed, the universal desire for safety, security, respect, and dignity observed among people across cultures suggests why the modern human rights project has resonated so strongly throughout the world. The tendency among modern commentators, however, is to treat the question of human rights as a political process and as a movement of recent origin. Indeed, if we want to study humanitarian and human rights organizations as such, we needn't go back much further than the middle of the 19th century when the first efforts to establish private humanitarian and human rights organizations occurred. Before that time, human rights organizations, as such, did not exist. Even humanitarian agencies tended to be conceived in light of religious and individual charity. So why did human rights and humanitarian organizations come into existence in modern times? What moral ideas, historical developments, intellectual currents, and political and legal events might have converged to stimulate their emergence? And to what do we attribute their spectacular growth in the 20th century? Such questions can be answered only if we consult the origins of this conception. We do so in recognition that while human rights and humanitarian organizations are a recent manifestation of modernity, they rest on ideas and basic ethical conceptions that have truly ancient origins.

HUMAN RIGHTS AND HUMANITARIAN AID IN HISTORY

Modern conceptions of human rights rest fundamentally on the notion of the dignity of human persons. This notion of dignity in turn requires each human being to see and treat other human beings with dignity and respect. Of course, throughout history countless examples can be cited where this basic notion was ignored, where acts of great brutality were perpetrated with impunity, and where peoples of many lands faced conditions of great misery. Still, after more than a century of evolving human rights organizations, the same observations could be made concerning the world today.

Yet from very early times and in many places, including ancient India and China and the ancient Near East, the human ethical sensibility can be seen in the writings and sacred texts of different civilizations. In ancient India, for instance, the *Bhagavad-Gita* (circa 5000 B.C.E.) celebrates virtues such as nonviolence, purity of mind, freedom from anger and envy, and the goods of gentleness, modesty, truth, and personal rectitude. In China, Confucius (551–479 B.C.E.) and his subsequent interpreters, such as Mencius (372–289 B.C.E.), emphasized the inherent good of individuals, the centrality of the family and of family relationships, and the importance of society in cultivating the person's innate moral sense. In these Eastern traditions, the idea existed that people should grow in virtue, show compassion to the needs of others, and treat others with respect. In Confucianism as well as in many other ancient moral codes, the Golden Rule was seen as a paramount principle for guiding human action and promoting self-control and temperance.

Of the ancient traditions having the most direct impact on the development of human rights as we know them today, the Hebrew tradition is the oldest and most influential. Ranging back to around 1200 B.C.E., it captures the essence of the Golden Rule and the Ten Commandments. The Decalogue calls upon human beings to recognize their creaturely status, to worship their maker with reverence, and to recognize God's desire that they act uprightly toward one another. Living in families, societies, and nations, people were obligated to behave ethically toward one another. They were enjoined to respect and protect human life, rather than murder the innocent. Stealing and lying were also prohibited as violations of human dignity, as was adultery. In sum, the person and property of others deserved respect. Positive inducements to give aid and comfort to the homeless, the old, the helpless, the widows, and the orphans could also be found in the Old Testament. The similarities found between the Decalogue and the Code of Hammurabi, as well as in the ethical systems of Hinduism, Buddhism, and Confucianism, suggest that a common natural law was accessible to human beings in a variety of cultural contexts and that it demanded piety, honesty, fairness, respect for persons, property, and for marriage and family obligation. Similarly, the Hebrew scriptures and other ancient writings also paint a stark picture of human weakness, of vice and ambition. The lessons to be drawn from such texts are manifold in their richness. As a totality, they point to an understanding of humanity as being in need of correction but capable of correction, as being capable of doing unspeakable evil and yet also of doing great good. That there are important philosophical variations in these ancient treatments on human rights and obligations is not in dispute, but the important commonalities are often not sufficiently recognized.

If in the Hebrew ethical system we find one taproot of Western human rights reflection, then in Greek philosophy we discover yet another major source, especially in Hellenic political and ethical science. Socrates, the founder of Greek ethical science, averred certain basic ethical principles, including the notion that one should never knowingly do harm to another. To return harm for harm, he deemed unjust. Personal integrity and a thirst for knowledge as virtue was for him the ultimate good of a fully human life. The Greek ethical philosophers who followed Socrates, including Plato and Aristotle, understood the social and political nature of human beings. They appreciated the fact that persons were born into families, that they formed their deepest friendships there, and that these friendships later translated into wider society and into the civic arena. In these social settings it was necessary for the city to encourage the development of virtuous citizens, for soldiers to show courage and to seek honor, for politicians and officeholders to display justice and to be good-tempered, for the prestigious and wealthy to display liberality and magnanimity, and for the masses to practice temperance, to persevere in work, and to practice honesty. Moral virtues, then, as conceived by Aristotle, involved seeking a middle way between extremes of vice, although some actions by their very names—such as adultery, theft and robbery, murder, shamelessness, and envy—could never be done in the right way. Thus, while ethics was a science for the most part of circumstances and situations amenable to standards and principles that relied heavily on good judgment forged in experience, certain kinds of things were seen as being intrinsically evil.

For people to become virtuous, they needed good examples and good education or training in order to establish good habits. Primarily, the function of raising good citizens rested in the family. Aristotle made this important observation in books 8 and 9 of his *Nicomachean Ethics*. Family bonds between spouses, between parents and children, and between siblings constituted the most intense bonds of love and friendship, and good political regimes modeled themselves after spousal, parental, filial, and fraternal relations. Moreover, the political regime could not with impunity ignore the development of moral and noble citizens. Aristotle went so far as to say that a regime that left such things to chance was most imprudent, since it "makes all the difference" to the excellence of a regime that its citizens be capable of good and noble deeds. In such a regime, the goal is not merely to survive but also to live nobly and well.

With the downfall of the city-states as politically independent entities in Greece, there arose a new and even broader conception of human duties and obligations. Whereas previously one's principal duty as an Athenian was to the defense and preservation of Athens and fellow Athenians, Stoic philosophy began to argue that one owed obligations to humanity as a whole. With city-states fallen and the world-state emerging, Stoics conceived of people as being part of a single, universal human society. Human beings, in this emerging view, possessed souls, divine sparks participating in and part of the divine soul that united all humanity. This philosophy of universality, so well suited to the growth of empire, pointed the way toward a conception of toleration, and identified common links between various and diverse human communities, all conceptions very directly related to our modern conception of human rights. That some Roman intellectuals readily embraced such philosophy was not surprising, as it suited the conditions of empire.

The Roman Empire was not an unmitigated example of virtuous rule. Indeed, Rome, like all societies, produced paragons of great virtue as well as examples of egregious vice. Stoical ideology never permeated all levels of Roman society. Indeed, some Stoical schools were decidedly skeptical about the role of politics and power and thus urged virtuous men to seek lives of private contemplation, while others nevertheless counseled adherents to embrace lives of active public service. Amidst the cruelties and barbarities of Roman imperial rule, and the reality that this rule had been achieved by conquest, the Roman legal system provided a mechanism for peaceful and prosperous relations among diverse peoples across a large geographical area. From the standpoint of human rights, Rome's legal practice would prove to be its greatest and most lasting legacy.

Indeed, the genius of Roman law was its ability to preserve the core of the *lex urbanus*, or of Roman law proper, while acknowledging the diversity of laws and customs to be found among conquered peoples, the *lex civile*, or law of cities. But the Romans also noticed that many common legal customs and principles of justice could be found throughout the empire. Thus developed the notion of *lex gentium*, or law of nations or peoples, a body of law that was common to all places. Closely related to this concept was the idea of the *lex naturalae* or law of nature. The Roman Stoics and philosophers who posited this concept believed that the existence of so many common principles of justice among different peoples was a result of the innate human capacity, through right reason, to deduce exact and universal principles of justice and of right and wrong. Cicero was an especially important figure who taught that human beings have natural inclinations to the truth, to happiness, and to an awareness of the good of life and the need to protect, preserve, and procreate new life. Hence, human beings are drawn into the society of the family and of political communities. The natural law concept, coupled with the *lex gentium* idea, strongly influenced the development of legal thinking and of international law down through the Middle Ages to our own time. The conception of natural law, bequeathed to us by the Romans, anticipates the modern human rights project, in which human rights are ideals that are not scrupulously practiced in the positive law of nations but toward which they aspire as a matter of principle.

Growing out of the Hebrew tradition, even as Roman imperial sway reached its peak, Christianity emerged from Palestine and spread inexorably throughout the Roman Empire. Fundamental to the Christian ethic were such conceptions as the dignity of the human person, the universal brotherhood of man, the basic equality of human beings (men and women alike) as creatures of God, the requirement of service to others, the need for compassion, the commandment to love one's neighbor, and obedience both to lawful civic authority and to the Ten Commandments, which in turn call for individuals to show scrupulous ethical comportment toward one another. Absolutely critical to any full understanding of the Christian contribution to moral philosophy and ultimately to the progress of human rights was the Sermon on the Mount of Jesus, where the beatitudes are tersely enumerated and offered as the pinnacle of human dignity. The Sermon on the Mount articulates the inner logic of the Sinaitic Code recorded in the Ten Commandments. The person who humbles himself to orient his interior life toward well-ordered love, justice, and forgiveness is one who achieves ultimate happiness, joy, and peace, and is able to spread such peace in acts of charity.

Although Christianity called for its adherents to be good citizens, it was often perceived as a subversive movement, and Roman political authorities alternatively permitted local persecution or sponsored empirewide persecution of Christians. Early Christian apologists, facing such persecution, articulated a series of ringing condemnations of persecution in a fairly wide body of literature. These apologetic works anticipated in large measure arguments that have been made in the 19th and 20th centuries on behalf of persecuted peoples and of their right to freedom of religion.

By far the most influential writer of early Christianity was St. Augustine. His works developed a number of themes of importance for later development of humanitarian law. First, Augustine taught that slavery was a conventional result of sin rather than a natural condition. In his view, God could not have made any rational human being by nature to be the property of another. Still, he was not confident, given the fallen state of humanity, that slavery was capable of eradication. Second, Augustine, like the Romans, believed in natural law. This natural law was inscribed by God on the hearts of human beings and could be discerned by reason. Kings and rulers were obliged to discover the natural law through careful deliberation. Indeed, kings had special duties and responsibilities to their subjects. They were, in Augustine's view, the servants of the servants of God. Kings could not claim unrestrained rights or assert that they were above the law, nor could they simply make law by fiat. Justice demanded that they serve the common good. Even their acts of war were subject to the moral restraints of the just war doctrine, which was influential in the development of later laws of war. Augustine's theory of Christian kingship echoes the principles of restraint found in the Old Testament treatment of kingship.

The principal consequence of the Christian era for the later development of human rights was rooted in the radical conception of Christian equality and the requirement to tend to the needs of one's neighbor. This propelled individuals and local communities to undertake works of charity toward those in need. The establishment of hospitals, hospices, and orphanages can be traced to the earliest Christian centuries. The emergence of monastic orders, especially in the West from the fifth century onward, precipitated a spreading web of monastic foundations emanating from Italy and from Ireland across the territories of Western and Northern Europe. Monasteries became islands of civilization and learning, and centers of agricultural productivity. The earliest schools, libraries, and pharmacies were located in them. They served as way stations for weary travelers and as sanctuaries of safety. The Benedictine and Celtic activity in monasteries and convents represented some of the most effective humanitarian agents in Western Europe. Diocesan bishops and parish churches also served as centers for settled civilization and active works of charity, at a time when governments largely left such activity to the work of the Church. Monastic establishments did not always flourish, and often experienced periods of corruption and decay, but renewal movements also periodically rejuvenated monastic life, as during the Cluniac revival of the 10th to 11th centuries, and the Cistercian renewal of the 12th century. Moreover, during the Cluniac revival, the Holy Roman emperors cooperated with Cluny and the papacy to spread the Peace of God and Truce of God as means of restoring greater security to many parts of Western Europe. All of this tended to the greater humanitarian good.

Growing out of the Judeo-Christian monotheistic traditions and rooted in their sacred books, Islam emerged in the seventh century. It regarded Jews and Christians as "Peoples of the Book." Like them, Muslims embraced the Ten Commandments as a basis for human rights, viewing all human rights as divinely ordained, rather than of human origin as such. Islam likewise embraced the themes of almsgiving, compassion, and mercy as divine ideals. In Islam is an acknowledgment of the core aspects of the natural law common to other religious and ethical systems.

Institutional developments occurred in both Christian and Islamic practice to provide alms and charity and to assist human needs. By promoting the development of the moral sensibility in people, Christian and Islamic thinkers and writers hoped to mitigate the inhumane and perverse conditions that marked so much political life. The state in Christian lands and the caliphate in Muslim ones were concerned with promoting the development of virtuous citizens. Thus virtue, as for the classical Greeks, remained an important object of civic education in Christian Europe, and Islamic scholars also imbibed and even transmitted some of these ancient writings to the Western world.

Medieval Christendom's tradition of corporatist obligation gradually dissolved during the high Middle Ages and the Renaissance. The Protestant Reformation challenged the dominance of the Roman Church, and emerging states, which claimed sovereignty, also rebelled against the notion of a universal religious authority that could meddle in the political life of nations. In the 16th and 17th centuries, new theories of state sovereignty were worked out as the medieval synthesis fell apart. Bloody religious and political wars raged across the face of Europe. These devastating conflicts were finally brought to resolution in 1648 with the signing of the Peace of Westphalia, which underscored the doctrine of state sovereignty, emphasizing that no higher legal authority existed than the monarchs or princes of nations, who had the sole right to determine what religion would be acknowledged, supported, or tolerated within their realms. All matters domestic were seen to lie solely within the discretion of the sovereign state, and each had the right to determine its own foreign policy as well. In time, after further legal development, such states were considered independent and equal, at least in legal terms, and interference within the territorial jurisdiction of the state was considered a violation of the norm of sovereignty. These seemingly absolute principles, however, were qualified with the understanding that the sovereign governments of territories would be obliged to respect the rights of religious minorities. From this understanding grew the notion in customary international law that a sovereign who mistreated his subjects so egregiously as to "shock the conscience" of humanity would be subject to correction and intervention. Indeed, a *duty* for other sovereigns to intervene could arise if a sovereign flagrantly disregarded the duty to respect the fundamental dignity of those under his suzerainty. This principle was rooted in an older natural law appreciation of the nature of human beings.

Although these principles brought a new stability to the international politics of Europe, they did not always promote the rights of the subjects of the sovereigns. Indeed, it was at this time that the notion of the divine right of kings was asserted most vigorously by sovereign authorities to justify and legitimize their rule. The new theory of sovereignty allowed kings to assert broad authorities and powers. Thus, while Europe enjoyed greater stability, this was achieved at the price of greater authoritarianism. Once the revolution of legal positivism was given impetus under the writings of Emmerich de Vattel and others, the human rights of the subjects of these "divinely" ordained monarchs and sovereigns fell prey to the will of the sovereign. Indeed, law itself came to be seen as an act purely of the will of the sovereign.

However, in the realm of political philosophy, radically different conceptions of political legitimacy were being asserted by such figures as Thomas Hobbes and John Locke. The former, though supportive of absolute monarchy, took the bold step of asserting that authority to rule did not come from God but rather from the individual subjects who alone could consent to be placed under the authority of a sovereign. Hobbes held that people were driven by fear for their lives into a social contract with one another to hand total authority over to a sovereign whose principal responsibility was to provide for their security and preservation. Hobbes, then, developed an individual consent principle for government. Moreover, he held that individuals had a natural right to preserve themselves, a right that government could not take away, but this natural right was not grounded in the older notion of natural law and its assertions of natural inclinations. Rather, a careful reading of Hobbes demonstrates that the numerous natural laws he cites do not exist in the "state of nature," in which there is only a war of all against all. Rather, these natural laws come only into existence through the will of the sovereign. The natural condition of human beings is one of violent self-aggrandizement. Indeed, human beings have only an animal instinct for survival, and fear of losing life becomes the basis for a new-found trust in the social contract, whereby each individual gives up his natural right to preserve himself to the overpowering Leviathan who will at last establish order.

Although Hobbes may be viewed as the modern source of the notion of natural rights and thus of human rights in general, the authoritarian tendencies of his thought are not popular. More congenial to modern sympathies is the political philosophy of John Locke, whose ideas provide the basis of the modern development of democratic political systems. Like

Hobbes, Locke held that human beings possessed certain inalienable rights, including the rights to life, liberty, and property. For Locke, individuals enjoyed these rights as persons, not as citizens or subjects of a state. Governments might protect and preserve these rights—indeed, the principal role of governments in Locke's view was to do precisely that— but they had no legitimate right to ignore or violate the natural rights of individuals. Indeed, for Locke, the only kind of civil government that was legitimate was the kind of government that acknowledged and protected individual rights. He considered all forms of tyranny illegitimate. Still, in Locke, who acknowledges the existence of natural law in the state of nature itself (unlike Hobbes), we find a preference for the idea of contractual rather than natural arrangements of basic human institutions.

The political thought of what came to be known as the Enlightenment represented a revolutionary new conception that became the basis for state claims to sovereignty. The ideas were not brand new, since they could be seen at least in germ form in Aristotelian theory and in the writings of William of Ockham, and even in such famous documents as the Magna Carta. The latter—though promulgated in 1215 by English nobles and clergy to assert their rights in the face of monarchical authority—became a much-adverted-to source for the rights of all Englishmen. Still, the emphasis on the individual as the locus of inalienable rights and the source of all political legitimacy was quite novel. Generally, individual rights were previously viewed in religious terms or as conventional statutory or customary norms that could change with the vagaries of time and history. The family, not the individual, was generally seen in the tradition as the basic unit of society, though the individual was clearly important. Now the claim was that some individual rights were immutable and rooted in the autonomous individual. This claim had the strong scent of natural law surrounding it, even if it seemed revolutionary in character. But as legal experts and scholars as well as governments began to embrace legal positivism, the natural law source of claims to individual rights gradually became more obscure, even as governments gradually began to democratize and adopt constitutions and bills of rights.

Important examples of such basic law include the founding documents of several American colonies, in particular the Body of Liberties of the Massachusetts colony (1641), which laid out the specific rights of their citizens. The American Declaration of Independence, suffused with Lockean references to individual rights, was a classical defense of the notion of natural rights. But it is also the case that the Declaration of Independence grounds the rights of individuals not in any contract as such, but by virtue of human beings being creatures given by God a dignity that must be recognized. The Constitution of the United States and the Bill of Rights to the U.S. Constitution were landmarks in the evolution of citizen rights, and by implication in the development of human rights as well. So too was the Declaration of the Rights of Man, which emerged during the early years of the French Revolution. In this important document, the term "human rights" is explicitly used to denote rights common to all human beings as part of their birthright as reasoning creatures of God. Thus, while concerned with the specific rights of French citizens, the declaration casts a larger shadow as a universal assertion of rights. This was the ideological groundwork laid in the late 18th century for the later development of the conception of human rights, even though human rights organizations as such did not exist.

Rather, representative bodies of peoples and republican governments began to take over the role of asserting human rights principles upon which their regimes would be based, at least in principle. Hitherto, the main guarantors of human rights were the religious organizations, the churches, the parishes, and the religious orders. Indeed, most of the human welfare activity undertaken throughout human history has been undertaken precisely by those animated by a spirit of charity who sought to mitigate the misery and uphold the dignity of their neighbors. Human rights were seen as being protected in the primary institutions of societies, whereas governments were seen as being responsible largely for the safety and security—and perhaps to some extent the prosperity—of the nation. Only in the 20th century did governments begin to supplant the family and religious bodies in the great tasks of education, health, welfare, and social development. Before then, schools, universities, hospitals, orphanages, pharmacies, hostels, and even guilds and other humane associations were the work of private or religious action.

The gap between principle and practice in human affairs has often been rather wide. It should be no surprise, then, that the earliest efforts to assert human rights principles would not always meet with success. The Constitution of the United States tolerated slavery in the early years, and the French Revolution devolved into almost childish pantomimes and a nightmare of senseless bloodshed, only to be followed by the conservative reaction that brought Napoleon to power. But important manifestos such as those just mentioned, if they did not always take root immediately, did seem to fire the imagination and hold out a better possibility for human aspiration. Gradually during the 19th century, fragile democratic governments, rooted in lofty ideals of civil and political rights, consolidated themselves and moved toward broader conceptions of participation and inclusion. During that century, the British interdicted the slave trade through the use of its maritime power, and in the United States a bloody civil war made possible the emancipation of slaves. Full citizenship rights in practice would be denied American blacks until the civil rights revolution of a century later, but both in the United States and in Europe democratic ideology and human rights notions were taking firmer root. Moreover, it was during the 19th century that the first modern international organization, the Rhine River Commission, was fashioned by European states in the wake of the Napoleonic Wars, as governments acknowledged that certain problems required continuous transnational cooperation. This modest beginning set the stage in the latter part of the 19th century for the creation of dozens of intergovernmental organizations, including some that dealt with humanitarian issues.

THE EMERGENCE OF HUMANITARIAN AND HUMAN RIGHTS ORGANIZATIONS

The 1800s saw the emergence of the first modern humanitarian and human rights organizations *as intergovernmental bodies*. In the early 1800s in the United States, the abolitionist movement was active in opposition to slavery. Later in the same century, a variety of women's suffrage organizations were formed to lobby for the expansion of the political rights of women. The 19th century was a period of active formation and consolidation of national labor unions that sought to advance worker interests and rights. In the area of humanitarian activity, the Red Cross was founded by Gustave Moynier and several other humanitarians inspired by the work of Jean-Henri Dunant in 1864. The Red Cross organization rapidly spread from Switzerland to a number of countries. This development in the advancement of humanitarian principles during time of war was matched by similar governmental efforts to codify the international customary laws of war. Both public and private awareness of human rights issues were on the increase.

At the beginning of the 20th century, the world was poised at the verge of significant human rights development. Unfortunately, it was also at the brink of major political upheavals and devastating global conflicts. Indeed, the growth of human rights and humanitarian organizations is inextricably intertwined with the story of war, persecution, violence, and the contest of authoritarian states with fledgling democratic ones. The 20th century has witnessed some of the most horrific and blatant violations of human dignity and also the first sustained global efforts to promote human rights at the international level.

In Europe, significant political upheavals and massive population movements in the Balkans resulted in two distinct Balkan conflicts in 1912 and 1913, variously involving Serbia, Turkey, Greece, Bulgaria, Macedonia, and Russia. Hundreds of thousands of people were uprooted in these wars of ethno-nationalistic division. In turn, unresolved aspirations for self-determination in the Balkans presaged the onset of the World War I. Indeed, even by the end of the 20th century, the Balkans remained a hotbed of ethnic division, dispute, and bloodshed, underscoring the tenacity of unresolved desires for self-determination. Recognizing this tendency, numerous world leaders gathered at the Versailles Peace Conference of 1919 and, in addition to setting terms for the defeated Central powers, also agreed to create the first potentially global international organization, the League of Nations. Apart from serving as a collective security institution to maintain and enforce global peace, the League took steps through its mandate system to encourage the self-determination and independence of peoples. A war in Europe served as the wedge for the end of European colonial domination. With many European states having adopted parliamentary and democratic forms of government, the inherent inconsistency of their maintaining overlordship of colonial peoples grew increasingly obvious.

World War I and its aftermath stimulated a tremendous expansion in the number of international organizations, some of which were independent of the League, and others closely tied to its work. The postwar breakup of the Ottoman Empire and the 1917 Bolshevik Revolution in Russia produced millions of displaced persons and refugees. This, coupled with the adoption by most states of a visa and passport regime regulating travel and immigration across borders, left uprooted peoples in a legal limbo. Facing huge humanitarian problems throughout the Near East and in Russia, the International Committee of the Red Cross appealed on behalf of many private relief agencies to the League of Nations for formal international assistance. The League responded by creating the first humanitarian office for refugees, the High Commissioner for Russian Refugees, which dealt not only with Russian refugees but also Armenians and Assyro-Chaldean refugees displaced by events surrounding the dissolution of the Ottoman Empire. Never conceived of as a permanent agency, the High Commissioner's Office, to which Fridtjof Nansen, the famous Norwegian explorer and philanthropist, was named the first high commissioner, was later reformulated on several occasions. Its work, together with its successor and related organizations (the Nansen International Office for Refugees, the High Commissioner for Refugees Coming from Germany, and the High Commissioner of the League of Nations), laid the foundation for even more extensive international efforts on behalf of refugees after World War II.

The League's work on behalf of displaced persons and its effort to encourage the just treatment of non-self-governing peoples did not exhaust its efforts on behalf of human rights broadly understood. The covenant of the League empowered the organization to supervise the traffic in women and children, to regulate the traffic in dangerous drugs, to supervise the arms trade, to promote freedom of communications and transit, and to establish measures for the prevention and control of disease. Several technical and advisory organizations were established by the League to study such problems, to issue reports, and to make recommendations.

Independent of the League, but working closely with it on humanitarian and refugee resettlement issues, was the International Labour Organization (ILO), which was established in 1919 by governments to address issues of common concern to labor, employers, and governments. The ILO survived the League to become a specialized agency in the United Nations (UN) system in 1946. Its sponsorship of treaties and agreements setting international labor standards marked some of the earliest and most significant advances in human rights work.

World War II (1939–1945) and the events connected to it greatly accelerated international awareness of and attention to human rights issues. The devastation wrought to human life and property during the war was incalculable. Cities lay in ruin. In Europe alone, 30 million people were displaced from their homelands. Millions had perished during the war, some in bombing raids that devastated not only the military and industrial bases but also the homes of the participants in the war. The close connection that had arisen between industrial production of military weapons and the civilian work force blurred the lines that traditionally separated the civilian population from military operations. Persistent violations of the laws of war—by the Germans in Europe and the Japanese forces in the Pacific, but common enough among participants on both sides elsewhere—displayed how fragile the tendons of humanitarian policy were in time of war. More horrendous still was the systematic Holocaust that Adolf Hitler and the Nazis had directed against Jews and other peoples in Europe. All of this constituted a great shock to the consciences of people throughout the world.

At the same time, international efforts at cooperation had begun to take shape during the war years. The Declaration of the United Nations, talks at Dumbarton Oaks, and further wartime conferences at Yalta and Potsdam led to agreements among the Allies leading toward the promulgation of the United Nations Charter. Relief and assistance agencies also took shape during the war. These included the Food and Agriculture Organization (FAO) in 1943, as well as the International Bank for Reconstruction and Development (IBRD or World Bank) and International Monetary Fund (IMF), which were established by the Bretton Woods agreements of 1944. In 1943 the United Nations Relief and Rehabilitation Administration (UNRRA) was established to deal directly with populations displaced by war. In Europe the logistics of humanitarian relief were undertaken by the Displaced Persons Branch of the Supreme Headquarters of the Allied Expeditionary Force (SHAEF), which turned over humanitarian operations to UNRRA in 1945. In 1947 UNRRA and the Intergovernmental Committee for Refugees (IGCR), which had assisted in the resettlement of refugees and displaced persons, ceased to exist and their functions were transferred to a new but temporary agency called the International Refugee Organization (IRO). Five years later the IRO was replaced by the United Nations High Commissioner for Refugees (UNHCR). In the Middle East a separate refugee agency, the United Nations Relief and Works Agency for Palestine (UNRWA), was created to deal specifically with the Palestinian refugees.

As humanitarian protection and assistance were being provided to refugees and displaced persons, governments pursued other human rights objectives through various UN bodies. The United Nations Charter itself contained numerous references to the obligations of states to respect the human rights and fundamental freedoms of all people. The charter cites these as central principles of the UN system. At the same time in Article 68, it called upon the Economic and Social Council (ECOSOC) to create such commissions as might be necessary to promote human rights. ECOSOC responded with the establishment of the United Nations Commission on Human Rights (CHR). This body, in turn, rapidly recommended to the General Assembly the adoption of a Universal Declaration of Human Rights, which was approved in 1948. In the same year, the Genocide Convention was adopted by the United Nations General Assembly. Within three years of the end of World War II, governments, acting through the cooperative mechanisms of the UN, had taken steps to embark on the more systematic promotion of human rights.

Still, there was a wide gap between the stated desire of governments to abide by and promote respect for human rights and their actual practice. Moreover, governments were reluctant, even where committed in their domestic systems, to create international law and institutions that might infringe on their sovereignty. There was disagreement, too, over the content of human rights and the respective importance of civil and political rights versus economic, social, and cultural rights. Some states, particularly those of the West, gave greater priority to the former over the latter, while states of the Eastern bloc and newly independent developing countries in the Third World often emphasized the latter, even to the exclusion of the former. Ideological disputes had their impact on the human rights debate as the Cold War deepened. Facing these complications, work at the international level to draft binding instruments to give legal, in addition to moral, effect to the rights contained in the Universal Declaration was slow. Nonetheless, governments began to rely on the Universal Declaration as a definitive source of human rights in their condemnations of one another's behavior. Newly independent governments, not infrequently, incorporated parts or all of the declaration's provisions into their domestic constitutions or law.

Thus, the Universal Declaration began through an evolutionary process to become more than a mere hortatory document, as it had been originally intended to be. Eighteen years after the declaration, drafts of the International Covenant on Civil and Political Rights and the International Covenant on Economic, Social, and Cultural Rights were finally adopted by the United Nations General Assembly in 1966. Another 10 years passed before either had entered into force, illustrating the ongoing reluctance of governments to enter into binding agreements on the subject of human rights. The International Covenant on Civil and Political Rights was supplemented with an optional protocol offering tougher, though still rather modest, measures of enforcement. Governments were reluctant to hold their own feet to the fire. Nonetheless, with the adoption of the covenants, students of human rights began to speak about the emergence of an International Bill of Human Rights, consisting of the Universal Declaration, the covenants, and several other human rights instruments. The covenants also created committees to hear complaints and receive reports submitted from member-states in compliance with their treaty obligations, adding a degree of international oversight to the endeavor of promoting and protecting human rights. The Optional Protocol to the International Covenant on Civil and Political Rights provided the first global mechanism for individuals to file complaints against their own governments.

If progress at the international level in achieving enforceable legal instruments to protect human rights was slow, more dramatic progress was demonstrated at the regional level, particularly in Europe. With the adoption of the European Convention on Human Rights in 1950, the Council of Europe set in motion the evolution of an increasingly sophisticated human rights machinery. The convention created a European Commission of Human Rights that, in addition to permitting state-to-state complaints, also permitted individuals to file petitions against their own governments, provided those governments had declared their readiness to accept the petition regime. Through a variety of protocols, this system was streamlined and extended. The convention also established a European Court of Human Rights (ECHR), which could hear cases brought to it by the commission or states parties, and interpret and apply the provisions of the convention to the cases. Together, the commission and the court provided mechanisms through which state compliance with the convention could be monitored.

Although the original convention was limited to civil and political rights, the Council of Europe later adopted a European Social Charter, in which states, with a degree of selectivity, could agree to be bound by various economic and social rights provisions. European member-states of the Council of Europe, for the most part, had already attained a high degree of compliance with human rights under their domestic constitutional and statutory law. Thus, it is difficult to say how much the human rights provisions of the convention and social charter led to improvements in human rights in Europe. No doubt the effect was interactive. The fact that the regional instruments existed only reinforced domestic tendencies toward observance of human rights principles by European governments, and fear of the adverse publicity accorded to violations probably gave governments additional incentives to work amicably within commission and court structures to resolve complaints about human rights abuses. With the enlargement of membership and the crowding of dockets, the commission was disbanded and the European Court restructured in the late 1990s.

Other regional structures existed in other parts of the world. The Charter of the Organization of American States (OAS), coupled with the American Declaration of the Rights and Duties of Man, both adopted in 1948, set the tone for protection of human rights in the Western Hemisphere. At the fifth OAS Meeting of Consultation of Ministers of Foreign Affairs in 1959, the Inter-American Commission on Human Rights (IACHR) was established. The commission's statute identified it as an autonomous entity of the OAS, and it was charged with promoting respect for human rights in the Americas. This body from its inception has undertaken country studies to this end, and in 1965 was given authority to receive and act upon petitions by individuals concerning violations by OAS governments of the provisions of the American Declaration of the Rights and Duties of Man. Added to these American efforts on behalf of human rights was the Inter-American Convention on Human Rights of 20 November 1969. While the human rights provisions of the OAS charter bound all member-states of the OAS, the convention's provisions applied only to ratifying governments. This convention established an Inter-American Court of Human Rights (IACT), tying it to the IACHR. Like the now-defunct European Commission, the IACHR may receive, examine, and act upon both individual petitions and interstate complaints. Unlike the European system, both the individual petition system and interstate complaint system are mandatory rather than optional. The right to file complaints is given not only to individual victims but to any group, such as nongovernmental organizations. The IACT has jurisdiction over both disputes concerning violations of the convention and to render advisory opinions. Enforcement mechanisms for court judgments, however, are lacking.

Efforts to establish a similar regional regime in Africa have centered on the innovative African Charter on Human and Peoples' Rights and the African Commission on Human and Peoples' Rights established by the charter. The functions of the commission permit it to study and promote human and peoples' rights in Africa, to prepare draft legislation to be used as a model by African governments in terms of codifying and implementing human rights standards in their domestic legal orders, and to hear interstate and individual complaints. Its work, however, was not enforceable, and organizational and budgetary weaknesses hampered both its endeavors to promote and to protect human rights. Efforts to expand and strengthen the African human rights system took a step forward in 1998 with the adoption of a Protocol to the African Charter aimed at establishing an African Court on Human and Peoples' Rights, which entered into force in 2004, and into operation in January 2006 with the election of judges.

HUMAN RIGHTS IN INTERNATIONAL LAW: DILEMMAS AND DEVELOPMENTS

Even as regional systems of human rights emerged, the international arena witnessed a proliferation of human rights conventions, many adopted by annual meetings of the United Nations General Assembly. The proliferation of human rights instruments is not viewed by all as an entirely helpful phenomenon. Some believe that the large number of agreements, many of which lack effective means of enforcement or are routinely ignored by many of the very states that voted for their adoption, creates an atmosphere of cynicism. Others believe that the sheer number of such agreements and their routine adoption represents an increasing awareness of human rights among governments, even where their compliance may fall short of the ideals espoused in the instruments. Whichever view is correct, there can be little doubt that there has been an explosion of human rights activity at the international level and that countless examples of violations of human rights continue to occur throughout the world.

Nonetheless, that both phenomena coexist should probably not be surprising. What they reflect are two very strong but potentially contradictory realities, that is, that people and governments desire to achieve greater respect for human rights and that governments prefer to retain as much sovereignty over their affairs as possible, including cases where disputes over sovereignty and territorial jurisdiction exist. The late 20th and early 21st centuries have been a period of intense nationalism and civil war. These conflicts have been marked by a good deal of bloodshed, hatred, violence, brutality, and inhumanity. The international community as a whole—sometimes fecklessly, at other times with greater determination and success—has sought to mitigate these situations through the application of humanitarian assistance and humanitarian law. In doing so, they consistently use the language of human rights to urge governments to resolve disputes and to call upon them to observe more humane standards of treatment in respect to their populations. Still, there is a rub. As organizations proliferate, so too do violations of human rights, often on a grand scale.

Thus, on the one hand, the international community routinely has approved a multitude of successive human rights declarations and conventions, including, to name just a few, the 1952 Convention on the Political Rights of Women; the 1954 Convention Relating to the Status of Stateless Persons; the 1958 Convention on the Nationality of Married Women; the 1959 Declaration on the Rights of the Child; the 1960 Declaration on the Granting of Independence to Colonial Countries and Peoples; the 1963 Declaration on the Elimination of All Forms of Racial Discrimination; the 1965 International Convention on the Elimination of All Forms of Racial Discrimination; the 1967 Declaration on the Elimination of All Forms of Discrimination against Women; the 1969 Declaration on Social Progress and Development; the 1973 Convention on the Suppression and Punishment of the Crime of Apartheid; the 1974 Universal Declaration on the Eradication of Hunger and Malnutrition; the 1975 Declaration on the Protection of All Persons from Being Subjected to Torture and Other Cruel, Inhuman, or Degrading Treatment or Punishment; the 1975 Declaration on the Rights of Disabled Persons; the 1977 Declaration on the Rights of Deaf-Blind Persons; the 1979 Convention on the Elimination of All Forms of Discrimination against Women; the 1981 Declaration on the Elimination of All Forms of Intolerance and of Discrimination Based on Religion or Belief; the 1984

Convention against Torture and Other Cruel, Inhuman, or Degrading Treatment or Punishment; the 1985 Declaration of Basic Principles for Victims of Crime and Abuse of Power; the 1986 Declaration on the Right to Development; and the 1989 Convention on the Rights of the Child.

This is only a partial list. Still, it helps to illustrate how extensive (and at times redundant) much of the international activity in the name of human rights has been. On the other hand, the vast majority of the declarations carry no legal weight, and several of the conventions that do establish legal obligations enjoy only sparse ratification among states. Others, such as the Convention on the Rights of the Child, though enjoying rapid and extensive ratification, do not contain effective enforcement mechanisms. Some of the declarations and conventions are highly contentious and controversial, while others merely reiterate rights that are stated in the International Bill of Human Rights, the Universal Declaration of Human Rights, and the International Covenants on Civil and Political and Economic, Social, and Cultural Rights. Some of the conventions do create enforcement mechanisms, such as committees to examine complaints regarding the violation of human rights and to receive reports from governments concerning their efforts to promote human rights, but in most instances such mechanisms are weak, lacking the teeth necessary to ensure state compliance. Many states are willing to ratify such agreements, knowing that they cannot actually be held to account for violations. Even state endorsement of the primary human rights instruments, the International Covenants on Civil and Political and Economic, Social, and Cultural Rights, has been slow. However, after three decades, about three-quarters of the governments have subscribed to them. In the case of the Optional Protocol to the International Covenant on Civil and Political Rights, a little more than half of the governments have ratified it. Other major treaties have been supplemented by protocols in an effort to establish more effective oversight and enforcement mechanisms, as with the Convention on the Rights of the Child and the Convention against Torture, but in these cases, too, ratification is sparse.

Coordinating the growing number of committees that receive state reports and complaints concerning human rights abuses is the United Nations High Commissioner for Human Rights (UNHCHR), which was established in the wake of the 1993 World Conference on Human

Rights. The UN recognized that the increasingly wide range of international human rights oversight committees and human rights activities needed coordination and overall promotion by a body dedicated specifically to these tasks. Thus, while ECOSOC and the United Nations General Assembly continue to serve as the bodies to which human rights agencies ultimately report, the UNHCHR now functions as the immediate mechanism for the coordination and promotion of human rights activities throughout the world, not only in the United Nations (UN) system as a whole but also in the field, where UNHCHR maintains a presence in many countries and where it offers technical assistance to them regarding human rights education and promotion. Moreover, in 2006, a further reform was initiated to address the ineffectiveness often evidenced in one of the UN's oldest human rights bodies, the United Nations Commission on Human Rights (CHR), which too often included member-states that ignored even elementary human rights principles in their own countries. Thus, a somewhat streamlined and new Human Rights Council was established for the purpose of achieving more credible oversight and to encourage a membership of governments more inclined to respect fundamental human rights.

It is easy to become too cynical or too optimistic about the progress of human rights in the modern world. What must be recognized, ultimately, is that as long as we have a sovereign state system, the observance of human rights principles is something that must be practiced by governments in their own domestic legal systems. The entire human rights apparatus of the UN system is predicated on this notion, however much the detractors of state sovereignty may wish to deny it. Governments might be prodded by advocacy groups, by the spotlight of world opinion, or by pressure from other governments to a better observance of human rights, but they cannot be forced to sign agreements with which they have reservations. As the contentious debates at the 1993 World Conference on Human Rights illustrated, there is sufficient cultural and ideological variance about which human or peoples' rights are most important to fuel continuing controversies in both domestic and international politics concerning which rights should be given priority when they clash with other rights. These kinds of problems are fundamentally philosophical and cultural ones that defy centralized global efforts at codification.

Still, when one broadens the view slightly and begins to examine international efforts on behalf of the humanitarian needs of victims of disaster, war, famine, and persecution, one cannot help but be impressed both by the staggering size of the needs and the correspondingly large degree of energy, time, and resources that go into the alleviation and mitigation of those needs. Here, the UN system is often at its best, in coordination with countless nongovernmental organizations dedicated to the preservation and improvement of human life. Thus, during the course of the six decades in which the UN has labored to respond to growing global problems, there has emerged a state-mandated and authorized system for meeting the needs of the poor, hungry, sick, and homeless of the world, as well as the needs of victims of war, disaster, and political feuding. Much of this international structure, as we have already seen, was erected in the immediate aftermath of World War II in order to meet the overwhelming needs of 30 million displaced persons in the continent of Europe alone. But the number of organizations has increased since then. To the FAO, World Bank, IMF, ILO, World Health Organization (WHO), the United Nations Educational, Scientific, and Cultural Organization (UNESCO), UNHCR, and the United Nations Children's Fund (UNICEF) have been added the Intergovernmental Committee for European Migration (ICEM) in 1952, now known as the International Organization for Migration (IOM); the World Food Programme (WFP) in 1961; the United Nations Fund for Population Activities (UNFPA) in 1969; the United Nations Disaster Relief Organization (UNDRO) in 1971, the functions of which were shifted in 1992 to the newly created United Nations Department of Humanitarian Affairs (DHA), and again in 1998 to the United Nations Office for Coordination of Humanitarian Affairs (UNOCHA); the United Nations Development Programme (UNDP) in 1971; the United Nations Environment Programme (UNEP) in 1972; and the International Fund for Agricultural Development (IFAD) in 1977.

As the number of humanitarian assistance agencies has grown, so too have their budgets, in part in response to greater needs. The UNHCR at the opening of the 1980s managed budgets of $300 to $400 million to assist and protect refugees. In subsequent decades, the budgets rose to more than a billion dollars annually, in part as a reaction to the increased number of refugees throughout the world. UNICEF's programming budget on behalf of children has seen a similar growth, with recent budgets approaching the $2 billion level. Helping such agencies to deliver this vast bulk of assistance is an army of international and indigenous nongovernmental organizations (NGOs), which do much of the actual grassroots implementation of humanitarian assistance. NGOs, in turn, serve as an advocacy community in defense of humanitarian interests and human rights. They are often the groups that first detect human rights abuses and report them more broadly to the international community. Here, the international humanitarian and human rights networks intersect.

But with increased needs, increased numbers, and bigger budgets, there has been a crisis of coordination within the UN system, especially in the area of humanitarian assistance but also increasingly in the development assistance area. With UN budgets hard-pressed to meet new and larger responsibilities, pressures have built for a more streamlined, less redundant, and better articulated system of achieving humanitarian policy objectives. For more than a decade, the UN system has struggled to coordinate its response to international emergencies and disasters. In 1991, the UN took the first steps toward promoting a more centralized coordination of the humanitarian assistance agencies with the establishment of the Department of Humanitarian Affairs (DHA) and the establishment of the post of Emergency Relief Coordinator (ERC). The ERC in turn supervised an Interagency Standing Committee (IASC) composed of prominent international assistance agencies such as the UNHCR, UNICEF, UNDP, and the WFP among others. But the traditional independence of the member agencies of the IASC was not easily brought under central management, and the system—though improving communication—did not always result in effective consolidated appeals. In 1998, a further reorganization of the UN system saw UNOCHA replace the DHA, and continue to advance the cause of consolidated appeals processes and greater degrees of coordination among UN humanitarian assistance bodies, both of which have proved to be difficult endeavors.

Even as the number of intergovernmental bodies offering humanitarian aid has grown, there has been an even more impressive proliferation in the numbers of nongovernmental agencies. The NGO sector is one of the liveliest and most extensive features of the humanitarian assistance regime, as well as of the human rights arena. Major humanitarian assistance NGOs include religious agencies such as Caritas Internationalis (CI), Islamic Relief, World Vision, and American Jewish Relief Service (AJWS), among many others. Among the major nonreligious NGOs are such well-known agencies as Cooperative for Assistance and Relief

Everywhere (CARE), Concern, Oxford Committee for Famine Relief (OXFAM), and the Save the Children Alliance. In turn, hundreds of NGOs have joined coalitions and networking bodies such as Interaction, the International Council of Voluntary Agencies (ICVA), and European Solidarity towards Equal Treatment of People (EUROSTEP), among others. These umbrella organizations help to promote contact and collaboration among NGOs. In addition to these more traditional charitable agencies, one must also recognize the work of the more visible philanthropic agencies that often have command over substantial resources. Modern philanthropy has also established foundations to pursue charitable works. Most familiar are the long-standing organizations such as the Carnegie Foundation, the Rockefeller Foundation, and the Ford Foundation. A more recent entry into this world is the Gates Foundation, founded by Bill and Melinda Gates, which emphasizes equitable global access to health and education. Private charities such as these often bring billions of dollars of assets to bear on humanitarian problems.

Another more modern manifestation of the charitable instinct is found in the now common tendency for well-known entertainers to organize fund-raising events for famine relief, AIDS prevention, and elimination of poverty and disease. Often forgotten in this area are figures such as Danny Thomas, founder of the St. Jude's Children's Research Hospital, and Jerry Lewis, founder of the Muscular Dystrophy Telethon. More recent manifestations in popular rock culture include the efforts by Irish rock star and gadfly Bob Geldof, who initiated the Band Aid album in 1984 to raise money for famine relief in Ethiopia, and his even more famous Live Aid concert of 1985, which raised tens of millions of dollars for famine relief throughout Africa. More recently, another Irish rock star, Bono, collaborated with Geldof in organizing a reprise of Live Aid, in the Live 8 concerts held in 2005. Bono took his work in the humanitarian arena seriously enough to found his own NGO known as DATA, which stands for Debt, AIDS, Trade in Africa. The compelling nature of human misery in the midst of natural disaster, civil war, and human rights abuses has drawn the increasing attention, then, not only of governments and international governmental bodies but also of the private nonprofit sector, and even the icons of business, industry, and popular culture.

Although intergovernmental organizations, NGOs, and private philanthropic bodies are increasingly common and visible features of the humanitarian and human rights fields, they have not displaced the foundational role of families and religious groups and churches as bearers of human and humane civilization. These basic institutions have persisted despite the rapid intrusion of secular institutions into areas where these traditional institutions once dominated, such as in education and social welfare. Indeed, when the modern human rights instruments were taking shape after World War II, the role of the family and of churches was widely recognized as being critical to the socialization of people. They were accorded basic rights under the principle of subsidiarity. Indeed, the traditional ethical precept of subsidiarity, together with the principle of solidarity, should be at the basis of all international organizational activity in pursuit of human rights.

STRATEGIES FOR PROMOTING HUMAN RIGHTS

That governments often display a desire to abide by and promote human rights can be seen in the welter of conventions, declarations, and recommendations they have entered into since the end of World War II. During the 1960s and 1970s, efforts to give these aspirations greater legal force were reflected in efforts to design reporting and complaint mechanisms into the agreements. This is one strategy governments have adopted in order to strengthen human rights agreements. Reporting and complaint procedures vary from agreement to agreement, but the basic pattern is to set up a committee to which either states parties or individuals, and sometimes even NGOs, may bring complaints regarding a member-state's failure to abide by its obligations under the treaty.

Typically, optional protocols to human rights treaties have been drafted to allow governments to voluntarily subject themselves to greater degrees of scrutiny, outside inspection, or individual complaints. This is the case with the Optional Protocol to the International Covenant on Civil and Political Rights. Ratification of the optional protocol constitutes member-state acknowledgment of the committee's competence to hear individual complaints. Similarly, an Optional Protocol to the Elimination of All Discrimination against Women establishes a system for hearing of individual or group complaints, as does the Optional Protocol to the African Charter on Human and Peoples' Rights, which establishes a court that may hear complaints from states, individuals, or

NGOs. A slightly different approach is taken in the Optional Protocol to the Treaty against Torture, which, pending ratification by 20 member-states, will permit an independent investigative subcommittee to visit detention facilities of member-states to monitor their compliance with treaty norms. In the case of many human rights treaties with such complaint mechanisms, the states party to the agreement are only subjected to the complaint procedure if they have declared their willingness to submit to it.

In some treaties, such as the International Covenant on Economic, Social, and Cultural Rights, governments are only required to submit reports on the measures they have taken through their domestic legal system to give effect to its provisions. These forms of human rights enforcement do not guarantee state compliance—even where the fairly radical step of allowing individuals to carry complaints against a state is allowed. Some of them, such as the European Convention on Human Rights and its recently renovated court, work because governments do not relish having the spotlight on their human rights foibles. In the European states, where sensitivity to the protection of human rights is quite significant, most governments seek responsibly to respond to complaints about human rights abuses before they are broadly publicized. In turn, the complaint review processes in Europe and in other contexts attempt to screen out frivolous and anonymous claims and to ensure that all complaints have run their course through all available local remedies. Even in the European system, which is the most highly developed and longest in duration, there is little capacity to use sanctions or coercive measures against a recalcitrant government that refuses to desist from, correct for, or compensate for human rights abuses. Most of the pressure is of the hortatory kind. This brings us to another important point. If the legal development of human rights at the international level has yet to develop truly effective mechanisms for enforcement, the political pressure that can be brought to bear by habit or general monitoring can be a significant inducement to states to observe basic human rights principles.

This means that the mass media, by pointing out abuses and focusing public attention on them, can have an important impact. Media throughout the world are increasingly adopting such a role, as reflected in the work of media-related NGOs, such as the Institute of War and Peace Reporting and Reporters without Borders.

A major step forward in the attempt to prevent and to punish the most outrageous violations of human rights took place with the adoption of the statute of the International Criminal Court (ICC) in 1998 and its entry into force in 2002. The ICC, building upon the ad hoc success of the United Nations Security Council in establishing criminal tribunals for Yugoslavia and Rwanda, attempts to establish a universal system for jurisdiction over and prosecution of war crimes, crimes against humanity, genocide, and other major violations of international humanitarian law. Governments still retain, under the ICC, the primary right and first responsibility to bring accused criminals to trial, but the ICC may institute proceedings against accused criminals if it believes that the member-states have been unable or unwilling to do so responsibly. The United States advanced serious reservations during the negotiation of the ICC statute and has since refused to ratify it on several grounds. Still, a large number of states have ratified the ICC statute, and the United States, though unlikely to do so, has sophisticated legal systems in place to try and punish serious breaches of law. International criminal law has thus taken a major leap forward, and no longer may even heads of state feel free to egregiously violate human rights norms with impunity, a fact underscored by the trial to which former Serbian president Slobodan Milosevic was subjected before his death, the trial of Saddam Hussein in Iraqi courts, and the trial of Charles Taylor for the crimes against humanity he is alleged to have committed during his tenure as president of Liberia.

Even as governments have taken steps to increase the prospect of greater human rights oversight and enforcement mechanisms, there has always been a further political reality at work in the form of wider world opinion. The international human rights advocacy community plays an important role in this regard. Groups such as Amnesty International (AI), Human Rights First (HRF; formerly known as the Lawyers' Committee for Human Rights, LCHR), Human Rights Watch and its regional affiliates, and a host of other nongovernmental agencies serve as monitors of human rights violations, investigating and publicizing them. Through their advocacy work and their lobbying with governments and international agencies, they stimulate pressure on governments to promote and respect human rights. They do this directly and indirectly: they do so directly by embarrassing governments with poor human rights records; indirectly, they do so by placing additional pressure on governments traditionally concerned about human rights issues to exert their influence with the offending states. This, then, is a highly political process that, though imperfect, can be made to uphold the ideals of human rights and fundamental freedoms.

The NGO sector is exceptionally diverse. As a general rule, those involved in human rights advocacy are not engaged in providing large amounts of aid. On the other hand, many of the large aid-giving NGOs have recently seen the need to develop advocacy dimensions to their work. There is, then, a wide array of NGOs representing a range of intellectual, religious, and philosophical perspectives. Indeed, even the past decade has witnessed a huge expansion in the number of NGOs, and especially so those working in the human rights field. This has been made possible largely by new information technology, in particular the emergence of the Internet. Whereas the costs of NGO formation and activity has in the past limited such organizations to those operating in the more developed and wealthy parts of the world, now even small groups, such as Derechos Human Rights, the South Asia Human Rights Documentation Centre (SAHRDC), and Widows Rights International, for instance, can acquire computers and Internet access, thus putting them into touch with the entire world. Thousands of indigenous NGOs have emerged in the past decade, and they serve as the eyes and ears and voices of peoples who experience repression and even persecution.

Human rights issues increasingly have come to dominate agendas of international forums, through intergovernmental activity and through the activity of the nongovernmental sector. The connections between civil war, political instability, and international conflicts and human rights abuses are noticed. In resolving such disputes, it is often necessary to anticipate the humanitarian and human rights agenda, especially in terms of reestablishing human populations displaced by the violence and persecution. Thus, even in such inveterate conflicts as the Afghanistan civil war, the Mozambican civil war, the Cambodian-Vietnamese conflict, the Bosnian conflict, the Central American conflict, and the conflicts in Sudan and the Congo, resolution of the disputes has depended on or will depend on addressing the refugee and displaced persons flows resulting from years of conflict. Governments and international agencies are recognizing the linkages and taking steps to anticipate them.

Another growing trend in our time is the gradual, if halting and imperfect, spread of democracy throughout the world. Modern democracies have their problems and their blind spots, but they represent major improvements over tyrannical and authoritarian governments. A democratic Afghanistan is far preferable from a human rights standpoint to Taliban repression. A democratic Iraq may be more chaotic than a Saddam dictatorship, but the desire for freedom and the sense of self-determination in which the majority rules is preferable to a jackboot regime. Indeed, with every passing year, more countries adopt democratic forms of government, often imperfectly at first—but then, first steps are often uncertain and wobbly. Even many nondemocratic countries under the pressure of a globalization of democracy have become less oppressive and more amenable to international human rights norms and outside political pressure. There is reason, then, to hope that in the future larger numbers of people will enjoy greater levels of respect for their basic human rights than was true during the tumultuous, brutal, and deadly century through which we have just passed.

There is, however, a major discordant trend, in what otherwise can be viewed as a positive future for human rights. September 11, 2001, marked a day on which international relations changed. The shocking and brutal terrorist attacks on that day illustrated that there is a price to be paid for the expanding freedom of movement, and of global communication and transportation. Modern terrorism has shown that it can use the vehicles of freedom and technology for destructive purposes. Moreover, terrorist organizations, not being governments and working in the shadowy interstitial tissue of international relations, cannot be easily interdicted or held accountable for callous acts of inhumanity and disregard of basic human rights. Governments, on the other hand, do have a primary responsibility to protect and preserve the lives, safety, and prosperity of their peoples. International efforts to repress and punish terrorist activity, then, are an increasingly urgent need. Human rights treaties recognize that certain rights may be derogated from in times of national emergency, and the terrorist attacks on and after September 11 point to the ongoing need for international diligence in preventing such heinous acts against innocent people. However, even as nations and peoples recognize that security will constrain freedom of movement and certain privacy rights, governments must also weigh how the common good can be secured without unnecessarily restrictive policies.

At no time in human history have more public and private resources been expended in the name of promoting human rights. Still, the human rights situation remains far from perfect. Like Sisyphus, we push away the rocks of prejudice, discrimination, and cruelty, only to see them reappear. So, part of our task is to keep the struggle for human rights alive, even where we admit that success is likely to be only partial and temporary. The quest for a perfect world is perhaps chimerical, but the quest for a better world is an eminently human and achievable endeavor where both the aspiration and determination exist.

The Dictionary

– A –

ADDAMS, JANE (1860–1935). The founder of Hull House was born in Cedarville, Illinois, on 6 September 1860. Addams' father was active in state politics as a Republican and encouraged his daughter's pursuit of education. Addams graduated from Rockford College in 1881 and subsequently entered the Woman's Medical College in Philadelphia. Ill health forced her to drop out. Addams later traveled throughout western and central Europe. During the English part of her trip, Addams conceived her "scheme" to establish a settlement house in a poor neighborhood in Chicago.

With Ellen Gates Starr, Addams established Hull House in September 1889. Addams and Starr were influenced by Toynbee Hall and the People's Palace, both in London, the novels of Walter Besant, and the writings of John Ruskin and Leo Tolstoy. Hull House became both a real community center and a place where reformers and academicians could meet and discuss their ideas on a range of topics such as industrialization, labor relations, municipal politics, crime, and **education**. Addams and other residents worked for the passage of many pioneering laws and urban programs such as the first juvenile court and "mother's pension" laws, the first playground in Chicago, eight-hour laws for working **women**, establishment of workman's compensation, regulatior. of tenements, and inspections of factories. Addams also worked for the abolition of child labor and for women's suffrage and the legal recognition of labor unions. Throughout the 1890s until World War I, Addams was regularly included in lists of both the greatest American women and the greatest American citizens.

In 1912 Addams seconded the nomination of Theodore Roosevelt for president at the Progressive Party convention and campaigned vigorously for the party since it endorsed many reform measures, including women's suffrage. From 1911 to 1915 Addams was the vice-president of the National American Woman Suffrage Association.

Addams devoted herself primarily to pacifism from 1914 onward. For her, war was the highest form of wasteful conflict. Addams helped form the Chicago Emergency Federation of Peace Forces in December 1914 and the Women's Peace Party, later the Women's International League for Peace and Freedom (WILPF) in January 1915. Addams chaired the International Congress of Women at The Hague in April 1915. Throughout 1915 Addams unsuccessfully toured the belligerent European capitals to urge the acceptance of neutral mediation. She was heartily denounced for continuing her pacifist position after the entry of the United States into World War I, and was accused of being a German militarist and Bolshevik sympathizer. Addams presided over a conference of the WILPF in Zurich that denounced the Versailles Treaty but supported the **League of Nations**.

During most of the 1920s, Addams was considered by many to be a dangerous radical and part of a worldwide communist conspiracy. She denounced the Palmer raids, worked against immigration restriction, and continually supported the United States joining the League of Nations and recognizing the Soviet Union. By the late 1920s she regained the esteem her countrymen once held for her and was awarded the Nobel Peace Prize in 1931.

In her last years, Addams accepted one of the vice presidencies of the American Association of Social Security and supported many social causes. She died of cancer in Chicago on 12 May 1935.

AFRICAN CHARTER ON HUMAN AND PEOPLES' RIGHTS. This unique human rights document was adopted at Nairobi, Kenya, on 28 June 1981 by the Assembly of Heads of State and Government of the Organization of African Unity (OAU), now known as the **African Union (AU)**. It entered into force among ratifying African governments on 21 October 1986. As the title of the charter suggests, it deals both with the rights of individuals as well as peoples. These are identified in Part I, Chapter I of the charter. Unlike most human rights documents, the charter, in Part I, Chapter II, identifies the duties of individuals, including among others, the duty to preserve the **family**, to respect parents and maintain them in case of need, to serve the national community, to contribute to the community's physical preservation and territorial integrity and defense according to law, and to pay taxes.

The charter established an **African Commission on Human and Peoples' Rights**, comprised of 11 highly reputable private individuals serving in their personal capacities for renewable terms of six years. Unlike other regional human rights systems, the African Charter did not provide initially for the establishment of a full-fledged court but only for a commission, on the principle that this preserved an African legal tradition of seeking political resolution of disputes. It also protected African member-states in their **sovereignty**. The commission sits twice annually at Banjul, Gambia, having commenced its work on 2 November 1987.

The charter is unique among regional conventions protecting human rights in that it includes economic, social, and cultural rights, in addition to civil and **political rights**. Moreover, unlike other regional systems, the African Charter recognizes the rights of peoples, as well as those of individuals. Otherwise, it protects a wide range of conventional rights common in both regional and global human rights conventions.

After several years of experience, it became evident that the commission could not adequately perform either its promotional or its protection functions, leading the OAU in 1994 to move toward the establishment of a court. On 10 June 1998, 30 OAU heads of state and government signed the text of the Protocol to the African Charter on Human and Peoples' Rights, calling for the establishment of an **African Court on Human and Peoples' Rights**. The protocol entered into force in 2004 after the 15th African government ratified the protocol. Eleven judges for the new African Court on Human and Peoples' Rights were elected in January 2006 and sworn in before the African Union Summit at Banjul, The Gambia, on 2 July 2006. For a text of the charter, see OAU Doc. CAB/LEG/67/3/Rev.5.

AFRICAN COMMISSION ON HUMAN AND PEOPLES' RIGHTS. The African Commission on Human and Peoples' Rights was established by the **African Charter on Human and Peoples' Rights**, which was adopted in 1981 by member-states of the Organization of African Unity (OAU), but did not enter into force until

October 1986. The commission held its first session in November 1987, and has met twice annually since then at Banjul, Gambia. It is authorized to promote human and peoples' rights, to collect documents, to conduct studies and conferences, to disseminate information, to encourage the development of human and peoples' rights organizations, and to make recommendations on such matters to governments. It may also formulate principles to be used by governments as a basis for human rights legislation and conduct investigations concerning abuses of human rights. It may receive communications from any state party concerning violations of the charter committed by other states parties. These may be handled through bilateral negotiation. If after three months the matter is not resolved, it may be submitted to the commission. The commission may also receive complaints directly. In either case, it may investigate the complaint, hold hearings, and submit a report of its findings to the states involved in the situation. The commission first seeks to determine that all local remedies have been exhausted or that pursuit of such remedies would involve an unreasonable delay, prior to taking up a question itself. Reports remain confidential until such time as the Assembly of Heads of State and Government decides to permit the chairman of the commission to publish them. Since its establishment in 1987, the commission has adopted rules of procedure and other guidelines for its work, and it holds workshops on the development of national strategies to promote and protect human rights in Africa.

After several years of experience, it became evident that the commission could not adequately perform either its promotional or its protection functions. It lacked the financial resources to aggressively pursue its promotional functions, and it was too often silent in the face of obvious governmental abuses of human rights, including terrible abuses in the Democratic Republic of the Congo, to name but one example. Rarely did the commission field investigations into human rights abuses, and the process for consideration of complaints was ponderous and slow. As with its promotional agenda, its small budget limited its ability to pursue its protection function. Even where it attempted to exercise its functions, member-states routinely denied it the right to enter their territory. These and other concerns prompted the OAU in June 1994 to launch exploratory work for the establishment of a court. On 10 June 1998, 30 OAU heads of state and government signed the text of the Protocol to the African Charter on Human and Peoples' Rights, calling for the establishment of an **African Court on Human and Peoples' Rights**. The protocol entered into force in 2004 after the 15th African government ratified the protocol, but preparations for launching the court's work have been complicated by the decision of the **African Union (AU)** to merge it with the AU's own Court of Justice.

AFRICAN COURT ON HUMAN AND PEOPLES' RIGHTS. Established by the Protocol to **African Charter on Human and Peoples' Rights** of 1998 by the Organization of African Unity (OAU), the African Court on Human and Peoples' Rights came into existence on 25 January 2004, after the 15th member-state ratified the optional protocol. The original member-states included Algeria, Burkina Faso, Burundi, Ivory Coast, Gambia, Lesotho, Libya, Mali, Mauritius, Uganda, Rwanda, Senegal, South Africa, Togo, and the Comoros. After experience showed that the **African Commission on Human and Peoples' Rights** was unable fully to perform its promotional and protection functions, the OAU decided that the establishment of a new court could pave the way toward the establishment of a more efficient and effective system for the protection of human rights, along lines more consistent with the experience of regional human rights regimes in Europe and the Americas.

Currently, slated to be seated at Banjul, Gambia, the court is to be composed of a contentious arm consisting of judges and an administrative arm, which is the registry. The judges may hear complaints from the commission, from states parties, and from individuals and even nongovernmental organizations if the state subject to the complaint as a state party has given the court the explicit competence to hear such complaints. The court may only hear cases involving situations occurring after the state party in question has ratified the protocol. However, none of these provisions have come into full effect as of yet. While, the **African Union (AU)**, which is the successor to the OAU, has endorsed the court as a conventional organ within the African Union, it is still considering how to merge it with its own Court of Justice. The AU is responsible for financing the operations of the court. The judges are to be elected by the Assembly of Heads of State and Government of the AU and the AU Council of Ministers is empowered to monitor the execution of the court's judgments. The court, in turn, is to report to the assembly, a body that has the capacity to amend the protocol establishing the court.

Owing to the fact that the AU also has a Court of Justice, which primarily addresses interstate complaints and serves as a constitutional court for the AU itself, some confusion arose concerning the relationship of the two bodies, especially since human rights provisions are included in the 2000 Constitutive Act of the African Court of Justice, that potentially overlap with those of the African Court on Human and Peoples' Rights. In July 2004, the AU decided to fuse the two courts, and in July 2005 it decided that the completed draft instrument accomplishing this merger should be considered at its session in January 2006. A complicating factor is that the protocol establishing the African Court of Justice has yet to be formally ratified by AU member-states. Nonetheless, the decision has been made by the AU that the African Court on Human and Peoples' Rights should proceed and the election of 11 judges, including two **women**, took place in January 2006, with the court registry to be subsequently placed in operation. It is likely that the seat of the court will be shifted to East Africa from Banjul, leaving open the possibility that the commission and the court may operate from different locations.

AFRICAN UNION (AU). Originally founded in 1963 as the Organization of African Union (OAU) by 32 African governments, the AU took its new name in 2002 as part of a renewed effort by African governments to enhance their multilateral cooperation. It is a comprehensive regional organization with broad functional authorities, including the areas of human rights and humanitarian issues. Among the purposes mentioned in the charter of the OAU were the promotion of unity and **solidarity** of African states, coordination of cooperation to achieve a better life for African peoples, the eradication of colonialism, and promotion of international cooperation toward the goals of the **United Nations Charter** and the **Universal Declaration of Human Rights**. These were to be achieved through political, diplomatic, economic, educational, cultural, scientific, technical, defense, security, **health**, sanitation, and nutritional cooperation. Human rights and humanitarian concerns broadly were affected by cooperation in all these areas.

Almost immediately, the OAU was faced with humanitarian situations concerning **refugees**. In 1967 it convened the Conference on the Legal, Economic, and Social Aspects of African Refugee Problems at Addis Ababa, Ethiopia. The conference concluded that refugees had to be treated as a humanitarian problem, that granting **asylum** should not be viewed as an act of hostility, and that assistance should be provided not only to refugees but also to their hosts in refugee-affected areas. The conference's recommendations were later incorporated into the OAU **Convention Governing the Specific Aspects of Refugee Problems in Africa**, which broke new ground in international regional refugee law by defining refugees more broadly than other international instruments. As refugee situations multiplied in Africa throughout the late 1970s and into the 1980s, the OAU participated in several international conferences to heighten international awareness of the humanitarian situation and to attract resources. These included the two conferences on assistance to refugees, notably the Second International Conference on Assistance to Refugees in Africa (ICARA II), cosponsored by the OAU with the **United Nations High Commissioner for Refugees (UNHCR)** and other **United Nations (UN)** agencies. The OAU's Bureau for Refugees, its Commission of Fifteen on Refugees and its Coordinating Committee on Assistance to Refugees all deal with various aspects of the African refugee problem.

In the broader realm of human rights, the heads of state and government of the OAU adopted the **African Charter on Human and Peoples' Rights** in 1981. That charter created an **African Commission on Human and Peoples' Rights**, which is now an integral part of the AU. The **African Court on Human and Peoples' Rights** is also in the process of being made operational by the AU. Also emanating from the work of the OAU was the African Charter on the Rights and Welfare of Children, which entered into force in November 1999.

The movement toward a more intense effort at continental unity began in 1999 when African heads of state decided to establish the AU. At that and three subsequent summits of the heads of state, concluding at Durban in 2002, the new African Union took shape and was finally launched. Its purposes are comprehensive, embracing efforts to promote greater peace and security, economic prosperity and development, democratic participation in political life, and promotion of human rights. The new AU Commission, which is the chief executive body, embraces a political affairs portfolio that promotes human rights, democracy, good governance, electoral institutions, civil society organizations, humanitarian affairs, refugees, returnees and internally displaced persons. One of its first great challenges was to address major conflicts and humanitarian/human rights crises around the continent, including the situations in the Democratic Republic of the Congo and in the Darfur region of Sudan. In the latter case, the Peace and Security Council fielded the African Union Mission in Sudan to oversee implementation of the Abuja Peace Process, to monitor the human rights situation, and to provide security for provision of humanitarian assistance. Address: P.O. Box 3243, Addis Ababa, Ethiopia. For more information see www.africa-union.org.

AFRICARE. Founded in 1971, this U.S. nongovernmental organization provides development and relief assistance predominantly in sub-Saharan African. Africare promotes development **education** programs in the United States with a special view to mobilizing African American support for grassroots development projects in Africa. Its programs and projects include the development of pharmaceutical supplies, water resources, improved **food** production, reforestation, and emergency assistance to **refugees**. A reliable humanitarian and development assistance agency, it has attracted large sums of private resources as well as large U.S. government grants for rural development programs. Over the life of the agency, 36 African countries have benefited from its relief and development programming. Today it operates programs in 26 African countries, with special emphasis on food security and agriculture, **health** and HIV/AIDS, development of civil society, environment and natural resource management, and ongoing emergency relief, refugee aid, and humanitarian assistance. Its annual program services have exceeded $40 million in recent years, making it an agency of considerable stature in the African continent, where it strives to promote human dignity and advance human development. Address: 440 R Street, NW, Washington, DC 20001, USA. Website: www.africare.org.

AGA KHAN, SADRUDDIN (1933–2003). Sadruddin Aga Khan was born on 17 January 1933 in Paris, France. An Iranian **national**, Prince Sadruddin's schooling was international in flavor. His early education was received in Switzerland, while his collegiate studies were done at Harvard University, from which he graduated in 1954, later studying at its Center for Middle Eastern Studies. Following a family tradition begun by his father, who served two terms as president of the **League of Nations**, Prince Sadruddin devoted his life to international service by working for a number of international organizations. Prince Sadruddin joined the **United Nations Educational, Scientific, and Cultural Organization (UNESCO)** in 1958, becoming executive secretary to its International Action Committee for the Preservation of Nubia. The committee brought together Eastern bloc and Western archaeologists in an attempt to save ancient artifacts, temples, and churches of the area. He later served as deputy high commissioner for refugees from 1962 to 1965 and as **United Nations High Commissioner for Refugees (UNHCR)** from 1965 to 1977. As high commissioner, he coordinated the international relief efforts to Bangladesh, Chile, Cyprus, Sudan, and Uganda and widened the UNHCR mandate to aid refugees from Algeria, Angola, Palestine, and Vietnam.

Prince Sadruddin served as special consultant and chargé de mission to the United Nations (UN) secretary-general, and as convenor and cochairman of the Independent Commission on International Humanitarian Issues and the Independent Working Group on the United Nations Financial Emergency. He was the coordinator for the United Nations Humanitarian and Economic Assistance Program for Afghanistan from 1988–1990. He also served as the personal representative of the United Nations Secretary-General for Humanitarian Assistance Related to the Iraq-Kuwait Crisis in 1990–1991. Later he served as the executive delegate of the secretary-general for a UN Interagency Humanitarian Program for Iraq and Kuwait and the Iraq/Turkey and Iraq/Iran border areas. With Denis de Rougement and other friends, he established the Groupe de Bellerive, a think tank, and the Bellerive Foundation, a grassroots action group, both in Geneva, to promote environmental protection and natural resource conservation. Bellerive was one of the first organizations to alert people to the potential human health hazards of modern, intensive farming practices. The prince was also a former vice president and a long serving trustee of the World Wide Fund for Nature International. Prince Sadruddin died in Boston, Massachusetts, after a short illness on 13 May 2003.

ALIENS' RIGHTS. Historically, the rights of aliens have been preserved in accordance with the international customary law of **state responsibility**. Aliens in general cannot expect to enjoy rights greater than those enjoyed by the citizens of the country in which they reside or are traveling through. Some countries, however, have maintained that there is a minimum standard of justice that should be accorded all persons, whether citizens or aliens, and many argue that that minimum standard is found in the so-called **International Bill of Human Rights**, which includes such international pronouncements as the **Universal Declaration of Human Rights** and the **International Covenant on Civil and Political Rights**. Although the minimum standard of justice idea is still controversial, the progress of international human rights instruments and their widespread acceptance by states as declaratory statements of international obligation give some credence to the notion that a minimum standard of justice is an evolving reality. This has implications for the rights of aliens.

In general, aliens who exhaust local remedies and who claim that a government has shown either a lack of due diligence in protecting their rights or actual complicity in the injury to them may seek redress through the **nationality** of claims by requesting their country of nationality to press a case for redress on their behalf against the offending state. Such a case remains, essentially, a state-to-state action, since individuals do not have the power under most circumstances in **international law** to sue a **sovereign** government. Still, by invoking their nationality ties, individuals may seek redress for wrongs committed against them while under the jurisdiction of foreign states, first through the legal avenues available to them in that state, and then by recourse to legal action undertaken by their country of nationality on their behalf. Still, many aliens, such as **refugees** and those seeking **asylum**, are unable to avail themselves of the legal protection of their home state. This leads to complications that are only partially remedied by international agreements relating to refugees and **stateless** persons.

Apart from efforts to provide for the protection and assistance to refugees and stateless people, the **United Nations (UN)** has, in its

Declaration on the Human Rights of Individuals Who Are Not Nationals of the Country in Which They Live, reaffirmed the fundamental human rights of aliens. In doing so, it has acknowledged that aliens have a duty to abide by the laws of the country in which they reside and that states have a right to control illegal immigration. The condition of migrants and alien populations, especially in the case of **minorities**, constitutes an ongoing concern for advocates of human rights.

AMERICAN DECLARATION OF THE RIGHTS AND DUTIES OF MAN. The Ninth International Congress of American States adopted the American Declaration of the Rights and Duties of Man on 2 May 1948 in Bogotá, Colombia. The declaration was only a statement of principles, and because it was not part of the charter of the **Organization of American States (OAS)**, it was not considered to be binding as law.

The introduction of the declaration recognized the dignity of the individual and that essential human rights were not derived from citizenship but were attributes of a person's human personality. The preamble asserted that all men are born free and equal and are naturally endowed with reason and conscience. Further, rights and duties are interrelated, and one of the highest duties is the preservation and strengthening of culture, the "noblest flowering" of which is embodied in moral conduct.

The two chapters laid out the rights and duties of persons. In 28 articles, the declaration listed numerous rights. These include the **right to life**, liberty, and personal security; **equality** before the law; **freedom of religion**; freedom of expression, inquiry, and dissemination; and freedom of **movement and residence**. Other civil and **political rights** stipulated were the right to a **fair trial**; to a **nationality**; to participation in free elections; to **freedom of assembly** and **freedom of association**; to **property**, petition, and protection from **arbitrary arrest**; and to due process of law and **asylum**. Other rights mentioned include the right to a **family**, to protection for mothers and children, and to private life, as well as the inviolability of the home and correspondence. Rights to **health, education**, and culture, to **work** and to fair remuneration, as well as to leisure and **social security** are also listed.

The declaration also articulates several duties of individuals in 10 articles. Every person has a duty to society, to children and families, to acquire education, to vote, to obey the law, to serve one's country, to cooperate with state and community, to further social security and welfare, to pay taxes, to work, and to refrain from political activities when one is an **alien** resident in a country.

Although the OAS ruled a year after the adoption of the declaration that it did not create any legal obligation, actions since then have strengthened the juridical status of the declaration. The **Inter-American Commission on Human Rights Statute** declared that for the purposes of the commission "human rights" were those listed in the declaration. During its history, the commission has consistently used the articles of the convention as its standards for promoting and protecting human rights. In fact, the Second Special Inter-American Conference in 1965 explicitly asked the commission to emphasize those human rights referred to in Articles I–IV, XVIII, XXV, and XXVI of the declaration. This request was then incorporated into the commission's statute. The revision of the OAS Charter in 1970 also has been seen as strengthening the declaration's normative character.

AMERICAN JEWISH WORLD SERVICE (AJWS). AJWS was founded in 1985 and motivated by the Jewish ethical imperative to promote justice. Its programs focus on elimination of **poverty** and the promotion of development, regardless of religion, race, or **nationality. Health, education**, HIV/AIDS, and sustainable agriculture programs are among its major efforts to promote community development and civil society. It also undertakes emergency assistance and humanitarian relief. Another major focus supports empowerment of **women** in nearly 40 projects throughout the world. In total its program assistance reaches 40 countries through 250 grassroots programs. Address: 45 West 36th Street, 10th Floor, New York, NY 10018-7904, USA. Website: www.ajws.org.

AMERICA'S DEVELOPMENT FOUNDATION (ADF). This U.S.-based nongovernmental organization (NGO) was founded in 1980 for the purpose of encouraging the development of democracy in the developing world, consistent with the particular needs of democratic groups in those nations. It supports the development of independent private sector groups, especially those devoted to the protection and extension of fundamental rights and freedoms. It works with such indigenous groups in the Americas, Southeast Asia, and Africa. It supports electoral reform and civic **education** in democratic principles. It also provides technical assistance to improve the administration of the justice system, to protect human rights, and to promote democratic governance. The agency began work in the area of civil society as its major focus, before the wider nongovernmental humanitarian sector fully appreciated the need for attention to the connection between political stability and economic development in their specific programming. ADF's emphasis on civic education, institutional development, and local democratic government thus placed it in the forefront of these activities at an early time. It currently works in more than 30 countries in Eastern and Central Europe, the Middle East, the Caribbean, Central America, and Africa. Address: 600 South Lee Street, Old Town, Alexandria, VA 22314, USA. For further information, see www.interaction.org, member profiles. Website: www .adfusa.org. *See also* INTERACTION.

AMNESTY. Governments have long used amnesty as a means of forgiving individuals held for punishment of both political and nonpolitical offenses or crimes. It is within the **sovereign** prerogative of a country to undertake blanket or individual extensions of amnesty consistent with its domestic law and practice. Amnesty is sometimes extended by a government to reduce public tensions after periods of emergency rule. Many countries routinely issue amnesty proclamations for political prisoners on special national holidays or anniversaries. Changes of government often lead new governments to free prisoners, especially political prisoners, incarcerated by the previous regime. At other times, amnesty is extended in order to fend off international diplomatic pressure. In this connection, **Amnesty International (AI)** and other human rights advocacy groups often prove effective by scrutinizing and publicizing governmental treatment of prisoners and by organizing both private and governmental campaigns for the release of prisoners. Amnesty is also used by states to encourage the return of those who fled from their country of **nationality** to avoid prosecution, induction into the military service, or because of desertion from the armed services.

Amnesty is an ameliorative tool that governments may use to heal national divisions, to forgive old wounds and offenses, and to encourage the reintegration of former citizens. More recently, amnesty is often closely associated with the formation of **truth commissions**. Whether people take advantage of amnesty offers, particularly in the case of expatriated citizens or exiles, is another matter. Whether they do so or not depends in part on their perception of the reception they will receive not only from the government but also from the society at large. Yet the passage of blanket amnesty laws in countries with such disparate governments as that of Auguste Pinochet in Chile, the Sandinistas in Nicaragua, and the **apartheid** regime in South Africa is regarded by some as a weakening of the rule of law insofar as they undermine the legal protection of human rights throughout the world, and inhibit the capacity of victims of human rights abuse from obtaining redress and justice, especially in egregious cases of **torture** or murders.

AMNESTY INTERNATIONAL (AI). Peter Benenson, a British lawyer, inadvertently created AI in 1961 when he urged people in a newspaper article to work peacefully to release prisoners of conscience. Thousands of letters poured in from people in many different countries offering to collect information, to publicize cases, and to approach governments to release their prisoners. AI is a recognized international nongovernmental organization (NGO) and has consultative status with the United Nations **Economic and Social Council (ECOSOC)** as well as with regional bodies.

AI's primary mandate is to help effect the release of prisoners of conscience—those who are prisoners because of their beliefs, race, gender, ethnicity, language, or religion and who have not used or counseled violence. Additionally, AI works to support the principle of **fair trial**, as well as prompt hearings, the abolition of the **death penalty**, and the eradication of **torture**.

AI's successes have resulted from its ability to mobilize local groups who work to better the human rights conditions of specific prisoners. AI's secretariat selects these prisoners for the local groups who then write letters to prison officials, judges, and other government officials. These local amnesty groups also ask lawyers and NGOs to intervene and to try to send letters directly to the prisoners.

It has been estimated that since 1961 AI has helped to release thousands of prisoners of conscience. AI was in large part responsible for the **United Nations General Assembly** Declaration on Torture, which culminated in the 1984 Convention on Torture.

AI was awarded the Nobel Peace Prize in 1977 and the United Nations Human Rights Prize in 1978. It publishes an annual world report, a monthly bulletin that updates information from fact-finding missions, and other research materials. AI has also published books on numerous topics related to its work. More recently, it has been an active watchdog of governmental restrictions on human rights of detainees in the international effort to repress global **terrorism**. In this connection, AI joined other human rights NGOs in 2005 in calling on the **Organization for Security and Cooperation in Europe (OSCE)** to carefully scrutinize extradition procedures to ensure that individuals subjected to **extraordinary rendition** or "interrogation outsourcing" are not secretly subjected to torture in countries where suspicions of such activity are high. AI has recently drawn attention to the problem of forced evictions throughout Africa, most notably and egregiously in Zimbabwe and Sudan, but also in Ghana, Nigeria, Angola, and Kenya. It continues to express concern about human rights abuses in Myanmar and Uzbekistan, and has criticized Palestinian groups for terrorist attacks and endangerment of civilians. AI is a member of the **Coalition to Stop the Use of Child Soldiers**. Address of AI's International Secretariat: 1 Easton Street, London, WC1X0DW, UK. Website: www.amnesty.org.

ANDEAN COMMISSION OF JURISTS. This international nongovernmental organization was established in 1982 with headquarters in Lima, Peru. It seeks to protect human rights and to promote democratic government in the Andean region of South America. It sees the legal profession as having a special vocation to modernize and develop political institutions and civil society. The commission has consultative status with the United Nations **Economic and Social Council (ECOSOC)**, and cooperation agreements with related intergovernmental organizations such as the **United Nations High Commissioner for Refugees (UNHCR)**, the **United Nations High Commissioner for Human Rights (UNHCHR)**, the **United Nations Educational, Scientific, and Cultural Organization (UNESCO)**, and the **Organization of American States (OAS)**. It is also affiliated with the **International Commission of Jurists**. It is composed of jurists from Bolivia, Chile, Colombia, Ecuador, Peru, and Venezuela. To achieve its goals, the commission provides counseling and educational programs dealing with human rights and legal issues, conducts research, and hosts seminars periodically. It publishes the *Andean Newsletter*, which is now available electronically on the commission's website, and a host of other reports and other works. Through this work, the commission hopes to strengthen democratic institutions, to promote the rule of law, and to advance the protection of human rights in the Andean region. Address: Andean Commission of Jurists, Los Sauces 285, Lima 27, Peru. Website: www.cajpe.org.

ANTHONY, SUSAN B. (1820–1906). Susan B. Anthony, "commander-in-chief" of the **women**'s rights movement after the U.S. Civil War, was born on 15 February 1820. Anthony began her adult life as a schoolteacher and was soon a leader in the women's temperance movement. By 1853, Anthony was devoting her efforts to the antislavery and women's rights movements. She worked as an agent for the American Antislavery Society from 1856 until the Civil War broke out.

From the early 1850s on, Anthony worked closely with **Elizabeth Cady Stanton** in both the antislavery and women's rights movements. Stanton considered her own speeches to be the "joint products of our two brains." From 1853 to 1860—driven by her belief that women could not be free politically without possessing economic rights—Anthony canvassed New York State on petition drives in support of giving women **property** rights. A New York law passed in 1860 allowed married women to own and keep property independently of their husbands, to carry on a trade, and to enter into contracts. It provided for joint guardianship of children and it gave wives rights over husband's property. This law overturned centuries of common law practice.

Anthony worked to remove the word "male" from the Fourteenth Amendment to the **Constitution of the United States**, which caused a breach between her and other antislavery leaders such as **Wendell Phillips, Frederick Douglass**, Horace Greeley, and **William Lloyd Garrison**. After the amendment's passage, Anthony traveled throughout the country speaking on behalf of women's suffrage. From 1868 to 1870, Anthony and Cady Stanton published a New York weekly primarily devoted to women's rights.

Wanting to test the constitutionality of denying women's suffrage, Anthony registered and voted in 1872. She was arrested, tried, convicted, and fined. The Supreme Court in 1875 upheld the constitutionality of denying women the right to vote. In the meantime, Anthony worked for a federal women's suffrage amendment through the National Woman Suffrage Association until 1890 and with the National American Suffrage Association from 1890 to 1906.

Anthony, with her close colleagues, published the four-volume *History of Woman Suffrage (1881–1902)*. She organized the **International Council of Women (ICW)** in 1888 and the International Woman Suffrage Alliance in 1904. Her last effort on behalf of women's rights was her successful battle to make Rochester University coeducational in 1906. The "Napoleon" of the women's rights movement died on 13 March 1906.

APARTHEID. For many years, especially after the emergence of Third World majorities in the **United Nations General Assembly**, concern was voiced over the practice of apartheid by the government of South Africa. Apartheid referred to the official policy of separation of the races, the establishment of a color bar, and the separation of public facilities, transportation, recreational areas, **housing** areas, eating facilities, and washrooms. It prohibited intermarriage and the free movement of nonwhites, and severely restricted **property** rights. The black homeland (or Bantustan) policy represented the most ambitious aspect of the apartheid system in which the majority black population was to be consigned to about 10 percent of the land area of South Africa. The system perpetuated the nonextension of political and economic rights to the black population. Deeply racist in its content and effects, the apartheid policy was equally deeply resented by African peoples and governments, and broadly condemned by the international community.

Opposition to apartheid in the **United Nations (UN)** eventually led in November 1973 to the adoption by the **United Nations General Assembly** of the **International Convention on the Suppression and Punishment of the Crime of Apartheid**. The convention defined apartheid as a crime, and held those individuals practicing it criminally responsible, whether they engaged in apartheid as members of private organizations or public institutions. Though widely ratified by developing countries, the vast majority of major powers, excepting the Soviet Union, abstained on the vote adopting the convention and later refrained from ratifying the convention itself. This reluctance centered on concern that many provisions of the convention constituted illegal interference in the domestic affairs of a member-state of the UN. Still, even the United States, which did not become a signatory, passed separate legislation in which economic sanctions were imposed on South Africa because of its racist practices.

In a less well-known action of December 1985, the United Nations General Assembly approved the International Convention against Apartheid in Sports. This convention entered into force in 1988, though only a relatively small number of states became signatories. The convention established a 15-member Commission against Apartheid in Sports that reported to the General Assembly on matters within the purview of the convention.

The issue of apartheid has become largely a closed if regrettable chapter in the history of South Africa, as a result of the dramatic reforms that were initiated in the early 1990s and that culminated in the election of **Nelson Mandela**, leader of the formerly banned African National Congress, as president of the country. Economic sanctions against South Africa were revoked by the UN and by other countries, which had imposed them unilaterally. Although localized and criminal violence still plagues parts of the country, the apartheid system as a legal structure has been dismantled. In an effort to put apartheid behind them, the people of South Africa engaged in the first, and a very major, **Truth and Reconciliation Commission (TRC)**.

ARAB LAWYERS' UNION. Also referred to as the Arab Federation of Lawyers, this body was founded in Cairo in 1958. Its members include the bar associations and law societies of 15 countries, including Algeria, Bahrain, Egypt, Iraq, Jordan, Kuwait, Lebanon, Libya, Mauritania, Morocco, Palestine, Sudan, Syria, Tunisia, and Yemen, as well as Palestine. Its individual members include more than 200,000 lawyers and 27 bar associations. The union promotes contact between Arab lawyers, seeks freedom for lawyers and magistrates to do their **work**, and promotes the right of Arab lawyers to take cases in any Arab country. It also seeks to promote and protect human rights in Palestine and throughout the Arab world. It promotes the development of the legal profession and the emergence of genuinely independent judiciaries in the Arab world. It enjoys consultative status with the United Nations **Economic and Social Council (ECOSOC)**. Address: 13 Arab Lawyers' Union Street, Garden City, Cairo, Egypt.

ARBITRARY ARREST. The notion that individuals should be free from arbitrary arrest hails back to the early development of natural rights principles. The notion is captured in the **Constitution of the United States** and the **Bill of Rights**, which affirm the notion that a person has a fundamental **right to life**, liberty, and **property**, as well as a right to be charged for a crime before a judge, and a right to due process of law if any of these rights is to be abridged. In **United Nations (UN)** parlance, the right to freedom from arbitrary arrest is usually coupled with the right to be free from arbitrary detention and arbitrary exile. The **Universal Declaration of Human Rights** and the subsequent **International Covenant on Civil and Political Rights** both emphasize these fundamental freedoms, as do a variety of regional human rights instruments.

ASSOCIATION FOR THE PREVENTION OF TORTURE (APT). Founded in 1977 by Jean Jacques Gautier, this private, nongovernmental organization (NGO) seeks to identify, publicize, and prevent incidences of **torture**, as well as to assist the victims of torture. It enjoys consultative status with the United Nations **Economic and Social Council (ECOSOC)**, the **Organization of American States (OAS)**, the **Council of Europe (COE)**, and the **African Commission on Human and People's Rights**. Address: Route de Ferney 10 C.P. 2267, 1211 Geneva 2, Switzerland. Website: www.apt.ch.

ASSOCIATION OF PROTESTANT DEVELOPMENT ORGANIZATIONS IN EUROPE (APRODEV). One of three major nongovernmental coalitions of European agencies, such as **European Solidarity towards Equal Participation of People (EUROSTEP)** and **International Cooperation for Development and Solidarity (CIDSE)**, that exercise major influence on humanitarian and human rights issues throughout the world, APRODEV unites 17 significant Protestant humanitarian and development aid organizations, including Hungarian Interchurch Aid; the Swiss agencies Bread for All and HEKS/EPER; the German agencies Bread for the World, EAEZ, and EED; the British agency Christian Aid; the Belgian agency Protestant Solidarity; the French agency CIMADE; the Dutch agencies ICCO and Global Ministries; and a number of Scandinavian agencies, such as the Church of Sweden, Diakonia, Danchurchaid, Finnchurchaid, Icelandic Church Aid, and Norwegian Church Aid. The **World Council of Churches (WCC)** and the **Lutheran World Federation (LWF)** enjoy observer status with APRODEV. APRODEV serves as a forum and coordinating body for its members and their work, which includes emergency relief aid, rehabilitation and development aid, capacity building, and human rights and humanitarian advocacy. Website: www.aprodev.net.

ASSOCIATION OF SOUTHEAST ASIAN NATIONS (ASEAN). Founded in 1967, ASEAN was formed in order to promote political, economic, and cultural ties among its member-states, which initially included Indonesia, Malaysia, the Philippines, Singapore, and Thailand. Its membership has since expanded to include Brunei Darussalam (1984), Vietnam (1995), Laos and Myanmar (1997), and Cambodia (1999). ASEAN has on occasion tackled human rights and humanitarian issues, as it did in attempting to resolve the Cambodian situation during the 1980s, in keeping with one of its founding objectives, which is to promote regional peace and stability "through abiding respect for justice and the rule of law in the relationship among countries in the region." ASEAN has taken an interest in **refugees** and in the effects of refugee flows on the region as well as in promoting research on natural disasters. ASEAN has a Committee on Social Development and a Population Program, and increasingly has addressed issues concerning **terrorism** and transnational criminal activity. It has been less successful in addressing human rights issues plaguing its members Myanmar (Burma) and Cambodia.

Situated in a growing and dynamic region with a population of about 500 million, a combined gross domestic product of nearly U.S.$740 billion, and trade activity of some U.S.$720 billion, ASEAN has emerged as a major regional organization, with a capacity to encourage promotion of peace, justice, and prosperity among its member-states. The highest decision-making body of ASEAN is the meeting of the ASEAN heads of state and government, which occurs annually. Numerous ministerial meetings are also held to address a variety of sectorial concerns, including legal matters, rural development, and **poverty** alleviation, social welfare matters, and transnational criminal issues. The ongoing work of ASEAN is conducted through 29 committees and 122 technical working groups, and it maintains official relations with 53 nongovernmental organizations, and a variety of governments, **United Nations (UN)** agencies, and professional organizations. Address: ASEAN Secretariat, 70A Jalan Sisingamangaraja, Jakarta 12110, Indonesia. Website: www.aseansec.org.

ASYLUM. The practice of providing protection and hospitality to people seeking refuge from persecution or harm in their homeland comes down to us from ancient times. In modern usage, asylum is granted by states to individuals who have suffered from persecution or fear that they will be persecuted by their government of **nationality** or citizenship. By refusing to grant a request for **extradition**, a government tacitly extends asylum to the individual fugitives. Asylum, as currently constituted, is not yet a legal right of individuals. Governments alone have the right to grant asylum. Individuals have a right to seek and enjoy asylum, but governments have no corresponding duty to grant it.

Governments acknowledge the existence of two forms of asylum: territorial and diplomatic. Most governments subscribe to the principle of territorial asylum, which may be granted by them to individuals who have fled into their territorial jurisdiction and claimed asylum status. Only in Latin America is diplomatic asylum widely recognized. It imposes on governments a duty to allow safe passage out of their territory for those individuals, including their own citizens, who have sought asylum in the embassy of another country that accepts diplomatic asylum. Most governments outside of Latin America do not acknowledge the legitimacy of this principle. In Latin America, the **Inter-American Convention on Diplomatic Asylum** codified the regional customary norm. In addition, an **Inter-American Convention on Territorial Asylum** codified regional practice in the area of territorial asylum claims.

Efforts to develop a universal (as opposed to a regional) right of asylum include the abortive Convention on Territorial Asylum, which in turn was stimulated by the **United Nations General Assembly Declaration on Territorial Asylum** adopted in 1967. The latter is not a legally binding agreement among governments. Indeed, governments are primarily responsible for determining asylum claims and alone enjoy the privilege of granting asylum, but the **United Nations High Commissioner for Refugees (UNHCR)**, under its statute and various international and regional conventions and declarations, has the capacity to advocate on behalf of **refugees**, in order to ensure their protection and assistance, and to discourage illegal repatriation or **nonrefoulement** of individuals who have been granted refugee status, or who are prevented from seeking asylum.

ATLANTIC CHARTER. Formally drafted by British Prime Minister Winston Churchill and later revised by him with U.S. President Franklin Delano Roosevelt during negotiations held between them from 9–12 August 1941 at Placentia Bay, Newfoundland, this statement served as the initial groundwork for Allied cooperation during World War II, and enunciated the principles by which a more peaceful and just postwar world order could be established. It was later incorporated into a **Declaration by the United Nations** on 1 January 1942. Among the principles asserted in the Atlantic Charter were several dealing essentially with human rights including the notions of the **self-determination** of peoples, of access to international trade, and of the securing of improved labor standards, as well as the reaffirmation of the territorial integrity of states, a largely settled principle of **international law**. It also emphasized the need for economic advancement, **social security**, freedom of the seas, and peaceful settlement of disputes.

AUNG SAN SUU KYI (1945–). Aung San Suu Kyi was born in Rangoon, British Burma, in 1945. Her father, General Aung San, was Burma's leader at independence and established the modern Burmese army. He was assassinated in July 1947. Suu Kyi studied at Oxford University, where she met and married Michael Aris, who was a professor of Tibetan studies at Oxford. They have two sons.

In April 1988, Daw Suu Kyi returned to Burma to be with her mother who was ill and who died in January 1989. General Ne Win, who took control of Burma in a military coup in 1962 and instituted "the Burmese way of socialism," which has led to economic ruin, resigned the presidency in July 1988. Riots over the poor economic conditions broke out in August 1988 and led to a 19-member military junta taking control in September 1988 and subsequently renaming the country Myanmar. In response, Daw Suu Kyi helped organize the National League for Democracy (NLD), dedicated to democratic reform. By 1989 the NLD had two million dues-paying members.

Influenced by the civil disobedience campaigns of Dr. **Martin Luther King** and the Satyaghraha movement of **Mohandas K. Gandhi**, Daw Suu Kyi during 1988 and 1989 traveled the country speaking on behalf of democracy and the end of military dictatorship. In doing so, she regularly violated government regulations that prohibited meetings of more than five people. In 1989, she publicly attacked the continued control of the country by General Ne Win, and in June 1989 she called on the armed forces to overthrow him.

On 20 July 1989, Daw Suu Kyi and 42 other leaders of the NLD were arrested, offices of the league throughout the country were ransacked, and NLD files were confiscated by the government. It is estimated that 2,000 party members were put in detention in July through August of 1989. Daw Suu Kyi was placed under house arrest. In elections in May 1990, the NLD won 82 percent of the vote and 392 of the 495 seats in the National Assembly. The league's first demand after this victory was for the freedom of its leadership, including Daw Suu Kyi. The military government annulled the elections. In September 1990, the junta announced that it would release Daw Suu Kyi if she agreed to leave the country. She refused.

Daw Suu Kyi was awarded the 1991 Nobel Peace Prize for her nonviolent campaign to bring democratic government to Myanmar (Burma). She used the $1.3 million prize to establish a trust for the **education** and **health** of the Burmese people. On 21 September 1994, she was allowed to leave her home for the first time since her arrest for a televised meeting with two leaders of the junta. On 10 July 1995, the junta freed her from house arrest. However, many other leaders of the NLD remained in prison while others were afraid to speak publicly.

Daw Suu Kyi announced that she would resume her work to restore democracy to Myanmar (Burma) and that she was open to negotiations with the junta toward the end of installing a transition government composed of both civilians and military officials. Suu Kyi did not attend the United Nations International Women's Conference in Beijing, China, owing to her concern that Burma's military dictatorship would not allow her to return to the country, yet she was able to send a videotaped address, which was shown in Beijing. In her videotaped address, Suu Kyi called for a reduction in military spending, improvements in **women**'s education, and the empowerment of women throughout the world.

The Burmese government denied an entry visa to her husband, Michael Aris, after he was diagnosed with prostate cancer in 1997. Suu Kyi did not visit her husband in Great Britain because the Burmese government made it plain that if she left the country, she would be denied a reentry visa. Aris died in March 1999.

In September 2000, the Burmese government put her under house arrest again. After negotiations led by the **United Nations (UN)**, she was released on 6 May 2002. After her release, Suu Kyi made seven trips to supporters in different parts of the country. On the seventh trip, to northern Burma, near the town of Dipeyin, Suu Kyi and her supporters were viciously attacked by a progovernment gang of about 5,000, who used rocks, slingshots, nail-studded clubs, bamboo sticks, and iron bars to beat to death nearly 100 of her supporters. Suu Kyi narrowly escaped serious injury and even death.

The Burmese government arrested her when she reached Ye-U and she was imprisoned in Yangon (Rangoon). After surgery in September 2003, Suu Kyi was put under house arrest in Yangon. In response, the U.S. Congress passed economic sanctions against Myanmar that are the toughest sanctions since those imposed on Cuba. The Burmese government extended Aung San Suu Kyi's house arrest in December 2004 and she was still confined as of the spring of 2006.

– B –

BIKO, STEVEN (1946–1977). Leader of the Black Consciousness Movement and arguably the most important black South African leader of the early and mid-1970s, Steven Biko was born in King William's Town on 18 December 1946. Biko's father died when he was four and his mother raised him alone. Biko attended school at Brownlee Primary, Lovedale Institute, and then transferred to Marianhill, a Catholic school in Natal. In 1966, he enrolled in the "non-European" section of the medical school at the University of Natal. Initially earning good grades, Biko's academic program suffered as he increased his political activity and he was officially terminated from the university in 1971.

Biko and some fellow students established the South African Students Organization (SASO) in order to develop black leadership out of the shadow of white student organizations. As a SASO resolution phrased it, "SASO is a black student organization working for the liberation of blacks first from psychological oppression by themselves through inferiority complex and secondly from the physical oppression accruing out of living in a white racist society."

Biko was the first president of SASO and then went to work for Black Community Programs in Durham and helped establish the Black People's Convention in 1972. Projects of the former were started in cities in South Africa in the 1970s with the aim of launching black self-help initiatives such as literacy classes and services such as **health** clinics. Biko was also the driving force behind Black Consciousness, the movement and ideas, which provided the foundation for the Black People's Convention.

Biko was banned in March 1973. Under South Africa's **apartheid** law, a person was banned without trial. The banned person was restricted to a small geographic area; could not be published or quoted; and was not allowed to speak to more than one person at a time. Further, banned people, such as Biko, were under constant surveillance and subject to searches.

In 1976, Biko was detained for 101 days without charge. Many times after that, detention the authorities charged Biko but he was never convicted. Biko was appointed honorary president of the Black Community Program in 1977. In the same year, conversations began between the Black People's Convention and the African National Congress (ANC), a development that worried the South African government. On 18 August 1977, Biko was stopped at a security checkpoint and arrested for being in violation of his banning order. He was taken to the Port Elizabeth prison. On 6 September, Biko was taken to Room 619 in handcuffs and leg irons. Naked, he was manacled to a grill and subjected to 22 hours of interrogation, being beaten and **tortured** throughout his questioning. During those hours, he received a severe head injury. One of the district surgeons allowed Biko to be transferred to Pretoria Central Prison, hundreds of miles away, where he died on the floor of his cell, naked and alone, on 12 September 1977. Members of South Africa's **Truth and Reconciliation Commission (TRC)** Amnesty Committee reviewed Biko's case and refused to grant **amnesty** to the former security police applicants because of the applicants' lack of full disclosure.

For many, Biko's murder at the hands of the security police was a turning point. The anniversary of his death was commemorated for years afterward and his death marked the beginning of the eventual demise of the apartheid regime.

BILL OF RIGHTS (U.S.). The term "Bill of Rights," in U.S. constitutional parlance, refers to the first 10 amendments to the **Constitution of the United States**. These amendments are different from any of the other amendments in that they are seen to be an integral part of the U.S. Constitution because of the fundamental nature of the liberties protected by them and because they were proposed and adopted as part of a promise by Federalists to citizens who were troubled by the omission of such protection of liberty in the Constitution drafted in Philadelphia. To attract citizen support in the face of a strong antifederalist challenge, the Federalists prudently determined to include such a charter of rights in the Constitution immediately after and in return for the ratification of the Constitution itself.

The ten amendments comprising the Bill of Rights were adopted in 1791. The First Amendment prohibits Congress from establishing a religion or prohibiting religious freedom, abridging **freedom of speech, freedom of the press, freedom of assembly**, and petition. The Second Amendment provides for the right of people "to keep and bear arms" in order to keep state militias functioning. The Third Amendment prohibits the quartering of soldiers in homes during peacetime and allowed it in wartime only under written law. The Fourth Amendment protects people from unreasonable searches and seizures.

The Fifth Amendment provides that a grand jury indictment was necessary for a person to be charged for a capital offense, prohibits double jeopardy and forced self-incrimination, provides that private **property** could be taken for public use only with "just compensation" and that no person could "be deprived of life, liberty or property, without due process of law." The Sixth Amendment protects people in criminal prosecutions by ensuring the accused has the right to a public and speedy trial, to be told of the charge against him, to confront witnesses against him, and to have legal counsel for his defense. The Seventh Amendment provides for jury trials. The Eighth Amendment prohibits excessive bail, excessive fines, and "cruel and unusual punishment." The Ninth Amendment, the "forgotten ninth" as it is sometimes referred to, provides that people's unenumerated rights are protected. The Tenth Amendment reserves the powers not delegated to the United States or prohibited to the states to the states and to the people.

Although Congress is mentioned only in the First Amendment, all of the amendments comprising the Bill of Rights were intended to be applicable only to the federal government. James Madison, the floor manager of the amendments in the U.S. House of Representatives, soon held after adoption that the amendments should be applicable to the states as well as to the federal government. Yet, for most of U.S. history, the Bill of Rights did not protect citizen rights from state action. This outcome resulted from the decision of the Supreme Court in *Barron versus Baltimore* (1833). Chief Justice John Marshall spoke for the Court when he said that the Fifth Amendment specifically restrained the federal government, not state governments. Further, to Marshall, there was no intention on the part of those who wrote and adopted the Bill of Rights to have it applied to the states.

After *Barron*, the issue of the applicability of the Bill of Rights has been a contentious one because it strikes at the heart of the federal system of the United States and because of the fundamental freedoms protected by the amendments. The Court dealt with the issue again after the Fourteenth Amendment (1868) was passed in the wake of the U.S. Civil War. The amendment included the words "nor shall any state deprive any person of life, liberty, or property, without the due process of law," which were lifted verbatim from the Fifth Amendment. Even with this language of the Fourteenth Amendment, the Court in the *Slaughterhouse Cases* (1873) decided that the Fourteenth Amendment did not incorporate the Bill of Rights into the amendment's meaning of "life, liberty, or property." Therefore, the 1868 amendment did not protect citizens from any state action that the Bill of Rights would protect them from if committed by the federal government.

The decision of the Court in the *Slaughterhouse Cases* was, in effect, overturned by a series of cases dealing with different freedoms from the mid-1920s to the late 1960s, wherein the Court used the constitutional doctrine of incorporation to decide that the Bill of Rights, via the due process and equal protection clauses of the Fourteenth Amendment, did protect people from state action. The Court began to accept incorporation at least partly in *Gitlow versus New York* (1925). The Court declared in *Gitlow* that "freedom of speech and of the press . . . are among the fundamental personal rights and liberties protected by the due process clause of the fourteenth amendment from impairment by the states." In following years, the Court used this logic to protect other provisions of the Bill of Rights from state and local government action, such as the liberties in the First and Fourth Amendments, most of the Fifth and Sixth Amendments, and the cruel and unusual punishment section of the Eighth Amendment.

– C –

CAIRO DECLARATION. Adopted by the Conference of the Heads of State or Government of Nonaligned Countries on 10 October 1964, the Cairo Declaration identified a comprehensive plan for international peace and cooperation. It addressed numerous issues concerning human rights, including statements on the elimination of colonialism, neocolonialism and imperialism, the need for respect of the right of peoples to **self-determination**, the condemnation of the use of force against the right of self-determination, and the condemnation of **racial discrimination** and **apartheid**. The Cairo Declaration is hortatory in nature, lacking the force of law, but it exhibits the views of numerous countries affiliated with the nonaligned movement. Some of its elements, particularly its affirmation of both state

sovereignty and the right to self-determination, are potentially contradictory.

CARE. A private nongovernmental organization (NGO), CARE was established in 1945 to provide assistance to the masses of displaced and homeless people in Europe after World War II. First headquartered in New York, CARE (which at first stood for Cooperative for American Remittances to Europe and now stands for "Cooperative for Assistance and Relief Everywhere") now is headquartered in Atlanta, Georgia, and operates relief and assistance programs in over seventy countries. CARE USA is one of the largest American NGOs in terms of its budget and volume of assistance. CARE is especially noted for its logistical skills in transportation, delivery, and rationing of humanitarian **food** aid, but its assistance activities extend far beyond the transportation sector. It engages in food-for-**work** programs, reforestation and conservation projects, irrigation and agricultural assistance schemes, as well as in emergency assistance activities.

Its work also focuses on the needs of children, especially in the areas of **education**, **health**, nutrition, and water sanitation programs. Its work on HIV/AIDS includes attention to care for orphaned children. It sponsors a special campaign for CARE for the Child, aimed directly at ending malnutrition, as well as a Children and Poverty Campaign, aimed at promoting education generally and at ending discrimination against the access of girls to education. This program also promotes the health of children. CARE USA budgets are typically balanced with 60 percent devoted to development and 40 percent to emergency aid and rehabilitation programs. Today, CARE is a truly transnational enterprise and operates as a confederation of 11 independent international members, with country offices in Australia, Canada, Denmark, Germany, France, Japan, The Netherlands, Norway, Austria, the United Kingdom, and the United States, as well as an International Secretariat Office in Brussels, Belgium. U.S. Address: 151 Ellis Street, NE, Atlanta, GA 30303-2440, USA. International Secretariat: Boulevard du Regent, 58/10, B-1000 Brussels, Belgium. Website: www.careinternational.org.

CARITAS INTERNATIONALIS (CI). Caritas Internationalis is a confederation of 162 national Catholic charitable organizations involved in the collection and provision of humanitarian aid and development aid, with assistance programs in more than 200 countries. CI serves as a coordinating mechanism for the promotion of social justice and charity by these national affiliates and their grassroots components. Founded in 1951 in the wake of the post–World War II humanitarian crisis, its roots can be traced back into the 1920s as various already-existing national Catholic charities perceived the need to collaborate at the international level. At its founding, 13 national CI organizations banded together. CI is headquartered in the Vatican and today constitutes a truly global system of humanitarian cooperation, with an ability to mobilize huge amounts of resources in response to emergency relief situations.

Advocacy in the human rights arena is an ongoing concern for CI, which attempts to influence policy makers at the international, national, and local levels to promote policies and programs conducive to peace and justice. Areas in which CI especially focuses include financing for international development, the indebtedness of poor countries, and the impact of globalization in trade on poor countries. It has also promoted peaceful reconciliation of disputes, an end to human trafficking, and the movement toward sustainable development. It enjoys consultative status with the United Nations **Economic and Social Council (ECOSOC)** as well as with a number of **United Nations (UN)** specialized agencies and with the **Council of Europe (COE)**. Address: Palazzo San Calisto, I-00120 Città del Vaticano, Vatican. Website: www.caritas.org.

CARTAGENA DECLARATION. Adopted in 1984, the Cartagena Declaration defined **refugees** as those "persons who have fled their country because their lives, safety, or freedom have been threatened by generalized violence, foreign aggression, internal conflicts, massive violations of human rights or other circumstances which have seriously disturbed public order." This language substantially broadens the language defining refugee status found in the United Nations **Convention Relating to the Status of Refugees**. It reflects rather the broader language found in the African regional definition incorporated into the **Convention Governing the Specific Aspects of Refugee Problems in Africa**. The declaration was approved by several Central and Latin American states, and it recognized that the condition of flight prevailing in the region called for a more expansive definition of refugees and of the circumstances in which they should be accorded **asylum**. The **Organization of American States (OAS)** later encouraged its members to implement the provisions of the declaration.

CARTER CENTER. The Carter Center was established in 1982 by former U.S. President James E. Carter Jr. and former First Lady Rosalynn Carter. The center's goals are to advance human rights and alleviate human suffering throughout the world. The center's Peace Program works to improve democracy in the Western Hemisphere. The Conflict Resolution Program strives to establish and maintain peace by preventing and/or resolving conflicts globally. The Democracy Program helps the development of democracies globally by observing elections, strengthening civic organizations, and supporting the rule of law. The Human Rights Initiatives act on behalf of human rights abuse victims and integrate human rights into all Carter Center program activities. The Carter Center has worked also to advance mental **health** care in various parts of the world, to eradicate guinea worm disease in Africa, and river blindness disease in the Western Hemisphere.

Former President Carter won the Nobel Peace Prize in December 2002 and has continued his life's work in defense of human rights. Known for his controversial efforts as president to base his foreign policy on human rights and humanitarian principles, Carter has continued since his one-term presidency to advance such principles not only through the Carter Center but also through his Habitat for Humanity program, which in the United States alone has made affordable **housing** available to thousands of low-income families. The Carter Center has become an important focal point as a think tank, a center for policy evaluation, and as an international nongovernmental organization actively engaged in the pursuit of human rights and humanitarian action. Address: The Carter Center, One Copenhill, 453 Freedom Parkway, Atlanta, GA 30307, USA. Website: www .cartercenter.org.

CENTRE FOR HOUSING RIGHTS AND EVICTIONS (COHRE). Since 1992, COHRE has worked with nongovernmental organizations

(NGOs) and the United Nations **Committee on Economic, Social, and Cultural Rights (CESCR)** to advance human rights issues related to **housing** and the prevention of evictions. It engages in research and publishing, in housing rights training, in monitoring and prevention of forced evictions, in promoting the special needs of traditionally disadvantaged groups including **women**, children, ethnic **minorities**, and indigenous peoples. COHRE is actively engaged in consultative activities with a variety of governments, **United Nations (UN)** agencies, regional organizations, and human rights bodies to promote housing rights. Address: 83 Rue de Montbrillant, 1202 Geneva, Switzerland. Website: www.cohre.org. *See also* VANCOUVER DECLARATION ON HUMAN SETTLEMENTS.

CHILDREN INTERNATIONAL. Founded in 1936, this well-established private humanitarian agency maintains **food** aid, **education**, and **health** programs in various regions of the world. It sponsors the "barefoot doctors" program and supports educational activities. Its activities center on child sponsorship programs in 11 countries: Chile, Colombia, Dominican Republic, Ecuador, Guatemala, Honduras, India, Mexico, Philippines, United States, and Zambia. Resources are used to ensure better sanitation, **housing**, clean water access, safe playgrounds, community centers, medical clinics, and income generation programs for **families** in **poverty**. Address: 2000 East Red Bridge Road, Kansas City, MO 64121, USA. For further information, see www.interaction.org, member profiles. Website: www.children.org. *See also* CHILDREN'S RIGHTS; INTERACTION.

CHILDREN'S RIGHTS. There are several human rights instruments in which the rights of children are affirmed. Children benefit from all of the rights stipulated in the **International Covenant on Civil and Political Rights**, sometimes to a more favorable degree than adults, as in the case of detention. Explicit rights for children are enunciated in Article 24 of the covenant, which provides that every child has a right to protection "as are required by his status as a minor, on the part of his **family**, society and the State." In addition, Article 24 provides that children are to be registered after birth and "shall have a name," and that every child has a right to a **nationality**. The **International Covenant on Economic, Social, and Cultural Rights** also enunciates a body of rights that broadly apply to the rights and well-being of children. More specifically, in Article 10, it affirms that the "widest possible protection and assistance should be accorded to the family . . . particularly for its establishment and while it is responsible for the care and education of dependent children." It further provides for special protection and assistance to mothers before and after childbirth, and for the special and nondiscriminatory protection and assistance on behalf of children and young persons, especially from economic and social exploitation. The article calls upon governments to undertake legislation to protect children with fair and humane child labor laws. Among the other rights of children enunciated is the right to a free primary **education**.

The most explicit and extensive enunciation of children's rights, however, is found in the 1989 **Convention on the Rights of the Child**, which in turn was preceded by a legally nonbinding **Declaration on the Rights of the Child** of 1959. The convention not only reiterated the range of rights children enjoy but also established a **Committee on the Rights of the Child (CRC)**, which meets to review reports of states parties concerning steps they have taken to implement provisions of the convention. Two important protocols to the convention were adopted in May 2002 protecting children involved in armed conflict and protecting children from trafficking and sale, prostitution, and pornography.

One of the first agenda items addressed by the **United Nations (UN)** was the status of children in the post–World War II setting. To address the needs of children, the **United Nations General Assembly** established the **United Nations Children's Fund (UNICEF)**, which is particularly devoted to the provision of emergency care to children and to the provision of educational opportunities. It, together with the **International Labour Organization (ILO)**, also takes concern in issues surrounding the child labor practices of states. Other assistance agencies, such as the **United Nations High Commissioner for Refugees (UNHCR)**, also undertake special assistance programs for vulnerable groups, such as children. Growing out of the dialogue establishing the Convention on the Rights of the Child, the UN established a special representative of the secretary-general for Children and Armed Conflict as a part of the **United Nations Secretariat** to serve as an advocate and facilitator for the mitigation of the terrible condition of children in civil war zones and to reduce incentives for their conscription into rebel groups. At the regional level, action to protect children's rights includes the African Charter on the Rights and Welfare of the Child, which entered into force in November 1999. A number of voluntary agencies also are engaged explicitly in assistance programs intended to meet the basic needs of children and to enhance their enjoyment of basic rights, such as **Children International** and the **Save the Children Alliance (SCA)**, Enfants Réfugiés du Monde, as well as the Young Men's Christian Association (YMCA) and the Young Women's Christian Association (YWCA), to name but a few.

COALITION AGAINST TRAFFICKING IN WOMEN (CATW). CATW is a nongovernmental organization (NGO) dedicated to the promotion of **women**'s rights and the elimination of all forms of sexual exploitation. It was founded in 1988 and was the first NGO dedicated to combating the problem of human trafficking, in particular sex trafficking of women and girls. It has consultative status with the United Nations **Economic and Social Council (ECOSOC)**. It monitors a variety of illicit activities, including prostitution, pornography, sex tourism, and other forms of sexual exploitation. It shares information with governments and international organizations, and attempts to modify international and national policies and legislation in order to advance the dignity of women and girls and free them from sexual exploitation. It is organized into six regional secretariats and more than 15 national coalitions. Website: www.catwinternational.org.

COALITION TO STOP THE USE OF CHILD SOLDIERS. Formed in 1998, the Coalition to Stop the Use of Child Soldiers represents an international effort by a number of nongovernmental organizations (NGOs), to draw attention to the particular plight of children in circumstances of conflict and civil war, and to protect **children's rights** in such situations. Among the member organizations of the coalition are **Amnesty International (AI)**, **Human Rights Watch**, the **Save the Children Alliance (SCA)**, and **World Vision**. The coalition works with intergovernmental bodies such as the **United Nations Children's Fund (UNICEF)** and the **International Committee of the Red Cross (ICRC)** to advance efforts to protect children from abuses in conflict-torn countries. It also establishes national coalitions in various regions in order to advance these goals, and to date 35 national coalitions exist along with regional coalitions in the Great Lakes region of Africa, in Latin America, the Middle East, and Southeast Asia.

Examples of the abusive treatment include children's abduction from their homes and forced induction into rebel groups, such as the Lord's Resistance Army in Uganda. Child soldiers are also drawn into paramilitary groups supporting governments, or as in the case of Myanmar, explicitly recruited by the government. More commonly, however, child soldiers are recruited or inducted by rebel groups, and sometimes into ethnic and interclan militias. It is estimated that about 300,000 children are engaged with military forces throughout the world, but most acutely so in Africa. Child soldiers are trained to carry arms, lay mines, and, in the case of girl soldiers, may be subject to rape and sexual abuse. All of these activities violate the basic rights of children, who often are deprived of adequate **food**, **health** care, and **education** in such situations. The use of child soldiers in civil wars in the Democratic Republic of the Congo, Liberia, and Sierra Leone has been especially common, and international bodies, including the **International Criminal Court (ICC)**, have instituted investigations into such ongoing criminal activity in Uganda and the Congo. The ICC statute forbids the conscription of children under the age of 15 for military purposes. The coalition advocates the application of the more strict standard of 18 years of age be observed as the minimum age for service in the military. This stricter measure is found in the Optional Protocol to the **Convention on the Rights of the Child**, which prohibits the involuntary conscription or induction of children under the age of 18, though children above the age of 16 may join voluntarily—a concession opposed by the coalition.

The work of the coalition and its members focuses on solutions to the abusive use of children in conflicts by encouraging demobilization, disarmament, and reintegration. The best results occur in the context of comprehensive peace agreements, but improvements are also possible, though with greater difficulty even in the midst of conflicts. The coalition is headquartered in London. Address: 2-12 Pentonville Road, 2nd Floor, London N1 9HF, UK. Website: www .child-soldier.org.

COMMISSION FOR SOCIAL DEVELOPMENT. A subsidiary body of the United Nations **Economic and Social Council (ECOSOC)**, the Commission for Social Development was established in 1946 under the name of the Social Commission. Its name was changed and its purview broadened in 1966. The commission has been involved in the drafting of various human rights instruments, including the **Declaration on the Rights of the Child**. The commission's work on such issues as **housing**, social welfare services, social development, and **education** is closely related to a variety of human rights issues and concerns.

COMMISSION ON CRIME PREVENTION AND CRIMINAL JUSTICE. Consisting of 40 member-states, this commission is devoted to the prevention of crime and promotion of stable criminal justice systems. It serves as a forum for discussion among governments about how best to fight crime at the global level. A subsidiary body of the United Nations **Economic and Social Council (ECOSOC)**, it was established in 1991 as a successor to the Committee on Crime Prevention and Control, which had been established in 1971 to encourage technical cooperation among governments. The commission meets annually in Vienna. It addresses crime prevention and criminal justice activities broadly, but much of its work deals with human rights concerns, including efforts to reduce trafficking in human persons, narcotics trafficking, and other forms of organized crime and **terrorism**. In addition, the commission seeks to improve the efficiency and fairness of criminal justice administration.

COMMISSION ON HUMAN RIGHTS (CHR). Article 48 of the **United Nations Charter**, authorizes the United Nations **Economic and Social Council (ECOSOC)** to establish subsidiary bodies to protect human rights. ECOSOC, acting under this authority, established the United Nations Commission on Human Rights in February 1946, calling upon it to submit proposals concerning the establishment of an **International Bill of Human Rights**, measures for preventing various forms of discrimination and for the protection of **minorities**, and draft proposals concerning the status of **women** as well as other human rights issues. The commission commenced work immediately on the drafting of the **Universal Declaration of Human**

Rights. It also later drafted the **International Covenant on Civil and Political Rights** and the **International Covenant on Economic, Social, and Cultural Rights**, thus fulfilling its duty to develop an International Bill of Human Rights. The commission has drafted numerous additional human rights instruments, including those dealing with **racial discrimination**, the crime of **apartheid**, and **torture**.

The commission's work has extended beyond the mere drafting of human rights treaties, important as this is. It has investigated and reported through various ad hoc or working groups on violations of human rights in various situations, promoted the availability of technical and advisory services to help reduce the incidence of human rights violations, and, under the authority of an ECOSOC resolution, received communications on patterns of human rights abuse through its Subcommission on Prevention of Discrimination and Protection of Minorities. The latter procedure is a confidential one, whereby the commission, through its subsidiary bodies, can deal on a confidential basis with cases of persistent human rights abuses, and report findings concerning them to ECOSOC.

Among the working groups established by the commission are the Working Group of Governmental Experts on the Right to Development, the Working Group on Contemporary Forms of **Slavery**, the Working Group on Enforced or Involuntary **Disappearances**, the Working Group on the Rights of Persons Belonging to National, Ethnic, Religious and Linguistic Minorities, and the Working Group to Examine Situations Which Appear to Reveal a Consistent Pattern of Gross Violations of Human Rights. The commission, in addition to forming working groups to help perform its work, also makes use of special rapporteurs to conduct studies or analyses of particular questions, such as indigenous rights, administrative detention, the problem of torture, the use of mercenaries, and the problem of religious intolerance. In 1994 the commission established a new special rapporteur to investigate violence against women. The commission, which met annually at Geneva, consisted of representatives of 53 member-states selected by ECOSOC, each of whom served for a term of three years. Several member governments of the commission over the years engaged in regular and flagrant abuse of human rights, leading to criticism of the body as being racked with conflicts of interest and hypocrisy that reduced its ability to focus international attention on countries where routine human rights abuse occur. In 2005, United Nations Secretary-General Kofi Annan proposed reforms to the commission in his "In Larger Freedom" Report on the **United Nations (UN)**. He urged reducing the size of the body and elevating it to the status of a council or making it directly report to the **United Nations General Assembly**, which, he argued, ought also to directly elect its members by a two-thirds vote. These measures, he asserted, would help to restore its credibility and professionalism. After months of contentious debate, the General Assembly adopted a reform package, terminated the commission, and established a new **Human Rights Council** in March 2006. Address: Office of the High Commissioner for Human Rights, United Nations Office in Geneva, 1211 Geneva 10, Switzerland. Website: www.ohchr.org.

COMMISSION ON THE STATUS OF WOMEN. The United Nations **Economic and Social Council (ECOSOC)** established the Commission on the Status of Women in June 1946 under its authority to create subsidiary bodies to assist in the performance of its work. The commission may be asked by ECOSOC to prepare studies and issue reports on a range of social, economic, and cultural issues, including issues related to the human rights of **women**. The commission may be asked to review or comment on draft declarations and conventions as they concern women's rights. It also serves as a preparatory body for major women's conferences. The commission normally meets once every two years in either New York or Vienna. Its membership has been expanded several times during its existence, and currently is composed of 45 members elected by ECOSOC for a period of four years. The commission's members are allocated by region to reflect the realities of global diversity. Each year it meets for 10 working days to conduct its business. Address: UN Secretariat, 2 United Nations Plaza, DC-2/12 Floor, New York, NY 10017, USA.

COMMITTEE AGAINST TORTURE (CAT). Established under the terms of Article 17 of the **Convention against Torture and Other Cruel, Inhuman, or Degrading Treatment or Punishment**, the CAT consists of 10 experts in the field of human rights elected to four-year terms by the states parties to the convention. The committee members serve in their personal capacities rather than as representatives of governments.

The committee, which first met in 1988 to establish its rules of procedure, is empowered under Article 19 of the convention to receive reports from the states parties, which are obliged within one year of entry to submit such reports through the United Nations secretary-general concerning steps they have taken to give effect to the provisions of the convention. Governments are thereafter required to submit supplementary reports in intervals of four years. The committee may make comments on such reports and forward them to the state party concerned.

Under Article 20 of the convention, the committee, upon receipt of reliable information of violations to the convention, is obliged to invite the concerned government to cooperate in an examination of such evidence and reply to it. If further investigation is warranted, the committee may initiate further inquiry and transmit any findings to the concerned government. Under Article 21 a state party may declare the competence of the committee to receive and consider communications from other states parties to the effect that it is not fulfilling its obligations under the convention. States parties may then attempt to resolve the complaint within a six-month period, after which, if the matter is unresolved, either government may refer the matter to the committee, which may take it up provided all domestic remedies have been invoked and exhausted. The committee may extend its good offices to resolve the matter or call for the creation of an ad hoc conciliation commission. After one year, the committee is charged to make a brief report to the concerned parties regarding the disposition of the complaint.

Under Article 22, states parties may declare that they "recognize the competence of the Committee to receive and consider communications from or on behalf of individuals subject to its jurisdiction who claim to be victims of a violation by a State Party." The committee is obliged in such instances to disregard anonymous or frivolous claims, and to refrain from action on complaints where local remedies have not been shown to be exhausted. Within six months of a valid complaint, the concerned state party is obliged to report to the committee on steps it has taken to deal with the complaint. The committee, after considering all the information and reports made available to it by the individual and the state party, is charged to forward its views to the complainant and the government involved. The committee meets in Geneva twice a year for three weeks in May and two weeks in November to conduct its work. Address: Office of the High Commissioner for Human Rights, United Nations Office at Geneva, 1211 Geneva 10, Switzerland. Website: www.ohchr.org. *See also* TORTURE.

COMMITTEE OF MINISTERS OF THE COUNCIL OF EUROPE. *See* COUNCIL OF EUROPE (COE).

COMMITTEE ON ECONOMIC, SOCIAL, AND CULTURAL RIGHTS (CESCR). This committee, which was created by and reports to the United Nations **Economic and Social Council (ECOSOC)**, was established in 1985 in order to help supervise implementation of the **International Covenant on Economic, Social, and Cultural Rights**. The covenant itself came into force nearly a decade earlier. The committee's predecessor, a working group of experts, performed the oversight functions until the CESCR's creation. The committee consists of 18 prominent experts in the field of human rights, who meet annually in Geneva, usually in two sessions a year. With the help of working groups, the committee screens and evaluates the reports submitted by governments pursuant to their obligations under the covenant. The CESCR is unable currently to hear direct complaints from individuals; however, a draft optional protocol to the covenant is under consideration, which would (if and when adopted) confer such competence on the committee. Address: Office of the High Commissioner for Human Rights, United Nations Office at Geneva, 1211 Geneva 10, Switzerland. Website: www.ohchr.org.

COMMITTEE ON MIGRANT WORKERS (CMW). The full title of the CMW is the Committee on the Protection of the Rights of All Migrant Workers and Members of Their Families. It is the monitoring body of independent experts established by the **International Convention on the Protection of the Rights of All Migrant Workers and Members of Their Families**, which entered into force in July 2003. The CMW held its first session in March 2004 in Geneva, where it sits. Under the convention, the states parties (to date 34) submit regular reports to the committee concerning national progress on the implementation of rights specified in the convention. The first report is due within a year of ratification and then in five-year intervals. A procedure for reception of individual complaints against governments is anticipated once 10 parties agree to such a procedure under Article 77 of the convention. Migration is an increasingly common phenomenon in international relations and although **international law** contains customary provisions for the protection of migrants in the law of **state responsibility**, migrants are often subjected to inhumane treatment and dangerous conditions both in the workplace and also in the process of migration. The Convention on Migrant Workers was intended to highlight the special predicament of such populations and to encourage governments to establish laws and policies that adequately preserve and protect their rights. Address: Office of the High Commissioner for Human Rights, 1211 Geneva 10, Switzerland. Website: www.ohchr.org.

COMMITTEE ON THE ELIMINATION OF DISCRIMINATION AGAINST WOMEN (CEDAW). Article 17 of the **Convention on the Elimination of Discrimination against Women**, adopted on 18 December 1979, called for the establishment of this committee as a mechanism for considering reports that states parties undertook to submit concerning the domestic policy measures taken toward implementation of the convention's provisions protecting **women** from discrimination. As of March 2005, 180 states had become party to the convention, while as of September 2005, 72 had ratified the optional protocol to the convention, which grants individuals the capacity to submit reports to the committee. States parties are directed to be present at meetings in which the committee examines a state's report in order to answer questions and participate in discussion on the report. After receiving and examining such reports, the committee may make "suggestions and general recommendations" to the states parties through the secretary-general of the **United Nations (UN)**. The committee is composed of 23 members nominated and elected to four-year terms by the member-states from among their nationals, who are experts of high moral standing in the field of human and women's rights. The committee meets annually in either New York or Vienna to consider the member governments' reports. Address: UN

Secretariat, 2 United Nations Plaza, DC-2/12th Floor, New York, NY, 10017, USA.

COMMITTEE ON THE ELIMINATION OF RACIAL DISCRIMINATION (CERD). Articles 8 and 9 of the **International Convention on the Elimination of All Forms of Racial Discrimination**, adopted on 21 December 1965, established this committee in order to review compliance of states parties to the provisions of the convention. States party to the convention now number 170. Under the convention, the committee is authorized to examine and review several different kinds of reports and complaints. First, each state party to the convention is obliged to submit periodic reports concerning domestic measures it adopts to comply with the provisions of the convention. The committee reviews these reports, may request further information from the reviewed states, and may make suggestions and recommendations to the state party. It reports its findings to the **United Nations General Assembly**. The convention also provides that any state party may lodge a complaint against another state party concerning a failure to comply with the convention. The committee is charged with transmitting such complaints to the party alleged to be in violation of convention provisions, to further consider the matter once it is determined that local remedies have been exhausted, to appoint an ad hoc conciliation committee to resolve the issue amicably, to ensure that the conciliation committee report is transmitted to concerned parties, and to report to other states parties and to the UN General Assembly the disposition of the matter once the concerned states have responded to the conciliation committee's report.

Under Article 14 of the convention, the committee may also receive and evaluate complaints made by individuals and groups, provided that states parties have given an explicit declaration permitting this. To date, 46 states have done so. The committee is authorized to bring such complaints to the attention of states parties, to consider information and explanations of the petitioner and the state party, to make suggestions and recommendations to the petitioner and the state party, and to report its findings to the General Assembly. Finally, under Article 15, the committee is entrusted to receive reports from appropriate **United Nations (UN)** bodies concerning the steps taken by administering authorities of non-self-governing territories regarding issues relevant to compliance with the convention.

The committee is composed of 18 experts on issues concerning human rights and **racial discrimination**. Members serve in their own individual capacities for terms of five years. They are elected by states parties to the convention and usually meet twice a year in Geneva to consider reports and petitions. Address: Office of the High Commissioner for Human Rights, United Nations Office at Geneva, 1211 Geneva 10, Switzerland. Website: www.ohchr.org.

COMMITTEE ON THE RIGHTS OF THE CHILD (CRC). Established under the terms of the 1989 **Convention on the Rights of the Child**, which entered into force on 2 September 1990, the CRC consists of 10 experts to which states parties agree to submit reports on the steps they have initiated to give effect to the rights set forth in the convention, and on the progress made in achieving those rights. The reports are made within two years of entry into force for each state party and thereafter at five-year intervals. In January 1993, the committee met to consider the initial reports of 57 states then party to the convention. As of October 2005, 192 states were party to the convention. The 18 members of the committee are elected by states parties from among their nationals. They are to be experts of high moral standing and of recognized competence in the area of **children's rights** and they serve in their own personal capacities. They serve for terms of four years. The committee establishes its own rules of procedure. In addition to reviewing and submitting a report to the **United Nations General Assembly** through the United Nations **Economic and Social Council (ECOSOC)** concerning the reports of the states parties, it also is charged with serving as an intermediary with **United Nations (UN)** specialized agencies such as the **United Nations Children's Fund (UNICEF)** regarding requests states parties may make concerning technical assistance needed to fulfill any aspect of the convention. The committee may make recommendations and suggestions based on the reports it receives from states parties. These are to be transmitted to the concerned state party and to the General Assembly. It may not hear individual complaints, but other human rights committees may hear individual complaints concerning violation of children's rights. The committee also oversees implementation of two

Optional Protocols to the Convention on the Rights of the Child, including one dealing with children in armed conflict and one on the sale of children, child prostitution, and child pornography. Website: www.ohchr.org.

CONCERN. Founded in the wake of the Biafran **famine** of 1968 during the Nigerian civil war, Concern was established in response to Irish missionaries working in the midst of the conflict. Originating in religious charitable instincts, the agency was first called Africa Concern, and its work moved beyond the humanitarian emergency in Biafra to encompass relief and development projects in other parts of Africa, and eventually in other parts of the world. In 1970, it responded to the cyclone disaster and civil war in Bangladesh, and to a subsequent famine in East Pakistan during 1971. Given the geographically expanded nature of its work, Africa Concern changed its name to Concern. The agency also adopted a secular approach to the provision of relief to **refugees**, emergency aid to disaster victims, and development aid to impoverished peoples, and it now works in 26 countries. It is a member of **European Solidarity towards Equal Participation of People (EUROSTEP)**. Address: 52-55 Lower Camden Street, Dublin 2, Ireland. Website: www.concern.org.ie.

CONFERENCE OF EUROPEAN CHURCHES (CEC). Founded in 1959, the CEC is a fellowship of 126 Orthodox, Protestant, and Old Catholic Churches from throughout Europe aimed at promoting ecumenical relations. It has promoted the rights of **refugees**, **asylum** seekers, and **women** over the years, and more recently addressed the growing problem of trafficking in women and problems associated with the growing migrant populations of Europe. The CEC has strongly supported the development of human rights treaties and institutions in Europe, including those associated with the **Council of Europe (COE)**, such as the **European Convention on Human Rights**, the **European Social Charter**, and the **European Court of Human Rights (ECHR)**, as well as human rights initiatives initiated by the **European Union (EU)** and the **Organization for Security and Cooperation in Europe (OSCE)**. The CEC promotes the **freedom of religion** and the right to conscientious objection to military service. It provides human rights training programs for its member churches, especially in the emerging states of Eastern Europe. The CEC maintains offices in Geneva, Brussels, and Strasbourg. General Secretariat Address: P.O. Box 2100, 150 route de Ferney, CH-1100 Geneva 2, Switzerland. Website: www.cec-kek.org. *See also* CONVENTION FOR THE SUPPRESSION OF THE TRAFFIC IN PERSONS AND OF THE EXPLOITATION OF THE PROSTITUTION OF OTHERS.

CONSTITUTION OF THE UNITED STATES. The human rights protections in the U.S. Constitution derive from the sense of the founders and their successors that the power of government needed to be limited if the liberties or freedoms of citizens were to be protected. Although the founders wanted to create a strong central (federal) government, the division of the government into separate branches, the checks that each branch had on the others, and the guarantees of personal liberties in the **Bill of Rights** were designed to blend governmental strength with protected liberties.

The federal government is compelled to respect some basic human rights by different constitutional principles. According to the original document, the writ of habeas corpus could only be suspended in cases of rebellion or other "invasions of the public safety." Secondly, bills of attainder (legislative trials) and ex post facto laws are forbidden. Trial by jury in criminal cases is guaranteed. Further, the crime of treason is spelled out, and two witnesses to the same act must testify to bring a conviction for treason. Fourthly, citizens of each state have the same rights as each other. Finally, no religious test may be required for anyone to hold public office.

The most important protections of human rights in the Constitution are the first 10 amendments to the Constitution, the so-called Bill of Rights, which was ratified in 1791. In these amendments, **freedom of religion, freedom of the press, freedom of assembly**, and **freedom of speech** and petition are protected. Further, people accused of crime are protected against unreasonable searches and seizures, double jeopardy, compelled self-incrimination, and excessive bail. They are also guaranteed a speedy trial, representation by legal counsel, and compensation for loss of private **property** for public use.

The greatest expansion of human rights protection in the Constitution followed the adoption of the Civil War amendments. The Thirteenth Amendment abolished **slavery**. The Fourteenth Amendment made all people born or naturalized in the United States citizens of the United States and prohibited the states from abridging "the privileges or immunities of citizens of the United States," depriving "any person of life, liberty, or property, without due process of law," and denying any person "the equal protection of the laws." The Fifteenth Amendment protected the voting rights of all citizens regardless of "race, color, or previous condition of servitude."

Other noteworthy amendments expanding the protection of human rights, specifically voting rights, are the Nineteenth Amendment protecting **women**'s suffrage, the Twenty-Fourth Amendment, which protected peoples' right to vote in absence of paying a tax, and the Twenty-Sixth Amendment, which granted people 18 years of age and older the suffrage.

The Supreme Court in its decisions also has expanded the protection accorded human rights. The Court has given groups such as the National Association for the Advancement of Colored People (NAACP) and the American Civil Liberties Union standing, which has led to, among other things, the Supreme Court decision on *Brown versus the Board of Education of Topeka* (1954) and *Heart of Atlanta Motel versus the United States* (1964), outlawing segregation in public schools and public accommodations, respectively.

Further, the Court has consistently enunciated since the mid-1930s the idea that some freedoms in the U.S. constitutional system are more important to the functioning of representative government than others. Hence, these "preferred freedoms" are accorded a much greater degree of protection than other freedoms. The "preferred freedoms" have included freedom of religion, speech, press, assembly, and petition. The Court has scrutinized more carefully laws that affect these freedoms than others.

Finally, the Court has discovered a right of **privacy** first enunciated by Justice William O. Douglas in *Griswold versus Connecticut* (1965). Douglas argued that many Court decisions established specific guarantees in the Bill of Rights that have created "zones of privacy." This right of privacy became the basis for the Supreme Court's controversial decision in *Roe versus Wade* (1975), striking down state laws prohibiting abortion. Initially, this argument was used unsuccessfully in *Bowers versus Hardwick* (1980) in an attempt to overturn state antisodomy laws. Yet in June 2003, the Supreme

Court in *Lawrence versus Texas*, overturned *Bowers* and declared that all remaining antisodomy laws were unconstitutional on the basis of the right of privacy first accepted by the Court in *Griswold*. On balance, the Court will probably interpret the Constitution and its amendments in such a way as to expand the future protection granted to human rights in the United States. *See also* BILL OF RIGHTS (U.S.).

CONSTITUTIONS. One of the principal means by which human rights provisions are given legal effect is through their incorporation into the constitutions of states. In this way, they are enforced as civil rights and individual liberties by governmental authority and often judicial guardianship. Because the nation-state system is grounded in the principles of national **sovereignty**, territorial integrity, and political independence of states, the ultimate realization of the protection of human rights is achieved when governments routinely incorporate such rights in their constitutional documents and legislative statutes. The constitutions of many countries frequently contain provisions specifying the rights of citizens, sometimes in the direct language of the constitution or sometimes through a specific bill of rights. The **Constitution of the United States** is a prime example of both such procedures. Sometimes countries incorporate international instruments, such as the **Universal Declaration of Human Rights**, into the constitution as a kind of bill of rights. In many countries the courts, often the highest court of the land, are responsible for reviewing cases where the constitutional rights of individuals have been infringed. In other countries, constitutional councils have been created to oversee legislation and ensure that parliamentary statutes do not violate civil or individual rights or other constitutional provisions.

Many international human rights treaties, declarations, and agreements explicitly call upon governments to incorporate constitutional or statutory provisions in order to give effect to the principles contained in them. Human rights treaties are not self-enforcing instruments. They require ongoing performance and execution by states, if their ultimate aims are to be achieved and given continuous effect. It is through the activity of sovereign states in their own domestic legal orders that this is most effectively done.

CONVENTION AGAINST TORTURE AND OTHER CRUEL, IN-HUMAN, OR DEGRADING TREATMENT OR PUNISHMENT. Adopted by the **United Nations General Assembly** on 10 December 1984, nearly a decade after the **Declaration on the Protection of All Persons from Being Subjected to Torture and Other Cruel, Inhuman, or Degrading Treatment or Punishment**, this legally binding convention entered into force in June 1987. The treaty reiterates the principal elements of the definition of **torture** contained in the declaration, obliges states parties to take domestic legal action to prevent acts of torture from occurring under their jurisdiction, and creates a **Committee against Torture (CAT)** to receive, study, and respond to reports submitted by states detailing their compliance with convention provisions. The convention defines torture as "any act by which severe pain or suffering, whether physical or mental, is intentionally inflicted on a person for such purposes as obtaining from him or a third-person information or a confession, punishing him for an act he or a third person has committed or is suspected of having committed, or intimidating or coercing him or a third person, or for any reason based on discrimination of any kind, when such pain or suffering is inflicted by or at the instigation of or with the consent or acquiescence of a public official or other person acting in an official capacity." It explicitly excludes from this definition pain or suffering arising only from, inherent to, or incidental to lawful sanction.

The convention enjoys the full ratification or signature of three-quarters of the world's governments. An optional protocol to the convention has been opened for ratification by states that wish to subject themselves to visits and oversight by an independent subcommittee of experts, which would have the authority to conduct visits to prison and detention facilities of member-states. Once 20 member-states have ratified the optional protocol, it will enter into force among the states parties. For a full text of the convention, with member-state reservations, and the optional protocol, see the Office of the High Commissioner for Human Rights website, www.ohchr.org.

CONVENTION FOR THE SUPPRESSION OF THE TRAFFIC IN PERSONS AND OF THE EXPLOITATION OF THE PROSTITUTION OF OTHERS. The international community has shown concern about the problem of illicit traffic in **women** and **children**

since the early part of the 20th century. In 1904, this concern led to the International Agreement for the Suppression of the White Slave Traffic. This was followed in 1910 with an international convention on the same subject. Still later, in 1921, an International Convention for the Suppression of the Traffic in Women and Children was promulgated and, in 1933, a related convention for the Suppression of the Traffic in Women of Full Age was concluded. The **League of Nations**, in turn, attempted in a draft convention of 1937 to consolidate and extend the scope of these agreements. This work was interrupted by the events of World War II. However, in 1948 the **United Nations (UN)** took up the matter and, on 2 December 1949, the **United Nations General Assembly** adopted the Convention for the Suppression of the Traffic in Persons and of the Exploitation of the Prostitution of Others, thus completing in spirit the draft convention prepared by the League of Nations in 1937.

The convention calls upon states parties to punish persons who lead others into prostitution or who own or keep brothels, to provide means for the rehabilitation of those victimized by prostitution, and to interdict the international traffic of prostitution through immigration screening procedures. In recent years, some European governments withdrew from the convention and passed national legislation legalizing prostitution, hoping by this means to reduce trafficking. However, evidence suggests that legalized prostitution has not reduced trafficking, and liberalized prostitution laws are again being called into question in light of this ongoing problem of trafficking in women. On 18 January 2002, the Optional Protocol to the **Convention on the Rights of the Child** on the sale of children, child prostitution, and child pornography offered another avenue for international cooperation in interdicting the sex trade. The United Nations Convention against Transnational Organized Crime resulting from the Palermo Conference of December 2000 also advanced international cooperation in this regard. For a text of this and related agreements, see the **United Nations High Commissioner for Human Rights (UNHCHR)** website, www.ohchr.org.

CONVENTION GOVERNING THE SPECIFIC ASPECTS OF REFUGEE PROBLEMS IN AFRICA. In 1966, facing growing problems with **refugees**, the Organization of African Unity (OAU), now known as the **African Union (AU)**, convened a meeting of legal experts to draft a refugee convention for Africa. This was followed in 1967 by the work of the Conference on the Legal, Economic, and Social Aspects of African Refugee Problems. In September 1969, the OAU heads of state and government adopted the final draft of the convention, which entered into force in June 1974. The most significant aspect of this agreement lies in its expanded definition of refugee status. While retaining the internationally accepted criteria of granting refugee status to those having a well-founded fear of persecution, African governments added the following language: "The term refugee shall also apply to every person, who, owing to external aggression, occupation, foreign domination or events seriously disturbing public order in either part or the whole of his country of origin or nationality, is compelled to leave his place of habitual residence in order to seek refuge in another place outside his country of origin or nationality." This definition enables most of those Africans transplanted by domestic turmoil and civil war to qualify for **asylum**, assistance, and protection. The convention calls upon member-states to regard the granting of asylum to refugees as a peaceful and humanitarian act rather than an unfriendly one. The convention also articulates the duty of refugees to refrain from subversive activities. The preamble to the convention acknowledged the importance of the **Universal Declaration of Human Rights** concerning the principle that human beings shall enjoy fundamental rights and freedoms without discrimination. Of the AU's 53 members, 44 have ratified this convention. For details, see the official documents section of the African Union website, www.africa-union.org.

CONVENTION ON CONSENT TO MARRIAGE, MINIMUM AGE FOR MARRIAGE, AND REGISTRATION OF MARRIAGES. Prompted by discussions emanating from the conference that drafted the **Supplementary Convention on the Abolition of Slavery, the Slave Trade, and Institutions and Practices Similar to Slavery**, the **Commission on the Status of Women**, at the behest of the United Nations **Economic and Social Council (ECOSOC)**, prepared a draft of this convention, which was adopted by the **United Nations General Assembly** on 7 November 1962 and which entered into force as between states parties on 9 December 1964. The title of the convention is descriptive of its provisions. It provides that marriages are to be legally entered into with the full and free consent of both parties. It calls upon states parties to take legislative steps to specify a minimum age for marriage, although it does not specify such an age. Finally, it stipulates that all marriages be registered with proper authorities. A total of 49 governments are parties to this convention. For a text of the convention, see *United Nations Treaty Series*, vol. 521, p. 231, or www.ohchr.org. *See also* CONVENTION ON THE NATIONALITY OF MARRIED WOMEN; WOMEN.

CONVENTION ON THE ELIMINATION OF ALL FORMS OF DISCRIMINATION AGAINST WOMEN. More than a decade after the **Declaration on the Elimination of Discrimination against Women**, this treaty provided enforcement mechanisms and institutional bodies to ensure the progressive compliance of member-states with the provisions for promotion of the human rights of **women**. Adopted on 18 December 1979, the convention calls for states parties to condemn discrimination against women in all of its forms, to adopt constitutional and statutory provisions to ensure the equality of men and women, and to repeal existing legislation prejudicial to the equal rights and treatment of women. It reiterates the **political rights** of women, and their rights to employment, **education**, and social services on an equal footing with men. The convention created a **Committee on the Elimination of Discrimination against Women (CEDAW)**, consisting of 23 experts to be elected by states parties and to serve in their own personal capacities. The committee receives reports from states parties concerning their progress in implementing the provisions of the convention, and may make recommendations on the reports of states parties. These recommendations may be made in the annual reports that the committee is charged to make to the **United Nations General Assembly** through the United Nations **Economic and Social Council (ECOSOC)**. As of 2005, 180 states had become party to the convention, and 72 had ratified an optional protocol to the convention, which grants individuals the capacity to submit complaints to the committee. For a full text of the agreement, with member-state reservations, see the Office of the **United Nations High Commissioner for Human Rights (UNHCHR)** website, www.ohchr.org.

CONVENTION ON THE NATIONALITY OF MARRIED WOMEN. National laws relating to the effects of marriage on **nationality** vary considerably. In the early part of this century, most governments uniformly provided that **women** marrying **alien** men would automatically acquire the nationality of their husband at marriage and lose their original citizenship. In the United States, this practice ceased with the passage of the Cable Act in 1922, which provided women with the free choice of their nationality upon marriage, either to retain their previous citizenship or to take on a new one, including that of their husband. Many countries, however, continued with the practice of having the woman's nationality follow that of her husband. The Montevideo Convention of the Nationality of Women (1933) was promulgated in order to address problems resulting from the conflict of national legislation on this subject and to give women free choice in determining their nationality upon marriage on an equal footing with men. Only a handful of nations ratified the Montevideo Convention. The United Nations **Commission on the Status of Women** recommended in 1949 that a new Convention on the Status of Married Women be drafted. It completed a draft Convention on the Status of Married Women in 1955. The convention was later adopted on 29 January 1955 by the **United Nations General Assembly**, and entered into force for states parties on 11 August 1958. The main feature of the convention is the principle shared by the Cable Act and Montevideo Convention that a mere celebration of marriage or the dissolution of marriage or a change in citizenship by a husband should not automatically affect the nationality of the wife. Women seeking to change their nationality are required to do so through normal naturalization procedures. After nearly five decades, only 70 countries have ratified the convention, a copy of which may be found at the **United Nations High Commissioner for Human Rights (UNHCHR)** website: www.ohchr.org. *See also* CONVENTION ON CONSENT TO MARRIAGE, MINIMUM AGE FOR MARRIAGE, AND REGISTRATION OF MARRIAGES.

CONVENTION ON THE POLITICAL RIGHTS OF WOMEN. Opened for signature on 31 March 1953, this treaty entered into force for states parties on 7 July 1954. The first three articles contain the substantive provisions of the convention. Article I provides that

women shall be entitled to vote in all elections on equal terms with men, without any discrimination. Article II provides that women shall be eligible for election to all publicly elected bodies, established by national law, on equal terms with men, without any discrimination. Article III stipulates that women shall be entitled to hold public office and to exercise all public functions, established by national law, on equal terms with men, without any discrimination. Reservations to the treaty are permitted under Article VII and states parties may denounce the convention under terms of Article VIII. The convention lacks effective enforcement mechanisms, although under Article IX, disputes arising between contracting states over the interpretation or application of the convention may, after negotiation, be submitted to the **International Court of Justice (ICJ)** or to some other mutually agreeable mode of settlement. For a full text of the convention, see *United Nations Treaty Series*, no. 2613, vol. 193, p. 135, or www.ohchr.org.

CONVENTION ON THE PREVENTION AND PUNISHMENT OF THE CRIME OF GENOCIDE. *See* GENOCIDE.

CONVENTION ON THE REDUCTION OF STATELESSNESS. After several years of deliberation initiated by the **United Nations (UN)** secretary-general under the authority of a **United Nations General Assembly**, this convention was concluded on 30 August 1961 in an effort to reduce the problem of **statelessness** and to address the predicament of stateless persons. Following the adoption of the 1954 **Convention Relating to the Status of Stateless Persons**, the Convention on Reduction of Statelessness provides for measures to expedite the attainment of a **nationality** by stateless persons, and it calls for the establishment of a framework within the UN to which "a person claiming the benefit of this Convention may apply for the examination of his claim and for assistance in presenting it to the appropriate authorities." In practice the **United Nations High Commissioner for Refugees (UNHCR)** has undertaken this role. Only 26 countries are parties to the agreement. For a text of the agreement, see www.ohchr.org.

CONVENTION ON THE RIGHTS OF THE CHILD. Thirty years after the **Declaration on the Rights of the Child**, the **United Nations**

General Assembly on 20 November 1989 concluded this convention, which not only reaffirmed the principles set forth in the earlier declaration, but provided for mechanisms to protect the rights of **children**, to monitor progress on the achievement of those rights, and to promote the improvement in the situation of children. The convention recognizes the primary right of the **family** as the natural and fundamental unit of society to take responsibility for the rearing, **education**, and formation of children, with the state and other private associations serving the needs of families in providing for the care, education, and security of children. The **Commission on Human Rights (CHR)** spent 10 years working on the convention prior to its adoption by the General Assembly. The convention entered into force on 2 September 1990, after being rapidly ratified by most states, within a matter of a few years. Like the declaration, the convention reiterates rights that children possess under various other international instruments. It reaffirms their **right to life**, to a name, to a **nationality**, to nondiscrimination, to family reunification upon separation, to be free from illicit trafficking, to protection of the law, and to a basis of economic support. They also have the right to be free from neglect or abuse, to have access to special services in cases of retardation or handicap, to an education, and to **health** services, among many others. By terms of the convention, those persons under the age of 18 at the time of having committed a capital crime may not be subject to the **death penalty**.

The convention established a **Committee on the Rights of the Child (CRC)**, consisting of 10 experts to whom states parties agree to submit reports on the steps they have initiated to give effect to the rights set forth in the convention, and on the progress made in achieving those rights. The reports are made within two years of entry into force for each state party and thereafter at five-year intervals. In January 1993, the committee met to consider the initial reports of nearly 60 states parties. Nearly all of the world's countries, a total of 192, have ratified this convention.

Important Protocols to the Convention on the Rights of the Child were established in May 2002. These include the Optional Protocol on the Involvement of Children in Armed Conflict, and the Optional Protocol on the Sale of Children, Child Prostitution, and Child Pornography. For a solid history on the drafting of the convention, see Lawrence

J. LeBlanc, *The Convention on the Rights of the Child: United Nations Lawmaking on Human Rights* (1995). For a full text of the agreement, with member-state reservations, see the Office of the **United Nations High Commissioner for Human Rights (UNHCHR)** website, www .ohchr.org. *See also* CHILDREN'S RIGHTS; COALITION TO STOP THE USE OF CHILD SOLDIERS.

CONVENTION RELATING TO THE STATUS OF REFUGEES.
Done at Geneva on 28 July 1951, this convention entered into force on 22 April 1954. The treaty legally defines **refugees** as persons who "as a result of events occurring before 1 January 1951 and owing to well-founded fear of being persecuted for reasons of race, religion, **nationality**, membership of a particular social group or political opinion, is outside the country of his nationality and is unable or, owing to such fear, is unwilling to avail himself of the protection of that country." The time restriction concerning events occurring before 1 January 1951 was later dropped in the **Protocol Relating to the Status of Refugees** of 31 January 1967. A total of 143 countries have ratified the 1951 convention and 143 have ratified the protocol, for a combined total of 146 countries that have ratified one or both of them. Under Article 35 of the convention, the **United Nations High Commissioner for Refugees (UNHCR)** is given the duty of supervising the application of the convention provisions. This fact, combined with the less restricted definition of the term *refugee* in the statute of the UNHCR, coupled with the requests by the **United Nations General Assembly** for the UNHCR to extend its good offices to persons in refugee-like situations, in practice extended the safeguards of the convention to large populations of persons, even before the adoption of the 1967 protocol.

After defining the term *refugee*, the convention, in the cessation clauses, identifies the conditions under which refugee status can be lost. The convention's provisions do not extend to persons who have committed crimes against peace, **war crimes**, **crimes against humanity**, or other serious nonpolitical crimes. Refugees have duties to the country in which they find themselves, including the duty to conform to its laws and regulations and the duty to abide by measures taken for the maintenance of public order. Under Article 3, refugees are not to be discriminated against on the basis of race, religion, or country of origin. Subsequent articles assert that refugees are to be treated no less favorably than **aliens** concerning **property**, rights of association, access to domestic courts in the host country, access to employment, professional activity, **housing**, public **education**, freedom of movement, and public relief. Refugees are to be accorded rationing and public relief at a level consistent with that accorded to the host country's nationals. Contracting states are obliged to provide identity papers and travel documents to refugees, except under compelling circumstances of national security.

Most importantly, refugees are not to be expelled from the country of **asylum** save on grounds of national security or public order, and only pursuant to a decision reached in accordance with due process of law. More particularly, states parties are enjoined from forcibly returning or refouling refugees to territories (i.e., their state of origin or nationality from which they fled on grounds of fearing persecution) in which their life or freedom would be threatened. This principle of **nonrefoulement** is considered by many **international law** experts to have ripened into a general norm of customary law. Governments also agree as far as possible to facilitate the assimilation or integration of refugees through naturalization. Article 11 of this agreement called upon contracting states to give sympathetic consideration to the establishment of refugee seamen on their territories, to issue travel documents to them, or to grant them temporary admission to their territory so that they might eventually pursue establishment in another country. For a text of the convention, see UN General Assembly Official Records, Fifth Session, Supplement No. 20 (A/1775), p. 48, or www.unhcr.ch.

CONVENTION RELATING TO THE STATUS OF STATELESS PERSONS. Adopted on 28 September 1954 by a special Conference of Plenipotentiaries under the aegis of the United Nations **Economic and Social Council (ECOSOC)**, this convention represented an effort to accord **stateless** persons protection under **international law**. A similar treaty had been earlier adopted by governments to cope with **refugees**. Indeed, the two subjects had originally been conjoined in the earlier conference that proposed the **Convention Relating to the Status of Refugees** of 1950, but the subject of statelessness was more complicated and set aside for later deliberation. The convention entered into force as among states parties in June 1960. It defines a stateless person as anyone "who is not considered as a national by any State under the operation of its law." Stateless persons are reminded that they have duties toward the countries in which they find themselves, including abiding by its laws and refraining from acts prejudicial to public order. Contracting states agree to refrain from any form of discrimination in applying the standards of the convention. They agree to respect a range of additionally specified rights of stateless persons, including their **freedom of religion** and **freedom of association**, their rights to own and dispose of **property**, to seek gainful employment or self-employment, and to enjoy other public benefits at a level no less favorable than that generally accorded to **aliens**. Importantly, the convention calls upon contracting parties to facilitate the process by which stateless persons can acquire a new **nationality**, either through naturalization as a citizen of the contracting party or a third state. *See also* CONVENTION ON THE REDUCTION OF STATELESSNESS; STATELESSNESS.

CONVENTION TO SUPPRESS SLAVE TRADE AND SLAVERY. Signed at Geneva on 25 September 1926, this convention called upon states parties to prevent and suppress the slave trade and to pursue the complete abolition of all forms of **slavery**. The convention explicitly called upon member-states to adopt measures to prevent and suppress the transport of slaves on their flag vessels and within their territorial waters as well as to eradicate such practices as the capture, sale, and transport of individuals for the purpose of placing them in bondage or slavery. The **United Nations (UN)** incorporated the convention in 1953 with the adoption of the Protocol Amending the Slavery Convention. For a copy of the convention, see www.ohchr.org.

COUNCIL OF EUROPE (COE). The Council of Europe has, since its inception in 1949, taken a consistent interest in human rights and humanitarian issues. Its original purposes included the defense of human rights, democracy and the rule of law, the articulation of European-wide agreements by member-states in their social and legal practices, and the promotion of a wider awareness of European identity and shared values, despite unique national and cultural experience. It is not to be confused with the **European Union (EU)**, which aims more explicitly at economic integration. From the outset of the Council of Europe, the problem of **refugees** loomed large after World War II, occupying the council's attention, especially as the Cold War deepened. In 1951, it convened a committee of experts to study the issue. In 1956, it established a Resettlement Fund to provide assistance to European refugees and displaced persons, in an effort to restore normalcy and stability to their lives.

The statute of the council sets forth the aims of the organization. These include achieving "a greater unity between its Members for the purpose of safe-guarding and realizing the ideals and principles which are their common heritage and facilitating their economic and social progress," and taking "common action in economic, social, cultural, scientific, legal and administrative matters and in the maintenance and further realization of human rights and fundamental freedoms." Members of the Council of Europe are required under Article 3 of the statute to "accept the principles of the rule of law and of the enjoyment by all persons within its jurisdiction of human rights and fundamental freedoms." The council was at first explicitly not concerned with matters of defense and security. Flowing from its statute, the institutional mechanisms of the council routinely engaged in humanitarian and human rights issues. (See the *European Treaty Series* No. 1, published by the Council of Europe for a text of the statute.)

The institutions of the council include a Committee of Ministers consisting of the foreign ministers of the member-states, which now numbers 46 and acts on behalf of the organization; a Consultative Assembly, now known as the Parliamentary Assembly, which is composed of 630 members of the 46 national parliaments, and which deliberates issues and makes recommendations to the Committee of Ministers; and a secretariat, of about 1,800 persons, which conducts the routine administration of the organization under the supervision of the Committee of Ministers. There is also a Congress of Local and Regional Authorities that meets.

These bodies have been actively involved in the preparation of numerous European human rights instruments, including, among others, the **European Convention on Human Rights** (1950) and subsequent protocols, the **European Social Charter** (1961) and subsequent protocol, and the **European Convention for the Pre-**

vention of Torture (1987). The European Convention on Human Rights created in turn a **European Commission on Human Rights**, which reported to the Committee of Ministers of the Council of Europe, and a **European Court of Human Rights (ECHR)**, which transmits its judgments to the Committee of Ministers of the Council of Europe for execution. The commission was eliminated in a reform of the European Court in 1998. The European Convention on Human Rights encompasses mainly civil and political rights, whereas the European Social Charter addresses protection and promotion of the economic and social rights first articulated in the **Universal Declaration of Human Rights**. The council awards a Human Rights Prize in three-year intervals to recognize outstanding service in defense of human rights.

With the momentous developments in Europe after the fall of communism, the council began acting as a major human rights watchdog in the former communist countries of Eastern Europe, assisting these countries in their efforts to engage in democratic and constitutional reforms. Responding to this new challenge, the Council of Europe, at its summit of heads of state and government in Vienna, emphasized that the organization should serve as the guardian of democratic security as a complement to military security. In its 1997 summit at Strasbourg, the heads of state and government identified four areas of ongoing activity and concern, including the persistent theme of democracy and human rights, but also the issue of social cohesion, the security of citizens, and the advancement of cultural diversity. In May 2005, at its third summit of heads of state and government at Warsaw, further goals were identified as major areas of future council concern, including the ongoing task of promoting human rights, the task of strengthening the security of citizens from **terrorism** and other attacks on human dignity from such sources as organized crime and trafficking in human beings, and finally in fostering cooperation with other European and international bodies. With the revolutionary developments in Europe, council membership has expanded from a largely West European organization to include 21 countries from Central and Eastern Europe, thus fulfilling one of its original aspirations to serve as a means of genuinely pan-European cooperation. Address: Avenue de l'Europe, 67075 Strasbourg CEDEX, France. Website: www.coe.int.

CRIMES AGAINST HUMANITY. This class of international crimes was established by the Nuremburg Tribunal after World War II, in order to try to punish those officials in the Nazi regime who participated actively in the efforts to exterminate civilian populations, including most obviously the Jewish people, in what is now referred to as the **Holocaust**. This act of **genocide** so shocked the conscience of the international community that the Allied governments were determined that an example should be made of those directly responsible for the formulation and execution of such heinous and unthinkable crimes, even though no specific prohibition against such enormities had hitherto existed under **international law**. One murder by government agents or soldiers, whether in time of peace or war, may constitute a criminal act or a war crime. To proliferate the killing of millions of innocent persons is so unthinkable as not to require an explicit prohibition, or at least so thought governments until such enormities became commonplace in the mid-20th century.

Technically, under an extreme interpretation of legal **positivism** and an exaggerated notion of absolute **sovereignty**, a government might claim a right to treat its population as it sees fit, including with great severity or even brutality, without interference from other governments or international bodies. But under the Westphalian system, the time-honored tradition of **natural law**, and the customary practice of states, no government could consider itself immune from international action if it pursued policies toward its own citizens that "shocked the conscience of humanity." Other governments, under customary international law, might then have not only a right but also even a duty to intervene in order to stop the inhumane activity. This notion gave governments permission under proper circumstances to justify action by way of humanitarian intervention, thus overriding the normal and prior right of the territorial integrity and independence of the culpable state.

The formal definition of crimes against humanity at Nuremburg served notice that governments could no longer hide behind claims of sovereign immunity to justify murder and persecution of their own citizens, or the citizens of other countries subject to belligerent occupation. Under international law, all persons have an obligation not to commit such crimes, and may be tried and, if convicted, punished for them by any government or international court that is able to exercise jurisdiction. Such international courts might include ad hoc tribunals such as the **International Criminal Tribunal for the Former Yugoslavia (ICTY)** and the **International Criminal Tribunal for Rwanda (ICTR)** or the recently established and permanent **International Criminal Court (ICC).**

CULTURAL SURVIVAL. Cultural Survival is a nongovernmental organization dedicated to the promotion and protection of **indigenous rights**. Since 1972 it has sought to promote global awareness and understanding of these rights and to help indigenous peoples become more effective advocates of their own rights. Examples of its programs in advancement of indigenous rights include its Guatemala Radio Project in which Cultural Survival cooperates with several local radio stations as a means of information dissemination and **education**, training of broadcast journalists, and promotion of indigenous news and programs, and its Human Rights Documentation project in Colombia, which works with indigenous peoples caught in the cross fire of Colombia's internal conflicts. In Africa, its Ituri Forest Peoples Project in the Congo promotes child literacy and **health** care, and in Asia its Tibet Project works with Tibetans in Tibet, India, Nepal, and the United States to promote small-scale carpet businesses. It publishes a quarterly periodical, the *Cultural Survival Quarterly*; a semiannual newspaper, *Cultural Survival Voices*; as well as the *Weekly Indigenous News*. Members numbering about 4,300 persons from more than 150 countries include professional anthropologists, university professors, and students, as well as activists and members of the public. Address: 215 Prospect Street, Cambridge, MA 02139, USA. Website: www.cs .org. *See also* MINORITIES; SURVIVAL INTERNATIONAL; WORLD COUNCIL OF INDIGENOUS PEOPLES (WCIP).

– D –

DATA. DATA was founded by Irish rock star Bono (born Paul David Hewson), the lead singer of the Irish rock band U2. Bono appeared at the 1984 Band Aid and at Live Aid in 1985, both organized by another Irish rock star, Bob Geldof. Thus, early in his career he brought his musical talents to the service of humanitarian relief efforts. In

1999, Bono became more intensely interested in the complex of problems surrounding the perverse effects of debt upon the poorest countries, especially those in Africa. To address more deliberately the humanitarian issues affecting Africa, he founded his own nongovernmental organization (NGO), DATA, in 2002. DATA stands for "Debt, AIDS, Trade in Africa," and it represents an effort to understand the problem of **poverty** in its political and economic dimensions. This moved Bono and his associates beyond thinking primarily in terms of charity to addressing human rights concerns as matters of justice and **equality**. Much of the strategy pursued by DATA involves networking between the wealthiest governments and those of Africa, and with the NGO sector. DATA attempts to publicize the problems in Africa and increase awareness as to appropriate solutions by using well-known celebrities and organizing highly visible events to attract attention. Addresses: DATA, 1400 Eye St. NW, Suite 1125, Washington, DC 20005, USA; DATA, 8 St James's Square, London SW1Y 4JU, UK. Website: www.data.org.

DEATH PENALTY. The use of the death penalty as the ultimate punishment for serious crimes was once a common practice of governments. Although widely used throughout history, in recent times the death penalty has been generally restricted by most governments to such crimes as murder and treason, following a legal process in which the persons accused of serious crimes have access to due process, such as a trial by judge or jury. More than two-thirds of the world's governments have abolished the death penalty in their domestic jurisdictions. As a matter of **international law**, each country is free either to retain or abolish the practice, although the trend in state practice continues to be toward its abolishment.

The **right to life**, which is generally regarded as the most basic of all human rights, if interpreted in a strict sense, would seem to be inconsistent with the use of the death penalty. However, in many legal settings the right to life is implicitly qualified to mean the right to "innocent" life, and criminals guilty of first-degree murder—that is, willful and premeditated murder—thus may be seen as having forfeited their right to life. Various killings short of this, such as those done in self-defense, in the heat of irrational passion, or by negligence or mere accident, have been long and widely regarded as not justifying the death penalty. Additionally, acts of murder by the young or the mentally handicapped have generally been regarded as not qualifying for application of the death penalty, although what constitutes mental handicap or the age of majority has varied in state practice.

Various human rights instruments have implied that no one may be arbitrarily deprived of his or her right to life. This principle is enunciated in the **International Covenant on Civil and Political Rights**, but it does not outlaw the use of the death penalty as such, as long as its application is not arbitrary. The Second **Optional Protocol to the International Covenant on Civil and Political Rights**, adopted by the **United Nations General Assembly** in 1989, has as its goal the eventual elimination of the death penalty, but only parties to the protocol are under an obligation to abolish the death penalty. About a quarter of the governments have ratified this protocol, although many more have already in practice abolished the death penalty. The **Convention of the Rights of the Child** prohibits the death penalty in cases involving those under the age of 18 at the time of the commission of the crime. Protocol XIII of the **European Convention on Human Rights** prohibits the death penalty in all circumstance to signatory nations, and a 1990 protocol to the **Inter-American Convention on Human Rights** outlaws the use of the death penalty by signatory states except during wartime. The **International Criminal Court (ICC)** bars the application of the death penalty concerning all cases tried under its jurisdiction. In addition to these restrictions in international and regional conventions, numerous nongovernmental organizations (NGOs) are active in the movement to abolish the death penalty. These include **Amnesty International (AI)** and **Derechos Human Rights**, among others.

Variances in state practice in the use of the death penalty continue, although abolishment or curtailment of its use is common and growing. The continuing variance in practice has affected the process of **extradition**. States having abolished the death penalty routinely refuse to extradite suspect fugitives to a country that still retains capital punishment without a guarantee that the death penalty will not be imposed upon the extradited person if he or she is subsequently found guilty of the crime.

DECLARATION BY THE UNITED NATIONS. On 1 January 1942, this declaration was issued by representatives of 26 nations allied against Axis aggression. Expressing the sentiments outlined in the **Atlantic Charter**, it signified the first formal step by nations toward the eventual establishment of the **United Nations (UN)**. In the preamble to this brief statement of **solidarity**, the representatives asserted their conviction that "complete victory over their enemies [was] essential to defend life, liberty, independence and religious freedom, and to preserve human rights and justice." The **United Nations Charter** and subsequent UN human rights documents reflected this concern for the protection of human rights. For a complete text of the declaration, see the *U.S. State Department Bulletin*, 3 January 1942, p. 3.

DECLARATION OF INDEPENDENCE (U.S.). The U.S. Declaration of Independence, which has come to be seen as the founding charter of the United States of America, was approved by the Continental Congress on 4 July 1776. The declaration was the official explanation for why the colonies declared independence from Great Britain on 2 July 1776. The vote in favor of independence on 2 July announced the existence of 12 new countries—New York abstaining on the independence resolution passed on 2 July. The declaration was made unanimous by all 13 of the former colonies on 15 July 1776, when New York agreed to it. Contrary to popular understanding, the declaration announced the independence of the colonies from each other as much as it did their mutual independence from Britain.

Thomas Jefferson, on behalf of a committee, drafted the declaration, which was amended by the Congress. The declaration reflected the English Whig tradition dominant since 1688. It argued for independence from the **natural law** tradition and the contract theory of government. The declaration charged King George III and the British Parliament with acts that violated natural law and oppressed the people of the 13 colonies. In the view of the declaration signatories, these and the other listed grievances justified the revolution.

In some ways, the declaration is a defense of the right of national **self-determination**. It argues on the basis of representative government, asserting that government is created by people to secure their rights, specifically, life, liberty, and the pursuit of happiness. These rights come from God, not from any government, and so cannot be alienated legitimately from individuals. Finally, the declaration refers to all men being created equal. This assertion of **equality** has become a hallmark of the U.S. political system and has consistently been appealed to as a value toward which the United States should strive.

DECLARATION ON TERRITORIAL ASYLUM. Efforts to arrive at a binding convention on territorial **asylum** by governments have proved elusive. The practice of governments strongly suggests that they wish to retain ultimate control over the granting of asylum, rather than creating an obligation on the part of states to grant it or to confer on individuals an unambiguous right of asylum, which could be claimed against any government. Adopted by the **United Nations General Assembly** on 14 December 1967, the declaration acknowledges that asylum is an act of states that must in turn be respected by other states. Individuals who are not war criminals or guilty of other acts contrary to the **United Nations Charter** have the right to seek and enjoy asylum, but the declaration notes that "it shall rest with the State granting asylum to evaluate the grounds for the grant of asylum." The declaration reaffirms principles contained in other international agreements relating to **refugees**, such as the United Nations **Convention Relating to the Status of Refugees**, that persons seeking asylum should not be subjected to involuntary repatriation, expulsion, or rejection at the frontier, except in cases of overriding national security or emergency.

DECLARATION ON THE ELIMINATION OF ALL FORMS OF RACIAL DISCRIMINATION. Adopted unanimously by the **United Nations General Assembly** on 20 November 1963, this nonbinding statement of principles set the stage for the adoption two years later of the **International Convention on the Elimination of All Forms of Racial Discrimination**. The declaration called upon states to speedily end all forms of discrimination on the basis of race, color, or ethnic origin through domestic public policy measures.

DECLARATION ON THE ELIMINATION OF DISCRIMINATION AGAINST WOMEN. Adopted by the **United Nations General Assembly** on 7 November 1967, this declaration, though nonbinding, represented a major step in the work of the **United Nations (UN)** on behalf of the rights of **women**. Article 1 of the declaration states that "Discrimination against women, denying or limiting as it does their **equality** of rights with men, is fundamentally unjust and constitutes an offense against human dignity." The declaration calls upon governments to eliminate all laws, customs, and practices that discriminate against women. It reiterates the **political rights** of women that had been set forth in the **Convention on the Political Rights of Women**. It underscores a woman's right to inherit, own, and dispose of **property**, the freedom to enter on an equal basis into marriage, to have equal opportunities for **education**, equal opportunities for employment, and fair compensation. The declaration contains no enforcement provisions, but urges governments and other bodies to observe the principles enunciated. The principles of the declaration were, however, later incorporated into the **Convention on the Elimination of All Forms of Discrimination against Women** of 1979, which did create certain implementing mechanisms.

DECLARATION ON THE HUMAN RIGHTS OF INDIVIDUALS WHO ARE NOT NATIONALS OF THE COUNTRY IN WHICH THEY LIVE. Growing out of the work of the **United Nations (UN)** Subcommission on Prevention of Discrimination and Protection of **Minorities**, this declaration represented a reiteration and clarification of the traditional laws of **state responsibility** concerning the protection and rights of aliens. Adopted by the **UN General Assembly** on 13 December 1985 as part of Resolution 40/144, the declaration acknowledges the right of states to control immigration across their boundaries and the duty of aliens to observe the laws of the nations in which they reside. On the other hand, it also stipulates a number of **aliens' rights**, including the **right to life**, freedom from **arbitrary arrest** or detention, due process of law, **privacy**, **equality** before the law, the right to marriage and a **family**, freedoms of thought, opinion, conscience, and religion, and freedom to transfer earnings abroad. Subject to the legitimate needs of the host state's national security and order, the alien has a **right to leave** the country, to freedom of expression, to peaceful assembly, and to own **property**. Aliens lawfully residing within a country have a right to safe and healthy working conditions, fair wages, the right to join unions and other organizations, and the right of access to **health**, educational, social, and welfare services. Although the declaration is nonbinding, many of the elements of the declaration are widely practiced by governments, some as universally binding customary **international law**.

DECLARATION ON THE PROTECTION OF ALL PERSONS FROM BEING SUBJECTED TO TORTURE AND OTHER CRUEL, INHUMAN, OR DEGRADING TREATMENT OR PUNISHMENT. Adopted by the **United Nations General Assembly** on 9 December 1975, upon the recommendation of the Fifth United Nations Congress on the Prevention of Crime and the Treatment of Offenders, this nonbinding declaration urged states to abolish the use of **torture** and other excessive forms of punishment. Torture is defined as a deliberate and aggravated form of cruel, inhuman, or degrading treatment or punishment, intentionally inflicted by or at the instigation of a public official for the purpose of extracting information or a confession, or for punishment of an act that the tortured person is suspected to have committed or actually committed. States are called upon to eliminate such practices by law, to treat torture itself as a criminal offense punishable by law, to train police forces in such a manner as to comply with the prohibition of the use of torture, and to monitor and investigate reported incidences of torture. The declaration was followed in 1984 by a legally binding **Convention against Torture and Other Cruel, Inhuman, or Degrading Treatment or Punishment**.

DECLARATION ON THE RIGHTS OF DISABLED PERSONS. Adopted by the **United Nations General Assembly** on 9 December 1975, this declaration drew attention to the special needs of persons with disabilities. Disabled persons were defined as those "unable to ensure by himself or herself, wholly or partly, the necessities of a normal individual and/or social life, as a result of a deficiency, either congenital or not, in his or her physical or mental capabilities." The principle of nondiscrimination was enunciated as applicable to all disabled persons, along with the inherent rights to respect for their human dignity and the right to a decent life. They should be accorded the same civil rights as any citizen, have the right of access to medical, psychological, and functional treatment, to economic and **social security**, and to the benefits of **family** living and foster care where possible.

DECLARATION ON THE RIGHTS OF MAN (FRANCE). Adopted by the French National Assembly in August 1789 as the preamble to the revolutionary republic's **constitution**, this declaration was an important statement in the evolution of the human rights tradition. The term "human rights" is explicitly referred to in the preamble to the declaration, which asserts that the failure to acknowledge and promote such rights is the principal cause of "public misfortune" and "corruptions of government." Influenced heavily by the English rights tradition, the bills of rights of various American state constitutions, and the American **Declaration of Independence**, as well as the political thought of French philosopher Jean-Jacques Rousseau, the Declaration of the Rights of Man was in turn an influential source for the development of numerous democratic constitutions in Europe during the 19th and early 20th centuries, and undoubtedly ranks high in the pantheon of human rights documents throughout history.

The declaration acknowledges the existence of a Supreme Being and of certain sacred and unalienable rights, including the rights of fundamental freedom and **equality**, of liberty, **property**, security, and resistance to oppression, the right of political participation, of due process of law, and of the presumption of innocence until conviction of a crime. Further, the declaration asserts the principles of the **freedom of religion**, and of unrestrained communication of thoughts, **freedom of opinion and expression**. But the declaration also asserts the principle of national **sovereignty**, the notion that citizens have duties as well as rights, and that force used in the interest of the common good will be necessary.

Although the declaration is a ringing endorsement of freedom and a clarion call to oppose and prevent tyranny, the realization of all of its principles was not immediately achieved in French political life. The French Revolution soon lost sight of its high-minded first principles and devolved into a brutal and bloody affair that culminated in the authoritarian reign of Napoleon. The gulf between principle and practice was quite wide, and in this sense the Declaration of the Rights of Man was a harbinger of later human rights pronouncements, which also suffer as statements of principled aspiration amid a lack of widespread observation. See **Thomas Paine**, *Rights of Man* (1987) for a text of and commentary on the French Declaration of the Rights of Man.

DECLARATION ON THE RIGHTS OF MENTALLY RETARDED PERSONS. In this declaration, adopted on 20 December 1971, the **United Nations General Assembly** highlighted the special needs of mentally retarded persons in the human rights context. Such persons should be accorded appropriate medical attention, **education**, social services, and a decent standard of living. They have a right to a qualified guardian to protect their well-being and interests, and their normal human rights should not be deprived without proper legal safeguards against abuse. The declaration acknowledges that it is best wherever possible for mentally retarded people to live with their own parents, and failing that, in contexts that approximate a normal life. In the preambulatory paragraphs, the declaration acknowledges that many countries have limited resources to achieve the full realization of the principles enunciated.

DECLARATION ON THE RIGHTS OF THE CHILD. Proclaimed by the **United Nations General Assembly** on 20 November 1959, the Declaration on the Rights of the Child is a nonbinding **United Nations (UN)** resolution containing 10 principles in which individuals, private organizations, and local and national governments are called upon to recognize and to strive to observe through appropriate legislation. The first principle prohibits discrimination against children or their families on grounds of race, color, sex, language, religion, political or other opinion, national or social origin, **property**, birth, or other status. Under principle 2, children are said to enjoy special protection under law to develop physically, mentally, morally, spiritually, and socially in a healthy and normal manner and in conditions of freedom and dignity. Principle 3 provides that children are entitled from birth to a name and a **nationality**. Principle 4 provides that children shall enjoy the benefits of **social security**, adequate prenatal and postnatal care, and rights to adequate nutrition, **housing**, recreation, and medical services. Principle 5 provides that handicapped children shall be given special treatment, **education**, and care. Principle 6 acknowledges that in most instances children are best cared for by their parents, and calls upon governments to care for orphans. Other children lacking adequate means of support should be assisted through their regular **family**. Principle 7 asserts that children are entitled to receive a free and compulsory education through the elementary level. Principle 8 stipulates that in all circumstances, children shall be among the first to receive protection and assistance. Principle 9 protects children from all forms of neglect, cruelty, exploitation, and trafficking. **Forced labor** by children before an appropriate minimum age is forbidden. Principle 10 reiterates the nondiscrimination provision stipulated in principle one. On the 30th anniversary of the declaration, the UN General Assembly concluded a **Convention on the Rights of the Child**, which reiterated and elaborated upon many of the rights set forth in the declaration as statements of aspiration. For a full text of the declaration, see UN General Assembly Resolution 1386 (XIV). *See also* CHILDREN'S RIGHTS.

DECLARATION ON THE RIGHT TO DEVELOPMENT. This controversial pronouncement of the **United Nations General Assembly** was approved on 4 December 1986. Like most declarations, it is a nonbinding statement that does not create legal rights as such. It was particularly controversial because of its association with the often rancorous ideological debate over the creation of a new international economic order, which preoccupied the **United Nations (UN)** bodies in the 1970s and early 1980s. Thus, although many of its principles are acknowledged and even practiced by some states, its assertion of a right to development cannot be said to have fully ripened into a binding principle of **international law**.

The declaration, in Article 1, asserts that "the right to development is an inalienable human right by virtue of which every human person and all peoples are entitled to participate in, contribute to and enjoy economic, social, cultural and political development, in which all human rights and fundamental freedoms can be fully realized." Article 2 does balance this claim with the recognition that human beings have a "responsibility for development" and "duties to the community," but nowhere is the term *development* itself precisely defined. Still, the recognition that development is a duty is an important qualification in a hortatory document asserting it principally as a right. As international law now exists, despite the declaration, no country or person has so widely acknowledged a right to development, that this imposes an enforceable legal claim against any other person or state, except insofar as the domestic legislation of a state might provide for such claims against fellow citizens. Absent the explicit formulation of such a right in treaty or custom, it remains an ideal and an aspiration rather than a clear, unmistakable, and enforceable right.

Efforts in the UN since the declaration's adoption suggest the recognition in UN circles that a declaration does not make a right as such. In 1990, a UN-sponsored conference, the Global Consultation on the Realization of the Right to Development as a Human Right, was held in Geneva on the subject. The title of the consultation suggested the tentative nature of the subject. In 1993, at the **World Conference on Human Rights**, debate on the right to development was expected to be quite heated. Surprisingly, the conference was able to achieve consensual language on the right to development as an inalienable right. However, the Vienna Declaration and Program of Action, which resulted from the conference deliberations, is not a legally binding agreement, and, lacking any kind of enforcement provisions, it still leaves the right to development in a hortatory stage of development.

DEPARTMENT OF HUMANITARIAN AFFAIRS (DHA). Established in April 1992, DHA served as the coordinating body for the work of the numerous **United Nations (UN)** agencies involved in disaster and humanitarian relief activities. It was led by an under-secretary-general for humanitarian affairs, who also served as the chair of the Interagency Standing Committee (IASC) and as the UN's Chief Emergency Relief Coordinator (ERC). DHA succeeded the United Nations Disaster Relief Organization (UNDRO), assuming the functions of the latter until it was, in turn, succeeded by the **United Nations Office for Coordination of Humanitarian Affairs (UNOCHA)** in 1998.

DERECHOS HUMAN RIGHTS. Located in San Leandro, California, this organization is an example of an Internet-based agency that has been established to advance human rights causes. It serves as a news outlet for human rights controversies, reports and links to various human rights and anti**torture** agencies, and promoting the prosecution of human rights violators and an end to the **death penalty**. It works in combination with a sister organization in Europe known as Equipo Nizkor, as well as Derechos Argentina, to disseminate information on human rights abuses and to protect the interests and memory of cases of **disappearances**. Lacking operational programs as such, its focus is on human rights advocacy through communication and information sharing. Website: www.derechos.org.

DEROGATION. This principle acknowledges the right of governments to suspend their obligations under provisions of a treaty during times of national urgency or grave threats to their existence. Several human rights treaties contain provisions for states to derogate from their obligations under such severe circumstances. The **International Covenant on Civil and Political Rights**, the **European Convention on Human Rights**, and the **Geneva Red Cross Conventions** are examples of treaties permitting derogation from certain treaty rights under certain circumstances. Some of these treaties also stipulate that certain rights may not be derogated under any circumstances. Normally, governments seeking relief from enforcement of their obligations under a treaty must take steps, under the terms of the treaty itself, to announce and justify steps taken in derogation of their otherwise binding legal obligations. *See also* PUBLIC EMERGENCY.

DIPLOMATIC ASYLUM. *See* ASYLUM.

DISAPPEARANCES. Although arrests without charge have been common in the 20th century, a new form of human rights violation— disappearances—emerged in Argentina in the 1970s. During the so-called Dirty War (1976–1983), the military rulers of Argentina implemented a violent antisubversion campaign. The Argentine military created a covert structure within the regular military security forces and divided this into "work groups" (*grupos de tarea*). These work groups engaged in disappearances, detention, **torture**, and extrajudicial execution of persons the military identified as subversives.

"Disappearances" can be understood simply to refer to situations in which government officials detain people and refuse to admit the detention in circumstances in which the detention raises fears for the safety or lives of the detainees. A legal definition employed by the National Commissioner for the Protection of Human Rights in Honduras has defined forced or involuntary disappearances as "the detention of a person by agents of the state or by others with the acquiescence of the state, without an order from appropriate authorities and in which the detention is denied and no official information on the fate or location of the detainee exists."

As can be seen, a disappearance needs arbitrary abduction or detention of a person by government agents who are tolerated or protected by the government, which then denies the abduction or detention. This permits the government to avoid responsibility for the arrest and for the fate of victims who are executed and surreptitiously buried to prevent discovery.

During Argentina's Dirty War, as many as 9,000 people "disappeared" after abduction by government security forces. Some estimates place the number at 15,000 executed but identified, and therefore not defined as "disappeared." Almost 70 percent of those who disappeared in Argentina were abducted from their homes or workplace, while only 25 percent were abducted on the street. There were also smaller numbers of disappearances in Chile and Uruguay.

Disappearances became very common in Central America in the 1980s especially in El Salvador, Guatemala, and Honduras. In Honduras, Argentine military advisers assisted the Honduran security forces. A secret intelligence division of the Honduran military, Battalion 3 16, carried out systematic disappearances mostly between 1981 and 1984. The battalion was commanded by General Gustavo Alvarez Martinez, its creator and chief of the national police force. After Alvarez was removed from office in 1984, the number of disappearances declined but still continued into the early 1990s. It is estimated that at least 200 people disappeared in Honduras from 1980 to 1992.

Disappearances violate many rights recognized in **international law**. First, they violate the **right to life**, specifically Article 3 of the **Universal Declaration of Human Rights**, Article 6 of the **International Covenant on Civil and Political Rights**, Article 1 of the **American Declaration of the Rights and Duties of Man**, and Article 4 of the **Inter-American Convention on Human Rights**. Second, disappearances violate the right to freedom and personal security. Specifically, forced detention violates Article 3 of the Universal Declaration of Human Rights; Article 9 of the Covenant on Civil and Political Rights; Articles 1, 8, and 25 of the American Declaration of the Rights of Man; and Article 7 of the Inter-American Convention on Human Rights. Third, those people who were abducted and then detained were also mistreated and tortured. Detention without contact with anyone outside of the facility and the realization that one is disappeared is an act of psychological torture. This, then, violates Article 5 of the Universal Declaration, Article 1 of the Covenant, and Article 5 of the American Declaration.

Many people were abducted, detained, executed, and examined for guilt by persons not competent under the law to render such judgments. The government officials served as judges, juries, and executioners. These acts violate Article 8 of the Universal Declaration, Articles 9 and 10 of the Covenant, Article 26 of the American Declaration, and Article 8 of the Inter-American Convention.

The practice of disappearances also violates a developing human right, the right to the truth that has not yet been explicitly advanced by any courts. The **Inter-American Commission on Human Rights (IACHR)**, in its annual report of 1985–1986, asserted that a society's right to know the truth is "inalienable" as it relates to motives and circumstances of "aberrant crimes" and it presupposes the existence of investigating committees or the judiciary to find the truth. The commission reiterated this in its 1992–1993 annual report dealing with Argentina when it established that victims and their relatives have a right to have a criminal court to conduct an investigation designed to establish individual guilt and punish those responsible.

The understanding of state accountability has been expanded in recent years. In the *Velasquez Rodriguez* case (1988), the **Inter-American Court of Human Rights (IACT)** decided that a government could be deemed culpable for a disappearance even if carried out by individuals neither employed by the government nor following its orders. The Court based this finding on Article 1 of the Inter-American Convention on Human Rights, in which states parties agree to "ensure" the exercise of the rights enumerated in the convention. This would appear to be sanctioned by the **Convention against Torture and Other Cruel, Inhuman, or Degrading Treatment or Punishment**, which defines torture as pain or suffering "inflicted by or at the instigation of or with the consent or acquiescence of a public official or other person acting in an official capacity." Other international activities in connection with disappearances include a draft declaration on the subject and a **United Nations (UN)** Working Group on Disappearances, which was established in 1980 and still operates. International opinion increasingly holds states legally and morally responsible for both acts of commission or omission that lead to disappearances, but punishment for such violations has not been easily secured.

Disappearances are not limited to Latin American. Indeed, long before the practice emerged there, disappearances were common in the Soviet Union, especially during the Stalinist years. During the 1980s until its demise in 2002, the Baathist regime of Saddam Hussein in Iraq was under constant criticism by human rights groups for the disappearance of large numbers of people. During the same time period, civil war in Sri Lanka produced more than 16,000 disappearances. More recently in Chechnya, the level of disappearances reached such a critical level as to evoke claims by human rights groups that it had attained the character of a **crime against humanity**, which is based on the treaty norm in the Rome Statute of the **International Criminal Court (ICC)** that forced disappearances qualify as such a crime that cannot be subject to a statute of limitation. Concern has been expressed about disappearances in the recent civil war in Nepal, which has put that country in the unenviable position as the top country for forced disappearances.

As noted above, the United Nations **Commission on Human Rights (CHR)** established a working group in 1980 to investigate the drafting of a legally binding instrument for the protection of all people from enforced disappearances. The working group continues to meet in Geneva under the auspices of the **United Nations High Commissioner for Human Rights (UNHCHR)**, on a task that has proved exceedingly protracted and complicated. *See also* DERECHOS HUMAN RIGHTS; FIGHTING AGAINST FORCED DISAPPEARANCES IN LATIN AMERICA.

DOUGLASS, FREDERICK (1818–1895). U.S. journalist, orator, and antislavery leader, Frederick Douglass was born a slave in Tuckahoe, Maryland, probably in February 1818. His original name was Frederick Augustus Washington Bailey. Sent to Baltimore to live with the Hugh Auld family, he was taught to read. In 1838, Douglass passed himself off as a sailor and escaped to New York. He later moved to New Bedford, Massachusetts, and he changed his name to Douglass.

His antislavery career began when an extemporaneous speech he gave in August 1841 at an antislavery meeting prompted the Massachusetts Antislavery Society to hire him as one of its agents. Douglass gave antislavery speeches throughout New England and the Middle Atlantic states for the next four years. To answer charges that he was an impostor, Douglass published his first autobiography in 1845. His increasing fame also brought increasing risk of recapture and Douglass traveled to Britain and lectured there from 1845 to 1847, strengthening British support for U.S. abolitionists in the process. During this time money was raised to obtain his legal manumission and he returned to the United States in 1847.

Douglass published a weekly newspaper, the *North Star*, later known as *Frederick Douglass' Paper* from December 1847 to 1860. The establishment of the paper marked the beginning of the estrangement between Douglass and **William Lloyd Garrison**, who had been the former's mentor. Douglass viewed the *North Star* as a specifically Negro newspaper while Garrison viewed it as a competitor to his *Liberator*. Secondly, and more importantly, by 1851 Douglass had rejected Garrison's refusal to work politically within the constitutional system to end **slavery** by aligning himself with the conservative constitutionalist abolitionists led by James G. Birney.

The *North Star* endorsed the Free Soil Party in the 1848 presidential election, openly endorsed working with the Constitution on behalf of emancipation in 1851, and urged the creation of a national antislavery party in 1853. Douglass had been committed to nonviolence, but the guerrilla warfare in Kansas Territory between antislavery and proslavery groups after 1854 led him to call on people to send guns to the Kansas abolitionists. John Brown kept Douglass abreast of his plans for a slave insurrection. While Douglass refused to take part in it, there is no evidence that he ever counseled against it until Brown changed his goal to that of seizing the Harper's Ferry arsenal. Douglass argued with Brown for two days to call off the attack to no avail. By 1860, Douglass wanted to enhance the power of the federal government to enable it to abolish slavery and publicly expressed hope for a Republican Party victory in the 1860 presidential election.

Douglass attacked the Lincoln administration's early failure to implement abolition, but after the Emancipation Proclamation he helped to recruit black troops for the Union effort. By the Civil War's end, Douglass had become the national leader of African Americans and a strong supporter of the Radical Republicans. Douglass argued for the adoption of both the Fourteenth and Fifteenth Amendments to the **Constitution of the United States**.

Douglass was assistant secretary of the U.S. Commission to Santo Domingo in 1871, marshal of the District of Columbia (1877–1881), recorder of deeds for the District of Columbia (1881–1886), and U.S. minister and consul-general to Haiti (1889–1891). He died in Washington, DC, on 20 February 1895.

DUNANT, JEAN-HENRI (1828–1910). Henri Dunant happened upon the battle of Solferino during the early wars of Italian unification in June 1859. Shocked both by the cries of the 40,000 wounded and by the lack of attention they received from their own armies, Dunant organized temporary medical aid for both the Austrian and French wounded. In his *Un Souvenir de Solferino* of 1862, Dunant advocated the establishment of voluntary relief societies in all countries, which would work to prevent human misery and care for all victims of war and those suffering in peace. He also called for an international treaty regulating the care and protection of the wounded in war. This led to the first Red Cross societies and the Geneva Convention of 1864.

Bankruptcy and expulsion from the Red Cross in 1867 prompted Dunant to leave Geneva and he spent most of the rest of his life in **poverty**. During his obscure years, he consistently advocated improved treatment of prisoners of war, emancipation of slaves, disarmament, arbitration between countries, and a national Jewish homeland. Dunant was rediscovered in 1895 by a newspaper reporter. During his last years, he received many honors and awards, including the first Nobel Peace Prize in 1901. Dunant died in Heiden, Switzerland, on 30 October 1910.

– E –

ECONOMIC AND SOCIAL COUNCIL (ECOSOC). One of six major organs of the **United Nations (UN)** ECOSOC is empowered under Chapters IX and X of the **United Nations Charter** and under the authority of the **UN General Assembly** to coordinate international cooperative efforts in the economic, social, cultural, educational, **health**, and related fields (including human rights). ECOSOC is empowered by the charter to "make recommendations for the purpose of promoting respect for, and observance of, human rights and fundamental freedoms for all" (Article 62b). ECOSOC is permitted, under the terms of Article 68, to create commissions in the economic and social areas, and also in the promotion of human rights. In this regard, ECOSOC established a **Commission on Human Rights (CHR)**, which in turn proceeded, as early as 1946, to draft multilateral instruments concerning human rights. ECOSOC has taken the lead in promoting the drafting of human rights conventions and submitting them to the General Assembly for adoption.

ECOSOC has established a number of subsidiary bodies for human rights over the years. Its **Human Rights Committee (HRC)** (established in 1966 pursuant to the terms of the International Covenant on Civil and Political Rights) and its **Committee on Economic, Social, and Cultural Rights (CESCR)** oversee various working groups. Until its termination and replacement by the **Human Rights Council** in 2006, the Commission on Human Rights reported to ECOSOC and oversaw a wide array of working groups, such as those dealing with indigenous rights and with the protection of persons from enforced **disappearances**. Most of these human rights bodies now operate under the supervision of the Office of the **United Nations High Commissioner for Human Rights (UNHCHR)** in Geneva, which was established in 1993, and now oversees the activities of the many treaty-based human rights committees. ECOSOC also monitors working groups on the right to development, on arbitrary detention, and on people of African descent. Its Group of Three Concerning the Convention against Apartheid, suspended operations in 1995, with the successful achievement of majority rule in South Africa.

ECOSOC also oversees the work of the **Commission on the Status of Women**, the **Commission for Social Development**, the Commission on Narcotic Drugs, the **Commission on Crime Prevention and Criminal Justice**, and the Commission on Population and Development, all of which in some form or another have a bearing on questions of human rights. For details on ECOSOC and its subsidiary bodies, see www.un.org/docs/ecosoc.

ECONOMIC, SOCIAL, AND CULTURAL RIGHTS. Unlike **political rights**, which can in practice be immediately observed by governments that will to do so, the realization of economic, social, and cultural rights depends heavily on the economic capacity of the country. These rights, first elaborated in the **Universal Declaration of Human Rights**, broadly include such elements as rights to **work**, to **social security**, to an adequate standard of living, to enjoy physical and mental **health**, to **education**, to have and be part of a **family**, and to development. Such rights, however, cannot simply be established by treaty. They involve not only policy changes but also frequently long periods of gradual improvement in overall economic conditions. For this reason the **International Covenant on Economic, Social, and Cultural Rights**, unlike its counterpart the **International Covenant on Civil and Political Rights**, did not initially include provisions for receipt and investigation of complaints or an **Optional Protocol**, but rather it provides that states parties should submit periodic reports on the steps they have taken to give effect to the goals enunciated in the covenant. However, in the 1990s, interest emerged to explore the feasibility of such an optional protocol in the arena of economic, social, and cultural rights. A working group continues to work on the draft text.

EDUCATION. The right to education is incorporated into a number of human rights instruments. The right was first articulated in Article 26 of the **Universal Declaration of Human Rights**, where the right to an elementary education was proclaimed. Such fundamental education, the declaration asserted, should be free and compulsory. Technical and professional education, though not mandatory, should be widely accessible, and higher education made available on the basis of merit. These notions were later further elaborated upon in Articles 13 and 14 of the **International Covenant on Economic, Social, and Cultural Rights**. Various statements regarding the elimination of discrimination in the educational arena are stipulated in the **International Convention on the Elimination of All Forms of Racial Discrimination** and in the **Convention on the Elimination of All Forms of Discrimination against Women**. Article 17 of the **African Charter on Human and Peoples' Rights** also stipulated that all persons have a right to education. The **United Nations Educational, Scientific, and Cultural Organization (UNESCO)** has attempted in a series of conventions, recommendations, and declarations to promote the right to education.

EQUALITY. Among the panoply of rights, the right to equality, coupled with that of liberty, is one of the most widely asserted and time-honored human rights. The U.S. **Declaration of Independence** of 1776 proclaimed that "We hold these truths to be self-evident, that all men are created equal." The French **Declaration of the Rights of Man** also asserts the fundamental freedom and equality of human beings. The **Universal Declaration of Human Rights** of 1948 asserts the equality of all people without regard to race, color, sex, language, religion, political or other opinion, national or social origin, **property**, birth, or any other status. Such equality extends to the individual's capacity before the law as well. The **International Covenant on Civil and Political Rights** reiterates these principles, as does the **International Covenant on Economic, Social, and Cultural Rights**. Similar provisions are found in various treaties calling for the elimination of discrimination, as well as a number of regional instruments, such as the **Inter-American Convention on Human Rights**, the **African Charter on Human and Peoples' Rights**, and the **European Convention on Human Rights**.

The right of equality is normally understood to refer to the right to equality before the law, equality in the administration of justice, the right to be free of discrimination, and the right to equality of opportunity, as opposed to the notion that all individuals have a right to equal standards of living. The right to liberty presumes that some inequalities of outcome will exist among people, and the notion of merit as a means of distinguishing between people does not constitute a form of impermissible discrimination.

ETHNIC CLEANSING. The term "ethnic cleansing" came into usage in the early 1990s to describe the policies of governments in the former Yugoslavia aimed at forcing the removal of various ethnic populations from the national territories of those governments or from territories in dispute and subject to civil war. Methods for encouraging the flight of populations include random killings, **disappearances**, rape, imprisonment, **torture**, and other forms of persecution designed to heighten fear and promote resettlement. Such methods and policies represent clear violations of the human rights of victims, and may constitute **war crimes** or **crimes against humanity** depending upon the circumstances. Although ethnic cleansing policies may fall short of the technical definition of **genocide** in their intention and scope, they are very much akin to genocide. Such policies were not invented by governments involved in the Balkans disputes, having been present in the behavior of nations long before then. However, the obvious adoption of such policies by governments in that region did give rise to the wider usage of the term, which unfortunately can be accurately applied to numerous countries with authoritarian regimes and widespread civil disturbance, including, for example, in such countries as the Sudan, where ethnic cleansing has been unleashed in the Darfur region, and in Iraq, where Kurds were subjected to an Arabization campaign by the former Saddam Hussein regime, until its demise in 2002. Those guilty of ethnic cleansing may be subject to trial and punishment not only by governments but also by such regional tribunals as the **International Criminal Tribunal for the Former Yugoslavia (ICTY)** and the **International Criminal Tribunal for Rwanda (ICTR)** or by the more recently established **International Criminal Court (ICC)**.

EUROPEAN COMMISSION ON HUMAN RIGHTS. Established by the member-states of the **Council of Europe (COE)** in its **European Convention on Human Rights**, the European Commission on Human Rights, which has been superceded by amendments to the European Convention and Court on Human Rights, consisted of individuals elected by the Committee of Ministers of the Council of Europe from a list of candidates drawn up by the council's Consultative Assembly. The commission received complaints from member-states regarding any breach of the convention by another member-state. It also received petitions addressed to the secretary-general of the Council of Europe from any person, nongovernmental organization (NGO), or group of individuals claiming to be the victim of a violation by a member-state of their rights as set forth in the convention, provided that the member-state in question had recognized the competence of the commission to receive such complaints. Mere ratification of the convention did not constitute such recognition; rather, the state had to acknowledge such recognition by explicit declaration. The vast majority of signatories did so. The commission was charged with determining whether the petitioners had exhausted available local remedies. Where this was not the case, it could not deal with the matter nor could it consider anonymous appeals. Only a small percentage of petitions made to the commission were found to be admissible.

When petitions were heard, the commission served as a fact-finding body and afforded good offices to encourage an amicable settlement. Whether or not a settlement was reached, the commission reported to the Committee of Ministers of the Council of Europe, which could then take enforcement measures it deemed suitable, although in practical terms these were limited to adverse publicity. In such reports to the Committee of Ministers, the commission made any observations and proposals it deemed appropriate. The commission took unresolved matters that it had reported to the Committee of Ministers before the **European Court of Human Rights (ECHR)**. If the commission or the states parties failed to take such a matter to the Court, the Committee of Ministers decided whether the European convention had been violated, and what, if anything, should be done about it. The Court, for its part, could deal with cases involving a potential breach of the convention only if the commission or member-states brought suit.

On 1 November 1998, the rather cumbersome mechanism for determining admissibility of complaints described above was revised by Protocol XI to the European Convention, by which the European Commission ceased to function, and the newly restructured ECHR was empowered to receive complaints directly. The changes were necessary owing to the huge increase in applications to the commission, from about 400 in 1980 to nearly 5,000 in 1997, just as the court's docket expanded from fewer than 10 cases a year around 1980 to over 100 by 1997. The crowded docket made it impossible for complaints to be acted upon in timely fashion by the commission and then by the Court, when complaints found admissible by the commission were referred to it. With the commission eliminated, the Court was enlarged in size to 46 judges, and divided into four sections, which in turn are composed of three-judge panels that determine the admissibility of complaints against member-states. The vast majority of complaints continue to be found to be inadmissible, but those complaints found admissible by the three-judge committees are referred to the full section chamber of seven judges, and potentially a matter of importance may be appealed to the 17-member grand chamber. Decisions by the Court are binding on member-states, and, as before, the Committee of Ministers of the Council of Europe may determine how to deal with states that refuse to comply with Court decisions. Further amendments to the admissions of complaints have been proposed under the yet-to-be-ratified and controversial Protocol XIV, which would among other things allow decisions on admissibility to be made by a single judge.

In 1999, the Council of Europe established the position of European Commissioner of Human Rights, which should not be confused with the previous commission. The commissioner has no direct connection to the Court, functioning rather as a human rights advocate, promoting awareness of human rights in Europe, encouraging the establishment of national human rights structures and institutions, and identifying gaps and shortfalls in state practice on human rights.

EUROPEAN CONVENTION FOR THE PREVENTION OF TORTURE AND INHUMAN OR DEGRADING TREATMENT OR PUNISHMENT. One of the regional instruments intended to eradicate the practice of **torture**, this convention went into force on 1 February 1989 having been adopted by the Committee of Ministers of the **Council of Europe (COE)** on 26 June 1987. The convention established a European Committee for the Prevention of Torture and Inhuman or Degrading Treatment or Punishment, which has the authority to visit and examine the treatment of incarcerated individuals, and to provide reports and make recommendations to states parties concerning its findings. Procedural amendments to the convention were effected through Protocol 1 and Protocol II, whereby adjustments were made to the election process of the committee. Forty-five governments have ratified the convention. For a text of the convention, see *European Treaty Series*, 126. For text of the protocols, see the European Treaty Series nos. 151 and 152. Texts of the agreements may be found on the COE website www .cpt.coe.int.

EUROPEAN CONVENTION ON HUMAN RIGHTS. Adopted on 4 November 1950 at Rome by the member-states of the **Council of Europe (COE)**, this groundbreaking human rights treaty entered into force on 3 September 1953, becoming the first international agreement to create mechanisms for the enforcement of elements of the **Universal Declaration of Human Rights**. To this end, the convention established a **European Commission on Human Rights** and a **European Court of Human Rights (ECHR)**. On 1 November 1998, by ratification of Protocol XI of the convention, the European Commission, which had served as a means for screening the admissibility of complaints, ceased to function. Instead, an enlarged Court was empowered to receive complaints directly. Under the new reforms, the Committee of Ministers continues to work with governments where violations of the convention have been shown to have occurred. The Committee of Ministers may call upon the state to undertake legislative action to rectify discrepancies with the convention. Coercive measures are avoided. The system has worked reasonably well over the years in encouraging states to respect human rights, because they typically wished to avoid the negative publicity that attends high-profile cases involving the violation of human rights. However, the cumbersome mechanism for reception of complaints through the commission led eventually to the recent reform and restructuring of the Court, to streamline the complaint procedure and bring it directly under the purview of the restructured Court, by which three-judge panels now decide whether complaints should be dismissed or heard.

The first part of the convention is a comprehensive list of political and civil rights and fundamental freedoms that the governments of member-states acknowledge they must respect and promote. The convention permits **derogation** from some of the listed rights during time of war or other **public emergency**; however, the **right to life**, the right to be free from **torture**, inhuman, or degrading treatment, the right to be free from **slavery**, and the right to be free from the application of ex post facto laws are not subject to derogation.

The convention has been amended, extended, or revised by numerous protocols. Some of the protocols brought new rights under the protection of the charter. These include Protocol I (1952), concerning the rights to peaceful enjoyment of one's possessions, the right to **education**, and the right to participate freely in elections; Protocol IV (1960), concerning the right to freedom of movement, choice of residence, to leave one's country and not to be expelled from one's country, and the right not to be deprived of liberty because of an inability to fulfill a contractual obligation; Protocol VI (1983), concerning the abolishment of the **death penalty**; and Protocol VII (1984), concerning various rights of aliens, certain protections for criminal defendants and those found guilty of criminal offenses, including rights of appeal, and certain **equality** of rights of spouses. Other protocols, including most significantly Protocol XI, amended the procedures and functions of the European Commission and the ECHR, eliminating the commission as the mechanism for complaints and empowering the Court to review individual complaints directly by three-judge panels. Protocol XIII (2002), building on Protocol VI, abolishes the death penalty under all circumstances without exception. Protocol XIII has been signed by 36 governments. A pending protocol XIV would provide for individual complaints to be heard by a single judge. For texts of the convention and protocols, see the website conventions.coe.int.

EUROPEAN CONVENTION ON SOCIAL SECURITY. This extensive convention consisting of 81 articles was adopted by the Committee of Ministers of the **Council of Europe (COE)** in December 1972. It went into force in March 1977. It was aimed at codifying **social security** policies and practices of member-states. Its provisions relate to a range of social welfare and employment benefits, including benefits for sickness and maternity, invalidity, old age and death, occupational injuries and diseases, unemployment, and other **family** allowances and benefits. As of 2006, only eight countries have ratified the agreement. For a text of the charter, see *European Treaty Series* 78 or the COE website, conventions.coe.int. *See also* INTERNATIONAL LABOUR ORGANIZATION (ILO).

EUROPEAN CONVENTION ON THE SUPPRESSION OF TERRORISM. Adopted by the Committee of Ministers of the **Council of Europe (COE)** on 27 January 1977, this convention entered into force on 4 August 1978. It calls upon contracting parties to extradite individuals who have committed terrorist acts such as the taking of **hostages**, air hijacking, kidnapping of or violence to diplomatic agents, overt or covert bombings, or the indiscriminate use of deadly weapons against persons. Such actions are not to be regarded as constituting political offenses but rather **terrorism**. Member-states agree to modify their bilateral **extradition** agreements to bring them into conformity with the convention. Forty-four governments have ratified the agreement. For a text of the convention, see *European Treaty Series* 90, at conventions.coe.int/treaty. *See also* INTERNATIONAL CONVENTION ON THE TAKING OF HOSTAGES; TERRORISM.

EUROPEAN COURT OF HUMAN RIGHTS (ECHR). Established under terms of the **European Convention on Human Rights** of 1950, the ECHR is authorized to interpret the convention and hear cases brought before it concerning the application of the provisions of the convention. In its role as interpreter of the convention, it serves as a kind of constitutional court for the European human rights system. In its capacity to hear individual complaints, it serves as a means of potential redress of individual human rights violations. The Court transmits its judgments and opinions to the Committee of Ministers of the **Council of Europe (COE)** for final action. A member-state may recognize the compulsory jurisdiction of the Court, as the vast majority of member-states have done, and the Court may under terms of Protocol II of the convention provide advisory opinions at the request of the Committee of Ministers of the COE.

Formerly, individual complaints were filed with the **European Commission on Human Rights**, but as of 1 November 1998, that body ceased to function. At the same time, the Court was restructured, revised, and enlarged. It now receives complaints directly. The revised Court has been enlarged to 46 judges, equivalent to the number of member-states of the COE. However, each state is not represented by a judge, nor are there formal limits on the number of judges by **nationality**. Judges do not represent nations as such but serve as impartial arbiters and independent actors. The Court selects a president and four section presidents to head the four separate sections, each of which forms a chamber consisting of the section president or vice president and a rotating bench of six additional judges to hear cases. A grand chamber of the Court may hear appeals from the four sections. Complaints are filed in Strasbourg, the seat of the Court, and are assigned to one of the four sections, where a three-judge panel determines their admissibility. The large majority of complaints, as in the past, are declared inadmissible for any number of reasons. However, complaints found to be admissible are then heard by the full section chamber, and if a matter of importance, may be appealed to the grand chamber of the full Court.

The judgments of the Court are not subject to appeal. They are final and binding on states parties to the European Convention on Human Rights. All decisions of the Court are transmitted to the Committee of Ministers of the Council of Europe, which may take actions deemed necessary to ensure their enforcement, although adverse publicity and possible exclusion from the COE constitute the only truly feasible measures. Still, most governments are reluctant to encounter negative international reaction, and so the system as a whole remains quite effective in promoting human rights, and has served as a model for other regional systems.

EUROPEAN SOCIAL CHARTER. Coupled with the **European Convention on Human Rights**, which incorporates civil and political rights only, the European Social Charter rounds out efforts by the **Council of Europe (COE)** to give regional legal effect in Europe to economic and social rights as provided for in the **Universal Declaration of Human Rights**. The European Social Charter does not, however, contain the same enforcement mechanisms contained in the European Convention on Human Rights.

Adopted on 18 October 1961 and entering into force on 26 February 1965, the charter gives European member-states options for compliance rather than providing for strong institutional enforcement mechanisms. Under Article 20 of the charter, states parties agree to take all "appropriate means" to attain as an aim of their domestic policies various social and economic rights articulated in Part I of the charter, which includes such matters as worker's rights, the right to social and medical assistance, the right to benefit from social welfare services, a right to safety and protection at **work**, a right to fair remuneration, and the like.

In addition to this general effort to reflect such rights in their national policies, contracting parties are to consider themselves bound by at least five of seven articles found in part II of the charter. The seven articles from which states may select are Article 1, the responsibility to maintain as high and stable a level of employment as possible; Article 5, to respect the right of workers to organize; Article 6, to respect the right of workers to collective bargaining; Article 12, to respect the right to **social security**; Article 13, to respect the right to social and medical assistance; Article 16, to respect the right of the **family** to social, legal, and economic protection; and Article 19, to respect the right of migrant workers and their families to protection and assistance. Finally, states parties are obliged to select additional articles or paragraphs in the charter to which they will agree to be bound, up to a minimum total of 10 articles or 45 numbered paragraphs. These options were meant to give states maximum flexibility in accepting those provisions of the charter acceptable to them.

Governments are obliged to report their decisions concerning the binding provisions to the secretary-general of the COE. The charter next establishes a system of reports whereby the Committee of Ministers of the Council of Europe and a Committee of Experts can monitor member-state compliance to the charter. The former, consisting of governmental representatives, has been reluctant to highlight cases of noncompliance, whereas the Committee of Experts, consisting of independent, nongovernmental representatives, has urged the Committee of Ministers to be more aggressive in its pronouncements and actions concerning cases of noncompliance. A Protocol to the European Social Charter of 1987 added four additional rights not mentioned in the original charter. The charter has been ratified by 27 governments. For a text of the European Social Charter, see the Council of Europe's *European Treaty Series*, 35 at www.conventions.coe.int/treaty.

EUROPEAN SOLIDARITY TOWARDS EQUAL PARTICIPATION OF PEOPLE (EUROSTEP). A coalition of 16 European secular nongovernmental organizations (NGOs), EUROSTEP serves as a network for interagency cooperation in pursuit of a politically progressive program of activities in Europe and abroad. This includes promotion of social justice, peace, democracy, and capacity building to promote the establishment of civil society throughout the world. The member agencies emphasize the achievement of economic and political development, the eradication of **poverty**, and the promotion of human rights. Individual agencies are heavily involved in assistance to **refugees**, emergency assistance, and humanitarian programming. Examples of member agencies with a substantial humanitarian program include **Concern**, Mani Tese, and **People in Need**, among others. With other European NGO coalitions, such as the **International Cooperation for Development and Solidarity (CIDSE)** and the **Association of Protestant Development Organizations in Europe (APRODEV)**, EUROSTEP is a major player in human rights and humanitarian assistance activities in terms of the combined resources its member agencies command. Member agencies are located in Belgium, the Czech Republic, Denmark, Finland, Germany, Greece, Ireland, Italy, The Netherlands, Portugal, Spain, and Switzerland. Address: Rue Stévin 115, B-1000 Brussels, Belgium. Website: www.eurostep.org.

EUROPEAN UNION (EU). Although the principal European body in the human rights arena is the **Council of Europe (COE)**, the EU, formerly known as the European Communities or EC, has engaged in considerable humanitarian assistance activities, as well as in the promotion of human rights. Its principal focus is on the economic integration of its member-states, but this has implications in turn for trade relations with developing countries, with which the EU member-states have had long-term economic relations. In agreements with developing countries, the EU abides by preferential trade agreements, and it acknowledges the need to link aid to **refugees** and humanitarian aid with long-term development assistance activities. The EU collectively and its member-states bilaterally have provided substantial amounts of humanitarian and disaster aid to areas of the world suffering from emergency situations. Coordination of EU humanitarian policy and action is undertaken by the European Community Humanitarian Office (ECHO), which was founded in 1992. ECHO assistance programs are undertaken in coordination with European nongovernmental organizations (NGOs). Recent ECHO programs have included assistance in the Indian Ocean region, especially for posttsunami reconstruction in the Aceh region of Sumatra, Indonesia, and a € 15 million program for victims of the Darfur conflict in Sudan. The EU maintains a Liaison Committee of Nongovernmental Development Organizations to the European Union (CLONGD-EU) as well as a European NGO body known as the Voluntary Organisations in Cooperation in Emergencies (VOICE).

In addition to its substantial activity in response to humanitarian situations, emergencies, and disasters, the EU addresses human rights questions as a core value of its work. In December 2000, the European Commission along with the Council and the Parliament proclaimed the Charter of Fundamental Rights, which enumerates many rights already contained in international instruments and in the European Convention on the Protection of Human Rights. The EU Charter enumerates a variety of human rights in connection with human dignity, including the **right to life** and a prohibition of the **death penalty**, various human freedoms, and principles surrounding **equality, solidarity**, citizen's rights, and general justice. The EU has also maintained a European Monitoring Centre on Racism and Xenophobia, but in December 2003, it decided to revise this body and convert it into a Fundamental Rights Agency, a process that is still underway. In an era of expanding members and new applications for membership in the EU, human rights are a major component in determining the admission of new member-states, as well as an ongoing concern in regard to EU relations with non-member-states throughout the world. Address: European Commission, rue de la Loi 200, B-1049 Brussels. Belgium. Website: europa.eu.int.

EXTRADITION. Extradition is the international legal process whereby a fugitive from criminal law is returned to the country and jurisdiction of the government where his crimes were allegedly committed. Most governments only honor extradition requests when they have an extradition agreement with the requesting state. Usually, an extradition request is followed by a hearing to determine if the request is valid under the terms of the treaty. In cases where a government believes that extradition is being requested for political crimes or in which the individual subject of the extradition request is likely to suffer political persecution, it may deny the extradition request and offer **asylum** to the fugitive. Although traditionally the obligation of a government to extradite fugitives depended on the existence of a bilateral extradition agreement, in more recent times multilateral agreements dealing with air hijackings and suspects of **terrorism** have also provided for extradition to signatory states, or even to international bodies such as the **International Criminal Court (ICC)**. *See also* DEATH PENALTY; EXTRAORDINARY RENDITION; NON-REFOULEMENT.

EXTRAORDINARY RENDITION. "Extraordinary rendition" refers to the transferring or "rendering" of **terrorism** suspects by the United States to other countries, even if those countries have a history of human rights abuses and/or mistreatment of prisoners. The number of prisoners so rendered is unknown but it is estimated to be between 150 and several hundred, and the number has increased after the terrorist attacks of 11 September 2001.

Those who argue in favor of the legality of the practice point to presidential authority as commander-in-chief during wartime; a series of legal precedents, usually referred to as state secrets privilege, supporting expanded presidential authority in times of war; and a National Security Directive signed by President George W. Bush after the terrorist attacks. The reasoning is that the terrorist attacks permitted the president as commander-in-chief and the United States under **international law** to send alleged enemy prisoners to other countries for interrogation.

Those who argue against the legality of such rendition point to the United Nations **Convention against Torture and Other Cruel, Inhuman, or Degrading Treatment or Punishment**, which the United States ratified, with reservations, in 1994, and then codified in U.S. federal law. The convention prohibits transferring a prisoner if there are "substantial grounds for believing" that the prisoner will be subjected to **torture**. It is alleged that the United States has transferred detainees to Afghanistan, Egypt, Jordan, Syria, and Uzbekistan, countries where the U.S. Department of State has reported abuse and torture of prisoners is relatively common. Given the record in such countries, critics of the policy of extraordinary rendition worry that the basic rights to humane treatment, enjoyed by all persons, even those alleged to have committed acts of terrorism, are being compromised. The practice of "extraordinary rendition" may stop if detainees acquire access to U.S. courts. In June 2004, the Supreme Court decided that U.S. citizens held as "enemy combatants" could legally challenge their detentions before judges and that prisoners other than U.S. citizens, held in Guantanamo Bay, may contest their imprisonment in U.S. courts, but those decisions did not apply explicitly to non-U.S. citizens. *See also* EXTRADITION.

– F –

FAIR FUND. Founded in 2002, FAIR Fund represents a new generation of human rights–oriented nongovernmental organizations (NGO) aimed at improving people's lives through grassroots activities and programs. Its work began with and continues to focus on the problems facing young **women** in Eastern Europe and the former Soviet Union, especially their vulnerability to human trafficking. FAIR Fund rapidly expanded its efforts from Eastern Europe, the Balkans, and the former Soviet Union to countries of Central Asia and East Africa. It offers technical support and programmatic assistance to thousands of young people in 11 countries, with emphasis on reducing gender violence and human trafficking, and increasing leadership and civic awareness among girls. Address: FAIR Fund, Inc. P.O. Box 21656, Washington, DC 20009, USA. Website: www .fairfund.org.

FAIR TRIAL. The right to a fair trial is provided for in the important human rights treaties. The **Universal Declaration of Human Rights** asserts in Article 10 that everyone is entitled to a fair hearing. Article XXVI of the **American Declaration of the Rights and Duties of Man** provides that every accused person has a right to an "impartial hearing." Article 14 of the **International Covenant on Civil and Political Rights** states that everyone is entitled to a fair hearing by an impartial tribunal. The **Council of Europe (COE)** in Article 6 of its **European Convention on Human Rights** asserts that everyone is entitled to a fair hearing. **The Inter-American Convention on Human Rights** declares that "every person has a right to a hearing" by an impartial tribunal. Similarly, the **African Charter on Human and Peoples' Rights** provides that every individual has a right to be tried by an impartial court or tribunal.

The American Declaration confines provisions for a fair trial to criminal proceedings. The other conventions extend it to civil suits as well. With some variation, the various instruments cited above provide that hearings should be public, as well as impartial or fair, and that they be conducted by duly constituted authorities. Exceptions are anticipated concerning public trials. Hearings are typically stipulated to occur within a reasonable time.

The fairness of a trial or hearing can be affected by the nature of the tribunal, how public it is, and by the rights accorded to the accused. The first element is seen by the treaty law as being quite significant, explaining why the instruments mandate that a tribunal should be independent and impartial, legally competent, or previously established by law. Despite the general right of public access to a trial, the instruments make exceptions to public trials in a number of situations in order to protect the rights of the accused. The accused have the right to be informed of the charges they face and to have adequate time to construct a defense and to communicate with counsel. The accused have a right to a speedy trial, to be present at their own trial, to cross-examine witnesses, to be provided an interpreter if necessary, as well as the right not to testify against themselves.

Although fair trials are protected in these treaties, there is often no such freedom in practice. Acts of **genocide**, incommunicado detention, assassinations of judges, and attacks on the independence of the judiciary are too common in some countries. On the other hand, some governments have paid reparations to people illegally subjected to detention, while others have placed their military under more stringent legal codes designed to ensure the rights of civilians. In these and other ways, the right to a fair trial has been secured.

FAMILY. The family is the basic human social institution, into which children are born and reared. Stable families are essential to the mature growth of children into productive and stable adults capable of recognizing the rights and duties of others. The most fundamental teaching in human rights, then, is conducted by the family, which prepares persons to become productive citizens and members of the wider society. It is in the context of family that the most intense bonds of **solidarity** are formed, and through families that these bonds of solidarity reach out to others in time of need. Respect for the fundamental rights of families, as expressed in the principle of **subsidiarity** is a key aspect of any healthy and just system for the promotion of human rights.

The natural basis of the family as the foundation of society is recognized in Article 16 of the **Universal Declaration of Human Rights**, which recognizes the natural right of adult men and women to enter into marriage and to found a family, which is defined in paragraph 3 as "the natural and fundamental group unit of society and is entitled to protection by society and the State." This acknowledges that the family is the basis of human solidarity, and that its place as the fundamental group of society must be respected by governments and other institutions of society, to the point of its prerogatives being protected by governments. Elements of this protective function is later explained as giving the state the capacity to work with families and to complete the work of families in providing for basic human needs and **education**.

In regard to meeting basic human needs, Article 25 stipulates that "Everyone has the right to a standard of living adequate for the **health** and well-being of himself and of his family, including **food**, clothing, **housing**, and medical care and necessary social services, and the right to security in the event of unemployment, sickness, disability, widowhood, old age or other lack of livelihood in circumstances beyond his control." Article 25(2) of the declaration further stipulates that "Motherhood and childhood are entitled to special care and assistance." Subsidiarity implies, as Article 26 of the declaration asserts, that "parents have a prior right to choose the kind of education that shall be given to their children." This right is coupled with the right of every person to an education, which other elements of society, including churches, private associations, and the state may provide, to assist families in their natural right to provide education for their children.

The implications of the family's role as the fundamental natural basis of society is further elaborated upon in the **International Covenant on Economic, Social, and Cultural Rights** where the role of the state is further and more specifically defined as supporting the work of families in providing basic human needs, education, and security, and in intervening when families fail to function in support of the safety and security of the child, as in the case of abuse and other dysfunctions of family life. The international **Convention on the Rights of the Child**, in Article 18, also recognizes the family as the primary institution responsible for the care, upbringing, and education of children, and of the secondary role of governments in assisting families in this primary responsibility. Although the declaration and these other legally binding instruments speak clearly on the natural rights and prerogatives of the family, more recent debate at international population conferences and **women**'s conferences has often grown controversial under the influence of modern ideological stances, which have often denied the natural basis of the family, and not infrequently have depreciated the value of motherhood and the role of parents as guardians and custodians of the intellectual and moral development of their children.

FAMINE. Famine is one of the ancient curses of humanity. It occurs with sufficient frequency in modern times to raise the question of why it still happens and how it can be prevented and alleviated. Simply put, famines result when there are insufficient local **food** sources to sustain the lives of local populations. The causes of famine can be traced to natural phenomena, such as extended droughts, desertification, blights on staple crops, locust infestations, and even floods, which can disrupt food harvests and supplies. In addition, man-made causes such as wars and forced migrations also contribute to famine by disruption of planting and harvesting cycles. Sadly, at times, the man-made sources of famine are intentional, reflecting the vicious policies of authoritarian regimes, although perhaps more frequently they reflect unintentional mistakes, incompetence, and incapacity. Famines are usually preceded by a variety of coping mechanisms as populations attempt to adjust to long-term climatic issues through trade and migration. The growth of large populations in areas with limited arable land or land susceptible to natural disasters increases the chance of famine, as local supplies of food are outstripped by population food needs.

In modern as in ancient times, some famines are induced or ignored for political reasons, by governments that may see famines as a way to eliminate or control opposition groups. Throughout history, famines have been dealt with by local institutions such as the **family**, extended clan-families, and also charitable relief offered by churches and religious institutions, and sometimes by government actions. In modern times, evidence suggests that enough food is grown to feed everyone, but that the distribution of global food production and supply is often uneven. The simple solution to modern famines, then, would appear to hinge on the logistical capacity to redistribute food to areas under stress, but this in turn continues to depend on the willingness of local governments and international bodies to act decisively when evidence of impending famine emerges.

The first modern efforts to address massive famines occurred in 1919 under the **League of Nations**, when Herbert Hoover, director of the American Relief Administration, proposed that an emerging famine in Russia should be addressed by a neutral international commission headed by Fridtjof Nansen. At first, the new Bolshevik government of Russia refused any assistance fearing that it could be a Western effort to interfere in Russia's civil war on the side of the White Russian rebels. However, once the Bolshevik's had eliminated the internal threat, they agreed in 1921 to accept massive amounts of food aid through the International Committee for Russian Relief, which was headed by Nansen. This first internationally organized famine response undoubtedly saved millions of lives. It also served as a harbinger of the kinds of famines and famine responses that would continue to mark modern international relations. Under Joseph Stalin only a decade later, famine followed the forced collectivization schemes of the communist government in the late 1920s. Grain production then fell precipitously, and the Ukraine, which had been a hotbed of nationalist resistance, became a target of Stalin's wrath. Long the breadbasket of Russia, even the reduced grain production from the Ukraine was removed for foreign export or for reallocation to other famine-affected areas of the Soviet Union. Because this atrocity was covered up by the government, only estimates can be made of the staggering human toll in the Ukraine during the years 1931–1933, but many experts believe that between 5 and 8 million people starved to death, in a thoroughly preventable famine. During the Great Leap Forward in Communist China, another massive state-induced famine occurred between 1958 and 1962, in which a staggering 30 million are believed to have died.

Numerous modern famines are the by-product of civil wars. The Biafran civil war of 1967–1970 produced about a million dead, most of whom were victims of starvation. Efforts by the **International Committee of the Red Cross (ICRC)** to address the needs of displaced persons inside Nigeria and Biafra relieved the necessity of some. Foreign governments and nongovernmental organizations (NGOs) sponsored airlifts of food into the famine-affected areas. However, these efforts failed to prevent widespread death. The devastating famine eventually forced rebel groups to abandon their effort to secede from Nigeria in 1970. Civil wars are often accompanied by droughts, floods, and other natural disasters that can intensify famines. Examples of this include the 1973 famine in the Tigray province of Ethiopia in which tens of thousands perished; the 1974–1975 famine in Bangladesh, following the 1971 war of independence and a series of cyclones, floods, and droughts, in which more than a million died; and the 1984–1985 famine in Ethiopia occurring in provinces affected by long-standing civil war, drought, and locust infestations.

In even more recent times, famines have broken out in North Korea, where from 1994–1999, as many as 3 million starved, although exact figures may never be known because of the repressive nature of the North Korean government, which did its best to prevent outside monitoring. Similarly, famine has been extensive in parts of Sudan, owing to long-standing civil wars and drought. In the Sahel region of Africa, which lies just below the Saharan desert, widespread regional famines have been fairly common. In the 1970s, a "creeping famine" began to emerge as an extended drought took its toll on populations in a number of countries, including Senegal, Mali, Mauritania, Niger, Chad, and Burkina Faso. Drought in the years 1968–1972 led to an extended famine in which around 100,000 died. A recurrence of famine in 1984–1985 again threatened lives, although international intervention was swifter, in part owing to the international awareness stimulated by the Ethiopian famine and the Live Aid concert, which stimulated robust international response. The food situation in Northern Africa has also often been further aggravated by invasions of locusts.

Clearly, then, even in present times, famines can occur when governments have no interest in preventing and perhaps even a stake in encouraging them. On the other hand, responsible governments seeking to avoid widespread death from famine now have international mechanisms to which they can turn to ensure the flow of emergency food supplies, and many localized famines are avoided, as was the case with one that was predicted but forestalled in southern Africa as recently as 2005. Cooperative action by the food assistance agencies of donor countries such as the United States and the **European Union (EU)**, among others, in cooperation with the **World Food Programme (WFP)** has frequently prevented large-scale famine from occurring. The work of local governments, NGOs, and local charitable agencies is also critical to averting famine. But when local resources are exceeded by the needs, international humanitarian assistance bodies, including the WFP, the **United Nations Children's Fund (UNICEF)**, the **United Nations High Commissioner for Refugees (UNHCR)**, and the **International Federation of Red Cross and Red Crescent Societies (IFRC)**, under the aegis of the **United Nations Office for the Coordination of Humanitarian Affairs** are now in place to respond effectively to famine. But such effective response still requires the cooperation of the host government.

FÉDÉRATION INTERNATIONALE DES DROITS DE L'HOMME/INTERNATIONAL FEDERATION OF HUMAN RIGHTS (FIDH). Headquartered in Paris, France, FIDH is dedicated to the dissemination of and respect for the principles of human rights found in such documents as the **Declaration on the Rights of Man** and the **Universal Declaration of Human Rights**. It fields missions of inquiry into areas where human rights abuses have occurred for the purpose of documenting, publicizing, and rectifying them. FIDH enjoys consultative status with the **Council of Europe (COE)**, the United Nations **Economic and Social Council (ECOSOC)**, and the **United Nations Educational, Scientific, and Cultural Organization (UNESCO)**. FIDH's mandate and priorities, which are set by its world congress and its international board with the support of its international secretariat, include protecting human rights and assisting human rights victims, mobilizing governments and intergovernmental bodies, supporting local nongovernmental organizations' (NGOs) capacity to defend human rights within their own countries, and raising human rights awareness. Address: 27 rue Jean-Dolent, 75014 Paris, France. Website: www.fidh.org.

FIGHTING AGAINST FORCED DISAPPEARANCES IN LATIN AMERICA (FEDEFAM). FEDEFAM was founded in 1981 at San José, Costa Rica, and formalized later in the same year at its second congress in Caracas, Venezuela. As a prominent nongovernmental organization (NGO) in the area of forced **disappearances**, it enjoys consultative status with the United Nations **Economic and Social Council (ECOSOC)**. It works to rescue victims of forced disappearances from clandestine detention centers, puts pressure on governments to investigate and punish those guilty of forced disappearances, and works toward international and national standards to outlaw and punish forced disappearances. Fourteen Latin American countries have member associations of FEDEFAM. FEDEFAM works with various human rights bodies within the **United Nations (UN)** system and with the **Inter-American Commission on Human Rights (IACHR)** of the **Organization of American States (OAS)**. It promotes **family** support groups for those families whose members are victimized by forced disappearances. Address: Edif. Aldomar Piso 7—Oficina 55, Marrón a Cují, Caracas, Venezuela. Website: www.desaparecidos.org/fedefam.

FOOD. The right of all people to food is proclaimed in the **Universal Declaration of Human Rights** in Article 25, paragraph 1, which states that "Everyone has the right to a standard of living adequate for the **health** and well-being of himself and of his **family**, including food, clothing, housing and medical care." The **International Covenant on Economic, Social, and Cultural Rights** in Article 11 reiterates this principle and further stipulates that every person has a fundamental right to be free from hunger. To this end, governments party to the covenant agree to take steps to improve the production and distribution of food and to disseminate knowledge of nutrition. **United Nations (UN)** agencies tasked to support the realization of this right include the **Food and Agriculture Organization (FAO)**, the **World Food Programme (WFP)**, and the **World Health Organization (WHO)**. In addition, the **United Nations High Commissioner for Refugees (UNHCR)** is charged to provide protection and assistance to **refugees**, which includes basic food aid. *See also* FAMINE.

FOOD AND AGRICULTURE ORGANIZATION (FAO). The FAO's activities affect humanitarian and human rights issues in a number of important material and philosophical respects. Founded in 1943 as a result of the **United Nations (UN)** Conference on Food and Agriculture, the FAO collects and disseminates information on **food** production, distribution, and marketing. It also seeks to improve agricultural capacities especially in developing country contexts, and to conserve fisheries and forestry resources. Subagencies, panels, and working groups under the supervision of FAO are engaged in pestilence and locust control, promoting nutritional standards, and even engage in disaster prevention and mitigation programs. To better handle emergency food aid situations, the **United Nations General Assembly** created the **World Food Programme (WFP)** in 1961 to complement FAO efforts to cope with food crisis areas. All of these efforts flow from the central aim of the organization, which is to ensure that all peoples can experience freedom from hunger and a right of access to adequate food resources. The FAO also addresses crisis prevention through the maintenance of food security programs and it maintains a Locust Watch Program to control locust and other migratory pest infestations in Africa, the Middle East, and South Asia. Address: via delle Terme di Caracalla, 00100 Rome. Italy. Website: www.fao.org. *See also* FAMINE.

FOODFIRST INFORMATION AND ACTION NETWORK (FIAN). Founded in 1986 by German **food** rights activists, FIAN is headquartered in Heidelberg, Germany, but has since built up a grassroots membership of about 3,300 individual members in 60 countries. Members meet in 40 active local groups, which are further organized into national or regional sections that choose delegates to the international council, which meets every two years to review and enact FIAN policy and to elect an International Executive Committee that oversees the work of the international secretariat. FIAN focuses exclusively on advancing the international human right to food. It promotes agrarian reform policies, human rights **education** as it relates to the right to food, and lobbies United Nations human rights and food bodies, such as the **Food and Agriculture Organization (FAO)**. Address: FIAN International e.V., Willy-Brandt-Platz 5, 69115 Heidelberg, Germany. Website: www.fian.org.

FORCED LABOR. The practice of forced labor is considered similar to that of **slavery**. Since shortly after its inception in 1919 the **International Labour Organization (ILO)** and its administrative office have studied the issue, and in 1930 the organization adopted the ILO Forced Labor Convention. In 1957 the ILO adopted a Convention on the Abolition of Forced Labor that, together with the 1930 Convention, is overseen by ILO bodies to which states parties to the conventions report concerning their compliance. A range of additional

ILO conventions supplement and complement those dealing with forced labor, to prevent abuses against workers, to ensure a right to **work**, and to work that is voluntary.

FREEDOM HOUSE. Founded by **Eleanor Roosevelt**, Wendell Wilkie, and others in 1941, Freedom House is an independent nongovernmental organization (NGO) dedicated to the promotion of democracy and peace through the spread of human freedom, in particular **freedom of opinion and expression, freedom of association, freedom of the press**, and **freedom of religion**, among others. These freedoms, along with the advancement of **political rights**, it believes, must preserve the rights of **minorities** and **women**. It is a vocal critic of authoritarian regimes of all colorations. Freedom House publishes a number of highly regarded reports on trends in human freedom and democracy throughout the world. In addition, it engages in advocacy for democracy at the **United Nations (UN)** and directly through contact with and training programs for governments. An example of the latter is its Africa Institute for Democracy, which provides training to government officials on human rights matters, promotion of civil society, and the rule of law. It promotes religious freedom through its Center for Religious Freedom. It supports democratic reformers throughout the world and encourages democracies to cooperate with one another in advancing the spread of freedom. It maintains offices in a number of countries, but operates with the conviction that the United States is particularly well situated to advance the cause of freedom by influencing other governments through its foreign policy. Address: 1301 Connecticut Ave., NW, Floor 6, Washington, DC, 20036, USA . Website: www.freedomhouse.org.

FREEDOM OF ASSEMBLY. The right of assembly is widely recognized in human rights treaties, including the **Universal Declaration of Human Rights**, the **International Covenant on Civil and Political Rights**, the **American Declaration of the Rights and Duties of Man**, the **Inter-American Convention on Human Rights**, the **European Convention on Human Rights**, and the **African Charter on Human and Peoples' Rights**. Most of the treaties acknowledge this right, provided the assembly is done peaceably, and most allow restrictions of the right where provided for by law. The legal grounds allowing for restrictions of this right include concern for the protection of public **health**, national security, public safety, and the rights and freedoms of others. Variously, the treaties allow restrictions to protect the ethics or morals of people, to preserve public order, or to prevent crime.

Although human rights advocates regard freedom of assembly as a fundamental component of political life, including the opportunity for persons to express their views in common with others through political parties, interest groups, campaigns, and elections, many countries routinely inhibit this right through requiring opposition groups to obtain licenses for meetings, refusing the extension of licenses, intrusive surveillance or disruption of meetings, and arrests. Not uncommonly, opposition parties and unions are banned altogether. Anonymous killings of community organizers have been documented in various parts of Latin America, while political activists in many countries are subject to detention. Abuses against the freedom of assembly have been reported with greater frequency in China, often allied with its repression of religious expression. Incidents of repressive acts have also been reported in India. Similar problems have grown in a number of Central and Eastern European countries and in former republics of the Soviet Union, as well as in North Africa and the Middle East, illustrating that the right of assembly remains tenuous in many countries.

FREEDOM OF ASSOCIATION. The freedom of association covers a wider range of activity than does the **freedom of assembly**, in that assembly implies a coming together for political purposes while association has been used to describe organizations that people form not only for political reasons but also for economic, religious, or cultural purposes.

The **Universal Declaration of Human Rights** recognizes everyone's right to freedom of association, including the freedom from belonging to an organization. The **American Declaration of the Rights and Duties of Man** permits every person to associate in order to promote one's cultural, economic, **work**-related, political, professional, religious, and social interests. These rights are reiterated in such instruments as the **International Covenant on Civil and Political Rights**, the **European Convention on Human Rights**, the **Inter-**

American Convention on Human Rights, and the **African Charter on Human and Peoples' Rights**. These agreements anticipate situations in which governments may legally limit this right in the interests of public order, safety, or national security.

Labor union activity is an area of association given special protections under the **International Covenant on Economic, Social, and Cultural Rights**, the **European Social Charter**, and the **International Labour Organization (ILO)** Convention 87 on Freedom of Association and Protection of the Right to Organize. The ILO adopted Convention 87 on 9 July 1948 and it went into effect on 4 July 1950. It includes the right to join a trade union or an employee's organization, and upholds the right of such organizations to write their own constitutions and rules, devise their own action plans, join national and international federations, and to do all these things without any interference from public authorities.

The freedom of association is not always and everywhere respected by governments. In many countries, people are persecuted or harassed because of their association with particular groups. Thus, in practice, states have a long way to go in realizing the widespread protection of this right.

FREEDOM OF OPINION AND EXPRESSION. The right to freedom of opinion and expression is affirmed in both the **Universal Declaration of Human Rights** and the **International Covenant on Civil and Political Rights**. Article 19 of the declaration states that "Everyone has the right to freedom of opinion and expression; this right includes freedom to hold opinions without interference and to seek, receive, and impart information and ideas through any media and regardless of frontiers." The covenant, while reaffirming this right, notes that it carries with it special duties and responsibilities, and thus it may be subject to some restriction concerning how the opinion and expression affects the rights or reputations of others and how it may impinge upon the need to protect national security, public order, public **health**, or morals. The **Inter-American Convention on Human Rights** also in reaffirming the right of freedom of thought and expression notes that certain restrictions may be legally appropriate, including prior censorship of public entertainments that may have an adverse moral effect on **children** and adolescents.

Similar language is found in the **European Convention on Human Rights**.

As noted above, this right is not an absolute one. It is qualified by Article 29 of the Declaration, which says that "1. Everyone has duties to the community in which alone the free and full development of his personality is possible. 2. In the exercise of his rights and freedoms everyone shall be subject only to such limitations as are determined by law for the purpose of securing due recognition and respect for the rights and freedoms of others and of meeting the just requirements of morality, public order and the general welfare in a democratic society."

The covenant follows the pattern of the declaration by asserting the right to expression but does not make the right absolute. Article 19 of the covenant declares that everyone has a right to hold opinions without interference, as well as the right to freedom of expression, and freedom to receive and impart information and ideas of all kinds, through any media of choice. Such rights are balanced against the duty to respect the rights and reputations of others as well as the duty to protect national security, public order and public health and morals. In Article 20 of the covenant, propaganda for war or advocacy of **racism or discrimination**, hostility, or violence is to be prohibited by states parties.

Such provisions treat freedom of expression as dealing with both rights and duties. The rights angle defends unrestricted dissemination of information. The duties position gives countries the right to restrict the flow of communication.

Additional instruments that protect freedom of expression include the **American Declaration of the Rights and Duties of Man**, which acknowledges the right to freedom of investigation, opinion, expression, and dissemination of ideas; the **European Convention on Human Rights**, which affirms the right to freedom of expression, to hold opinions, and to receive and impart information and ideas; and the Inter-American Convention on Human Rights, which states that everyone has the right to receive information and to express and disseminate opinions within the law. Other conventions implicitly acknowledge rights to disseminate information, while identifying situations in which this may be abridged. The **International Convention on the Elimination of All Forms of Racial Discrimination**, for instance, prohibits the dissemination of "ideas based on racial superiority or hatred" or that incite racial discrimination.

FREEDOM OF SPEECH. *See* FREEDOM OF OPINION AND EXPRESSION.

FREEDOM OF RELIGION. Nowadays, most national **constitutions** include protection of the freedom of religion and conscience, and provide for protection from discrimination on religious grounds. However, many states recognize a state or official religion, some of which, including certain Islamic and Buddhist countries, harshly impose this belief and repress others. Some states have no official religion or creed but practice favoritism toward a particular belief, while tolerating others. Certain former communist countries actively discouraged or even persecuted religious belief. A large number of states practice complete neutrality concerning religion, treating all beliefs, including nonbelief, equally before the law.

The idea of international protection of religious freedom began slowly in the 20th century in the Treaty of Versailles, which protected national **minorities**. Freedom of religion as such was only mentioned in the covenant of the **League of Nations** and only then in relation to certain mandate countries. The **Universal Declaration of Human Rights** in Article 18 included a right to freedom of religion. This right was strengthened in the **International Covenant on Civil and Political Rights** in Article 18, which states that freedom of religion "shall include freedom to have and adopt a religion or belief of . . . choice." The freedom to manifest one's religion is subject to regulation. Religious practitioners may not discriminate against people who adhere to other beliefs.

Other international legal texts also provide for freedom of religion. Article III of the **American Declaration of the Rights and Duties of Man** asserts every person's right to profess and practice a religious faith. Article 9 of the **European Convention on Human Rights** affirms every person's right of religious freedom, including the right to change one's faith and to practice it. The convention's first protocol of 1952 protects the right of parents to decide their children's **education** in conformity to their religious convictions. The **Inter-American Convention on Human Rights** in Article 12 defends the right to freedom of religion and conscience, including the rights to maintain or change one's religion and to practice and disseminate one's beliefs. The convention also protects parents' rights over the religious education of their children. Finally, the **African Charter on Human and Peoples' Rights** gives protection in Article 8 to freedom of conscience, including the profession and practice of religion.

It took the **United Nations General Assembly** almost 20 years to draft the Declaration on the Elimination of All Forms of Intolerance and of Discrimination Based on Religion or Belief. It resolved to enact all measures necessary for the eradication of religious intolerance and discrimination. Article 1 reiterates everyone's right to freedom of conscience and religion, including having, worshipping, observing, practicing, and teaching a religion. Article 2 forbids religious discrimination, and Article 3 labels such discrimination to be a violation of the Universal Declaration. All states parties promise in Article 4 to prevent and eliminate religious discrimination by law. Article 5 protects parents' wishes to provide religious education to their children, and Article 6 lists all the freedoms that could be understood to be included in the right of freedom, thought, conscience and religion.

FREEDOM OF THE PRESS. There are many international legal documents that lay down principles for communication, for **freedom of opinion and expression**, and for freedom of information, but not for the freedom of the press, per se. The principal **United Nations (UN)** agency for promoting freedom of the press is the **United Nations Educational, Scientific, and Cultural Organization (UNESCO).** One of its fundamental purposes is to advance knowledge and understanding through mass communication.

Numerous principles presumably should be applied to the process of global communication and information. Communications media should not be used for purposes of fomenting war or aggression, or to encourage intervention in the internal affairs of countries. The law may punish dissemination of ideas based on **racial discrimination**, superiority, or hatred, and punish incitement to destroy a national, ethnic, racial, or religious group, and states should modify practices based on inequality of the sexes. The media should educate and enlighten the public toward peace and disputes over communication and information should be resolved peacefully. States are sovereign equals in communication and information, and should make good-faith efforts to uphold global communication and information law. Peoples have **equal** rights and **self-determination** regarding communication and information.

These principles, however, lead to potentially contradictory situations. The appeal of the Nonaligned Movement for a New World Information and Communication Order reflected a split between the Western, liberal emphasis on individual rights and the Nonaligned Movement's emphasis on group identity and culture. Throughout the 1970s and 1980s, Western representatives argued that mass media should be independent of government control while representatives from developing and socialist countries argued that mass media should protect state interests and their peoples as a whole. Something of this latter position was reflected in the argument of several Asian countries in 1993 when they promoted an "Asian concept of human rights." These governments argued that Asians supported communal duties over individual rights, economic development over political freedom, and national over universal human rights standards.

If there is considerable variation in the rhetorical postures of governments regarding freedom of the press, there is a great deal of censorship of the press and the media in the actual practice of states. Ideas and information are often inhibited by governmental action. The variation of practice within national law is substantial, with some countries having only the weakest forms of censorship consistent with the needs of public order and morality, while other countries engage in widespread and significant censorship of the press and media. Worse still, there has been an increasing trend for imprisoning, kidnapping, and even killing journalists, especially in settings of civil conflict and in connection with the war on **terror**, eliciting the close inspection of human rights organizations dedicated to the freedom of the press, such as **Reporters without Borders** and the **Institute of War and Peace Reporting (IWPR)**.

– G –

GANDHI, MOHANDAS K. (1869–1948). Mohandas Karamchand Gandhi was born on 2 October 1869 in Porbandar, Gujarat, on the

Arabian Sea coast of India. His **family** was of the Vaishya or trading caste, but his father and grandfather were chief ministers in the princely states of the Kathiawar region. His mother, Putlibai, was a deeply religious woman who greatly influenced Gandhi. Gandhi married Kasturba Makanji in May 1881 and graduated from high school in January 1888. His father died in 1885, leaving his family in financial difficulty. Gandhi studied law in London from 1888–1891. He practiced law for two years in Bombay and Rajkot with little success.

Gandhi moved to Durban, Natal, in May 1893. Within weeks of his arrival, he left a courtroom rather than obey a judge's order to remove his turban, and on a business trip to Pretoria he was forcibly removed from the first-class compartment of a railroad car because he was not white. In Gandhi's words, "My active nonviolence began from that date," yet he did not organize the Natal Indian Congress until 1894, when he protested a proposed law that would have disenfranchised the Indians of Natal. Gandhi was almost lynched in early 1897 but refused to prosecute those responsible. During the Boer War, he established an Indian ambulance corps.

From 1902 to 1914, Gandhi developed all his most important ideas, achieved many political successes, and became internationally famous. He became a lawyer of the Supreme Court in Johannesburg, and he took control of a weekly publication, *Indian Opinion*, in 1904. He supported the British in the Zulu War. In his resistance to the Transvaal Draft Asiatic Ordinance, which required all Indians to be fingerprinted, he coined the idea of *satyagraha*, or nonviolent soulforce. At a protest meeting, 3,000 Indians swore an oath to go to jail rather than to obey the law. Gandhi was arrested, convicted, and jailed repeatedly during the campaign, as were thousands of Indians who disobeyed the law. The *satyagraha* in South Africa lasted until 1914 when the law was rescinded.

Gandhi wrote *Hind Swaraj* [Indian Home Rule] in 1909. In it, he condemned modern civilization as far too atheistic, materialistic, and devoted to machines, and he called for a society based on the dignity of human beings.

Gandhi returned to India in 1915, where he traveled two years to reacquaint himself with his country. In 1917, he used *satyagraha* for the first time in India to overturn a law that forced people in Bihar to grow indigo and sell it to English planters, reducing them to a type of serfdom. From 1916 to 1919, Gandhi developed his ideas on *swadeshi*, or reliance on indigenous products and spinning. He defined *swadeshi* as reliance on one's own heritage, political institutions, and religion, and the use of goods produced only in one's own country. As a means to this end, Gandhi proposed that every home acquire a spinning wheel (*charkha*) and that Indians only wear clothes produced by the wheel. In 1919 Gandhi was offered leadership of the Home Rule League. He refused, however, which led to a division of the Indian independence movement.

The British colonial government passed the Rowlatt Bills in March 1919, which legalized preventive detention without right of appeal. Gandhi began to edit two weeklies, *Young India* and *Navajivan*, as part of his noncooperation *satyagraha* campaign. On 13 April 1919, 6,000 people gathered in Amritsar to protest the laws. After failing to obey an army order to disperse, over 1,500 were gunned down. Gandhi called on all Indians to boycott the courts, the military, and to refuse to pay their taxes. On 13 April 1921, Gandhi began his campaign for *swadeshi*, or economic and cultural independence, causing British rule in India to totter. However, the murders of 21 policemen precipitated by a mob that chanted Gandhi's name led him to suspend his civil disobedience campaign because it was being transformed into a violent struggle. With the suspension of *satyagraha*, the threat to British rule collapsed, and Gandhi was convicted of sedition. He served only two years of a six-year term due to ill health.

Gandhi removed himself from politics until late 1928 when he resumed national leadership. He supported Jawaharlal Nehru for the presidency of the Congress Party and further sponsored the Congress Party resolution, which was adopted, demanding complete independence. In March 1930, Gandhi began a new civil disobedience campaign against the salt tax. He and 60,000 people were arrested. He was released when the government allowed the making of salt for personal use.

Gandhi was arrested again in early 1932 for planning a civil disobedience campaign called to protest the arrest of Nehru and others. Gandhi began a death fast when the government announced a law that would establish the Untouchables as a separate electorate. After the fifth day of the fast, the government relented. In early 1933 Gandhi established a weekly newspaper, *Harijan*, but for the most part in the mid-1930s he concentrated on the development of village industries and culture based on the *charkha*.

Although Gandhi was against all war, he wanted the Allies to defeat Germany during World War II, and he wanted to give Britain unconditional support. The Congress leaders made an offer of Indian support for Great Britain in the war in exchange for complete independence. When Britain refused to respond, the Congress officials in the Indian government resigned. In 1940, Gandhi began a *satyagraha* campaign in defense of **freedom of speech**, including speech against the war. He was arrested once again in 1942, along with 14,000 others, when he demanded that Britain "quit India." He was released from prison in May 1944.

The Labour government in Britain sent a mission to India in 1946 to decide British policy. Gandhi announced his opposition to a partition of India into Hindu and Muslim parts. The British mission initially recommended an independent united India but, in response to the Muslim League's Direct Action campaign, supported partition, which was accepted both by the league and the Congress Party. Riots broke out in August 1946 in Calcutta and spread throughout Bengal and Bihar. During 1946–1947 Gandhi lived in East Bengal and preached nonviolence to both Hindus and Muslims. The final partition plan was announced in June 1947 and was accepted.

On Independence Day, 15 August 1947, Gandhi was in Calcutta attempting to quell communal riots. On 1 September, he began a death fast to this end. The communal leaders worked out an agreement and there was no further major violence in Calcutta. Gandhi began another fast to force Nehru's government to send the $40 million to Pakistan that India had promised when it accepted partition. The Indian government yielded. On 30 January 1948, on his way to his daily prayer meeting, Gandhi was shot to death. His body was cremated and his ashes cast into the Ganges River.

GARRISON, WILLIAM LLOYD (1811–1879). William Lloyd Garrison was born on 12 December 1805 in Newburyport, Massachusetts. Garrison's father left the family in 1808 and, as a child, Garrison had to beg occasionally for **food**. In 1812, he went to live with the **family** of a Baptist deacon. Eventually, Garrison was apprenticed to the owner and editor of the *Newburyport Herald*, where he fell in love with the newspaper business.

Garrison published the *Free Press* in 1826 but it failed, and he later edited a temperance journal, the *Natural Philanthropist*, in Boston. In March 1828, Garrison met Benjamin Lundy, a Quaker abolitionist who supported gradual emancipation and freedmen colonization. Garrison quickly adopted the abolitionist cause. After a falling out with Lundy and a stint in jail for libel, Garrison eventually settled in Boston where he began to publish his newspaper, the *Liberator*, which reflected his harsh, uncompromising, and often accusatory editorials demanding immediate emancipation and denouncing freedman colonization. In the South, the *Liberator* was accused of fomenting Nat Turner's rebellion of 1831. Ironically, Garrison was a pacifist and opposed to all forms of violence, and his paper had little influence, even in Boston.

Garrison helped form the New England Antislavery Society (later the Massachusetts Antislavery Society) in 1832. He was elected as the organization's secretary, and the *Liberator* was designated an official organ of the new society. Garrison attended the World Antislavery Convention in London in 1833, where he was accepted as the leader of American abolitionism. This greatly increased his standing as an antislavery leader in the United States. In 1833, Garrison helped establish the American Antislavery Society and wrote its Declaration of Sentiments. By the mid-1830s, Garrison was the leader of New England abolitionism and about this time he renounced his allegiance to the U.S. government.

Garrison's position in the antislavery movement was continuously threatened because of his support for nonresistance (pacifism), **women**'s rights, anticlericalism, and his refusal to recognize the legitimacy of any government. He managed to take control of the American Antislavery Society in 1840, but in doing so he destroyed it as an effective abolitionist organization. Garrison's uncompromising attitudes extended to his refusal to acknowledge the **Constitution of the United States**, since it permitted **slavery**. He held to a position of disunion throughout the 1850s, and he publicly burned a copy of the Constitution, describing it as a "covenant with death and an agreement with Hell." Garrison was increasingly out of touch with the main currents of antislavery sentiment, especially after the formation of the Republican Party, which turned to political action strategies as opposed to mere moral suasion against slavery.

During the secession crisis, Garrison advised President Abraham Lincoln to allow the South to depart in peace. Yet after the firing on Fort Sumter, he threw his support to the Union cause, arguing that the South did not have a right to secede. He later supported Lincoln's Emancipation Proclamation. At the end of the Civil War, the abolitionist movement died a death of success, and Garrison turned his attention to post–Civil War issues such as reconstruction, voting rights, and the emergence of the Ku Klux Klan. He died on 24 May 1879 and was buried in Roxbury, Massachusetts.

GATES FOUNDATION. Officially titled the Bill and Melinda Gates Foundation, this organization was founded in 2000, and it represents a recent example of private sector philanthropy. Bill Gates is the founder of the wildly successful enterprise Microsoft Corporation. As one of the world's wealthiest persons, together with his wife and some associates, he decided to formalize the effort to share some of this wealth with those less fortunate. The foundation focuses on four main areas, including global **health, education**, public libraries, and the needs of vulnerable children in the Pacific Northwest. With an endowment of about $30 billion, the foundation spends around $1.5 billion annually in support of its humanitarian programs, about 60 percent of which is spent outside the United States in more than 100 countries, making its contribution to humanitarian work equal to that of many **United Nations (UN)** global agencies, such as the **United Nations Children's Fund (UNICEF)** and the **United Nations High Commissioner for Refugees (UNHCR)**. The global health programs focus on the most widespread causes of death, especially among children, including diarrheal illness, respiratory infections, HIV/AIDS, malaria, and tuberculosis. The foundation has its headquarters in Seattle, Washington, with offices in Washington, DC, and in Delhi, India. Address: Bill and Melinda Gates Foundation, P.O. Box 23350, Seattle WA 98102, USA. Website: www.gatesfoundation.org.

GENEVA RED CROSS CONVENTIONS (of 1929, 1949) AND PROTOCOLS. In 1929 representatives of nearly 50 governments met in Geneva in order to review the laws of war resulting from The Hague Conferences of 1899 and 1907. The conference produced two draft treaties dealing with topics of concern to the **International**

Committee of the Red Cross (ICRC): the Convention for the Amelioration of the Condition of the Wounded and Sick in Armies in the Field, and the Convention on the Treatment of Prisoners of War. These conventions enjoyed widespread ratification prior to the outbreak of World War II, but practices during the war illustrated the need for further international efforts to codify and strengthen international humanitarian law. Thus, in 1949, after failure by the Soviet Union to repatriate substantial numbers of prisoners of war it had captured, and owing to other violations of the 1929 conventions and customary **international law**, governments met again at the invitation of the Swiss government and the ICRC to elaborate further measures for the protection of prisoners of war and of civilians during time of war.

On 12 August 1949, the four Geneva conventions were adopted. They included the Geneva Convention for the Amelioration of the Condition of the Wounded and Sick in Armed Forces in the Field (No. I), the Geneva Convention for the Amelioration of the Conditions of the Wounded, Sick and Shipwrecked Members of Armed Forces at Sea (No. II), the Geneva Convention Relative to the Protection of Civilian Persons in Time of War (No. III, in 159 articles), and the Geneva Convention Relative to the Treatment of Prisoners of War (No. IV, in 143 articles). They were rapidly ratified and entered into force on 21 October 1950. They represented systematic and extensive codification of existing customary law, and they also relied on lessons learned in the recent practice of war to articulate new and expanded humanitarian principles. They are widely considered part of the modern law of war.

The development of widespread civil war and guerrilla conflict in the intervening years since the entry into force of the 1949 Geneva Conventions made necessary further refinements in the humanitarian principles applying in such situations. Over a period of four years, from 1974–1977, the Swiss government and the ICRC sponsored a diplomatic Conference on the Reaffirmation and Development of International Humanitarian Law. The conference ultimately adopted two protocols designed to revise and supplement the 1949 Geneva Conventions. Protocol I Relating to the Protection of Victims of International Armed Conflicts expanded the definition of armed conflict to include colonial wars and wars against racist or alien domination. It includes provisions on the treatment of the wounded, sick, and ship-wrecked; protection of medical transportation and facilities; principles for handling of missing and dead persons, combatant and prisoner-of-war status; protection of civilians; civil defense; relief in favor of the civilian population in time of war or under occupation; and measures in favor of **women**, children, and journalists. The protocol establishes an International Fact-Finding Commission of 15 members, which contracting parties are free to recognize as having competence to inquire into situations in which provisions of the protocol or the Geneva Conventions may have been violated, and to facilitate, through its good offices, respect for and observance of the principles of humanitarian law. However, unless a contracting party has acknowledged the competence of the commission to undertake such inquiries, they may be permitted only with the consent of the party or parties concerned.

Protocol II Relating to the Protection of Victims of Non-International Armed Conflicts applies the principles of international humanitarian law to civil war situations not encompassed by the 1949 Geneva Conventions. Unlike Protocol I, which establishes a weak enforcement mechanism in the form of the commission, Protocol II contains no enforcement mechanisms. Both protocols have enjoyed less rapid ratification than the Geneva Conventions, dealing as they do with more controversial types of conflicts. For texts of the conventions and protocols, consult the ICRC website, www .icrc.org.

GENOCIDE. Although instances of genocide have existed for centuries, the term *genocide* was first coined in a book by Dr. Raphaël Lemkin in 1944. Genocide is the act of destroying completely or partially a national, ethnic, racial, or religious group. Lemkin's book, *Axis Rule in Occupied Europe*, examined Nazi practices, which included the elimination of the Jewish population, the purposeful working to death of people in labor camps, and many other atrocities. As early as 13 December 1946, the **United Nations General Assembly**, reacting in part to the **Holocaust** perpetrated by the Nazis, adopted a resolution condemning genocide and classifying it as a crime under **international law**. The resolution called for the United Nations **Economic and Social Council (ECOSOC)** to prepare a draft convention on the subject. After two years of study, debate on a draft convention was concluded and the draft itself forwarded to the General Assembly for action. The Convention on the Prevention and Punishment of the Crime of Genocide was adopted by the Assembly in 1948.

The convention stipulates that genocide is a crime whether committed during peace or war. In Article 2, the convention defines genocide as "any of the following acts committed with intent to destroy, in whole or in part, a national ethnical, racial or religious group." Actions qualifying as genocide included "killing members of the group; causing serious bodily or mental harm to members of the group; deliberately inflicting on the group conditions of life calculated to bring about its physical destruction in whole or in part; imposing measures intended to prevent births within the group; and forcibly transferring children of the group to another group." The convention also stipulated that in addition to overt acts of genocide, conspiracy to commit genocide, complicity in the commission of genocide, as well as incitement to commit genocide and attempts to commit genocide were punishable. Trials of those charged with such crimes could be undertaken by appropriate domestic courts or international tribunals. The convention excludes genocide as a political crime in connection with requests for **extradition**, and states parties agreed to extradite those charged with genocide consistent with existing extradition treaties. Member-states may call upon relevant organs of the **United Nations (UN)** to prevent genocide. The Genocide Convention entered into force as between signatories in January of 1951, and well over 100 countries have since ratified it.

Despite the existence of the Genocide Convention, numerous cases of genocide have gone largely unpunished, suggesting that such treaties are not ultimately self-enforcing, despite their good intentions. However, the creation of an **International Criminal Tribunal for the Former Yugoslavia (ICTY)**, to hear cases involving charges of **"ethnic cleansing"** represents a recent effort to enforce aspects of the Genocide Convention. The United Nations Security Council also established an **International Tribunal for Rwanda (ICTR)** to deal with genocidal activities in that country, where elements of the Hutu government engaged in systematic efforts to slaughter Tutsis during 1994. The ICTR produced the first successful prosecution and sentence for the crime of genocide in 1998. After years of frustration in bringing those charged with the crime of genocide to trial, these recent efforts, coupled with the establishment of the **International Criminal Court (ICC)**, may mark a change in the international community's willingness and capacity to pursue alleged crimes of genocide with greater aggressiveness.

But at least in one key case, the Darfur situation in Sudan, the United Nations refused to invoke charges of genocide because it did not see sufficient evidence to show actual intent in governmental behavior and planning. A report issued, however, did admit that acts of a genocidal character were prevalent. In this, as in other cases where a political will to prevent and punish genocide is lacking, decisive action is not possible. For a text of the convention on genocide, see *United Nations Treaty Series* no. 1021, vol. 78, p. 277.

– H –

HEALTH. The right to health is proclaimed in Article 25 of the **Universal Declaration of Human Rights**, which states that "Everyone has the right to a standard of living adequate for the health and well-being of himself and his **family**, including **food**, clothing, **housing**, and medical care and necessary social services, and the right to security in the event of unemployment, sickness, disability, widowhood, old age or other lack of livelihood in circumstance beyond his control." Article 12 of the **International Covenant on Economic, Social, and Cultural Rights** also states that everyone has a right "to the enjoyment of the highest attainable standard of physical and mental health." Under the covenant, states parties agree to take steps to reduce infant mortality rates, promote children's development, improve environmental and industrial hygiene, prevent and control epidemics, and promote the availability of medical services. The principal agency through which the **United Nations (UN)** attempts to give practical effect to this right is the **World Health Organization (WHO)**, although a number of UN bodies are also active in the field, including the **United Nations Children's Fund (UNICEF)**, as well as a vast array of nongovernmental organizations (NGOs). In practical reality, governments vary widely in their ability to ensure the health and well-being of their populations. This fact is acknowledged in various human rights instruments.

HELPAGE INTERNATIONAL (HAI). HAI is a British nongovernmental organization (NGO) initially established in 1961 as Help the Aged. It has consultative status with the United Nations **Economic and Social Council (ECOSOC)**. HAI works through a number of nationally affiliated organizations to provide both emergency assistance and longer term development services to the elderly. Much of HAI's assistance in emergency contexts involves the provision of shelter, income generation opportunities, as well as water and sanitation assistance. Its work in more than 80 countries uniquely addresses the condition of life of older disadvantaged people, especially in natural disasters and complex emergencies, where the **family** and local community support structures for older people are often compromised. HAI attempts to rebuild and rehabilitate these structures while providing essential services to the elderly. It has published guidelines for relief agencies so that they might understand the special needs and vulnerabilities of older people in emergency relief settings. Current HAI regions of focus include those most affected by disasters, such as Sri Lanka's post-tsunami reconstruction effort, the Darfur crisis in Sudan, postemergency assistance in Northern Africa, and the food crisis in southern Africa, among others. Address: St. James's Walk, London EC1R 0BE, UK. Website: www.helpage.org.

HELSINKI ACCORD. In August 1975, representatives of 35 governments concluded two years of meetings and negotiations under the rubric of the Conference on Security and Cooperation in Europe (CSCE) in Helsinki, Finland. Many issues of security that had been left unanswered at the end of World War II and as a result of the events that immediately followed, such as the emergence of the Cold War, were discussed at the conference. Among these, human rights issues were prominent. In the Final Act of the conference, the principles of the sovereign **equality** of states, the inviolability of frontiers, the territorial integrity of states, the peaceful settlement of disputes, and the recognition of the principle of refraining from the threat or use of force, which was in turn integral to the **United Nations Charter**, were all reaffirmed. Coupled with these principles was that of nonintervention in the internal affairs of states.

The Final Act also emphasized the need to respect the human rights and fundamental freedoms of people, including freedom of thought, freedom of conscience, and **freedom of religion** or belief, and the principle of the equal rights and **self-determination** of peoples. In another part of the Final Act, known as Basket III, which is entitled "Cooperation in Humanitarian and Other Fields," the signatory states agreed to promote contact, ties, and reunification of families separated by events during and after World War II, to encourage freer travel and circulation of information, as well as cultural, educational, and scientific exchange opportunities. The Helsinki Act produced ongoing meetings of the Conference on Security and Cooperation in Europe, which in 1995 became a full-fledged intergovernmental organization, the **Organization for Security and Cooperation in Europe (OSCE)**. This new organization has been very active in protecting rights and offering humanitarian assistance to **refugees** and displaced persons in various East European nations and former Soviet republics. It monitors human rights issues and promotes the dissemination of international humanitarian law. *See also* HUMAN RIGHTS WATCH.

HOLOCAUST. The Holocaust perpetrated by the Nazi regime in Germany during World War II resulted in the incarceration, mistreatment, **torture**, and extermination of millions of Jews. Similar inhumane and brutal policies resulted in the deaths of millions of Slavic peoples, and smaller numbers of Roma (Gypsies) and homosexuals as well. The horrors of the concentration and death camps shocked the conscience of the international community. The writings of such literary figures as **Elie Wiesel** and others, in turn, has starkly portrayed for succeeding generations the horrible deeds that human beings are capable of inflicting on innocent people. In the wake of the growing awareness about the grave and unspeakable **crimes against humanity** committed by the Nazis, the international community embarked self-consciously on the path of protecting and preserving human rights. The earliest human rights instruments adopted by the **United Nations General Assembly** were promulgated in the spirit of preventing wanton **genocide** of the sort represented by the Holocaust. In the preamble of the **Universal Declaration of Human Rights**, an oblique but unmistakable reference to the Holocaust is found. It states that "Whereas disregard and contempt for human rights have resulted in barbarous acts which have outraged the conscience of mankind." Coupled with the Universal Declaration, the General Assembly also adopted in 1948 the Convention on the Prevention and Punishment of the Crime of Genocide. These early steps at the articulation of human rights agreements were directly related to the international revulsion at the crimes committed against innocent peoples in the Holocaust.

HOMELESSNESS. *See* HOUSING.

HOSTAGES. Hostage taking for public or private gain is a very old practice traceable to classical antiquity. The practice continues to exist despite international conventions and declarations. The first international conventions to explicitly prohibit the taking of hostages were the four **Geneva Red Cross Conventions** of 1949 that had a common provision on the subject (Article 3), which prohibited the taking of hostages during noninternational armed conflicts within the territories of high contracting parties.

Hostage taking is hostile to the spirit of the **Universal Declaration of Human Rights**. Although not specifically prohibited in the declaration as such, the declaration does assert the **right to life**, liberty, and security, freedom from **torture** and other degrading treatment, freedom from arbitrary detention, and the right to freedom of movement, all of which are violated by the taking of hostages.

The practice is also prohibited by the **International Convention on the Taking of Hostages** adopted by the **United Nations General Assembly** on 18 December 1979, and which entered into force on 3 June 1983. The convention recognized "that the taking of hostages is an offense of grave concern to the international community." States parties to the convention pledged to do all they could to secure the release of hostages held within their territory. Alleged offenders of the convention should be placed in custody for trial or **extradition**. If such persons are not extradited, they must be prosecuted.

In the *Teheran Hostages Case* of 1980, the United States government argued before the World Court that customary **international law**, in addition to affording diplomats special protection under long-standing norms, also provided minimum standards concerning the treatment of aliens more generally to be free of hostage taking. Moreover, various articles of the Universal Declaration were cited in further support of the case. The Court agreed, citing both the **United Nations Charter** and the declaration in its decision against the Iranian seizure of hostages.

The **United Nations (UN)** Security Council has condemned hostage taking and the United Nations **Commission on Human Rights (CHR)**, together with its Subcommission on the Prevention of Discrimination and Protection of **Minorities**, have repeatedly asserted that hostage taking is a grave violation of human rights.

The only regional agreement prohibiting hostage taking is the Declaration of the Basic Duties of Asian Peoples and Governments. In Article 11 of that instrument, no government may resort to or authorize the taking of hostages even under a valid **public emergency**. *See also* TERRORISM.

HOUSING. The right to housing is usually included as part of the right to an adequate standard of living. The **Universal Declaration of Human Rights**, Article 25, asserts a person's "right to a standard of living adequate for the **health** and well-being of himself and his **family**, including . . . housing." The **International Covenant on Economic, Social, and Cultural Rights** recognizes the right to an adequate standard of living, including housing, and the states parties promise to take appropriate steps to realize the right in Article 11. The **American Declaration of the Rights and Duties of Man** in Article XI places the right to housing within a person's right to preserve his or her health and to the extent permitted by community and public resources. The American Declaration also asserts every person's "right to the inviolability of his home."

The right of housing is described broadly to mean the right to live in dignity, peace, and security, as an aspect of the more fundamental **right to life**. The right to housing, then, is related to other rights. As such, housing advocates stress the "adequacy" of housing, insisting that "adequate shelter" means adequate privacy, space, security, lighting, ventilation, basic infrastructure, and location in regard to **work** and basic facilities. Other aspects of the right of housing that need to be considered are affordability and habitability.

In the early 1970s, various **United Nations (UN)** bodies and conferences addressed the problem of housing in connection with the environment. Concern both over the millions deprived of adequate shelter and over the effects of the unplanned growth of human settlements and urbanization on the environment eventually led in 1976 to the convening in Vancouver, British Columbia, of HABITAT, the United Nations Conference on Human Settlements. The **Vancouver Declaration on Human Settlements** noted that the quality of life was determined by the condition of human settlements and that the conditions in many settlements were "unacceptable" for "vast numbers of people." The declaration asserted that resources had to be used to create more livable settlements to ensure health and other basic human needs. In the Guidelines for Action produced by the HABITAT Conference, governments were called upon to adopt settlement policies as part of an overall development strategy and to provide for a minimally acceptable quality of life. The guidelines asserted that adequate shelter was a "basic human right" and that disparities in living standards needed to be reduced. The declaration did not carry binding force.

In the 1980s, various UN bodies were engaged in addressing the problems of homelessness and the provision of shelter. The **United Nations General Assembly** named 1987 the International Year of Shelter for the Homeless, and the HABITAT organized activities designed to renew national commitments to improving shelter. Later, the UN adopted guidelines for both national and international efforts in support of a Global Strategy for Shelter to the Year 2000.

At the regional level, the European Network for Housing Research (ENHR) was established in 1968 and as of August 2005 had more than 1,000 individual members and nearly 100 institutional members. The ENHR's main goals are to support research on housing and urban issues and to promote dialogue between researchers and practitioners in the fields of housing and urban development. Its General Assembly meets every two years and its secretariat is in Favle, Sweden. Nongovernmental organizations (NGOs) have also arisen to provide advocacy in the arena of housing rights, an example being the **Centre for Housing Rights and Evictions (COHRE)**.

HUMAN RIGHTS COMMITTEE (HRC). The Human Rights Committee was established in accordance with Article 28 of the **International Covenant on Civil and Political Rights**, which was adopted by the **United Nations General Assembly** on 16 December 1966 and entered into force on 23 March 1976. The committee is authorized to receive reports from the states parties concerning steps they have taken within their domestic jurisdictions to implement the provisions of the covenant. It reviews these reports and transmits them with comments and observations to the United Nations **Economic and Social Council (ECOSOC)** and to the states parties. The committee also is authorized to receive and investigate complaints made by any one state party regarding another's noncompliance with provisions of the covenant, provided domestic remedies have been exhausted in the state accused of the violation. Such complaints may be resolved by the states parties. If they are not, the committee is empowered to appoint an ad hoc conciliation committee in an effort to resolve the continuing dispute amicably. The ad hoc committee, in turn, may in its report on the matter suggest recommendations for resolution of the dispute. The concerned states may accept or reject the report, which in any case is transmitted to the UN General Assembly.

The Human Rights Committee may, under the terms of the **Optional Protocol to the International Covenant on Civil and Political Rights**, receive complaints from individuals. States that have ratified the optional protocol declare that such complaints can be made by their nationals to the committee, provided that all local remedies available to the petitioner have been exhausted. The committee rejects anonymous complaints and other complaints inconsistent with the covenant. Once a complaint is ruled admissible, the committee informs the accused state, evaluates evidence presented by both parties, submits its views to the petitioner and state party and reports on the outcome of the matter to the General Assembly through the ECOSOC. The committee also oversees compliance to the Second Optional Protocol to the Covenant concerning abolition of the **death penalty**. It is composed of 18 independent experts and meets three times a year in either New York or Geneva. For more information, see website www.ohchr.org.

HUMAN RIGHTS COUNCIL. In his report of March 2005, entitled "In Larger Freedom," **United Nations (UN)** Secretary General Kofi Annan proposed the termination of the United Nations **Commission**

on Human Rights (CHR) and the establishment of a new and re-formed Human Rights Council. The former had suffered from a long-term depreciation of its work owing to both its lethargy in dealing with major human rights abuses and the presence on the commission, sometimes as chair of the body, of some of the world's most notorious human rights abusers. Annan's proposal called for a smaller commission able to meet at any time rather than only at annual sessions, with its members elected directly by the **United Nations General Assembly** instead of by the United Nations **Economic and Social Council (ECOSOC)**, as was the practice under the commission. The Human Rights Council would meet in Geneva, where it could be in more direct contact with other UN human rights bodies, including the **United Nations High Commissioner for Human Rights (UNHCHR)**. In addition to the ongoing reporting mechanisms of human rights abuses, the new council would establish a voluntary peer review system.

Most of what the secretary-general proposed was ultimately adopted by the General Assembly, although the size of the Human Rights Council was put at 47, just six fewer seats than under the commission. To some critics, this did not streamline the council enough. Moreover, under the principle of equitable geographical distribution, the number of seats accorded to the Western European and Others category was reduced from 10 under the commission formula to seven under the council. Since human rights are more routinely observed in that geographical grouping than in others, critics of the new council complained that states grossly abusive in their domestic human rights practices are still likely to have little trouble winning seats on the new body, despite the new peer review system, since all that is really required is that candidates win a simple majority in the General Assembly. The United States, a major critic of the workings of the former commission on which it lost a seat in 2001, announced that it would not seek membership in the first round of elections for seats on the council, even as China, Cuba, and Iran announced their intention to vie for seats. The new council held its first meeting in Geneva in June 2006, but until it establishes a track record, the concerns of critics and the hopes of reformers will not be fully discovered.

HUMAN RIGHTS FIRST (HRF). Formerly known as the Lawyers Committee for Human Rights (LCHR), HRF changed its name in 2004 to reflect the fact that its work, though including lawyers, also involves people from many other walks of life, including scientists, doctors, academics, students, and many others. The LCHR was founded in Washington, DC, in 1978, and has worked on a range of issues related to human rights, including such issues as prisoner abuse, rights of **refugees** and **asylum** seekers, and the rights of **women** and **minorities**. HRF pursues its advocacy role by providing testimony to governments, working within the **United Nations (UN)** system with other nongovernmental organizations (NGOs) to promote a range of human rights, including labor rights. It seeks to highlight governmental abuses against the rights of detainees, including **torture**, and it has promoted a Hope for Darfur campaign to end human rights atrocities in that troubled region of Sudan. All of its revenue is derived from nongovernmental sources. New York Headquarters Address: 333 Seventh Avenue, 13th Floor, New York, NY 10001-5108, USA. Website: www.humanrightsfirst.org. *See also* LAWYERS WITHOUT BORDERS.

HUMAN RIGHTS FOUNDATION OF TURKEY (HRFT). Founded in 1990, in the aftermath of human rights abuses generated by the military coup in Turkey of 1980, HRFT provides medical and psychological assistance to victims of **torture**. It operates five treatment and rehabilitation centers where torture survivors receive therapy provided by physicians, psychiatrists, and social workers. It has also established a documentation center that publicizes ongoing human rights abuses. HRFT is unusual in the sense that most victims of torture receive treatment outside of the country where such abuse takes place, whereas its work takes place in the country of origin, indicating the current Turkish government's willingness to permit such activity in the nongovernmental organization (NGO) sector. It is the recipient of numerous international awards, including the European Human Rights Prize of the **Council of Europe (COE)**. HRFT publishes frequent reports on the human rights situation in Turkey. Address: Menekse 2 Sokak No: 16/5, 06440 Kizilay/ANKARA, Turkey. Website: www.tihv.org.tr.

HUMAN RIGHTS IN CHINA (HRIC). HRIC was founded by Chinese scientists and scholars in 1989 to galvanize efforts to press for democratic reforms, social justice, and promotion of human rights in the People's Republic of China. Its main headquarters is in New York, with a branch office in Hong Kong. It works through the **United Nations (UN)** system, governments, the media, and a number of multilateral organizations and corporations, as well as other nongovernmental organizations (NGOs), to advance its objectives of influencing political, legal, and social reforms in China. It works primarily as an advocacy body through research, publications, and dissemination of information concerning human rights in China. Headquarters Address: 350 Fifth Avenue, Suite 3311, New York, NY 10118, USA. Website: iso.hrichina.org.

HUMAN RIGHTS WATCH. Founded in 1978, Human Rights Watch, which is an independent nongovernmental organization (NGO) deriving its revenues solely from private sources without reliance on any government funds whatsoever, began its human rights monitoring and advocacy work in Europe in connection with follow-up to the **Helsinki Accord**. Over the years, its work as Helsinki Watch in Europe spread elsewhere, first to the Americas with the formation of America's Watch and then to other areas such as Africa, Asia, and the Middle East. In 1988, all of the Watch committees were unified with the formation of Human Rights Watch. Drawing on its legal, linguistic, and regional experts, it conducts systematic investigations of alleged human rights abuses, and documents and exposes them to public view. It examines the human rights performance not only of governments but rebel groups as well, and it has taken a special interest in the effects of communal violence on human rights. Its activities extend to more than 70 countries, across the political spectrum, and it maintains offices in New York, Los Angeles, Washington, DC, London, Brussels, Moscow, Dushanbe, Hong Kong, and Rio de Janeiro.

As an advocacy organization, Human Rights Watch seeks to widely publicize and denounce such violations of human rights as **disappearances**, murders, **arbitrary arrest** and imprisonment, **torture**, forced exile, censorship, and abuses of civil and **political rights**.

Its recent programs have included campaigns against the use of children soldiers, supplying evidence to the **International Criminal Tribunal for the Former Yugoslavia (ICTY)** and the **International Criminal Tribunal for Rwanda (ICTR)** concerning the alleged criminal activity of indicted persons, and gathering documentation of war crimes in Kosovo. It is a member of the **Coalition to Stop the Use of Child Soldiers**. Its work to advance the International Landmine Ban Treaty won it the Nobel Peace Prize in 1997. Human Rights Watch pressures governments into saving lives, refraining from abuses, freeing political prisoners, and observing widely acknowledged human rights. Apart from using adverse publicity to place pressure on abusive governments, it also attempts to convince powerful governments—in particular, the United States—to bring their influence to bear on governments that violate human rights. It publishes a wide range of reports, including an annual *Human Rights Watch World Report*, a *Human Rights Watch Update*, numerous country or regional studies, as well as thematic studies on human rights issues. Address: 45 Fifth Ave., New York, NY 10017, USA.

HUNGER PROJECT. Founded in 1977, the Hunger Project is dedicated to the achievement of low infant mortality rates, which are associated with elimination of hunger. It is principally a development **education** body devoted to grassroots citizen action, with its programs centering on 13 countries in Africa, Asia, and Latin America. Its highest priority is the empowerment of **women**, who are the primary vehicles for **health**, education, and nutrition. It publishes a number of newsletters and other public advocacy periodicals. Address: One Madison Avenue, New York, NY 10010, USA. For further information, see www.interaction.org, member profiles. Website: www.thp.org. *See also* FAMINE; FOOD; INTERACTION.

– I –

INDIGENOUS RIGHTS. Indigenous rights have been the subject of discussion in a number of international organizations. The United Nations **Commission on Human Rights (CHR)**, through its Subcommission on Prevention of Discrimination and Protection of **Minorities** authorized its Working Group on Indigenous Populations to prepare a draft declaration on the subject of indigenous rights. The draft, which was completed in 1993, echoed several principles already contained in the **International Labour Organization (ILO)** Indigenous and Tribal People's Convention of 1989, which in turn revised an earlier ILO convention of 1957 on the subject that had emphasized the principles of assimilation and integration, a notion that the 1989 convention sought to deemphasize in favor of the principle of distinct group identity.

The subject of indigenous rights is a controversial one for many governments since it potentially conflicts with their desire to preserve independence in their domestic policies toward native peoples. This panoply of human rights treaties applies to people belonging to indigenous groups. In addition to reiterating many of these rights, the 1989 ILO convention and the draft declaration seek to afford certain group rights to such peoples as well, including the right to maintain and develop their cultural identity and to be free from any form of forced assimilation or integration. This goes as far in the draft declaration as granting a group right that would require the states to provide, within available resources, assistance to ensure the maintenance of their identity and their development. Governments have displayed reluctance in ratifying such agreements or giving them effective mechanisms of enforcement even when acknowledging many of the principles they proclaim.

Nevertheless, at several international conferences, indigenous rights have figured prominently in discussions, including the 1992 Rio de Janeiro Conference on Environment and Development, where the international community acknowledged the necessity to recognize the traditional environmental practices of indigenous peoples and to promote the inclusion of indigenous peoples into national and international decision-making processes. Subsequent conferences on population and development at Cairo (1994), on social development at Copenhagen (1995), on **Women** at Beijing (1995), on human settlements at Istanbul (1996), and others have addressed indigenous peoples rights. The **United Nations General Assembly**, following a recommendation of the World Conference on Human Rights, which was attended by hundreds of indigenous people, proclaimed the International Decade of the World's Indigenous People (1995–2004). The subject of indigenous people's rights remains on the agenda of the Subcommission on Promotion and Protection of Human Rights even in the aftermath of the decade, and it is the primary concern of certain nongovernmental organizations (NGOs), such as **Cultural Survival** and **Survival International**. *See also* WORLD COUNCIL OF INDIGENOUS PEOPLES (WCIP).

INSTITUTE OF WAR AND PEACE REPORTING (IWPR). IWPR is an alliance of British journalists established as a charitable agency in 1991 to offer support to local journalists in war-torn areas to improve communication and reporting on key information concerning human rights and democratization. Specific programs for training of local journalists are operated in Afghanistan, the Balkans, the Caucasus, and Central Asia. IWPR programs are in turn funded by various governments, international organizations, and philanthropic agencies. IWPR maintains an extensive collection of information in nine languages on its website, along with a comprehensive training program for journalists. Website: www.iwpr.net. *See also* REPORTERS WITHOUT BORDERS.

INTERACTION. Interaction is an umbrella organization of more than 160 American nongovernmental organizations (NGOs) that are engaged in overseas humanitarian, human rights, and development assistance activities. It provides a mechanism for the member agencies to coordinate their activities and share information, as well as to speak with a larger voice on the shaping of national and international policies impinging on questions of social justice and the basic dignity of the human person. Its work centers on four main committees, including a Committee on Development Policy and Practice, a Committee on Humanitarian Policy and Practice, a Committee on Public Policy aimed at advancing development and humanitarian activity in the work of governments and intergovernmental organizations, and a Commission on the Advancement of **Women**. It seeks to increase public awareness of humanitarian needs, while serving as a mechanism for stimulating discussion of humanitarian public policy issues, for promoting member agency objectives, and for coordinating member agency activities. Especially helpful on the Interaction website is the Member Profiles section, which offers a summary of its members' programmatic activities. These are referenced in each entry of an Interaction member listed in this dictionary. Address: 1717 Massachusetts Avenue, NW, 8th Floor, Washington, DC 20036, USA. Website: www.interaction.org.

INTER-AMERICAN COMMISSION ON HUMAN RIGHTS (IACHR). The Fifth Meeting of Consultation of Ministers of Foreign Affairs in 1959 established the IACHR. The **Organization of American States (OAS)** approved the IACHR Statute and elected its members in 1960. The Second Special Inter-American Conference in Rio de Janeiro in 1965 by resolution expanded the authority of the commission. The Protocol of Buenos Aires in 1970 substantially amended the OAS Charter and transformed the commission into a major consultative organ of the OAS for the purpose of promoting the observance and protection of human rights. A new statute for the IACHR was adopted by the OAS General Assembly in 1979. It provided that the seven members of the commission were to be elected by a secret ballot by the council of the OAS from a list of up to three candidates proposed by each member-state. The commission members must be nationals of the member-states of the OAS and represent all of the members of the OAS. They serve a four-year term and may be reelected once.

The IACHR adopted regulations in 1967 and updated them in 1980. The regulations laid out the functions of the chairman; the composition and functions of the secretariat; rules governing the sessions, meetings, deliberations, and voting; the procedures used for the budget of the commission; and rules governing petitions. The regulations also established the procedures governing on-site observations, reports, hearings, the use of advisers, witnesses and experts, and for the commission to bring a case before the **Inter-American Court of Human Rights (IACT)**.

The 1970 Protocol of Buenos Aires added major amendments to the OAS Charter and thereby provided a strong constitutional basis for the commission making it one of the major organs of the OAS. Further, it recognized the **American Declaration of the Rights and Duties of Man** as a standard by which the OAS member-states would be judged. In 1978, the **Inter-American Convention on Human Rights** went into force. This convention codified the 1959 statute of the commission and permitted it to make recommendations concerning specific cases. The new commission under the 1978 convention has all of the powers of the old commission. Further, the 1978 convention permitted the commission to use the convention itself in its interpretation of the 1948 declaration.

To carry out its mandate to promote the practice and the defense of human rights, the commission investigates individual complaints of alleged human rights abuses; attempts to increase public awareness regarding human rights in the Western Hemisphere; and organizes conferences, meetings, and seminars. It makes recommendations to OAS members as to initiatives to increase protection of human rights. It formally requests states to adopt precautionary measures to deter serious harm to human rights and may formally request the IACT to order provisional measures in situations involving serious danger to persons. The commission submits cases to the Court, appears before it, and may request advisory opinions from it.

The IACHR's principal activities have been to prepare country studies and process individual complaints. The authority to prepare reports became the legal foundation for the commission to begin on-site country investigations. The first on-site inspection was in the Dominican Republic in 1961. The commission traveled throughout the country; met with the leaders of the government and the opposition, leaders of the church, businesses, and unions; held public hearings; and set up offices throughout the country. The actions adopted by the commission in 1961 are a model that is still followed. The commission adopted a "Resolution on On-Site Observation," which specified the actions a government had to take before the commission would visit a country. Newer rules of procedure have updated the resolution and made it a government obligation to protect the safety of commission staff, to provide facilities necessary for the work of the commission, and to promise not to punish those who cooperate or provide information to the commission. The rules of procedure also provide that the members and staff can travel freely and meet any individuals, including those in prison.

The commission saved hundreds of lives during the 1965 civil war in the Dominican Republic and it negotiated the release of diplomatic

hostages in Colombia in 1980. The commission's annual reports have at times caused governments to curtail practices condemned in the reports. The commission allows governments under investigation to review a draft report on human rights conditions, and they are invited to provide the commission with information. The commission is allowed to transmit its annual reports to the OAS General Assembly. These were not discussed in the assembly until 1975 when it debated and passed a resolution on the Chilean report. The assembly passed an even stronger resolution on the commission's Chile report the next year. Ultimately, the effectiveness of the commission's annual country reports is dependent upon the credibility of the commission, the intensity of public opinion, and the forcefulness of OAS resolutions.

The commission has been empowered since the 1978 convention to investigate all allegations of violations of any right in the American Declaration. If a state does not follow the recommendations of the commission, the latter may publish its findings in its annual report to the OAS General Assembly. The commission may ask the IACT for an advisory opinion, even if it concerns a state not party to the American Convention.

The commission's procedures for responding to individual complaints of human rights violations have not been very effective. The OAS General Assembly has rarely discussed the commission's findings on individual complaints. The commission itself has spent less time on individual complaints in the face of deteriorating conditions in the hemisphere, which forced it to increase the number of its country studies during the 1980s. The commission has not been selective in choosing petitions for investigation.

The commission has continued to take actions to improve its regional human rights regime. Following a meeting with the United Nations (UN) secretary-general's Representative on Internally Displaced Persons, the commission decided to create a special rapporteur on internally displaced persons. Unfortunately, it is a voluntary position with limited resources. On 20 October 2000, the commission approved a resolution recommending to OAS member-states that "they refrain from granting **asylum** to any person alleged to be the material or intellectual author of international crimes."

To strengthen the protection of human rights in the Americas, the OAS assembly could create a human rights committee to review the reports of the commission and advise it on what action to take. Further, the commission could adopt a new procedure whereby, in severe situations of internal displacement, it would send emergency missions, which would increase protection of the displaced. Alternatively, it could bring displaced persons issues to the attention of the Court, or increase cooperation with the **United Nations High Commissioner for Refugees (UNHCR)**. Such developments would strengthen the Inter-American human rights regime. Yet, the work of the commission is limited owing to its very small budget.

The Center for Constitutional Rights, the Human Rights Clinic at the Columbia Law School, and the Center for Justice and International Law formally petitioned the commission in February 2002 to act immediately to protect the rights of some 300 Al Qaeda and Taliban members detained at Guantanamo Bay by the U.S. government and suspected of **terrorism**. The petitioners asked that those detained should be treated as prisoners of war, that their international human rights should be protected, and that they should not be held incommunicado, subject to arbitrary or prolonged detention, unlawfully interrogated, or tried by military commissions legally empowered to issue a death sentence. The petitioners based their requests on the American Declaration of the Rights and Duties of Man and the powers granted to the commission to protect human rights. The U.S. government maintained that the detainees are "unlawful combatants," not prisoners of war under the terms of the Geneva Convention. Still, the George W. Bush administration acknowledged that the detainees were entitled to humane treatment, if not the full panoply of rights guaranteed formally to prisoners of war.

The commission ordered the U.S. government to "take urgent measures necessary to have the legal status of the detainees at Guantanamo Bay determined by a competent tribunal" on 13 March 2002. The commission notified the petitioners on 15 April 2002 that the U.S. government had rejected the commission's earlier order, arguing that the commission lacked the jurisdiction to interpret the Geneva Convention and to apply "precautionary measures."

The commission responded by letter to the U.S. government on 29 July 2004 saying that new information appeared to contradict claims that the U.S. government was treating and interrogating all detainees consistent with its obligations under the Treaty against Torture. The

U.S. government responded in December 2004, arguing again that the commission lacked jurisdiction and that domestic remedies had first to be exhausted. The petitioners asked the commission to extend its precautionary measures to forbid the use of information obtained through torture in legal proceedings against the detainees.

Here we see an example of how human rights advocacy groups attempt to use not only domestically available legal avenues to challenge government policies and approaches to detainment and interrogation of terrorist suspects but also to leverage regional or international bodies to the same end. Although efforts to block U.S. policies and procedures in regard to the detention and interrogation of terrorist suspects through the IACHR have proved unsuccessful, the high-profile nature of the case and the attention given to it required the U.S. government to justify in such forums the mechanisms and policies it was pursuing in the larger goal of providing security to its own people and in bringing genuine international criminals to justice without violating the rights of detainees not eventually found to be guilty of criminal activity. Address: IACHR, 1889 F Street, NW, Washington, DC 20006, USA. Website: www.cidh.oas.org. *See also* INTER-AMERICAN COMMISSION ON HUMAN RIGHTS STATUTE.

INTER-AMERICAN COMMISSION ON HUMAN RIGHTS STATUTE. The **Organization of American States (OAS)** adopted a statute for the **Inter-American Commission on Human Rights (IACHR)** and elected its members in 1960 in compliance with the resolution mandating the establishment of such a commission at the Fifth Meeting of Consultation of Ministers of Foreign Affairs held in Bogotá in 1959. The statute authorized the commission to promote respect for human rights and defined human rights as those enunciated by the **American Declaration of the Rights and Duties of Man**. The IACHR was granted only limited powers. These included the power to recommend to member-states new domestic laws to increase observance of human rights, to prepare annual country reports, to urge member-state governments to provide it with information on human rights, to advise the OAS on human rights, and to help develop awareness of human rights on the part of the inter-American public.

The IACHR ruled at its first session in 1960 that the statute did not give it the authorization to investigate and act upon individual petitions, but that it could use these in the preparation of the commission's annual country reports. A resolution of the Second Special Inter-American Conference in Rio de Janeiro in 1965 expanded the powers of the IACHR. This resolution in revised form became a part of the statute. It gave the commission the power to focus on the observance of the human rights referred to in Articles I–IV, XVIII, XXV, and XXVI of the American Declaration of the Rights and Duties of Man. It also gave the commission the power to investigate human rights abuses alleged in written communications, to request information from member-states, and to make recommendations and submit an annual report that would identify the progress made and the steps still needed to be taken to protect human rights.

Until 1970, the IACHR statute lacked an explicit treaty basis, being derived from OAS conference resolutions. The Protocol of Buenos Aires greatly amended the OAS Charter, however, and it thereby made the commission a major consultative organ of the OAS.

The commission drafted a new statute for itself, which the OAS General Assembly approved in 1979. The new statute explicitly authorized the commission to make on-site investigations with the permission of the governments. The new statute also restated that the human rights referred to in the OAS Charter are those expressed in the American Declaration of the Rights and Duties of Man.

INTER-AMERICAN CONVENTION ON DIPLOMATIC ASYLUM. The Inter-American Convention on Diplomatic Asylum was signed in Caracas, Venezuela, on 28 March 1954 at the Tenth Inter-American Conference and entered into force on 29 December 1954. The convention required a territorial state to respect the **asylum** granted by other states in legations, warships, military camps, and aircraft. All states may grant asylum, but they are not obligated to do so. States may not grant asylum under this convention to persons who are under indictment, on trial, or convicted for common offenses or to deserters from a state's armed forces unless actions leading to an asylum request are of a political nature. The grant of diplomatic asylum is temporary and should last only as long as it is necessary for the asylee to leave the territorial state.

The state granting asylum may require the territorial state to give guarantees of safe conduct in writing. It has a right to move the asylee out of the country and while en route the asylee is under the protection of the asylum state. The state granting asylum is not required to settle the asylee in its territory. The Dominican Republic, Guatemala, Honduras, and Uruguay expressed reservations to part of this convention. *See also* INTER-AMERICAN CONVENTION ON TERRITORIAL ASYLUM; REFUGEES.

INTER-AMERICAN CONVENTION ON HUMAN RIGHTS. The Inter-American Convention on Human Rights (the Pact of San José, Costa Rica) was signed at a Specialized Conference on Human Rights held in San José, Costa Rica, in November 1969 and it entered into force on 18 July 1978 when the official notice was received of the 11th country to ratify. By the late 1990s, the convention had been ratified by Argentina, Barbados, Brazil, Bolivia, Chile, Colombia, Costa Rica, Dominica, the Dominican Republic, Ecuador, El Salvador, Grenada, Guatemala, Haiti, Honduras, Jamaica, Mexico, Nicaragua, Panama, Paraguay, Peru, Suriname, Trinidad and Tobago, Uruguay, and Venezuela.

The convention resulted from a culmination of events that began in 1959, or in spirit as early as 1948. In 1948 the Ninth Inter-American Conference at Bogotá, which approved the Charter of the **Organization of American States (OAS)**, also adopted the **American Declaration of the Rights and Duties of Man** seven months before the United Nations **Universal Declaration of Human Rights** was adopted. Although the effect of the American Declaration has grown, it was not seen at the time to have created any legal obligation. The Fifth Meeting of Consultation of Ministers of Foreign Affairs in Chile in 1959 resolved that the Inter-American Council of Jurists should draft a Convention on Human Rights. Their 1959 draft was reviewed in 1965, 1967, and 1969 when it was finally approved. The Inter-American Convention is modeled on the American Declaration of the Rights and Duties of Man of 1948, the Universal Declaration of Human Rights of the same year, the Rome Convention of 1950, and the **International Covenant on Civil and Political Rights** and the **International Covenant on Economic, Social, and Cultural Rights**.

The preamble of the convention asserts that the essential rights of human beings are attributes of being human and exist "within the framework of democratic institutions." Part I of the convention defines the obligations of states; lists protected civil and **political rights**, and includes a promise of the contracting states to achieve economic, social, educational, scientific and cultural standards set in the OAS Charter and the Protocol of Buenos Aires.

Part II of the convention describes the mechanisms of protection. These include the **Inter-American Commission on Human Rights (IACM)** and the **Inter-American Court of Human Rights (IACT)**. The third and last part of the convention lays out the processes of ratification, reservations, amendments, protocols, and denunciations.

The convention specifies that the term "person," possessing the rights and freedoms protected by the convention, refers to "every human being." The convention protects 26 freedoms and rights, 21 of which are protected in the International Covenant on Civil and Political Rights. They include the **right to life**; the right to humane treatment, which means protection from **torture** and other types of inhumane treatment; freedom from **slavery**; the right to liberty, security, and a **fair trial**; freedom from ex post facto laws; the right to **privacy**; **freedom of religion**, conscience, thought, and expression; **freedom of assembly** and **freedom of association**; freedom to marry and to establish a **family**; the right to a name and to a **nationality**; freedom of **movement and residence**; the right to representative government; the right to equal protection and judicial protection; the right to compensation for false conviction; and the right of recognition as a person under law.

Other rights and freedoms guaranteed in the Inter-American Convention include the right of **property**, freedom from exile, and the right of **asylum**. The convention also prohibits the collective expulsion of aliens. Although the convention establishes a right to a nationality, it does not include explicit sanction for the right of **self-determination** or for the protection of **minorities**.

Although there has been substantial development in **international law** concerning all facets of human rights, including this convention, respect for human rights in Latin America does not have any greater security today than it had in 1948. As long as human rights treaties are not self-executing and states have the right to suspend provisions of such a treaty at any time, the protection of human rights will be fragile. State **sovereignty** has and will override human rights. The OAS General Assembly approved the Protocol of San Salvador in November 1988 and it came into force in November 1999. This additional protocol recognized cultural, economic, and social rights such as **work**, forming and joining trade unions, **social security**, **health**, **food**, **education**, and the benefits of culture; identified for protection, especially but not exclusively, were children, the elderly, the family, and the handicapped. In 1990, a further protocol to the convention outlawed the use by signatories of the **death penalty** except during wartime.

INTER-AMERICAN CONVENTION ON TERRITORIAL ASYLUM. The Inter-American Convention on Territorial Asylum was signed in Caracas, Venezuela, on 28 March 1954 at the Tenth Inter-American Conference and entered into force on 29 December 1954. The convention reiterated the right of a state to control who may enter its territory and the right of the state to have control over its inhabitants even if they were originally from another state. The convention allowed people to be protected from **extradition** when sought for political offenses, for illegal acts committed for political reasons, or in cases in which political motives were behind the extradition request.

A state's domestic law regulating aliens, freedom of expression, **freedom of assembly**, or **freedom of association** need not distinguish aliens from citizens, nor should such laws be grounds for complaint by another state unless such actions constitute systematic propaganda or foment use of force or violence against another state. Finally, an **asylum** state needs to regulate those to whom it has granted refuge and keep them a reasonable distance from sensitive borders. Numerous Latin American states have ratified this agreement, although some expressed reservations to portions of the convention. See the *Collection of International Instruments Concerning Refugees* (1979), from the Office of the United Nations High Commissioner for Refugees. *See also* INTER-AMERICAN CONVENTION ON DIPLOMATIC ASYLUM.

INTER-AMERICAN COURT OF HUMAN RIGHTS (IACT). The IACT was established by the **Inter-American Convention on Human**

Rights in 1969 with the explicit provision that its jurisdiction would be optional. The convention sets membership on the Court at seven judges who were to be nationals of member-states of the **Organization of American States (OAS)**. Judges would be elected by secret ballot by majority vote from lists of up to three provided by states parties to the convention. Upon election, judges serve for a term of six years, with only one reelection allowed. No two judges may be nationals from the same state. The Court's jurisdiction extends to all cases arising from the convention provided that the states recognize this jurisdiction. The Court sits in San José, Costa Rica.

On 22 May 1979, states parties to the IACT elected at the OAS General Assembly the first judges for the Court, which held its first hearing on 29 June 1979. Election procedures were laid out for the judges, as was the structure of the Court, including its officers and secretariat. Judges on the Court are granted diplomatic immunity from the time of their election through their term of office. The statute also established the duties of the judges as well as the Court's authority to oversee its judges. Finally, basic rules governing sessions, quorum, hearings, deliberations, and decisions were stated. The Court was given the authority to write its own rules of procedure.

The Court approved rules of procedure in 1980 establishing officers and their functions, voting procedures, and general rules. Further, the rules explained how to bring a case before the Court and the Court's procedure when a case is heard by it. The rules explain the form and procedures for the presentation of its judgment, and they describe the Court's advisory opinion process.

Only states parties to the convention and the commission are allowed to submit cases to the Court. The states parties to the convention may accept the jurisdiction of the Court unconditionally, on the basis of reciprocity, for an unlimited or a limited time, and on an ad hoc basis. If the Court finds that a violation has occurred, it may order a government to reinstate the injured party's rights and even order damages to be paid. The Court is mandated to present an annual report to the OAS General Assembly, including information about cases of noncompliance of states in its decisions.

The Court has the power to adjudicate disputes under its contentious jurisdiction powers, and it may issue advisory opinions. The latter has proved to be its more important function. Twenty-five states parties have ratified or adopted the convention, although Trinidad and Tobago denounced the Inter-American Convention on Human Rights in 1998. The judgment of the Court in a dispute is not subject to appeal. The Court also has the power to issue, in effect, temporary injunctions when asked to act by the IACHR or when asked by a party to a case pending before the Court.

Any OAS member-state may ask the Court for an advisory opinion and this opinion can deal with interpretations of any treaty, which concerns the protection of human rights in the Americas. All OAS organs are permitted to request an advisory opinion, as are OAS member-states when they have questions about the compatibility of domestic law to any human rights treaty. Since the Court's jurisdiction is optional and since individuals do not have standing before it, most of the Court's work has taken the form of advisory opinions. It is necessary, therefore, for the IACHR to bring contentious cases to the Court for the latter to function at its fullest potential. Address: P.O. Box 6906-1000, San José, Costa Rica. Website: www.corteidh.or.cr.

INTERNATIONAL ALLIANCE OF WOMEN (IAW). Dedicated to the preservation and extension of the **equal** rights of **women**, IAW was founded in 1902 in Berlin as the International Women Suffrage Alliance. At its Congress of 1926 in Paris, it changed its name to the International Women's Alliance, working closely with the **League of Nations** to advance the goals of universal suffrage. Its current name was adopted in 1946. It holds an international congress every three years, with interim meetings of its board and seminars on women's issues. It encourages its member organizations to work for the universal ratification and implementation of the **Convention on the Elimination of All Forms of Discrimination against Women** and its optional protocol. The alliance participates in **United Nations (UN)** Conferences on Women. It enjoys consultative status with the United Nations **Economic and Social Council (ECOSOC),** various UN specialized agencies such as the **International Labour Organization (ILO)** and the **United Nations Educational, Scientific, and Cultural Organization (UNESCO),** as well as with the **Council of Europe (COE)** and other regional organizations. With affiliate organizations from over 60 countries, it sponsors international and regional conferences concerning human rights issues generally and women's rights issues in particular. It publishes a newsletter, *International Women's News*, available at Editor, 10 Queen Street, Melbourne VIC 3000, Australia. Website: www.womenalliance.com.

INTERNATIONAL ASSOCIATION OF DEMOCRATIC LAWYERS (IADL). Initially founded as an association of European lawyers in 1946 who had resisted totalitarian ideologies and militarism during World War II, the IADL now enjoys a widespread international membership, in more than 90 countries. The organization seeks to promote respect for **international law** and human rights, especially through the promotion of democratic forms of government. It fields missions to investigate human rights abuses, attempts to promote the independence of judiciaries and bar associations, and to serve as a source for legal training and advice to international organizations and governmental officials. It attempts to restore and develop democratic rights and liberties in the legislation and practice of nations, and to promote the independence of national judicial bodies. It is also interested in the preservation of ecology and the right to development and economic **equality**. Its members were at the forefront of international efforts to end racism, colonialism, and **apartheid**. Members of IADL have brought actions at the **International Court of Justice (ICJ)**, the **European Court of Human Rights (ECHR)**, and the **Inter-American Court of Human Rights (IACT)**. It has consultative status with the United Nations **Economic and Social Council (ECOSOC)**. Address: Rue Brialmont 21, 1210 Brussels, Belgium. Website: www.iadllaw.org.

INTERNATIONAL BAR ASSOCIATION (IBA). Established in 1947, the IBA serves as a federation of national bar associations. With over 100 such national affiliates and thousands of members, it is an influential nongovernmental organization, which enjoys consultative status with the United Nations **Economic and Social Council (ECOSOC)**. It serves as a communications link between national bar associations, promotes the study of law and of practical legal issues, and publishes a host of periodicals, reports, and papers. Among the subjects of ongoing concern to the IBA are human rights, broadly understood including the promotion, protection, and enforcement of human rights, the promotion and protection of independent national judiciaries, national legal capacity building, and dissemination of legal knowledge and training. Address: 10th Floor, 1 Stephen St. London W1T 1AT, UK. Website: www.ibanet.org.

INTERNATIONAL BILL OF HUMAN RIGHTS. As early as the **United Nations (UN)** Conference in San Francisco, at which the **United Nations Charter** was negotiated, proposals were made to adopt an International Bill of Rights or a Declaration on the Essential Rights of Man. Although these proposals made little headway at San Francisco, the UN Charter did reflect the international community's concern with human rights and fundamental freedoms, and at the first session of the United Nations, the proposals resurfaced. Eventually, the United Nations **Commission on Human Rights (CHR)** was charged with producing an international bill of human rights. It became abundantly clear to members of the commission that achieving consensus on a nonbinding declaration would be much easier than negotiating a legally binding treaty, and so it divided its work into two phases, first in drafting a hortatory, nonbinding Declaration of Human Rights, and then in drafting binding treaties. The **Universal Declaration of Human Rights** was adopted in 1948 by the **United Nations General Assembly**. Not until 1966 did the General Assembly pass and open for signature two legally binding human rights treaties, the **International Covenant on Civil and Political Rights** and the **International Covenant on Economic, Social, and Cultural Rights**. Even then the Covenants lacked truly effective enforcement mechanisms, although an **Optional Protocol to the International Covenant on Civil and Political Rights** did contain measures that provided for more effective enforcement of that agreement. Taken together, the provisions of the UN Charter dealing with human rights, the Universal Declaration, the two covenants and the optional protocol comprise what is known as the International Bill of Human Rights. Some experts include the **International Convention on the Elimination of All Forms of Racial Discrimination** as part of the International Bill of Human Rights.

INTERNATIONAL CIVIL AVIATION ORGANIZATION (ICAO). This body was established in 1944 as a result of the International Civil Aviation Conference in Chicago, although it did not become fully operational until 1947. Its work was highly technical and took the form of establishing rules and regulations concerning the safety of air navigation. Though not directly concerned with human rights supervision, the ICAO has sponsored a number of conferences that have promoted suppression of criminal acts against the safety of aviation, including the Tokyo Treaty of 1963 on the punishment and deterrence of crime aboard aircraft; The Hague Convention of 1970 on the punishment and deterrence of air piracy; and the Montreal Convention of 1971 on the suppression of acts of violence against the safety of aviation. The rise of **terrorism** in recent times has been closely associated with crimes on board aircraft, including hijacking, the illicit use of bombs to destroy aircraft in flight, and on 11 September 2001, the use of aircraft themselves as weapons to destroy public buildings and innocent civilian populations. Address: 999 University Street, Montreal, Quebec, H3C 5H7, Canada. Website: www.icao.int.

INTERNATIONAL COMMISSION OF JURISTS. This nongovernmental body of eminent legal experts was founded in Geneva in 1952. Its purposes include promoting justice and the rule of law, the independence of judicial bodies and lawyers, as well as the promotion of human rights. It seeks to mobilize jurists to these ends and its membership is limited to 40 eminent jurists who represent the different contemporary legal systems.

The commission established a Centre for the Independence of Judges and Lawyers to promote the autonomy of these professions and to rally legal organizational support for people who are victims of harassment and persecution. The commission has regularly launched inquiries and issued reports concerning the situation of human, legal, and **political rights** in different countries as well as organized conferences, such as the African Conference on the Rule of Law in 1961, to further international legal principles. Growing out of the African Conference was a proposal for the establishment of an **African Commission on Human and Peoples' Rights** and the drafting of an African Convention on Human Rights, which culminated in the **African Charter on Human and Peoples' Rights** of 1981. The commission has conducted numerous investigations of human rights situations and published reports concerning them. Address: P.O. Box 216, 81a Avenue de Chatelaine, 1219 Geneva, Switzerland. Website: www.icj.org.

INTERNATIONAL COMMITTEE OF THE RED CROSS (ICRC).
The ICRC is one of the oldest humanitarian organizations in existence. Inspired by **Jean-Henri Dunant**, who began campaigning for more humane treatment of the sick and wounded from military conflict after his battlefield observations in Italy in 1859, the Red Cross commenced in 1863 and took up formal international activities with the adoption of the first Geneva Red Cross Convention in 1864. Ever since, the ICRC has continued its efforts on behalf of prisoners of war, the wounded, and other victims of armed conflict, whether civilians or soldiers. The Red Cross movement spread through the establishment of private national affiliate organizations. Its work at the national and international levels is guided by the principles of humanity, impartiality, neutrality, independence, voluntary service, unity, and universality. As a private rather than an intergovernmental organization, the ICRC has emphasized these principles in its work and thus gained an enviable reputation among governments. The organization has been rewarded on three occasions with receipt of the Nobel Peace Prize. The Red Cross movement includes not only the ICRC but also 183 national Red Cross or Red Crescent Societies, and an **International Federation of Red Cross and Red Crescent Societies (IFRC)**, which helps to coordinate and stimulate the work of the national organizations.

The ICRC is composed of 15 to 25 prominent Swiss nationals. They compose the assembly, which in turn selects an assembly council of five members. The council serves as a link between the assembly and the ICRC directorate, which manages daily operations. The ICRC has a staff of more than 12,000 based in approximately 80 countries.

The ICRC, apart from being empowered by governments to monitor and supervise the 1949 **Geneva Red Cross Conventions** and in more limited cases the 1977 protocols, continues to provide assistance and protection to persons displaced in war zones. The ICRC maintains a tracing and information service for prisoners of war and missing persons. It regularly visits political prisoners and detainees. It supplies assistance to **refugees** and displaced persons in even the remotest areas of the world where conflict occurs. It is funded by voluntary contributions from governments, which regularly entrust it with around $800 million of resources annually to carry out its work, depending on emergency needs. It enjoys consultative status with the United Nations **Economic and Social Council (ECOSOC)**, and it engages in an extensive public education program to disseminate information and promote knowledge and awareness of the Geneva Conventions, international humanitarian law more generally, and a host of human rights and humanitarian activities.

The ICRC's humanitarian and relief work is truly international in scope, but recent efforts have focused on the disaster reconstruction efforts in northern Sumatra's Aceh province, as well as promoting humanitarian law in Afghanistan, and other hotspots such as Nepal, Palestine, Indonesia, Colombia, the Democratic Republic of the Congo, Uganda, Sri Lanka, and Sudan. Address: 19 avenue de la Paix, CH-1202 Geneva, Switzerland. Website: www.icrc.org.

INTERNATIONAL CONFEDERATION OF FREE TRADE UNIONS (ICFTU). The ICFTU was founded by a congress of national trade unions that met in London in December 1949 to establish a permanent body for international cooperation. Its primary focus has been to promote the right to **work**, the right for workers to organize, and to improve conditions for workers. It has lobbied the **International Labour Organization (ILO)** and other **United Nations (UN)** bodies on matters concerning labor involving children, **health**, safety, and environment issues; the establishment of fair trade and labor standards; and promotion of the right of **equality**. It heightens public awareness to the abuse by governments of such rights, and attempts to influence governmental legislation and the development of international human rights law. Address: 5 Boulevard du Roi Albert II, Bte 1, 1210 Brussels, Belgium. Website: www.icftu.org.

INTERNATIONAL CONFERENCE ON POPULATION AND DEVELOPMENT. Convened by the United Nations **Economic and Social Council (ECOSOC)** in 1989, this conference was held after long preparation from 5–13 September 1994 in Cairo, Egypt. The conference broadly attempted to remind governments of the connection between population issues and the attainment of sustainable growth and development. It dealt with a range of human rights considerations, including the problems of migration, population displacement, the need for improving access to **health** care, **housing**, and **education**, the need to create greater economic opportunities for **women**, and, though highly controversial, the issue of broader availability of **family** planning methods. The Cairo conference was the fifth in a series of United Nations conferences dealing with population including technical meetings in Rome (1954) and Belgrade (1965), the World Population Conference in Bucharest (1974), and the International Conference on Population in Mexico City (1984). Its program of action, though not legally binding, represents a set of guidelines for governments to consider in their domestic policy settings. *See also* UNITED NATIONS FUND FOR POPULATION ACTIVITIES (UNFPA).

INTERNATIONAL CONVENTION ON THE ELIMINATION OF ALL FORMS OF RACIAL DISCRIMINATION. This convention was adopted unanimously by the **United Nations General Assembly** on 21 December 1965, two years after the adoption of the **Declaration on the Elimination of All Forms of Racial Discrimination**. The convention entered into force on 4 January 1969, a month after the deposit of the 27th instrument of ratification with the United Nations (UN) secretary-general, in keeping with Article 19 of the convention itself. The convention is divided into three parts, two of which are substantive in nature. The first substantive part provides a definition of **racial discrimination** and elaborates the fundamental civil rights available to all people without prejudice to their race or ethnicity. The convention defines racial discrimination as "any distinction, exclusion, restriction or preference based on race, color, descent, or national or ethnic origin which has the purpose or effect of nullifying or impairing the recognition, enjoyment or exercise, on an equal footing, of human rights and fundamental freedoms in the political, economic, social, cultural or any other field of public life." States parties to the convention agree to condemn and discourage racial discrimination, to outlaw organizations that practice racial discrimination or advocate racial hatred through propaganda, and to protect the rights guaranteed to peoples of all races.

The second substantive part of the treaty established the **Committee on the Elimination of Racial Discrimination (CERD)** composed of 18 experts. This committee in turn reviews reports submitted to the UN secretary-general by member-states concerning steps they have taken to comply with the convention. Member-states may report alleged violations of the convention by other member-states. The committee transmits such complaints to the state concerned, which is obliged to report back within three months with an explanation. Where such complaints remain unresolved, the committee is charged with appointing an ad hoc Conciliation Commission to serve in a good offices capacity to amicably resolve the dispute. The commission submits a report to the committee, which in turn reports to the disputing states. They must respond within three months to the committee's report, which they may or may not accept. States may also enable individuals or groups within their jurisdiction to submit complaints to the committee and create domestic entities to investigate and respond to such complaints. States may not be petitioned under the convention in this manner unless they have given an explicit declaration under Article 14 paragraph 1, permitting those under their jurisdiction to do so. This was the first human rights instrument to contain measures of enforcement and implementation apart from hortatory listing of rights to be observed. As of 2006, 180 countries had become parties to the convention, constituting over 90 percent of the members of the United Nations. For a text of the Convention see *United Nations Treaty Series* no. 9464, vol. 660, p. 195 or consult the United Nations High Commissioner for Human Rights website at www.ohchr.org.

INTERNATIONAL CONVENTION ON THE PROTECTION OF THE RIGHTS OF ALL MIGRANT WORKERS AND MEMBERS OF THEIR FAMILIES. Adopted unanimously by the **United Nations General Assembly** on 18 December 1990 after 10 years of negotiations, this treaty, consisting of 93 articles, reiterates a number of principles and human rights standards articulated in other human rights agreements, such as the **Universal Declaration of Human Rights** and a variety of **International Labour Organization (ILO)** conventions. The General Assembly determined that further emphasis needed to be given to the situation of migrants owing to their large numbers and to the global nature of the problems associated with migrant labor forces. Migrant workers are defined as persons who have been or are engaged in "a remunerated activity in a State of which he or she is not a national." Other kinds of workers, such as seasonal, itinerant, or frontier workers, are also defined as migrant workers under particular circumstances.

Among the rights protected under other treaties, but which are of special significance to migrant workers and their **families**, is the right to leave any state, including the state of origin, without restriction, as well as the right to enter and remain in their country of origin or **nationality**. These are all reaffirmed in the convention, along with other well-established rights such as the **right to life**, to freedom of thought and expression, to protection from arbitrary searches and confiscation of **property**, to freedom from subjection to **torture** or any other form of cruel, unusual, or degrading treatment or punishment, and to freedom from **slavery** or slavelike treatment. The convention also stipulates that the destruction of migrant workers' identity papers, work permits, or passports is unlawful. Collective expulsion of workers is forbidden, and individual expulsions, though permitted, must be undertaken through judicial means or must allow for an appeal to appropriate authorities.

The convention is monitored by a 10-member Committee on the Protection of the Rights of All Migrant Workers and Members of Their Families, known simply as the **Committee on Migrant Workers (CMW)**. The size of the committee is slated to increase to 14 members upon the 41st ratification. Committee members are elected by the states parties from among nominees and serve four-year terms in their own personal capacities. The committee is directed to receive reports from the states parties concerning steps the states have taken to give domestic effect to the convention's provisions. As of 2006, 34 governments had become party to the convention, which entered into force on 1 July 2003. For a text of the convention, see the United Nations High Commissioner for Human Rights website at www .ohchr.org.

INTERNATIONAL CONVENTION ON THE SUPPRESSION AND PUNISHMENT OF THE CRIME OF APARTHEID. First adopted by the **United Nation General Assembly** on 30 November 1973, this convention entered into force for contracting parties on 18 July 1976. The practices of **apartheid** in South Africa had for years excited the condemnation of the international community. Gradually, there being little evidence at the time that the government of South Africa might reform its objectionable policies, member-states of the **United Nations (UN)** General Assembly decided to take more formal steps to condemn the practice of apartheid. Parties to the agreement declared that apartheid is in the class of **crimes against humanity** and that inhuman acts resulting from the practice of apartheid—of racial segregation and discrimination—constitute crimes in violation of **international law**.

Article II defined the crime of apartheid to include all acts committed for the purpose of establishing and maintaining domination by one racial group of persons over any other racial group of persons and for the purpose of systematically oppressing them, thereby denying them the **right to life** and liberty of person; threatening members of a racial group with murder, serious bodily, or mental harm; or subjecting them to **torture** or to cruel, inhuman, or degrading treatment or punishment, or to **arbitrary arrest** and illegal imprisonment. Other acts characteristic of apartheid included deliberate imposition of living conditions on a racial group calculated to destroy them in whole or in part, and imposition of conditions intended to prevent the full development of the group or its capacity to enjoy human rights and freedoms, including rights to **work**, to form trade unions, to an **education**, to leave and to return to their country, to a **nationality**, to freedom of **movement and residence**, and to **freedom of opinion and expression**, **freedom of assembly**, and **freedom of association**. Policies intended to divide the population along lines of race, to create separate reserves or ghettos, to prohibit mixed marriages, and to allow the expropriation of **property** belonging to members of a racial group are declared criminal, together with **forced labor** and persecution of people for opposition to apartheid.

States parties to the convention agree to adopt legislative measures to suppress apartheid and prevent any encouragement of the crime of apartheid, and to bring to trial and punish any such persons who may fall under their jurisdiction who are responsible for or accused of the crime of apartheid. States parties to the convention agree to submit periodic reports to the Group of Three on Apartheid, which is appointed by and reports to the chairman of the United Nations **Commission on Human Rights (CHR)** concerning steps they have taken to implement the terms of the convention. The CHR is further charged by the convention to compile reports on and lists of individuals, organizations, institutions, and representatives of states that are alleged to be responsible for the crime of apartheid.

With the dramatic reforms that took place since 1990 and subsequent years in southern and South Africa, this convention has lost much of the ideological and political force that gave rise to its promulgation. Nevertheless, well over a dozen countries, including South Africa itself in 1998, have become parties to the convention since the collapse of the apartheid regime, so that now more than 130 governments are parties to it. For a text of this convention, see the Annex to UN General Assembly Resolution 3068 (XXVIII).

INTERNATIONAL CONVENTION ON THE TAKING OF HOSTAGES. Adopted by the **United Nations General Assembly** on 17 December 1979, this convention stipulates that "any person who seizes or detains and threatens to kill, to injure, or to continue to detain another person (hereinafter referred to as the 'hostage') in order to compel a third party . . . to do or abstain from doing any act as an explicit or implicit condition for the release of the hostage commits the offense of taking of **hostages.**" It also provides that each contracting party shall make such offenses punishable under its domestic law. The convention rests on the assumption that a person has an inalienable **right to life**, to liberty, and to security, and that hostage taking fundamentally violates such rights. The convention was signed by 39 states, and about 100 governments had ratified it. *See also* EUROPEAN CONVENTION ON THE SUPPRESSION OF TERRORISM; TERRORISM.

INTERNATIONAL COOPERATION FOR DEVELOPMENT AND SOLIDARITY (CIDSE). Formally established in 1967 after several years of preparatory work by several Catholic Cardinals in Europe, the acronym CIDSE originally stood for "International Cooperation for Socioeconomic Development," but took its new name International Cooperation for Development and Solidarity in 1981. The coalition initially involved Catholic nongovernmental charities from seven countries. The membership has grown to a total of 15 agencies, all but two of which—the American agency Center of Concern, which has associate member status, and the Canadian agency the Canadian Catholic Agency for Development and Peace (OCCDP)—are European. United by the social teaching of the Catholic Church, these agencies collaborate with one another through CIDSE through various working groups addressing a broad range of human rights and humanitarian concerns, including trade and **food** security, social justice, resources for development, and various regional groups focusing on issues in Africa, Asia, Latin America, Europe, and Southeast Asia. The combined revenues of the agencies comprising CIDSE make this coalition one of the major players in nongovernmental organization (NGO) advocacy and program assistance. With the **European Solidarity towards Equal Participation of People (EUROSTEP)**, a coalition of secular European agencies, and the **Association of Protestant Development Organizations in Europe (APRODEV)**, CIDSE rounds out the trio of Europe's most influential NGO coalitions lobbying and working for humanitarian and human rights causes. Address: Rue Stévin 16, B-1000, Brussels, Belgium. Website: www.cidse.org.

INTERNATIONAL COUNCIL OF VOLUNTARY AGENCIES (ICVA). Headquartered in Geneva, ICVA is the principal international coordinating body for more than 70 nongovernmental organizations (NGOs) engaging in humanitarian and development assistance activities throughout the world. It was founded in 1962 and enjoys consultative status with the United Nations **Economic and Social Council (ECOSOC)**, the **International Labour Organization (ILO)**, and the **United Nations Children's Fund (UNICEF)**. ICVA members and ICVA itself also have very close working relations with the **United Nations High Commissioner for Refugees (UNHCR)**. ICVA serves as a clearinghouse for information sharing among NGOs and as a liaison between NGOs and the variety of **United Nations (UN)** agencies headquartered in Geneva, in particular the Standing and Executive Committees of the UNHCR, but also the United Nations Interagency Standing Committee (IASC), through which the **United Nations Office for the Coordination of Humanitarian Affairs (UNOCHA)** endeavors to coordinate international humanitarian activities. ICVA also serves as a forum in which NGOs can work to promote humanitarian and human rights issues. Unlike the NGOs it serves, ICVA does not engage in operational programs as such. Its role is to coordinate NGO humanitarian and development assistance activities. It publishes a regular newsletter and other periodic reports on NGO-related activities and issues. Address: 48

chemin du Grand-Montfleury, 1290 Versoix Geneva, Switzerland. Website: www.icva.ch.

INTERNATIONAL COUNCIL OF WOMEN (ICW). This international nongovernmental organization (NGO) was originally founded in 1888 in Washington, DC, but now has its headquarters in Paris, France. It seeks to promote human rights in general, but in particular the equal rights of **women**, through coordination of the activities of dozens of national councils of women's groups. It also promotes efforts to achieve peaceful resolution of disputes, and the advancement of women in government and society, through the elimination of discrimination. It enjoys consultative status with the United Nations **Economic and Social Council (ECOSOC)** and with a variety of **United Nations (UN)** specialized agencies, including, among others, the **International Labour Organization (ILO)**, the **United Nations Development Programme (UNDP)**, and the **United Nations Children's Fund (UNICEF)**. It promotes this broad human rights agenda through organization of international meetings and through regional and national gatherings. It attempts to influence the drafting of United Nations General Assembly resolutions, and the work of many other UN specialized agencies. Address: 13 rue Caumartin, F-75009 Paris, France. Website: www.icw-cif.org.

INTERNATIONAL COUNCIL ON HUMAN RIGHTS POLICY (ICHRP). Established in 1998 at Geneva, the ICHRP is an independent body dedicated to analysis of and research on the policy implications of human rights issues. It works through conferences and workshops, commissioning of external research, and dissemination of its findings to **United Nations (UN)** bodies, and to other multilateral organizations, governments, and nongovernmental organizations (NGOs) actively working in the field of human rights. The council meets annually to establish the direction of its research program, which is carried out through an executive board. Through its research and gathering of international expertise for reflection on research findings, the ICHRP serves as an international think tank on human rights issues, bringing scholars and policy makers together in fruitful and wide-ranging dialogue. It issues recommendations and briefing papers for use in consultation with governments, intergovernmental organizations, and NGOs. Address: 48 chemin du Grand-Montfleury, P.O. Box 147, CH-1290 Versoix, Geneva, Switzerland. Website: www.ichrp.org.

INTERNATIONAL COURT OF JUSTICE (ICJ). The ICJ is one of six organs of the **United Nations (UN)**. It serves as the principal judicial organ of the UN and may also be used by member-states to seek adjudicated settlements or mutual disputes. The statute of the ICJ is an integral part of the **United Nations Charter** and thus any state party to the UN is party also to the ICJ statute. However, the Court exercises compulsory jurisdiction over cases involving states parties only if the government of the state has acknowledged such jurisdiction under Article 36. Under this article, the state recognizes the Court's compulsory jurisdiction involving cases in which the other party has also acknowledged its jurisdiction. Cases involving interpretation of treaties, any question of **international law**, disputes involving a breach of an international obligation, and determination of reparations are subject to the Court's compulsory jurisdiction in cases where both parties have acknowledged it.

The ICJ succeeded the **Permanent Court of International Justice (PCIJ)**, which was dissolved in 1946. Like its predecessor, the ICJ serves as a venue for contentious cases between governments who recognize its jurisdiction. Individuals, as such, have no standing to sue before the Court. However, the Court has heard a number of cases over the years involving human rights questions, offering not only advisory opinions but also judgments on contentious cases. For instance, in 2004 the court ruled in *Mexico versus United States of America* (Avena and other Mexican nationals) that the United States had been derelict in notifying Mexican consular officials about the arrest and pending prosecution of several Mexican nationals in capital murder cases under the terms of Article 36 of the 1963 Vienna Convention on Consular Relations. Similarly, the Court decided to exercise jurisdiction in the case of *Guinea versus Democratic Republic of the Congo*, in which Guinea alleges mistreatment of one of its citizens, Ahmadou Diallo, under the law of **state responsibility**. The court has also taken up a case filed by *Bosnia-Herzogovina versus Yugoslavia*, concerning the application of the **genocide** convention against Serbia as the successor state to Yugoslavia. In an advisory opinion to the **United Nations General Assembly** of 2004, the Court held that the Israeli government policy of building a wall to prevent terrorist attacks against innocent civilian populations violated international law. The Court has also ruled on the protection of diplomats, the trials of prisoners of war, **nationality** cases, as well as issues concerning treaty interpretation. The Court is composed of 15 judges elected by the United Nations General Assembly and the **United Nations** Security Council for nine-year terms. No two judges may be from the same state. The Court sits in The Hague. For a full record of its docket and decisions, consult the ICJ website at www.icj-cij.org.

INTERNATIONAL COVENANT ON CIVIL AND POLITICAL RIGHTS. Considered part of the **International Bill of Human Rights**, this covenant was adopted by the **United Nations General Assembly** on 16 December 1966, after some 10 years of drafting, discussion, and debate. In accordance with the terms articulated in Article 49, the covenant entered into force on 23 March 1976, three months after the 35th ratification was deposited. Together with the **International Covenant on Economic, Social, and Cultural Rights**, this covenant represented an effort by governments to move beyond the hortatory character of the **Universal Declaration of Human Rights** in order to give human rights binding legal character under **international law**. The states parties to the covenant, then, are legally bound to adhere to its terms. The rights listed and the terms of the covenant are not simply a matter of domestic jurisdiction. Rather, they constitute matters of international concern as between the parties, and states may take an interest in the compliance of other states to their human rights obligations.

Part I of the covenant reaffirms the collective rights of peoples, including the right of **self-determination** of peoples, and their right to dispose of their natural wealth and resources (Article 1). Governments undertaking to administer peoples in non-self-governing territories acknowledge their duty to promote the independence of such territories.

Part II of the covenant emphasizes that states parties have a duty to respect and ensure the rights of all individuals within their territorial jurisdiction regardless of race, color, sex, language, religion, political or other opinion, national or social origin, **property**, birth or other status. States parties agree to undertake whatever steps are necessary under their domestic law to give effect to the rights enumerated in the covenant, through appropriate legislation, judicial, or executive action. Article 4 of the covenant grants states parties the right to **derogation** from their obligations in regard to certain rights in times of **public emergency**, which threatens the life of the nation and the existence of which is officially proclaimed. Several rights, however, are not subject to derogation even in times of national emergency. These include the **right to life** and the right not to be arbitrarily deprived of life, the rights not to be subjected to **torture**, inhuman, or degrading treatment or punishment, the right not to be held in **slavery** or servitude, the right not to be imprisoned on grounds of inability to fulfill a contractual obligation, the right everywhere to be recognized as a person before the law and the right to freedom of thought, conscience, and religion. Also not subject to derogation is the prohibition of ex post facto legislation. All other rights listed in the covenant can be abridged or curtailed during times of national emergency. Any derogation must be announced and justified by states parties.

Part III, Articles 6–27, of the covenant identify the various rights protected. In addition to the rights listed above from which states may not derogate, there are numerous other rights. These include the right to liberty and security of person, the right not to be subjected to **arbitrary arrest** or detention, or to be deprived of liberty except in accordance with due process of law. Those deprived by law of their liberty are to be treated with humanity and respect. Persons lawfully within the jurisdiction of a state have a right of movement and freedom to choose a residence, and when outside their country, they have a right to return to it. People have a right of access to the courts and **equality** under the law as well as other legal guarantees such as the right to receive a statement of charges. They have a right to legal counsel (including free legal counsel if indigent), to a speedy trial, to confront and examine witnesses, and to nonselfincrimination. All persons have a right to appeal and a right not to face double jeopardy. Persons have a right to **privacy**, to hold opinions without interference, to **freedom of opinion and expression**, to **freedom of association** with others, to **freedom of assembly**, to participate in public affairs, to vote in elections based on the principle of equal suffrage, and to serve in public office. Persons have a right to marry and to have a **family**. Children have a right to protection, to a name, and to acquire a **nationality**. Finally, where **minorities** exist, they have a right to practice and enjoy their own culture, to profess and practice their own religion, and to use their own language.

Part IV of the covenant establishes the enforcement mechanisms and treaty monitoring machinery. Articles 28 to 45 specify the establishment, functions, and operation of an 18-member **Human Rights Committee (HRC)**. The committee's members are elected by states parties but serve in their individual capacities. The committee is empowered to hear reports from states parties concerning their compliance with the terms of the covenant. The committee, however, does not have the capacity to conduct its own investigations, but it may quiz governmental representatives concerning disturbing evidence contained in the state's reports to the committee. The committee reports annually to the **United Nations (UN)** General Assembly through the **Economic and Social Council (ECOSOC)**. The operation of this committee, though its jurisdiction and capacities are limited, serves to put pressure on governments to comply with their obligations under the covenant. Furthermore, under Article 41, governments may, at their voluntary discretion, declare the competence of the committee to receive and consider communications in which any one state party (including itself) may claim that another state party is not fulfilling its obligations under the covenant. Under Article 41 a series of possible committee actions are enumerated including the extension of the committee's good offices, its promotion of a directly negotiated settlement of the dispute, and its reporting procedures.

Further, under Article 42, the committee with the permission of the states party to the dispute, may establish an ad hoc Conciliation Commission, consisting of five persons mutually acceptable to the parties. The commission serves as a mechanism to encourage the amicable resolution of the dispute. When the dispute does not admit of amicable resolution, the commission may make its own recommendations concerning its disposition, although the states in dispute are not required to follow or accept the commission's findings. However, failure of the parties to cooperate may be duly noted by the **Commission on Human Rights (CHR)** in its annual report to the General Assembly. This function is now assumed by the United Nations **Human Rights Council**, which replaced the commission in 2006. The remainder of the covenant consists of the final clauses concerning ratification procedures, effects on federal states, and amendment procedures.

Governments party to the covenant have been extremely reluctant to take full advantage of the provisions of Articles 41 and 42 concerning the filing of complaints against other governments for noncompliance with the terms of the covenant. Involved in this, no doubt, is the concern that states filing complaints against other states may themselves be targeted for future complaints by way of retaliation. Although meant to provide a degree of enforcement or compliance to the covenant, these provisions have been largely inoperative for lack of state action. Clearly, governments were willing to commit themselves to strive toward the incorporation and domestic enforcement of the covenant's human rights principles, but they remain reticent to engage in a free-for-all exchange among themselves concerning how diligently they have complied. The actual practice of states, then, suggests that there was great wisdom in establishing a separate **Optional Protocol to the International Covenant on Civil and Political Rights**, which empowered individuals to lodge complaints against their own governments. The optional protocol was intended to put even more teeth into the enforcement and compliance aspects of the covenant. The fact that states have not been nearly so ready to ratify it (to date 104), as they have the covenant (to date 154), suggests that the exclusion of such measures from the covenant itself was a wise choice, at least from the point of view of attracting more rapid and widespread ratification of the covenant. A second optional protocol to the covenant outlawing the **death penalty** has attracted only 54 ratifications to date. For a complete text of the covenant, see appendix C.

INTERNATIONAL COVENANT ON ECONOMIC, SOCIAL, AND CULTURAL RIGHTS. Together with the **International Covenant on Civil and Political Rights**, the International Covenant on Economic, Social, and Cultural Rights was adopted on 16 December 1966 by the **United Nations General Assembly**. It entered into force a decade later, on 3 January 1976. Like the Covenant on Civil and Political Rights, it asserts the rights of peoples to **self-**

determination. Unlike the Covenant on Civil and Political Rights, states parties are not obliged immediately to adhere to the legal rights enumerated. Instead, recognizing that economic and social rights carry substantial economic consequences, the parties agree only to undertake steps "with a view to achieving progressively the full realization of the rights recognized in the present Covenant by all appropriate means, including particularly the adoption of legislative measures" (Article 2.1). This language is more permissive and is necessarily so, since states vary considerably in their capacity to tax and spend for the general welfare. Unlike civil and **political rights**, which can be normally guaranteed immediately by conscious choice of governments, guarantees to **education**, welfare services, **health** benefits, and so on are not only costly but often cumbersome systems to develop and sustain.

The rights enumerated under the covenant include the right to **work** and the right to just and favorable conditions of work, including fair wages, equal remuneration for work, equal opportunities for promotion based on merit and seniority, and appropriate opportunities for rest and recreation. States parties agree to ensure the right of everyone to form and join trade unions, to receive **social security**, to protection of the **family**, to have an adequate standard of living, to be free from hunger, to enjoy the highest attainable standard of physical and mental **health**, to receive a primary education, and to participate in cultural life. Apart from merely listing these rights, the covenant specifies in greater detail than the **Universal Declaration of Human Rights** the nature of the right and the particular steps that should be taken to enact them. This is apparent in the articles dealing with proper remuneration for work (Article 7), the right to associate in unions (Article 8), and the right to education (Article 13), which are spelled out in considerable detail.

From the standpoint of compliance, fewer measures are employed than in the Covenant on Civil and Political Rights, in recognition of the highly contextual and variable conditions existing among states parties. The latter agree in Article 16 to submit reports to the **United Nations (UN)** secretary-general regarding their progress in achieving observance of the rights recognized in the covenant. The reports are passed from the UN secretary-general to the **Economic and Social Council (ECOSOC)** for consideration, and to appropriate specialized agencies. ECOSOC may also refer reports and recommendations to the specialized agencies on matters falling within their competence as well as to the United Nations General Assembly, the **Commission on Human Rights (CHR)** (replaced in 2006 by the **Human Rights Council),** and other appropriate UN bodies. ECOSOC initially delegated the review of state reports on compliance with the covenant's provisions to its Sessional Working Group on the Implementation of the International Covenant on Economic, Social, and Cultural Rights. In 1985, ECOSOC established a **Committee on Economic, Social, and Cultural Rights (CESCR)**, which took over the Sessional Working Group's review of state reports. More than 150 governments have ratified the covenant. For a complete text of the covenant, see appendix B.

INTERNATIONAL CRIMINAL COURT (ICC). International law has long acknowledged that individuals are subjects of international law concerning their duties to refrain from commission of piracy, **war crimes**, and other international delicts. The protection of human rights implies that there are "human duties" that must be observed by individuals. Long before governments were prepared to acknowledge that individuals were anything more than objects of international law concerning acquisition of rights, they asserted that individuals were subjects of duties under international law. However, the successful prosecution of violations of international law by individuals depended largely on the will and capacity of individual governments to exercise jurisdiction and pursue prosecution, and more often than not they were unwilling or unable to do so.

The events of World War II, most specifically the **genocide** perpetrated by Nazi Germany, and the disregard of the laws of war by Japanese forces in the Pacific front, caused the victorious Allies to seek retribution against those guilty of war crimes and **crimes against humanity**, among others. Trials at Nuremburg and in Tokyo and other locations after the war led to the prosecution and punishment of war criminals, and established the principle that no one engaged in war crimes, whether their planning or commission, could expect to be immune from international prosecution and punishment. However, with the disbanding of the postwar tribunals, the legal systems of governments became the only available venue in which war crimes tribunals could be initiated. The Genocide Convention provided in Article 6 for such national trials as the primary means of giving effect to its provisions defining genocide as an international crime prosecutable by competent national tribunals.

The **United Nations General Assembly** called for the United Nations **International Law Commission** to explore the possibility of establishing a more permanent international judicial body to handle cases of genocide, and this inquiry later was expanded to include study of the desirability of such an international tribunal being established for other international crimes, such as war crimes and crimes against humanity and violations of international humanitarian law. In 1951 the commission reported that such a body was both desirable and possible, and the General Assembly appointed a committee that produced a draft statute in 1953. However, the committee postponed action on the draft statute pending resolution of the controversial and difficult question of defining aggression, and the momentum toward establishing any international criminal tribunal ground to a halt, not to gather renewed energy until 1989 when the General Assembly decided to explore the concept again with the inclusion of international drug trafficking as an additional prosecutable offense.

In 1993, in light of the **ethnic cleansing** associated with the Yugoslavian civil war, the **United Nations** Security Council established an **International Criminal Tribunal for the Former Yugoslavia (ICTY),** and in response to the genocide in Rwanda, it established an **International Criminal Tribunal for Rwanda (ICTR)** in 1994. These ad hoc tribunals had jurisdiction only over war crimes, genocide, crimes against humanity, and crimes committed in violation of international humanitarian law committed in the regions and during the times specified. Nevertheless, they represented an awareness that effective deterrence of human rights abuses required that steps be taken to try and punish those guilty of egregious violations of international law. Their limited scope, however, also led the international community to begin exploring the possibility of establishing an international criminal court of universal jurisdiction. The International Law Commission went back to work in 1994, and a long and difficult, and in the end not completely successful, effort to draft a statute for the ICC concluded with the adoption of the statute at Rome in 1998.

Among the controversial features of the treaty text was that the old problem of defining aggression remain unresolved, and in an unprecedented step the statute proposed that aggression would be a crime, although its definition would have to await a further consensus among members of the ICC. Those states not parties to the ICC statute, thus, could have no say about the ultimate definition of the crime of aggression. The drafting of the statute was not free of other controversy, and objections made by the U.S. government concerning features of tribunal and its operation were largely rejected by other governments, including those of Europe. The United States wished to have prosecution of individuals accused of war crimes more closely tied to Security Council decisions, as had been the ICTY and ICTR. Although the Security Council may refer cases to the ICC, so too may states party, nonstates party, and the prosecutor, acting under his or her own investigative powers. The U.S. position in regard to referrals to the ICC was largely rejected in favor of an independent prosecutor. In addition, the U.S. government raised concerns regarding the generation of frivolous suits even by non-ICC parties against American military personnel stationed abroad. Given the unique position of the United States as the main guarantor of international peacekeeping and peacemaking throughout the world, the U.S. government worried about how the ICC statute might be used as a mechanism to advance spurious and politically motivated legal claims meant to embarrass the world's lone military superpower. Other constitutional issues were also raised by U.S. negotiators. Thus, although the Bill Clinton administration was one of 120 signatory governments to the Rome Statute in 1998, it signed with significant reservations, and it recommended to the subsequent George W. Bush administration that the statute not be ratified by the United States, unless significant revisions could be secured. This was not to be, and the Bush administration announced that it would not ratify the statute.

Regardless of U.S. nonparticipation, the Rome Statute entered into force in July 2002, 60 days after ratification by the 60th member-state was deposited on 1 April 2002. The Court is seated at The Hague, Netherlands, in temporary quarters until permanent facilities are available. Unlike the ICTY and the ICTR, the ICC is an international organization independent of the **United Nations (UN)**. It consists of four organs, a presidency, the chambers, the office of the prosecutor,

Mrs. Eleanor Roosevelt presenting the Human Rights Charter. United Nations Office at Geneva Photo Collection.

Red Cross health educators give a demonstration to mothers outside on the proper way to prepare a nutritious weaning diet. United Nations Office at Geneva Photo Collection.

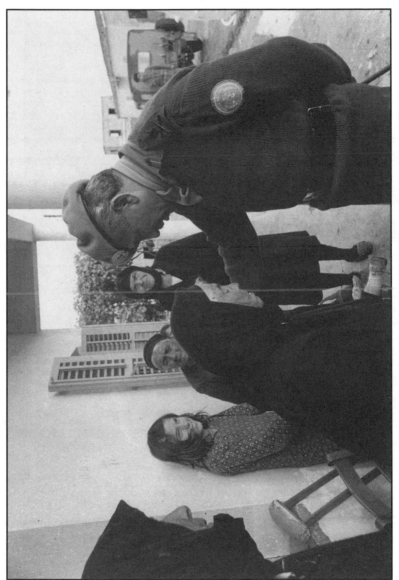

Humanitarian assistance in Cyprus. United Nations Office at Geneva Photo Collection.

United Nations Operation in Mozambique. United Nations Office at Geneva Photo Collection.

United Nations rushes to help children survive with this milk distribution organized by the United Nations International Children's Emergency Fund in Ecuador's devastated areas. United Nations Office at Geneva Photo Collection.

An International Committee of the Red Cross (ICRC) delegate in Colombia speaks with the local commander of the rebel group, ELN, prior to the release of a hostage being held by the group. ICRC/Boris Heger.

Following the signing of a cease-fire in Sri Lanka in 2002, both the government and the Liberation Tigers of Tamil Eleam (LTTE) requested that the International Committee of the Red Cross (ICRC) monitor two crossing points between government and LTTE-held areas. ICRC/Dominic Sansoni.

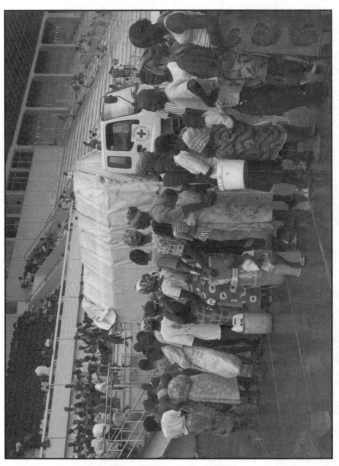

At the height of the fighting in Liberia in 2003, the International Committee of the Red Cross (ICRC) was able to help those affected because all the parties to the conflict accepted the organization's presence and way of working. ICRC medical delegates based at the John Fitzgerald Kennedy hospital worked around the clock to treat those hurt in the fighting, while food and other basic necessities were provided to tens of thousands of terrified civilians. ICRC/Virginia La Guardia.

and the registry. The president undertakes overall administration of the Court. The judicial activity of the court is undertaken by the chambers, including the Appeals Chamber, the Trial Chamber, and the Pretrial Chamber. The Pretrial Chamber issues warrants of arrest and summons to appear after evaluating requests by the prosecutor. The Trial Chamber actually hears and decides cases. The Appeals Chamber hears appeals initiated by the convicted person or the prosecutor of Trial Chamber judgments. The prosecutor is an independent and separate organ of the Court responsible for receiving requests for prosecution, investigating them, and where evidence supports the viability of prosecution, to bring them to the relevant chambers. The registry serves to advance the administration and servicing of the Court, such as provision of assistance and counseling to victims and witnesses.

Under the statute, the states parties are the actors with the first responsibility and opportunity to undertake prosecutions against suspected war criminals. Only when governments are unable or unwilling to do so may the prosecutor seek jurisdiction over persons accused of war crimes or other crimes that fall under the jurisdiction of the court, which include genocide, crimes against humanity, war crimes, and the crime of aggression. Each of these is further defined in greater specificity with the exception of the crime of aggression, which is left undefined by the statute. Members of the ICC are obliged to extradite individuals to the Court when they are unable or unwilling to assume jurisdiction or prosecution. The prosecutor and the Court may deem that any action taken by a relevant domestic tribunal was not seriously or properly pursued or was intended to shield an accused person from justice. In such cases, under the statute, the judgments and decisions of national courts may be disregarded, and the prosecutor may seek to exercise jurisdiction.

As momentum toward the full operation of the ICC has gained steam, the United States, which remains a nonmember, chose to enter into Status of Forces Agreements and Bilateral Immunity Agreements with countries in which its forces are stationed in order to shield them from potential **extradition** to the ICC, and to leave matters concerning judicial proceedings against U.S. military personnel for commission of war crimes under the authority of the U.S. government. These Status of Force Agreements have been enacted with states party to the ICC as well, under Article 98 of the ICC statute, which provides that ICC member-states are not obliged to violate agreements with nonparties to the statute. The nonparticipation of the United States in the ICC is regrettable, but it also reflects significant differences of legal and constitutional philosophy as well as the very different political situations of the United States compared to other governments. The larger goals of the ICC, however, can still be met in the sense that the U.S. government may cooperate with the ICC, as it has most recently through the Security Council to secure investigations into violations of international criminal law in the Darfur situation in the Sudan.

The U.S. government, along with other democratic governments, has the capacity to seek justice in cases involving violations of international law. Evidence of the capacity of national governments to take action against their own citizens is seen in the trial of Saddam Hussein and other members of his Baathist regime accused of genocide, war crimes, and crimes against humanity. The ICC provides that governments remain the first line of action in prosecution of international crimes. Thus, whether by national action, by ongoing efforts through ad hoc tribunals, and eventually through action by the ICC, one can expect that the larger goals of the ICC will be gradually achieved. These include a desire to ensure greater justice and to deter future commission of war crimes by reducing the prospects of immunity from prosecution. Address: Maanweg, 174, 2516AB, The Hague, The Netherlands. Postal Address: P.O. Box 19519, 2500 CM, The Hague, The Netherlands. Website: www.icc-cpi.int.

INTERNATIONAL CRIMINAL TRIBUNAL FOR RWANDA (ICTR). Established by the **United Nations** Security Council on 8 November 1994, under the powers granted to it by Chapter VII of the **United Nations Charter**, this tribunal has the power to prosecute persons for the commission of **genocide** and for violations of international humanitarian law, including **crimes against humanity** and **war crimes**, and violations of common Article 3 of the Geneva Conventions and the Additional Protocol II. Jurisdiction over such acts is limited to those committed during the year 1994 in connection with the ethnic violence in Rwanda and neighboring countries where Rwandese citizens fled. The tribunal consists of three principal organs, the chambers, the prosecutor, and a registry, which services the tribunal. The chambers include three Trial Chambers of three judges each and an Appeals Chamber of five judges. The ICTR has the distinction of being the first international criminal court in which an accused person—Jean Kambanda, former prime minister of Rwanda—admitted guilt for the crime of genocide before an international court. Kambanda's conviction marked the first time that a head of government was successfully convicted of the crime of genocide. The ICTR issued 20 convictions, many of them being high-ranking national or regional figures in the Rwandan government. For a text of the statute of the tribunal, see **United Nations (UN)** Security Council Resolution 955 (1994). Address: Arusha International Conference Center, P.O. Box 6016. Arusha, Tanzania. Website: www.ictr.org.

INTERNATIONAL CRIMINAL TRIBUNAL FOR THE FORMER YUGOSLAVIA (ICTY). This tribunal, established on 25 May 1993 by the **United Nations** Security Council upon the recommendation of the UN secretary-general, sought to give effect to the **Geneva Red Cross Conventions** and to punish persons guilty of serious **crimes against humanity** and **war crimes** in the civil conflicts in the former Yugoslavia. The secretary-general's report in turn was based on extensive study by the Commission of Experts established by the UN Security Council in October of 1992, which investigated charges of violations of international humanitarian law. The Commission of Experts concluded that the incidences of **ethnic cleansing**, sexual assault, rape, **torture**, murder, and mistreatment of civilians and prisoners of war had been so widespread and systematic as to be a product of policy rather than unrelated incidents. Whether these crimes rose to the level of **genocide** was a matter of dispute, but the criminal nature of such acts was not.

The International Tribunal, which was formally inaugurated on 17 November 1993, consists of three Trial Chambers of three judges each and an Appeals Chamber of seven judges. The tribunal has been very active, having issued more than 160 indictments and having achieved 43 final sentences. Others are yet to be taken into custody, await trial, or are at trial. The most important person under trial, Slobodan Milosevic, the former president of Serbia, died while in custody in March 2006. The current prosecutor is Carla del Ponte of

Switzerland, who was appointed in 1999. The objectives of the ICTY include bringing to justice those allegedly responsible for commission of acts since the onset of the Yugoslavian civil war in 1991, including crimes of genocide, war crimes, crimes against humanity, and serious violations of international humanitarian law. This primary objective is intended to render justice to the victims of proven crimes, and contribute to the deterrence of further crimes. The United Nations Security Council enacted the ICTY with the idea that it would contribute to the restoration of peace in a region marked by deep-seated historical animosities. Website: www.un.org/icty.

INTERNATIONAL FEDERATION OF RED CROSS AND RED CRESCENT SOCIETIES (IFRC). Part of the Red Cross movement, formerly known as the League of Red Cross and Red Crescent Societies (LICROSS), IFRC is a federation of national Red Cross and Red Crescent Societies founded in 1919 and growing out of the Red Cross movement that traces its roots to the work of **Jean-Henri Dunant** and other principal organizers in dealing with the humanitarian consequences of warfare. The IFRC promotes the sharing of information among and coordinates the emergency assistance activities of the numerous national societies, while strengthening their capacity to provide humanitarian assistance to **refugees** and to other victims of man-made and natural disasters. The bulk of Red Cross activity is undertaken by the various national societies, which now number 183, making the IFRC the world's largest international humanitarian organization. The combined resources of the national societies include nearly 100 million members and volunteers and 300,000 employees who assist more than 230 million beneficiaries annually.

The work of the national societies is extensive and varied, including disaster relief; **health** and social programs; first aid training; maintenance of national and local blood supplies; disaster preparedness; **family** reunification programs during emergencies; water and sanitation programs; and emergency shelter, **food**, and medical assistance. The IFRC itself promotes contact and cooperation among its national societies and publishes an online directory of these societies, along with a profile of their various programs and activities. Operating on the principles of **solidarity** and **subsidiarity**, the IFRC attempts to strengthen and promote the work of its national societies, and to facilitate the flow of assistance to areas hit by disaster and facing emergency situations. Its chief function, then, is to coordinate and mobilize relief activities when international emergencies strike, and to facilitate the cooperative interaction of the various national societies in such situations.

The IFRC works closely with the **International Committee of the Red Cross (ICRC)** as well as with the **United Nations High Commissioner for Refugees (UNHCR)** and other humanitarian agencies. It is a standing invitee to meetings of the United Nations **Office for Coordination of Humanitarian Affairs (OCHA)** Interagency Standing Committee, which deals with coordination of international responses to humanitarian emergencies. Address: 17 chemin des Crêts, P.O. Box 372, CH-1211 Geneva 19, Switzerland. Website: www.ifrc.org.

INTERNATIONAL INSTITUTE OF HUMANITARIAN LAW (IIHL). Focusing principally on the legal protection issues in time of war with respect to combatants, civilians, **refugees**, and displaced persons, the IIIIL seeks to promote, protect, develop, and disseminate the principles of international humanitarian law. Founded in San Remo, Italy, in 1970, it is a nongovernmental organization (NGO) with consultative status with the United Nations **Economic and Social Council (ECOSOC)**, the **United Nations Educational, Scientific, and Cultural Organization (UNESCO)**, the **Council of Europe (COE)**, and the **United Nations High Commissioner for Refugees (UNHCR)**. IIHL performs a useful **education** function for government and intergovernmental officials through offering courses on the laws of war and on the status of refugees, disaster victims, and migrants. These courses are offered to government officials, military personnel, lawyers, and teachers. It also publishes reports on its various conferences, colloquies, and seminars. It has strong institutional ties to the **International Committee of the Red Cross (ICRC)**, the International Organization for Migration (IOM), and the **International Federation of Red Cross and Red Crescent Societies (IFRC)**. Address: Villa Ormond, C. so Cavollotti 113, 18038 San Remo, Italy. Website: www.iihl.org.

INTERNATIONAL LABOUR ORGANIZATION (ILO). Established in 1919, in accordance with the International Labour Constitution, the ILO is unique to international organizations in that both its international conference composed of all member-states and the smaller ILO governing body composed of 56 titular members (including 28 governments, 14 employers, and 14 workers) and 66 deputy members (including 28 governments, 19 employers, and 19 workers) ensure representation not only of governments but of employers and employees. Member-states—now 178 in number—maintain a four-person delegation to the international conference, which meets annually to review the work of the organization. These delegations consist of two governmental representatives and one each for employers and workers. The governing body is elected by the international conference and meets three times annually. This unique structure is intended to forge working relationships between government, employers, and workers. In addition to the international conference and the governing body, the ILO has a permanent secretariat headquartered in Geneva, known as the International Labour Office.

The ILO's field of activities is rather broad, including the maintenance of fair labor practices, the promotion of the right of workers to **work** and to join trade unions, the protection of the right of collective bargaining, the eradication of various forms of compulsory labor, the assurance of humane working conditions and fair wages, and the extension of **social security**, **health**, and welfare benefits to workers and their families, among others. The ILO even in its earliest years took an interest in the problems of **refugees**, refugee resettlement, and the provision of employment opportunities for displaced peoples. It provided training programs for refugees in cooperation with the **League of Nations** prior to World War II. It has continued to address the growing concern of migrant labor in a series of conventions.

The ILO maintains two standing committees of direct relevance to human rights concerns. These are the ILO **Freedom of Association** Committee and the ILO Committee of Experts on the Application of Conventions and Recommendations. The former is particularly concerned that the right of workers to freely associate is not infringed by governments. Of special concern in its work is protecting the right of workers to join trade unions. To this end, it investigates complaints by workers concerning claims of infringement of this right. More ambitious yet is the work of the Committee of Experts on the Application of Conventions and Recommendations. This body oversees member-state compliance with the large number of ILO instruments dealing with various aspects of workers' rights. Collectively, the conventions and recommendations made by the ILO conference are known as the International Labour Code. It consists of dozens of instruments too numerous to mention fully here.

Among the more prominent of the 185 ILO treaties in connection with human labor rights are the following: the Right of Association Convention of 1921, **Forced Labor** Convention of 1930, Forty-Hour Week Convention of 1935, Protection of Wages Convention of 1949, the Right to Collective Bargaining Convention of 1949, Migration for Employment Convention of 1949, the Equal Remuneration Convention of 1951, Social Security Convention of 1952, Forced Labor Convention of 1957, Discrimination Convention of 1958, Social Policy Convention of 1962, Invalidity, Old Age, and Survivors' Benefits Convention of 1967, Minimum Age Convention of 1973, Equality of Treatment Social Security Convention of 1962, Migrant Workers Convention of 1975, Working Environment Convention of 1977, Collective Bargaining Convention of 1981, Occupational Safety and Health Convention of 1981, and the Indigenous and Tribal Peoples Convention of 1989. In 1990, the ILO adopted conventions on chemicals and on night work. In 1994, it further produced conventions on part-time work and in 1995 on safety in mines. These were followed in 1995 with conventions on home work and on seafarers' rights, and in 2000 on maternal protection. Address: 4 Routes des Morillons, CH-1211 Geneva 22, Switzerland. For copies of the ILO conventions mentioned above, among many others, consult the ILO website, www.ilo.org.

INTERNATIONAL LAW. International law may be defined as that body of rules, customary norms, treaties and principles that governments of states observe in their mutual relations. States, being sovereign entities, are not bound to observe rules or law that they do not voluntarily agree to observe. However, once states enter into obligations with one another, whether by customary rules or by treaties, they are bound to adhere to such obligations. Resting firmly on the principle of **sovereignty**, international law does not presume to dictate to states their domestic policies. However, enforcement of international agreements is usually accomplished through the legislative, executive, and judicial actions of domestic political institutions. Treaties and customary norms are not typically self-enforcing. Governments often incorporate treaties or customs into their domestic law through legislation that can then be enforced and subjected to the adjudication of domestic courts.

These principles generally apply to the area of human rights. The vast majority of human rights declarations, treaties, and agreements are only effective insofar as governments give them legislative effect within their own domestic legal systems. Indeed, many human rights instruments remain only expressions of legal aspiration to the extent that governments do not incorporate them or enforce them through their domestic legal orders. In those cases where states habitually violate human rights principles, international law provides only weak remedies. The primary norm of international law continues to be that of sovereignty, which includes the notion of noninterference in the domestic affairs, the territorial integrity, and the independence of states. A government has a legal right to intervene in another state's territory when its own citizens are being threatened or persecuted, but the right to intervene on behalf of the other state's nationals is severely circumscribed. Under traditional customary international law, such intervention might be justified if the actions of the state against its own nationals were so abhorrent as to "shock the conscience of mankind." Despite the predominance of the sovereignty norm, the fact that international law developed from the **natural law** tradition rooted in principles of natural justice has mitigated absolute claims to sovereign control over people and territory, and offered arguments for intervention and for curtailment of a state's sovereignty—as, for example, when the **League of Nations** imposed **minorities** treaties upon Iraq and Yugoslavia.

With the advent of the **United Nations Charter**, the presumption is that intervention should be done collectively, under the aegis of the **United Nations** Security Council, and that somehow the actions taken by a state against its own populations constitute a threat to international peace and security. The international intervention in Iraq in 1991 on behalf of Kurdish **refugees** and displaced persons was justified on these grounds, as were later interventions in the Balkans and elsewhere. However, international practice has not ripened to such an extent that international intervention to prevent human rights abuses by a government against its own citizens is considered a legal norm. The norm of nonintervention still remains a powerful one.

Still, governments may agree to various forms of international scrutiny, reporting mechanisms, and protocols, which indicate their willingness to be held to higher human rights standards. Such actions are voluntary in nature, but they represent a trend by some governments to hold themselves to a higher standard of scrutiny and enforcement. Moreover, political pressure can be brought to bear by governments and human rights bodies on refractory states that habitually or episodically violate human rights principles.

Human rights treaties have become an increasingly common feature of modern international law. They have proliferated in number, and in certain regional contexts they have evolved to the point where they have some enforceability. Still, the very fact that we refer to "human rights" suggests that the evolution is not yet complete. Until they become enforceable legal rights, many human rights treaties and declarations will remain more a statement of legal aspiration than a vehicle of routine legal fulfillment.

INTERNATIONAL LAW COMMISSION. This commission was authorized by the **United Nations General Assembly** in November 1947. It was established under Article 13 (1a) of the **United Nations Charter** for the purpose of promoting the development and codification of **international law**. In this capacity, the commission is charged to study and prepare draft agreements on matters submitted to it by the General Assembly. It consists of 34 members elected by the **United Nations (UN)** General Assembly for five-year terms and serving in their individual capacity. Its work on human rights has included the preparation of draft treaties, such as the **Convention on the Nationality of Married Women**, the **Convention on the Reduction of Statelessness**, the **Convention Relating to the Status of Stateless Persons**, and more recently, the draft statue of the **International Criminal Court (ICC)**. In doing this work of drafting conventions, the commission works closely with governments at every stage of the drafting process. Website: www .un.org.law.ilc.

INTERNATIONAL LEAGUE FOR HUMAN RIGHTS. First formed in 1941 as the International League for the Rights of Man, this non-governmental organization (NGO) seeks to promote the human rights articulated in various human rights treaties, including the **Universal Declaration of Human Rights**. It enjoys consultative status with the United Nations **Economic and Social Council (ECOSOC)**, the **Organization of American States (OAS)**, the **Council of Europe (COE)**, the **International Labour Organization (ILO)**, and the **United Nations Educational, Scientific, and Cultural Organization (UNESCO)**. Its influence is fairly broad. It investigates human rights violations, assists victims of human rights abuses, publishes reports, monitors human rights situations, engages in networking with other human rights agencies, and makes direct appeals to governments and international bodies. It has been an annual participant in sessions of the United Nations **Commission on Human Rights (CHR)**. In recent years, the league has worked extensively with the **Organization for Security and Cooperation in Europe (OSCE)** in efforts to cope with human rights situations and conflicts in the newly independent former Soviet Republics. Address: 228 East 45th Street, 5th Floor, New York, NY 10017, USA. Website: www.ilhr.org.

INTERNATIONAL MEDICAL CORPS (IMC). The IMC was established in 1984 by Robert Simon, MD, and various American volunteer doctors and nurses. It promotes programs for training and **health** care in countries at risk of health problems, and it also participates in emergency assistance where natural disasters have disrupted local health care capacity, such as in major floods, earthquakes, or **famine** situations. Although offering emergency assistance care, IMC works toward reestablishing local health care capacity. Since its formation, IMC has responded to natural disasters in more than 40 countries throughout the world. Its services include primary health care, maternal and child health care, war and trauma surgery, water sanitation, nutrition programs, reconstructive and rehabilitative surgery, and hospital reconstruction and rehabilitation. In connection with the latter, for instance, IMC rehabilitated the Kailahun Government Hospital in Sierra Leone, after it was looted and destroyed during the decade-long civil war in Sierra Leone. IMC fielded medical teams in the year 2000 to the district, setting up mobile clinic teams; then, in cooperation with the government once order was restored, it began the full-scale reconstruction of the hospital itself as well as satellite health clinics.

The IMC also offers medical assistance to **refugees** and displaced persons. Recently it has been active in Chad and the Darfur region of Sudan, where it provides emergency medical assistance through health clinics in refugee and displaced persons camps. The IMC's total global resources coming from **United Nations (UN)** grants as well as private funds and donations in kind totaled more than $96 million in 2004. IMC works with the **World Health Organization (WHO)**, the **World Food Programme (WFP)**, the **United Nations High Commissioner for Refugees (UNHCR)**, the **United Nations Children's Fund (UNICEF)**, and a host of nongovernmental organizations (NGOs) and professional groups and foundations in promoting its humanitarian work. The IMC keeps its headquarters in Santa Monica California, with an office in Washington, DC, and in the United Kingdom. Address: 1919 Santa Monica Blvd., Suite 300, Santa Monica, CA 90404, USA. Website: www.imcworldwide.org.

INTERNATIONAL REFUGEE ORGANIZATION (IRO). *See* UNITED NATIONS HIGH COMMISSIONER FOR REFUGEES (UNHCR).

INTERNATIONAL RESEARCH AND TRAINING INSTITUTE FOR THE ADVANCEMENT OF WOMEN (INSTRAW). Headquartered in Santo Domingo, Dominican Republic, INSTRAW was established in principle in 1975 by the **United Nations General Assembly**, on the recommendation of the World Conference of the International Women's Year held in Mexico City. However, it did not commence operations until 1980. It conducts research and training to enhance the integration of **women** into the development process and develops strategies for the advancement of women generally. INSTRAW is an autonomous **United Nations (UN)** body governed by a board of trustees nominated by its member-states and approved by the United Nations **Economic and Social Council (ECOSOC)**. It works with UN development agencies to highlight gender perspectives in the development arena, and to ensure the integration of women in the development process. It supports research activity on a range of topics including the political advancement of women, the role of women in human rights, in the promotion of peace, and in the migration phenomenon. It also provides training on gender-related issues for UN agencies, nongovernmental organizations, governments, and educational institutions. Website: www.instraw.org.

INTERNATIONAL SOCIETY FOR HUMAN RIGHTS (ISHR). ISHR was founded in 1972 in Frankfurt, Germany, by 13 people dedicated to the nonviolent pursuit of the preservation of human rights under the principles enunciated in the **Universal Declaration of Human Rights**. It originally addressed the violation of human rights in the former Soviet Union. In 1982, ISHR began more determined international activity with an expanded membership, although much of its work continued to be centered on human rights issues in the Soviet bloc. With the collapse of communism in the early 1990s, ISHR initiated efforts to promote the emergence of democracy in the newly independent states that formed out of the old Soviet Union. At the same time, its membership and activity expanded into Africa and Latin America. It campaigned for the establishment of the **International Criminal Court (ICC)** and has promoted **freedom of religion** and **children's rights**. ISHR's international membership has grown to more than 30,000 in 26 countries. At the practical level, ISHR sponsors military training programs in several countries to ensure that military personnel understand their obligations to protect human rights. It enjoys consultative status with the **Council of Europe (COE)** and observer status with the **African Commission of Human and Peoples' Rights** and associated status with the **United Nations (UN)** Department of Public Information. International Secretariat Address: Borsigalle 9, D-60388 Frankfurt/M., Germany. Website: www.ishr.org.

INTER-PARLIAMENTARY UNION (IPU). Founded in 1889, the IPU has one of the longest traditions of modern nongovernmental organizations (NGOs) in terms of promoting peaceful resolution of conflicts between states through law and arbitration. The IPU now enjoys a membership of national parliamentary groups in 143 countries, and seven associate members from regional based organizations such as the Andean Parliament, the European Parliament, and the Parliamentary Assembly of the **Council of Europe (COE)**, among others. IPU has investigated numerous alleged violations of the rights of parliamentarians involving cases concerning freedom of expression, murder, exile, and **disappearances**. Apart from its activity in defense of parliamentarians, IPU has sponsored conferences and meetings to study a range of international issues, including human rights concerns. It attempts to foster contact and collaboration among the parliaments of various countries, promotes the defense of human rights, and disseminates knowledge of the working of representative governments. It maintains consultative status with the United Nations **Economic and Social Council (ECOSOC)** and with other agencies. Address: 5 chemin du Pommier, CP 330, CH-1218 Grand-Saconnex, Geneva, Switzerland. Website: www.ipu.org.

ISLAMIC RELIEF. Founded in 1984 by Dr. Hany El Banna, Islamic Relief is an independent nongovernmental organization (NGO) dedicated to provision of humanitarian and development assistance to people of all races and religions, especially among the world's poorest populations. It has consultative status with the United Nations **Economic and Social Council (ECOSOC)**. Its work began first in dealing with the **famine** situation in Ethiopia and other African countries, and it has since expanded widely to other parts of the world where people are facing emergencies, or where **poverty** is daunting. Its projects supporting emergency needs, and **health**, **education**, and **housing** assistance are undertaken in 20 countries in Africa, Asia, Europe, and the Middle East. It has field offices in 13 of these countries and carries out projects through national partners in the other seven. It has extensive programs in support of orphaned children. Address: 19 Rea Street South, Birmingham B5 6LB, UK. Website: www.islamic-relief.com.

– J –

JEFFERSON, THOMAS (1743–1824). Thomas Jefferson, first secretary of state and third president of the United States, was born in Virginia on 13 April 1743. Jefferson was raised on a plantation near the frontier and entered the College of William and Mary. He soon became a member of a small intellectual group consisting of William Small, George Wythe, and its leader, the lieutenant governor of Virginia, Francis Fauquier. Dr. Small introduced Jefferson to the world of the Enlightenment, while Wythe became his instructor of law. Jefferson was admitted to the bar in 1767.

Jefferson served as a delegate from Virginia to the continental congresses called to protest British laws and decrees. His first important essay, *A Summary View of the Rights of British America* (1774) denied the power of parliament over the colonies and articulated the original argument that the American colonists "possessed a right . . . of departing from the country in which chance, not choice, has placed them, of going in quest of new habitations, and of their establishing new societies, under such laws and regulations as to them shall seem most likely to promote public happiness." He argued that the first colonists, by immigrating to North America, had dissolved their allegiance to Britain by organizing themselves as separate governments. Jefferson attempted unsuccessfully to place this argument in the U.S. **Declaration of Independence**.

Jefferson worked as a member of the Virginia legislature and as governor in the late 1770s and early 1780s to abolish any trace of aristocracy and to build the basis for representative government. He reformed **property** laws, championed **freedom of religion** and the disestablishment of the Church of England, sought reform of the penal code, and sought to establish a publicly funded system of **education**. Jefferson also promoted the gradual emancipation of slaves and prohibition of the importation of slaves.

Jefferson served as U.S. envoy and minister to France in 1784–1785 and subsequently joined George Washington's cabinet as secretary of state for a stormy term of office until his resignation in 1793. In 1796, he was elected vice president and joined with James Madison in the formation of a new political party, the Democratic-Republican Party, which he rode to the presidency in 1800. His conciliatory policies won him a second, less successful, term. He lived out his retirement from national office pursuing wide-ranging intellectual interests and founding the University of Virginia. He died on the fiftieth anniversary of the Declaration of Independence on 4 July 1826.

Jefferson's importance to human rights lies in his defense of representative government and in his ideas on the sanctity of the individual in society. Jefferson accepted the concepts of **natural law** and natural rights. People, in his view, had a **right to life**, liberty, and the pursuit of happiness because of their fundamental **equality** and in their moral capacity to judge right from wrong. Government existed to increase the happiness of its people and, failing to do this, the people could change or abolish the government. He feared that powerful government was the single greatest threat to individual liberty. Liberty was best guaranteed by limited and constitutional government. He was a strong advocate of the **Bill of Rights** and state's rights. Although he called for limited government, he also believed that only an educated citizenry could act responsibly in political life, especially in representative governments. He therefore advocated the availability of free public education.

Finally, Jefferson was convinced that people needed to be motivated by tolerance to ensure the success of representative government. This tolerance had to be exhibited in both religious and political matters. He promoted tolerance of both change and diversity, while recognizing the imperfections of human social life. Still, if change was inevitable, government needed to be representative and flexible to the considered judgment of the people. Jefferson was in this sense fully a democrat.

JOHN XXIII. Angelo Guiseppe Roncalli was born in the small village of Sott il Monte, Italy, on 25 November 1881 of peasant parents. He decided at an early age to become a priest and entered the seminary at Bergamo when he was 11 years old and was ordained a priest in 1904. During World War II, Archbishop Roncalli helped save thousands of Jewish people in occupied Europe and facilitated their journey to Palestine. He also convinced Kemal Ataturk, the president of Turkey, to allow a shipload of Jewish children to be sent to another neutral country instead of being sent back to Germany as its government demanded. In 1941 Roncalli arranged the shipment of Allied wheat across enemy lines to help save Greece from starvation.

Pope Pius XII appointed Roncalli apostolic nuncio to France in 1944. He also was the Vatican observer to the **United Nations Educational, Scientific, and Cultural Organization (UNESCO)** from 1946 to 1953. Pius XII named Roncalli a cardinal and in 1953 appointed him patriarch of Venice, where he very much enjoyed his pastoral duties and soon became a beloved Venetian institution. Roncalli was elected pope in the conclave of 1958. As Pope John XXIII,

Roncalli showed his independence quickly by increasing the size of the College of Cardinals and including many more non-Italian representatives.

The most important act of Pope John's papacy was his calling of the Second Vatican Council, which opened on 11 October 1962 and allowed its members unprecedented freedom of debate. The pope charged them to discover ways to relate the faith to the modern world and to work for Christian unity.

Pope John XXIII wrote five major encyclicals, the two most important being *Mater et Magistra* (May 1961) and *Pacem in Terris* (April 1963). *Mater et Magistra* commemorated the seventieth anniversary of Pope Leo XIII's *Rerum Novarum* by calling for economic activity to be governed by charity and justice and for a juridical order that ensures economic actions to be "in conformity with the common good." Further, John XXIII invoked the principle of **subsidiarity**—leaving decision making to the lowest level of society that works best for the common good. In addition, he called for taxes, **social security**, and public services, which would improve countries' economies and emphasized the necessity of international cooperation. Finally, he called for the strengthening of social relationships and emphasized "the cardinal point" of the social thinking of the Church: "individual men are necessarily the foundation, cause, and end of all social institutions."

In *Pacem in Terris*, the pope said that the world was in a new historical moment marked by "the conviction that all men are equal by reasons of the natural dignity." This reflected a truly global community that must be dedicated to the protection and advancement of basic human rights. These rights emanated from norms transcending any government and reflected peoples' reason and free will. These rights included life, religious liberty, association, and cultural, economic, and social goods, including **education**. Pope John XXIII was not able to see the work of the Second Vatican Council to completion. He died on 3 June 1963.

JOHN PAUL II (1920–2005). Karol Jozef Wojtyla was born in Wadowice, Poland, on 18 May 1920. The death of his parents and siblings left him alone to face life in Poland under Nazi occupation in 1941, during which he took part in many different underground religious, theatrical, and university activities. In October 1942, he entered an underground seminary and was ordained a priest in 1946. Wojtyla became auxiliary Bishop of Krakow in July 1958 and Archbishop of Krakow in December 1963. He participated in the Second Vatican Council, where he spoke on religious liberty, among other subjects. Pope Paul VI named him a cardinal on 29 May 1967. He took part in the papal conclave that elected John Paul I in August 1978, but the new pope died shortly thereafter and Cardinal Wojtyla was then elected pope on 16 October 1978, taking the name John Paul II.

Human rights were at the core of John Paul II's pontificate from the beginning. In his first encyclical, *Redemptor Hominus* (4 March 1979), he supported the **United Nations (UN)** and the **Universal Declaration of Human Rights**. He emphasized that the state, as a political community, consists of its people who are **sovereign**. Power can only be legitimate if it respects "the objective and inviolable rights of man," including the right to religious freedom and freedom of conscience. Addressing the **United Nations General Assembly** on 2 October 1979, he pleaded for human rights to remain the basic core of the UN activity. In his encyclical *Laborem Exercens* (September 1981), the pope continued the Catholic Church's teachings on **work** as a basis of human life and a source of human dignity. He warned that labor cannot be viewed as merely a factor of production but that it supports human persons who should be permitted to make work a calling that can enrich their lives. Specifically, he called for just benefits, labor-management relations, **education**, job training, child welfare, and the use of skills of immigrants and disabled people.

Although many factors prompted the collapse of the communist world in 1989, many experts believe that John Paul II's pontificate and his visits to Poland precipitated the beginning of the end of communism in Eastern Europe. He adroitly assisted the peaceful transformation to a noncommunist government by keeping consistent pressure on the communist authorities and by his counseling of nonviolence to those who opposed them.

In May 1981, the pope was wounded in an assassination attempt by a Turkish terrorist. His travels were subsequently curtailed but he continued writing a number of human rights–related documents. In December 1987 he issued *Sollicitudo Rei Socialis* to provide a positive vision for people who are faced with the appalling problems of underdevelopment, and to remind everyone that development should not be viewed solely in material terms. In *Centesimus Annus* (May 1991), issued to commemorate the centenary of Pope Leo XIII's *Rerum Novarum*, John Paul II rejected utilitarianism as a guide for societies, suggesting instead that rights permit us to fulfill our duties. He also rejected socialism since in it "the individual is completely subordinated to the functioning of the socio-economic mechanism." He endorsed a market economy conjoined to a representative polity and based on an ethical culture limiting the actions of both. In *Veritatis Splendor* (August 1993), he again spoke of human freedom and its connection to moral duty. In *Evangelium Vitae* (May 1995), he outlined steps to organize a "new culture of life" in the face of increasing threats to life. The pope also condemned **poverty**, malnutrition, hunger, war, capital punishment, and the arms and drug trade so common in the mid-1990s. As part of the Vatican's participation in the Fourth World Conference on **Women**, John Paul issued his *Letter to Women* on 29 June 1995, calling for an end to discrimination against women and urging the need for "real **equality**." In his *Letter to Families*, he emphasized the importance of the **family** as the basis of human society. In a series of famous "remembrances," in particular a remembrance on the **Holocaust**, he reflected on the past sins of individuals in the Church, seeking purification and forgiveness.

John Paul II continued a vigorous schedule of writing and pastoral visits right up until the final months of his life. Always mindful of the needs of the poor, he called upon Western nations to forgive the huge accumulated debt of poor countries, an appeal that governments began seriously to entertain only a few months after his death in 2005. In a series of Youth Conferences, he gathered young people from throughout the world in the largest gatherings known to human history, even in Paris at the heart of Europe's secular project. The huge upwelling of popular devotion on the occasion of his death on 2 April 2005 was a further testimony to the impact he had made in the 20th century, not only as one of the chief players in the collapse of international communism but also as a voice for the moral and spiritual basis of human dignity during the bloodiest century in human history. Millions paid their last respects to a man who, despite obvious physical suffering, continued to work intensely for the good of his fellow man.

– K –

KHARTOUM DECLARATION. The Khartoum Declaration (UN Doc. A/43/430) was made at the conclusion of the International Conference on the Human Dimension of Africa's Economic Recovery and Development in March 1988, as part of the **United Nations (UN)** Program of Action for African Economic Recovery and Development (UNPAAERD) in the wake of the **famine** and development emergencies that wracked the continent during the early to middle 1980s. The declaration noted that the human dimension of development in Africa had deteriorated dramatically during the decade. It noted that an urban bias had arisen in economic policy. This together with rapid population growth and rampant civil violence and instability had contributed to this deterioration. The declaration criticized the structural adjustment programs being implemented by the **World Bank**, the International Monetary Fund (IMF), and the donor community as contributing to the decline of essential services to people. It noted that, although such programs may be necessary for economic recovery, they take a large human toll in the interim. Such programs, it urged, need to include mechanisms for meeting the basic needs of the most seriously affected and vulnerable groups in society, including the disabled, **refugees**, and displaced persons. It called for urgent international action by governments, international agencies, and nongovernmental organizations (NGOs) to meet the humanitarian needs of millions of Africans. Substantial international assistance has since been delivered, but **poverty** remains a problem in many parts of Africa, especially those still torn by civil conflict.

KING, MARTIN LUTHER (1929–1968). U.S. clergyman and civil rights leader, Dr. King was born on 15 January 1929 in Atlanta, Georgia. He graduated from Morehouse College, Atlanta, in 1948 and took a bachelor of divinity from Crozer Theological Seminary in 1951. He received his PhD in theology from Boston University in 1955. King became prominent in the United States in 1956 when he successfully led a boycott of the public buses in Montgomery, Alabama, to abolish segregation on the public transportation system. On 13 November 1956, the U.S. Supreme Court declared Montgomery's bus segregation unconstitutional and its order to desegregate was presented to Montgomery officials on 20 December 1956.

To create a base of operation, King organized the Southern Christian Leadership Conference (SCLC). To raise money for the SCLC, to fight Southern segregation, and to preach his message of nonviolent direct action, he spoke throughout the country during the mid- and late 1950s and early 1960s.

An important influence on King's life and thought were the works of Reinhold Niebuhr, especially *Moral Man and Immoral Society* (1932). In this book, Niebuhr argued that the way to break out of the "endless cycle of social conflict" was through nonviolent resistance. This included a "spiritual discipline against resentment," which differentiated "between the evils of a social system . . . and the individuals who are involved in it," avoidance of claims of moral superiority, and recognition of the humanity of adversaries, which united people of differing interests. King came to believe that only in this way could blacks in the American South be truly emancipated.

King built the civil rights movement on the indigenous black community institutions of the South and preached the need for African Americans to confront segregationist adversaries as equals and to challenge segregation through nonviolent direct action: boycotts, sit-ins, civil disobedience to segregation law, marches, and acquisition of real voting rights. He constantly appealed to the white community for support on the basis of common regionalism, religion, or **nationality**.

King played a major role in the March on Washington in 1963 and his speech at the Lincoln Memorial transformed the civil rights movement into a national movement. His antisegregation and voting rights campaigns in Birmingham and Selma, Alabama, were instrumental to the passage of the Civil Rights Act of 1964 and the Voting Rights Act of 1965. He traveled to Chicago to work against school and housing segregation in 1966. He publicly opposed the Vietnam War in 1967. Later that year, King launched a poor people's campaign that attempted to forge an interracial coalition of blacks, Mexican Americans, Native Americans, and Puerto Ricans.

King received the Nobel Peace Prize in 1964 for his nonviolent direct action on behalf of racial **equality**. He wrote *Stride toward Freedom* (1958), *Strength to Love* (1963), *Why We Can't Wait* (1964), and

Where Do We Go from Here: Chaos or Community? (1967). King, one of the greatest apostles of nonviolence, was assassinated on 4 April 1968 in Memphis, Tennessee.

– L –

LAWYERS COMMITTEE FOR HUMAN RIGHTS. *See* HUMAN RIGHTS FIRST (HRF).

LAWYERS WITHOUT BORDERS. Founded in January 2000, this relatively young nongovernmental organization (NGO) provides a variety of services aimed at promotion of human rights. It mobilizes volunteer lawyers from around the world to offer pro bono services to other NGOs, including human rights advocacy groups. It promotes programs for the strengthening of the rule of law, promotes human rights training programs for legal professionals, and advances programs to enhance political stability in countries emerging from civil conflict. Currently, its work focuses on countries of Africa and the Middle East. It has consultative status with the United Nations **Economic and Social Council (ECOSOC)**. Address: 330 Main Street, Hartford, CT 06106, USA. Website: www.lwob.org. *See also* HUMAN RIGHTS FIRST (HRF).

LEAGUE OF NATIONS. Founded after the Paris Peace Conference of 1919, the League of Nations was the first nearly universal organization established by modern governments, partly based on principles enunciated by U.S. President Woodrow Wilson. Although the United States did not become a member, many other large powers and other countries did. Its principal function was to introduce collective security mechanisms in international relations to regulate the use of force. International efforts to maintain peace and security among nations clearly had human rights implications, though these were perhaps secondary. Still, the League of Nations soon found itself having to cope explicitly with both humanitarian and human rights issues, especially in dealing with the consequences of the collapse and reorganization of the Ottoman Empire and the implications of the Bolshevik Revolution in Russia.

Vast numbers of people were displaced by the Balkan Wars and World War I in the former territories of the Ottoman Empire and in Central and Eastern Europe. In numerous treaties between the Allied powers and the governments of Eastern Europe, such as Austria, Bulgaria, Czechoslovakia, Greece, Hungary, Poland, Romania, Turkey, and Yugoslavia, the latter countries agreed to respect the rights of **minorities** within their territories. Other countries were later admitted to the League of Nations on the condition that they would promise to respect the rights of religious, ethnic, and linguistic minorities. The League Council took note of such promises made by Albania, the Baltic States, and Iraq, thus acknowledging that the international community took an interest in the preservation of human rights for minority populations.

But apart from the minorities problem within countries, there was a related humanitarian problem of increasingly major scope concerning **refugees** fleeing from persecution in their homelands. Such people often lacked protection or legal documentation, and they presented a growing problem to the states of Europe. Private agencies bore the brunt in the immediate aftermath of World War I, in terms of tending to the humanitarian needs of these displaced peoples. From Russia alone, some 1.5 million people had fled, fearing persecution by the Bolshevik government, which had seized control of the government after the withdrawal of Russia from the war. The private agencies were overwhelmed by the vast scale of the need, and eventually, led by the **International Committee of the Red Cross (ICRC)**, they appealed to the League Council for a coordinated international response. The League reacted by creating an Office of the High Commissioner for Russian Refugees. Fridtjof Nansen was selected as the first high commissioner. His work was conceived as being primarily coordinative in nature. The office was to have a temporary duration and it would not have significant operational or financial responsibilities. These were to be left to the private charities and agencies. The high commissioner's role would be limited to legal protection and coordination of assistance activities.

Almost immediately, however, the League Council found it necessary to broaden the scope of Nansen's office beyond that of the Russian refugee situation. Greek and Armenian refugees in Turkey as well as Bulgarian, Assyrian, Assyro-Chaldean, and other refugees gradually fell under the orbit of Nansen's office, which, though heavily involved in the early years in coordinating humanitarian assistance to the Russian **famine**, gradually concentrated on the political and legal aspects of refugee protection. It left assistance activities to governments, private agencies, and such international bodies as the **International Labour Organization (ILO)**, which was active in promoting settlement and **work** opportunities for refugees consistent with its larger purpose of promoting fair and human conditions of labor for men, **women**, and children, itself a human rights focus of considerable importance.

The League of Nations reorganized and reconstituted its humanitarian operations concerning refugee populations several times. The Office of the High Commissioner was terminated in 1929. It was succeeded by the Nansen International Office for Refugees, which in turn ceased functioning in 1938. Faced with growing Jewish immigration from Germany, the League established a separate and autonomous body, the High Commissioner for Refugees Coming from Germany. This body and the Nansen Office were then later consolidated in 1939 into the High Commissioner of the League of Nations, but the threat of renewed war hung over Europe, and most of the League's humanitarian efforts from that time on were overshadowed and frustrated by the subsequent upheaval wrought by war.

Still, in the late 1930s toward the end of the League's existence, the Bruce Report (so-named after Stanley Bruce of Australia, who chaired a committee on the reorganization of the League) was published, in which it was urged that the economic, social, cultural, and humanitarian functions of the League should be consolidated into a separate agency or agencies, rather than being constantly subject to the simultaneous work of the council and the assembly. This report, in turn, served as the basis for the creation of the United Nations **Economic and Social Council (ECOSOC)**, which was later granted primary coordinating authority for such humanitarian and human rights issues. In addition, the League's mandate system, which had been created with a view toward encouraging the **self-determination** and eventual independence of peoples who had been under the colonial administration of Axis powers prior to World War I, served as the model for the **Trusteeship Council** of the United Nations. Thus, the League, in several important respects, broke new ground in dealing with human rights issues, and it paved the way for its successor, the **United Nations (UN)**, to undertake more ambitious strides in the protection of human rights and the promotion of self-determination.

LEAGUE OF RED CROSS AND RED CRESCENT SOCIETIES (LICROSS). *See* INTERNATIONAL FEDERATION OF RED CROSS AND RED CRESCENT SOCIETIES (IFRC).

LUTHERAN WORLD FEDERATION (LWF). LWF is the coordinating body of national Lutheran Church humanitarian organizations. Headquartered in Geneva, it provides a means for immediate contact with the wide international agency relief community located there. Its Office for International Affairs and Human Rights focuses its advocacy and program efforts in three main areas, including international advocacy, peacemaking and reconciliation, and capacity building. Its advocacy of human rights and humanitarian welfare focuses both on interaction with **United Nations (UN)** agencies and nongovernmental bodies centered in Geneva and through the frequent public statements and letters on issues of human rights, humanitarian need, and basic justice. LWF studies, conducts seminars, and documents matters related to these areas, publishing an e-mail bulletin to disseminate human rights information. In the arena of peacemaking and reconciliation, LWF has been especially active in promoting interfaith action for peace in Africa, and in reducing the incidence of violence against **women**. In the area of capacity building, LWF sponsors human rights training workshops and offers financial support to local churches to develop such training programs. In the area of humanitarian assistance, LWF provides assistance to **refugees** and promotes refugee settlement and repatriation programs, in addition to emergency assistance programs and development-related activities. Its national affiliates are engaged in a wide variety of community development, economic development, social welfare, vocational rehabilitation, and administrative services. Address: 150 route de Ferney (P.O. Box 2100), CH-1211 Geneva 2, Switzerland. Website: www .lutheranworld.org.

LUTHULI, ALBERT JOHN (ca. 1898–1967). Chief Albert John Luthuli was born in 1898 in Northern Rhodesia, now Zimbabwe, to

John Luthuli, an African Christian missionary from an elective chieftain family, and Mtonya Gumede, both of Zulu heritage. Luthuli's father died when he was about six months old and as a child his mother sent him to live with his uncle Martin in Groutville, Natal, the hometown of the Luthuli family.

After finishing his studies at Adams College in **education**, Luthuli taught there for the next 15 years, until 1935. During this time, Luthuli became secretary and then president of the African Teachers' Association. Luthuli organized the Zulu Language and Cultural Society as an auxiliary to the association to help preserve Zulu culture, and deepened and broadened his Christian faith. In late 1935, Luthuli was elected chief in Groutville and took his position in the beginning of 1936. He helped revive the Groutville Cane Grower's Association and later helped establish the Natal and Zululand Bantu Cane Growers' Association, which improved the economic well-being of sugar growers in the region. In 1938, Luthuli was a delegate to the International Missionary Conference in Madras, India, and in 1948 he went on a lecture tour to the United States on Christian missions in Africa.

Luthuli joined the African National Congress (ANC) in 1945 and supported its Programme of Action, adopted in 1949, which called for nonviolent civil disobedience against the **apartheid** system. Luthuli was elected president of the Natal ANC in 1951 and helped organize the national ANC's Defiance Campaign, a campaign of civil disobedience against apartheid laws, in 1952. The Native Affairs Department of the South African government removed Luthuli as chief after he refused its request to resign from the ANC. In December 1952, Luthuli was elected president of the ANC at its national conference, serving for 15 years, the longest presidency in ANC history.

Luthuli supported the Freedom Charter, which was endorsed by the ANC in April 1956. The charter called for universal suffrage, **equality** before the law, and fundamental liberties such as **freedom of religion**, **freedom of assembly**, and **freedom of speech**, as well as **privacy**, and an end to all laws of apartheid. Luthuli, along with **Nelson Mandela** and others, were arrested on 5 December 1956 on the charge of high treason based on the Defiance Campaign and the Freedom Charter. The treason charges against Luthuli were dropped but he was banned for five years in June 1959.

Although the banning order made it difficult for Luthuli to maintain contact with members of the ANC, his burning of his passbook on 26 March 1960, as part of an ANC protest against the Sharpeville massacre, was photographed and sent throughout the country. Luthuli also defended Mandela's actions at the time of the latter's conviction and life sentence in June 1964. In spite of the banning order prohibiting travel, the government allowed Luthuli to accept in person the Nobel Peace Prize in 1961.

Luthuli, in poor health and with deteriorating eyesight, was hit by a train and killed in Stanger, South Africa, on 21 July 1967. While some viewed him as merely a figurehead, Mandela always regarded Luthuli as his leader and a hero of the antiapartheid movement.

– M –

MAATHAI, WANGARI (1940–). The first African woman to win the Nobel Peace Prize, Wangari Muta Maathai was born in Nyeri, Kenya, in 1940 to a peasant family. She studied in the United States before returning home to earn her PhD in veterinary medicine from the University of Nairobi, where she was appointed professor for veterinary anatomy. She joined the National Council of Women of Kenya in 1976 and founded the Green Belt Movement in 1977. The movement was designed to aid poor, rural **women** in Kenya through a sustained tree-planting program, thus addressing an environmental concern while advancing the rights and welfare of women. Maathai sees a close relationship between environmental degradation and malnutrition, and between mismanagement of natural resources and the problems of **poverty** and unemployment. The programs she helped initiate increased firewood supplies for the poor and gave women gainful employment, while encouraging reforestation.

As a human rights activist, Maathai has been arrested, beaten, and even hospitalized for injuries incurred during various protests of government policy. Her dedication and determination have won many plaudits and accolades, including most notably the Nobel Peace Prize. She was elected to Kenyan parliament in 2002 and after President Daniel arap Moi resigned. She was elevated to assistant minister of Environment, Natural Resources, and Wildlife in 2003. In

March 2005, she was elected the first president of the Economic, Social, and Cultural Council of the **African Union (AU)**.

MAGNA CARTA. Also known as the Great Charter, the Magna Carta is considered one of the essential components of the English Constitution. Presented to King John at Runnymede in 1215 by noblemen who sought to defend their rights against widening monarchical powers, the Magna Carta asserted the rights of nobles, the clergy, and citizens. It granted freedom to the Church in England, reaffirmed the liberties of citizens of London, regulated monarchical authority concerning taxation, and called upon the king to acknowledge an expanded conception of justice, which should apply to all in such matters as imprisonment and deprivation of **property**. The notion of due process and access to a jury of peers was asserted in the lengthy bill of particulars. Implicit in the documents are the inchoate right to a trial by jury, the conception of the right of habeas corpus, and the conception of freedom from arbitrary taxation. The Magna Carta remains for all time a symbol of a people standing up against abusive actions by a sovereign and asserting principles of justice.

MANDELA, NELSON (1918–). Rolihlahla Nelson Dalibhunga Mandela was born on 18 July 1918 at Mbhashe in the Umtata district in the Transkei, South Africa. In 1942 Mandela received a bachelor's degree and studied law at Witwatersrand University. In 1944 he joined the African National Congress (ANC) and along with others established the ANC Youth League. Mandela was elected secretary of the league in 1947, and later its president.

Mandela was appointed volunteer in chief to oversee a Defiance of Unjust Laws Campaign organized by the ANC and the Indian Congress in 1952 to protest the **apartheid** laws. He was arrested, jailed, and later charged under the Suppression of Communism Act. Although released from jail, Mandela and 52 other people were banned from all meetings and rallies, and were not allowed to leave Johannesburg. In 1954, in the face of government repression, he reorganized the ANC into small, street-level cells.

In March 1960, police fired into a crowd of peaceful demonstrators, killing 69 and wounding 180. This Sharpeville massacre led to a two-week-long strike in the Western Cape. With the Pan Africanist-Congress

(PAC) in control of two townships, the government instituted a state of emergency and banned the ANC and the PAC.

In 1962, Mandela traveled widely outside the country and met numerous African dignitaries. On his return to South Africa, he was arrested and sentenced to five years imprisonment for traveling outside the country without a passport and for inciting strikes. The government banned all meetings relating to Mandela's situation. In October 1963 Mandela and others were charged with sabotage and with attempting revolution. In June 1964, Mandela was found guilty of sabotage and given a life sentence.

The Release Mandela campaign began in 1980. Prime Minister P. W. Botha later offered Mandela a conditional release, which he refused. Soon all the people connected with Mandela were released from prison and in December 1989 Mandela met with the new state President F. W. de Klerk, arguing that the ANC should be legalized, the state of emergency lifted, political prisoners released, and exiles allowed to return. On 2 February 1990, de Klerk announced the lifting of the bans on the ANC, PAC, and 31 other illegal organizations, the release of nonviolent political prisoners, and the end of many restrictions of the state of emergency. Mandela was released from prison on 11 February 1990.

Mandela refused to call for the end of economic sanctions until apartheid was completely dismantled and a transition government was established. In August 1990 the ANC agreed to suspend armed struggle while the government promised the release of more political prisoners and the review of its Internal Security Act. Mandela worked throughout 1990 and 1991 to end the violence between the ANC and the Inkatha Party, a Zulu tribe-based rival. In July 1991, the ANC held its first annual conference in South Africa since 1960 and elected Mandela president. On 17 March 1992, the voters in an all-white referendum supported de Klerk's reform policy. In February 1993, the ANC and the government announced agreement to a five-year national unity government, a proportional multiparty cabinet, and an executive council. For their efforts at peaceful reform, Mandela and de Klerk were awarded the Nobel Peace Prize in 1993.

The first one-person, one-vote election allowing blacks to vote took place in April 1994 and Mandela was elected president. As president, Mandela's priorities were to improve the economic well-being of South Africans, aid racial reconciliation and healing, and established a permanent democratic constitution. President Mandela implemented his Reconstruction and Development Plan immediately on taking office. This included a public works program, a plan for residential electrification, and free medial care in government hospitals and clinics for both pregnant **women** and for children up to five years of age. On 19 July 1995, President Mandela signed the Promotion of National Unity and Reconciliation Act, which established the **Truth and Reconciliation Commission (TRC)**, chaired by Archbishop **Desmond Tutu**. It held 140 hearings, took 22,000 victim statements, received more than 7,000 applications for **amnesty**, and published a final report in October 1998.

The Constitutional Assembly adopted a new constitution for the country on 8 May 1996 and it was certified by the new Constitutional Court and signed into law in December of the same year. The new constitution included a bill of rights, which guaranteed rights to adequate **education**, **food**, **health** care, including emergency medical treatment, **housing**, **social security**, and water. Every worker has a right to form and join a trade union and to strike. Further, it is unconstitutional to discriminate against anyone on account of race, gender, sex, pregnancy, marital status, ethnic or social origin, color, sexual orientation, age, disability, religion, conscience, belief, culture, language, or birth. All people in the country have a right to equal protection of the law, to bodily and psychological integrity, to **freedom of religion**, **freedom of expression**, and the freedom and security of the person, including protection from detention without trial, from deprivation of freedom without just cause, and freedom from **torture** and cruel, degrading, and inhuman punishment.

In August 1997, Mandela announced that he would not serve another term as president of the ANC and in December 1999 Thabo Mbeki was elected to succeed him. Throughout his career, Nelson Mandela has viewed his mission as one of reconciliation, building trust and confidence, bridging the racial divide, and building a multiracial democratic South Africa. *See also* LUTHULI, ALBERT JOHN (ca. 1898–1967); TRUTH COMMISSIONS.

MAP INTERNATIONAL. This U.S.-based private agency was founded in 1954 for the purpose of distributing medical supplies to

Christian medical institutions located overseas or engaged in emergency assistance activities. MAP International works with more than 300 partners throughout the world, providing free medicines. In a given year, MAP medical and **health** supply donations amount to about $200 million. In addition, it promotes community development activities aimed not only at providing health services and nutrition but also **family** planning, agricultural productivity, and water resource development. It sponsors fellowships for medical students to work at missions to address both emergency aid and development-related needs of local populations. It engages in long-term or short-term activities in 115 countries, providing rapid response to humanitarian emergencies, identifying local community health promoters to implement total health programs, and mobilizing local churches to promote HIV/AIDS **education**, prevention, control, and care. Address: 2200 Glynco Parkway, P.O. Box 50, Brunswick, GA 31520, USA. See www.interaction.org, member profiles. Website: www.map .org. *See also* INTERACTION.

MÉDECINS SANS FRONTIÈRES/DOCTORS WITHOUT BORDERS (MSF). MSF was founded in 1971 to provide medical aid in humanitarian emergencies throughout the world. A second major goal of the organization is to engage in public advocacy in favor of the populations it assists, drawing attention to and raising awareness of the plight of the populations it serves. Its work currently extends to 68 countries in Africa, Asia, the Americas, and Europe. Originating in France, this well-known nongovernmental organization (NGO) maintains **health**-related programs throughout the world in both emergency assistance and long-term development settings. Its humanitarian work includes the fielding of surgical teams, controlling the spread of epidemics, establishing health facilities of all varieties, training rural health personnel, mitigating malnutrition, addressing mental health needs, and providing for the special needs of the handicapped. A sample of its recent work includes the deployment of emergency medical teams to the earthquake in Pakistan that killed tens of thousands, providing nutritional aid to children in Niger, offering medical assistance in the slums of Haiti, and reaching thousands of displaced persons in the Ituri region of the Democratic Republic of the Congo, where documented mass rape campaigns have occurred. MSF personnel work in some of the most remote and dangerous areas of the world to bring medical relief and health assistance to distressed populations. Major national MSF offices exist in major donor countries such as Australia, France, Germany, Japan, the United Kingdom, the United States, among others, and its international headquarters are now located in Geneva, Switzerland. MSF International Office Address: Rue de Lausanne 78, CP 116-1211 Geneva 21, Switzerland. Website: www.msf.org.

MIGRANTS RIGHTS INTERNATIONAL (MRI). MRI came into existence in 1994 as a result of the **International Conference on Population and Development** in Cairo, where it began as the International Migrants Watch Committee. It consists of experts in migration and migrants' rights, along with practitioners engaged in work with migrants, including those in a wide variety of nongovernmental organizations (NGOs) such as trade unions, churches, legal organizations, and human rights agencies in all parts of the world. Its goals include promotion of migrants' rights, universal ratification of the **International Convention on the Protection of the Rights of All Migrant Workers and Members of Their Families**, facilitating the formation and work of migrant associations, and monitoring trends affecting the welfare of migrants. Address: C.P. 135 route des Morillons, 1211 Geneva, Switzerland. Website: www.migrantswatch.org. *See also* COMMITTEE ON MIGRANT WORKERS (CMW); DECLARATION ON THE HUMAN RIGHTS OF INDIVIDUALS WHO ARE NOT NATIONALS OF THE COUNTRY IN WHICH THEY LIVE.

MILLENNIUM DEVELOPMENT GOALS. The **United Nations (UN)** hosted a special Millennium Summit in New York in September 2000, at which representatives of governments discussed the future of the world in the third millennium, as well as the UN's role in addressing the pressing global needs. In the Millennium Declaration produced by the summit, human rights and humanitarian concerns loomed large. The values placed at the center of international activity included **freedom**, **equality**, **solidarity**, and tolerance, all of which have significance for human rights and humane action. Peace and security were presented in larger terms than initially conceived in the **United Nations Charter** as requiring concerted action against

terrorism, drug trafficking, transnational crime, proliferation of weapons of mass destruction, and illicit trafficking in small arms. In the realm of development the pressing concerns of **poverty** eradication, of basic **health** and **education**, and for meaningful **work** were identified. Increased globalization of the economy was seen as both an opportunity to eradicate poverty and as a challenge to ensure that the needs of least developed countries did not get lost in the increasingly open system of international trade and finance.

The declaration included a section devoted specifically to human rights, democracy, and good governance. It acknowledged and reaffirmed the need to fully respect and uphold the **Universal Declaration of Human Rights**. It called for wider practices of democracy and respect for minority rights, the protection of **women** from violence and discrimination, the protection of migrants, and the freedom of information. Another section of the declaration called for protection of the vulnerable, especially those engulfed by complex emergencies, such as **refugees** and displaced persons. Special attention was given to the need for protection of children from trafficking, from impressments into armed conflicts, and from prostitution and pornography. The declaration also included goals for protection of the environment. For a text of the Millennium Declaration, see the *UN Chronicle*, vol. 27, no. 3, pp. 42–47.

MINORITIES. One of the earliest assertions of human rights in the 20th century, apart from the development of the laws of war and **war crimes**, was the inclusion of clauses protecting minorities in a number of Eastern European states and former parts of the Ottoman Empire. Persecution of religious, ethnic, and linguistic minorities in the late 19th and early 20th centuries had unleashed massive flows of populations across changing national boundaries. The Balkan Wars that preceded World War I had been especially disruptive in this regard. Thus, after World War I, the Allied Powers, cognizant of the underlying problems facing minorities, concluded treaties with Austria, Bulgaria, Czechoslovakia, Greece, Hungary, Romania, Turkey, and Yugoslavia, in which just and equal treatment of minority groups was guaranteed, at least by law. Later, other states that sought entry into the **League of Nations** (Albania, the Baltic States, and Iraq) were placed under similar restrictions in regard to their treatment of minority populations.

Presumably, each state acknowledged that protection of minorities was both an international responsibility and a fundamental duty reflected in their domestic law. But most of the countries affected by these minorities treaties and clauses came in time to resent them as an intrusion on their national **sovereignty**. In a number of advisory opinions, the **Permanent Court of International Justice (PCIJ)** upheld the obligations governments had incurred toward minority populations, including prohibition of both *de jure* and *de facto* discrimination against them. Gaining national compliance with the minorities treaties and clauses, however, was increasingly problematical.

After World War II, with some limited exceptions, efforts to protect minorities by enforced treaties of peace were abandoned, although protection of minority rights has continued to be prominently discussed by **United Nations (UN)** human rights bodies. The **Universal Declaration of Human Rights** does not assert the rights of minorities. However, in other human rights instruments, such as the **International Covenant on Civil and Political Rights**, the **Convention on the Prevention and Punishment of the Crime of Genocide**, and the **Convention on the Elimination of All Forms of Racial Discrimination**, among others, a concern for protecting minority rights has been shown. The United Nations **Commission on Human Rights (CHR)** maintains a Subcommission on Prevention of Discrimination and Protection of Minorities.

Ongoing problems in Eastern and Central Europe as well as among newly independent republics formerly a part of the Soviet Union highlight the questionable treatment of minorities. Ethnic and linguistic minorities in many parts of Africa and Asia also face considerable hardship and persecution. Many of the most egregious human rights abuses in the world are perpetrated against minority populations. Fair and humane treatment of minorities is part and parcel of the growth of democratic political institutions within nations. The role that the international community should play in preventing or punishing gross violations of the rights of minorities has been, in turn, controversial. Some argue for the sovereign prerogatives of states and the idea of nonintervention. Others argue that intervention to protect citizens from their government's predatory actions is permissible and sometimes necessary. UN-authorized interventions in Iraq (to protect Kurds and Shiites) in the 1990s were justified on human rights grounds, and also on the grounds that these situations represented threats to international peace and security. *See also* ETHNIC CLEANSING; MINORITY RIGHTS GROUP INTERNATIONAL (MRG).

MINORITY RIGHTS GROUP INTERNATIONAL (MRG). MRG has been active in promoting **indigenous rights** and the rights of **women** and **minorities** for more than 30 years. Its advocacy of these rights is pursued at the national, regional, and international levels, including with such bodies as the **African Commission on Human and Peoples' Rights**, the **European Union (EU)**, the **Organization for Security and Cooperation in Europe (OSCE)**, the **World Bank**, and the **United Nations (UN)**, where it enjoys consultative status with the **Economic and Social Council (ECOSOC)**. It offers training for individuals so that they can effectively participate in and raise concerns at the United Nations Group on Minorities annual meetings in Geneva. Its work addresses ethnic, religious, and linguistic minority groups, promoting forums where minority populations can meet with government officials and representatives of majority populations to pursue constructive dialogue. MRG works to promote peaceful resolution to ethnic and religious conflicts and to bring an end to conflicts producing **ethnic cleansing** and **genocide**. MRG also offers concrete programs to promote educational curricula to overcome prejudice, and promote access of minority children to **education**. It seeks to ensure that minority issues are raised in governmental development planning to overcome **poverty** among minorities and indigenous groups. Address: 54 Commercial Street, London E1 6LT, UK. Website: www.minorityrights.org.

MOTT, LUCRETIA (1793–1880). Lucretia Mott was born on 3 January 1793 on Nantucket Island. Her father was a China merchant and sea captain. Both her parents taught her that **women**'s rights was the most important public issue. She taught school briefly and in 1811 married James Mott. The death of her first son prompted an increased interest in religion and she was ordained a Quaker minister in 1827.

Mott boycotted goods produced by slave labor from 1825 to 1863. She attended the meeting at which **William Lloyd Garrison** founded the American Antislavery Society and she herself established the Philadelphia Female Antislavery Society in 1833 and organized the

Antislavery Convention of American Women in 1837. Mott met **Elizabeth Cady Stanton** at the First World Antislavery Convention in London in 1840 and became Stanton's role model.

In July 1848, Mott along with Stanton and three other women decided to hold a convention to discuss women's rights. Mott insisted that the Declaration of Rights and Sentiments include a listing of economic and social injustices under which women suffered. In 1849, in a *Discourse on Women*, she argued that lack of access to **education**, differing wage rates, employment restrictions, and the lack of **political rights** together established female bondage. For Mott, **equality** in the economic realm would lead to equality in all other spheres of a woman's life. Mott did shy away from including a suffrage plank in the declaration, but she supported it in the end.

Mott served as the acknowledged leader of the new women's rights movement and as the equal to male leaders in the abolition movement. She worked throughout the 1850s on behalf of abolition and her home was a sanctuary for runaway slaves. Still, as a pacifist, she was appalled at the great violence of the American Civil War.

Mott helped to establish the Woman Suffrage Association and the National Women Suffrage Association in 1868–1869, and she fought unsuccessfully to avoid a split in the women's suffrage movement. She died on 11 November 1880.

MOVEMENT AND RESIDENCE. Article 13 of the **Universal Declaration of Human Rights** proclaims the right of all persons to "freedom of movement and residence within the borders of each State, and the right to leave any country, including his own, and to return to his country." The **International Covenant on Civil and Political Rights** elaborates on this in Articles 12 and 13. This right is not always acknowledged in state practice, particularly in the cases of forced expulsions and refugee flows. Treatment of legal aliens may also be problematical. The covenant stipulates that legal aliens may not be expelled from their country of residence without due process of law, while the **European Convention on Human Rights** explicitly forbids the collective expulsion of aliens, although under Protocol VI to the convention, aliens, on an individually determined basis, can be expelled provided that this is done through due processes of law for legally acceptable reasons.

– N –

NAIROBI FORWARD-LOOKING STRATEGIES FOR THE AD-VANCEMENT OF WOMEN. This lengthy manifesto, which resulted from the World Conference to Review and Appraise the Achievements of the **United Nations (UN)** Decade for Women, held in Nairobi, Kenya, from 15 to 26 July 1985, listed numerous strategies to achieve progressive **equality** for **women**, to enhance the role of women in development, to ensure that the benefits of development were shared by women, and to promote the role of women in the maintenance of peace. The document addressed the specific needs of women living under repressive regimes; of women living under conditions of drought and **famine**; of migrant women; of elderly, young, abused, and destitute women; of women who are victims of trafficking and involuntary prostitution; of refugee women; and of women with physical and mental disabilities. The document identified both obstacles to the attainment of full women's rights and basic strategies for their attainment, including mechanisms for monitoring women's rights, provision for technical cooperation, training and advisory services through national and international channels, and appointment by governments of women to positions of decision-making prominence. The strategies put forward by the conference were endorsed by the **United Nations General Assembly** at its 40th Session in December 1985.

NATIONALITY. The right of all people to a nationality is affirmed in the **Universal Declaration of Human Rights**. Several aspects of this right are also affirmed in the declaration, including the right to change nationality and the right not to be arbitrarily deprived of nationality. The **International Covenant on Civil and Political Rights** reaffirmed that every child has the right to acquire a nationality. Nationality is normally first acquired at birth, although conflicts of nationality laws can lead to situations in which children are born stateless. Nationality is often synonymous with the acquisition of citizenship, although in some countries it is possible to acquire the country's nationality without having the full **political rights** reserved for citizens. Nationality is acquired first at birth, based either on the principle of the place of birth or of the blood ties to the parent. In some instances, children born to parents of a country that only recognizes the *jus soli*, or place of birth principle, but born in a country that only recognizes the *jus sanguinis*, or parental blood tie principle, may be stateless. This is particularly a problem for **refugees**. The problem of **statelessness** has been dealt with by international conventions, including the **Convention Relating to the Status of Refugees**, the **Convention Relating to the Status of Stateless Persons**, and the **Convention on the Reduction of Statelessness**.

Nationality may also be acquired by a legal process known as naturalization. Immigrants may seek to change their original nationality and adopt that of their new home. Upon marriage, **women** or men may choose to adopt the nationality of their spouse. Historically, women have faced problems in connection with changes in nationality upon marriage. Most states in the early 20th century observed the principle that a woman's nationality automatically changed to that of her husband if her nationality differed from his. The Montevideo Convention of 1933 and later the **Convention on the Nationality of Married Women** of 1957 attempted to reverse this practice to ensure that women had a free and equal opportunity with men to determine their choice of nationality.

NATURAL LAW. In the ancient Roman experience of building an empire, both theoretical and practical questions arose about the origins of law and justice as understood and practiced by divergent peoples and as enforced by their various legal codes. The Romans, pragmatic in their dealings with newly conquered peoples, did not impose Roman law upon them, rather permitting the civil codes and often even the criminal codes of each people to persist. Each city had a *lex civile*, or written civil law. However, as Roman legal scholars and practitioners began to inspect the apparently divergent codes of city law, they began to find underlying universal patterns and principles, which led them to see how the preexisting Stoical notion of a law of nature (*lex naturalae*) or underlying principles of natural justice (*jus naturale*) might explain the common patterns and principles they perceived between and among the *lex civile* of peoples. This gave rise to their notion of a *jus gentium* (rights of nations, or loosely, a law of nations), which in the course of centuries became the basis of the formation of **international law**. Underlying all these manifestations of law, Roman philosophers saw a *jus naturalae* (a natural law rooted in principles of natural justice).

The most sophisticated and systematic treatment on natural law in the Middle Ages is found in the thought of St. Thomas Aquinas, which came under attack in the 14th century with the emergence of nominalism, as expressed in the thought of William of Ockham, who denied the existence of "nature" as real or objective, and who insisted that all terms were merely names invented in the human mind. In this perspective law has no basis in nature, but only exists as a voluntary act of the will of the sovereign who could coerce agreement through the application of power and authority. Law, then, was either rooted in the will of the sovereign or formed by some common agreement. The positivist tendencies of Ockham's thought did not immediately displace the traditional understanding of natural law. Indeed, many great legal minds, including Grotius, who is considered the father of modern international law, continued to accept the idea that law could be rooted in nature as well as in the voluntary acts of sovereigns. However, the triumph of legal positivism in the 19th century led to a depreciation of natural law thinking, at least as traditionally understood.

Generally, three modern schools of thought can be discerned among the many thinkers who have articulated natural law ideas. Two of these schools seek to avoid any theological grounding for natural law, arguing alternatively that the basis for human rights are to be found either in the human mind and or in the natural material/physical order only. Natural law, then, could be grounded in the mind of man and achieved through common agreement. Another school asserted that natural law was grounded in nature itself, a nature whose origins were too obscure to determine or that were assumed to be rooted in entirely physical and material causes, rather than through supernatural agency. A third school of thought argued that the ancient roots of natural law needed to be recovered if the stability of the ethical, moral, and political order of Christendom, which was grounded in the providential and superabundant work of a creating intelligence, was to be attained once again. The modern philosophical understanding of human rights and the assumptions upon which they are logically based remains contentious. Some positivists continue to regard all natural law claims as irrelevant, and the human rights project as an ongoing experiment in unachievable idealism. Many human rights advocates, looking for a way to ground an argument for human rights, seek to root the project in a human-centered or a nature-centered sense of ethics, but the more ancient traditional natural law perspective has won increasing numbers of adherents as well.

NONREFOULEMENT. The principle whereby those granted status as **refugees** are protected from being involuntarily repatriated to their country of **nationality** or origin, where they have a well-founded fear of being persecuted. Rooted in the statute of the **United Nations High Commissioner for Refugees (UNHCR)** and in the **Convention Relating to the Status of Refugees**, this principle is now widely regarded as customary **international law**. The logic for the existence of this protective right is that refugees are effectively cut off from the legal protection of their country of nationality or origin and that they plausibly fear that if returned to the jurisdiction of their government they will be persecuted. Individuals not found to be refugees, of course, are subject to deportation to their country of nationality, but not so with refugees. States are not bound to provide permanent **asylum** to refugees. However, they are forbidden to repatriate them forcibly. States may send refugees to a third state or, without granting permanent asylum, provide temporary haven with the understanding that on the improvement of the situation in their homeland they will return.

NUREMBURG TRIBUNAL. *See* WAR CRIMES.

– O –

OPTIONAL PROTOCOL TO THE INTERNATIONAL COVENANT ON CIVIL AND POLITICAL RIGHTS. In an effort to supplement and strengthen the implementation and compliance measures of the **International Covenant on Civil and Political Rights**, the **United Nations General Assembly** adopted an optional protocol to the covenant on 16 December 1966. The protocol entered into force on 23 March 1976. Under the terms of the protocol, individuals claiming to be victims of a violation by a state party of rights enumerated in the covenant could file communications with the

Committee on Human Rights against that state, provided it had ratified both the covenant and the protocol. Such petitions are legitimate if the individual complainant has exhausted all available domestic remedies. The Committee on Human Rights, under Articles 3 and 5, is directed to reject anonymous communications and, under Article 5, to defer considering communications that are being examined under "another procedure of international investigation or settlement." Subsequent to the filing of a legitimate complaint, the committee is directed to inform the state party about the alleged violation and the state is called upon to respond within six months to the committee regarding steps it has taken to clarify or remedy the matter. The committee's deliberations on communications from the parties are closed and after its deliberations the committee forwards its views to the state party and the individual concerned. The committee is also directed to report on its activities under the protocol in its annual report to the **United Nations (UN)** General Assembly through the **Economic and Social Council (ECOSOC)**.

A fairly large number of complaints have been received by the committee since the entry into force of the protocol in 1976, but many have been ruled inadmissible for failure to exhaust local remedies or because the matter was being actively investigated by other international bodies. Still, in those cases ruled admissible, the committee has developed a growing body of case law in which both the provisions of the covenant and the protocol have been interpreted, clarified, and applied. The optional protocol has been ratified by 105 countries. For a full text of the protocol, see appendix D.

ORGANIZATION FOR ECONOMIC COOPERATION AND DEVELOPMENT (OECD). The OECD is an outgrowth of post–World War II Marshall Plan assistance to Europe. It succeeded the Organization for European Economic Cooperation in 1961. Its membership expanded from European states, the United States, and Canada to include Australia, New Zealand, and Japan in 1964. Although its principal focus has been on promoting economic ties and growth among its member states, the OECD, through its Development Cooperation Directorate and Development Assistance Committee (DAC), has long been engaged in the studies and evaluation of both emergency humanitarian aid and development assistance to countries of the developing world. The DAC also sponsors an international forum known at the Network on Conflict, Peace and Development Cooperation that promotes consultations between experts from the United Nations system on the process of peace-building and conflict prevention that targets the most conflict prone countries of the developing world. The OECD currently has a membership of 30 countries and active relationships with some 70 other countries. The OECD was active in promoting the idea of the establishment of **Millennium Development Goals** that later formed the targets agreed to by nearly all of the world's governments in the Millennium Declaration of 2000. Address: 2 rue André Pascal, F-75775 Paris CEDEX 16, France. Website: www.oecd.org.

ORGANIZATION FOR SECURITY AND COOPERATION IN EUROPE (OSCE). The OSCE grew out of the Conference on Security and Cooperation in Europe (CSCE), which produced the **Helsinki Accord** of 1975. The accords included a major section on the promotion and protection of human rights. The CSCE continued to meet periodically to review the implementation of the Helsinki Accords and to respond to political and security developments in Central and Eastern Europe. The collapse of communism in Eastern Europe and the breakup of the Soviet Union created a climate of instability that the CSCE found itself dealing with extensively, including the humanitarian assistance needs that accompanied the political instability. At its 1994 session in Budapest, the CSCE recognized that it no longer resembled a periodic conference but rather a full-fledged intergovernmental organization, and the member-states reorganized to form the OSCE, which officially assumed its functions on 1 January 1995.

The OSCE was involved heavily in support of the implementation of the Dayton Accords in the former Yugoslavia. It sponsored conferences on the issues of migration and **refugees** in the Commonwealth of Independent States, in order to promote the principles of international humanitarian law. It supplied human rights monitors in the late 1990s in the difficult Kosovo situation. It engaged in operational programs in the civil war in Tadjikistan, and maintained a presence in other conflict-prone situations, including Armenia, Azerbaijan, Chechnya, and Georgia. The OSCE attempts to prohibit human trafficking, to combat **terrorism**, and to promote a range of human rights among its 55 member-states, with priority focus of **freedom of religion** and **freedom of movement**, and also on the **freedom of assembly** and **freedom of association**, the right to liberty, and to a **fair trial**. Its programs emphasize training of government officials and law-enforcement officers. It is especially engaged in programs for democratization and in monitoring of elections to ensure that they are free and fair. Website: www.osce.org.

ORGANIZATION OF AFRICAN UNITY (OAU). *See* AFRICAN UNION (AU).

ORGANIZATION OF AMERICAN STATES (OAS). The constitutional basis for an Inter-American human rights regime is the charter of the OAS. The original 1948 charter had few and very general provisions relating to human rights. The fundamental reference to human rights was in Article 5(j) of the original and Article 3(j) of the amended charter. These articles assert that the "fundamental rights of the individual without distinction as to race, **nationality**, creed or sex," is a fundamental principle of the OAS. However, the charter did not define what the "fundamental rights" were, nor did it establish any type of means to protect them. There was an announcement of an **American Declaration of the Rights and Duties of Man**, but this was only adopted as a resolution of the Bogotá Conference, which had drafted the charter and it explicitly was not part of the charter.

The first tangible result of efforts to make the OAS more protective of human rights was a resolution of the 1959 Fifth Meeting of Consultation of Ministers of Foreign Affairs that mandated the creation of an **Inter-American Commission on Human Rights (IACHR)**, which was to further respect for human rights. The OAS adopted a statute for the commission and elected its members in 1960.

The 1970 Protocol of Buenos Aires amended the OAS Charter and thereby provided a stronger constitutional basis for the IACHR by making it one of the major organs of the OAS. The OAS General Assembly did not discuss the IACHR annual country reports until 1975 when it debated and passed a resolution on the Chilean report. The assembly passed a stronger resolution on the IACHR's Chile report the next year. The effectiveness of the IACHR's reports is in part dependent upon the subsequent action of the OAS. The OAS General Assembly has rarely discussed the IACHR's findings on individual complaints. In 1979, the General Assembly of the OAS also adopted a statute of the **Inter-American Court of Human Rights (IACT)** with the adoption of the **Inter-American Convention on Human Rights**. IACT, which reports to the General Assembly of the OAS, entered into force on 1 January 1980.

With the end of the Cold War, as numerous Latin American states took substantial strides toward the establishment of democratic governance, the OAS has placed more emphasis on democracy as a hemispheric norm and as a structural means to advance human rights. It has taken three main actions to promote democracy. In 1990, the OAS General Assembly established the Unit for the Promotion of Democracy. In June 1991, the assembly approved Resolution 1080, establishing automatic procedures for meetings of the OAS foreign ministers in response to threats to overthrow or overthrows of democratic government. Finally, the assembly promoted an Inter-American Democratic Charter, which was eventually adopted as a result of negotiations at the Summits of the Americas in 1994, 1998, and 2001.

The Unit for the Promotion of Democracy has helped strengthen democracy by helping member-states to develop political institutions and by promoting democratic political culture. In addition, it has organized a number of election observation missions. Resolution 1080 was invoked several times during the 1990s during threats to democratic governance in the region. The Inter-American Democratic Charter envisions democracy being linked to economic development, human rights, and the evolution of civic culture. The charter also established response procedures in the case of unconstitutional changes of government or when democracies are substantially altered and it provides for election observer missions. The charter has been applied in Venezuela in 2002 and in Haiti in the early 2000s. Address: 17th Street and Constitution Ave., N.W., Washington, DC 20006, USA. Website: www.oas.org.

OXFAM. This well-known and highly regarded British nongovernmental organization (NGO) was founded in 1942 as the Oxford Committee for Famine Relief, as a means of encouraging **food** supplies into Greece where **famine** had struck during the Nazi occupation of that country. It later raised funds and advocated for relief of war **refugees** throughout Europe. After the war it continued to offer relief aid, expanding beyond Europe to the entire world. In 1963, the first of its national committees was founded in Canada. It formally adopted the name of OXFAM in 1965. It was active in Africa during the Sahel drought and famine of the 1970s, and was the lead agency in response to the humanitarian emergency inside Cambodia in 1979. In the 1980s, its work expanded greatly in response to the famine in Ethiopia and other parts of Africa, where its work in water and sanitation programs won it considerable distinction. In the mid-1990s, its work focused heavily on the refugee and humanitarian problems precipitated by the **genocide** in Rwanda. At this time, it joined with nine other OXFAM national committees to form OXFAM International.

It now operates in over 70 countries and, through its sister organizations in OXFAM International, its work has evolved to reach more than 100 countries of assistance. Much of its work continues to center on the provision of emergency assistance in disaster and refugee situations, but it also broadly attempts to deal with the relief of **poverty** through long-term development programs. It has consultative status with the United Nations **Economic and Social Council (ECOSOC)** as well as working ties with a number of **United Nations (UN)** agencies. It is one of the largest and most influential European NGOs.

OXFAM has naturally gravitated toward work in the human rights arena to complement its historical emphasis on humanitarian assistance and poverty reduction. It has worked to strengthen the voices of the poor, men and **women** alike, in being heard within their own local and national settings. This is done by increasing access to information and by promoting **freedom of opinion and expression** and **freedom of association**. Its work in the area of community development emphasizes the productivity of women and the preservation of **indigenous rights**. It produces reports and publications on such human rights issues as the right to land, discrimination against women, and the adverse impacts of corruption. It supports a wide range of programming and assistance in such areas as **education, health**, and HIV/AIDS, in addition to its traditional and ongoing work in response to conflicts, disasters, and refugee situations. Address: OXFAM House, John Smith Drive, Cowley, Oxford OX4 2JY, UK. Websites: www.oxfam.org.uk and www.oxfam.org.

– P –

PAINE, THOMAS (1737–1809). Author and humanitarian, Paine was born in Thetford, Norfolk, England, on 29 January 1737. He held a variety of jobs in England but was not happy in his native country. With a letter of recommendation from Benjamin Franklin, Paine migrated to America in November 1774. In Philadelphia, Paine edited the *Pennsylvania Magazine* for a year and a half.

Although he had been in the colonies for only about a year, Paine, in *Common Sense* (January 1776) was able to articulate the arguments for independence from Great Britain in a language understandable to literate colonists. The pamphlet, appealing to both reason and emotion, is credited by most U.S. historians as being decisive in molding public opinion in favor of independence.

After the Revolutionary War began, Paine drifted to General Nathaniel Greene's army and served as a volunteer aide-de-camp. Here, Paine began writing *The Crisis Papers*, which exhorted patriots to continue the struggle for freedom. In 1780 he published *Public Good*, which argued for the calling of a national convention to create a stronger constitution than that provided for in the Articles of Confederation. For his public services, New York State gave Paine a 300-acre farm in New Rochelle, New York.

In response to Edmund Burke's *Reflections on the Revolution in France* (1790), Paine wrote the *Rights of Man* (1791–1792) in Britain. The book defended the early actions of the French Revolution and laid out and defended republican principles. Paine was charged with treason by William Pitt's government and he fled to France where he was elected as a delegate to the French Convention. He argued for the exile rather than the execution of King Louis XVI and for this he was jailed by Robespierre from December 1793 to November 1794. Paine wrote the *Age of Reason* (1794/1796) as a way to uphold morality and a sense of justice in a time of revolutionary upheaval.

Paine in the above works and others consistently defended republican principles, denigrated monarchy, and appealed to people to accept and protect what we today call human rights. From 1792 on, he regularly advocated that government, through a progressive income tax, should care for the aged and those unable to care for themselves. Paine's ideas reflected the sensibilities of the Enlightenment in that he argued that laws of nature (or **natural law**) exist and these were a reflection of divine providence. He promoted the power of reason as an ordering principle in human affairs, defended tolerance, and strongly affirmed that all persons' dignity and human rights should be protected. His religious beliefs were akin to what later became Unitarianism.

Paine returned to the United States in 1802 an unpopular figure, and he died in New York City on 8 June 1809.

PEOPLE IN NEED. People in Need is an award-winning Czech nongovernmental organization (NGO) dedicated to the provision of humanitarian aid and the promotion of human rights. Founded in 1992, its first assistance programs for **refugees** and displaced persons were initiated in Bosnia-Herzegovina and Chechnya. Later programs for reconstruction aid were aimed at other war-torn or disaster-prone areas such as Kosovo, Iran, Iraq, and Afghanistan. It has sponsored tens of millions of dollars worth of programs in 33 countries, with much of the aid taking the form of **food, health** supplies, and resources for reconstruction of schools, and other forms of emergency assistance. Its human rights advocacy work includes support of dissidents and other activists from countries governed by authoritarian regimes. It promotes the goal of spreading democratic governance. It is a member of **European Solidarity towards Equal Participation of People (EUROSTEP)**. Website: www.clovekvtisni.cz.

PERMANENT COURT OF INTERNATIONAL JUSTICE (PCIJ). Predecessor to the **International Court of Justice (ICJ)**, the PCIJ was established by the **League of Nations**. Article 14 of the League covenant had specified that the council submit plans to League members for the establishment of such an international court. A group of international jurists met to devise a draft scheme for the Court, which was debated and approved by the League assembly on 13 December 1920. Unlike the ICJ, however, the PCIJ was not conceived as an organ of the League. League members were not bound by the assembly approval of the PCIJ unless they signed and ratified the Protocol of Signature of 16 December 1920. More than fifty countries eventually did so, although the work of the PCIJ was severely constrained by the events of World War II. The PCIJ was disbanded in January 1946, and the ICJ commenced its work shortly thereafter.

The PCIJ, like the ICJ, was constituted to adjudicate complaints made by member-states and to issue advisory opinions to the League of Nations rather than as a court to which individuals could appeal for protection of human rights. However, several of its rulings had a direct bearing on disputes or treaties that had human rights implications, in particular its opinions dealing with the duties of governments to refrain from discrimination against **minorities**. Its advisory opinions included such issues as the operation of minority schools in Albania and Upper Silesia, acquisition of **nationality** in Poland, the competence of the ILO to regulate the personal **work** of employers, and the interpretation of the 1919 Convention Concerning Employment of **Women** During the Night, among others.

PHILLIPS, WENDELL (1811–1884). Wendell Phillips was one of the great U.S. abolitionists of the 19th century. He was born on 29 November 1811 in Boston, to one of Boston's prominent families. A graduate of Harvard, Phillips practiced law for a time before devoting his energies to the abolitionist movement. He married Anne Terry Greene, a dedicated abolitionist in 1837. He met **William Lloyd Garrison** in the same year, and became president of Boston's Anti-slavery Society. He worked closely with Garrison in the abolitionist movement until the Civil War, and he also participated in the promotion of **women**'s suffrage. Phillips was opposed to involvement in partisan politics and sought to advance the abolitionist cause through affecting public opinion. He favored the position of disunion prior to the Civil War, holding that free states ought not to remain in union with slave-holding states. However, when the Civil War began, he justified the war as a national atonement for the sin of **slavery**, as a way to destroy the Southern slave-holding aristocracy, and as a means of achieving universal and immediate emancipation.

During the war, Phillips proposed the vote for all blacks, worked for the freedom of blacks to be given land and tools to enable them to be economically self-sufficient, and called for the establishment of a Freedman's Bureau. He also supported the formation of Negro regiments to fight in the war, and he argued in favor of constitutional amendments to abolish slavery and to prohibit **racial discrimination**. He split with Garrison over support of the Lincoln administration, and he replaced Garrison as the president of the American Antislavery Society in 1865. Phillips worked tirelessly for the passage of the Fifteenth Amendment, which was finally adopted in 1870. He then turned his attention to other political and social causes, including labor reform laws such as the eight-hour day, a progressive income tax, workers' right to organize and to strike, and government regulation of corporations. He also supported women's rights, the abolition of capital punishment, prison reform, and more humane treatment of Native Americans. Phillips died on 3 February 1884.

PHYSICIANS FOR HUMAN RIGHTS (PHR). Founded in 1986, the members of PHR have been dedicated to the elimination of **torture**, **disappearances**, and political killings. The members of PHR work to improve sanitary conditions in all kinds of detention facilities, to ensure access to medical services during time of conflict, and to protect **health** professionals who have been subjected to human rights abuses. PHR operates an International Forensics Program to mobilize the medical and scientific community to provide expertise in recovery of the dead, the identification of remains, and generation of medical evidence for use in national judicial bodies or international **war crimes** tribunals. It offers a wide range of reports and publications on particular countries and various human rights issues, such as hunger, **asylum**, AIDS transmission, landmine injuries, and the like. Address: 2 Arrow Street, Suite 301, Cambridge, MA 02138, USA. Website: www.phrusa.org.

PIERRE, ABBÉ (1912–). Born in Lyon and christened Henri-Antoine Groués, Abbé Pierre was a deeply devout youth who entered the Capuchin order before being ordained to the priesthood in 1938. During World War II, he demonstrated great courage as a member of the French Resistance helping Jewish families escape into Switzerland. His code name was Abbé Pierre, a moniker that has followed him ever since. Pursued by the Gestapo, he escaped from France and continued to work with the Free French in North Africa. He was elected to the French Constituent Assembly as an independent and focused his energies on alleviating the **poverty** and **homelessness** so common after the war. In 1949, he founded the first of his Emmaus communities for homeless men, imitating the charitable work of the great French saint of charity, St. Vincent de Paul. As the number of Emmaus communities grew, Abbé Pierre decided to resign from Parliament in 1951 to assist the teeming numbers of unemployed and homeless **refugees** and displaced people. From that time forward, even into his declining years, Abbé Pierre has continued to serve the needs of the poor, publicizing their plight and pleading their cause before the entire French nation, winning him the popular title of "the conscience of France." President Jacques Chirac awarded him the Legion of Honor in 2001, as one of the country's leading voices in defense of humanitarian concern and human dignity.

POLITICAL RIGHTS. Political rights, as reflected in the **Universal Declaration of Human Rights** and the **International Covenant on Civil and Political Rights**, guarantee individuals the capacity to take part in the government of their country either directly or through elected representatives. The Universal Declaration additionally provides that everyone shall have equal access to public service in their country and that governmental legitimacy hinges on periodic and genuinely free and fair elections through universal suffrage. These provisions are also asserted in the covenant and echoed in regional instruments such as the **African Charter on Human and Peoples' Rights** and the **Inter-American Convention on Human Rights**. The latter provides that eligibility to exercise political rights can be legally regulated concerning such criteria as "age, **nationality**, residence, language, **education**, civil and mental capacity or sentencing by a competent court in criminal proceedings." The inclusion of political rights, together with civil rights, in human rights instruments has drawn considerable support from democratic governments that generally provide such guarantees to their citizens. That many nondemocratic states have ratified such agreements as well suggests that there is still a wide gap in many parts of the world between the ideals of political rights and their realization in the practice of many governments. In many countries, the political rights of **women** fall well short of the ideal of **equality**.

POVERTY. To be free from poverty is not a right per se in any international covenant, although the right may be inferred from several international agreements that deal with the issue of standard of living. The **Universal Declaration of Human Rights** asserts that "Everyone has a right to a standard of living adequate for the health and well-being of himself and of his **family**." According to Article 25, this standard of living includes clothing, **food**, **housing**, medical care, and any "necessary social services" as well as the right to such security when faced with disability, old age, sickness, unemployment, or widowhood. The **International Covenant on Economic, Social, and Cultural Rights** recognizes everyone's right "to an adequate standard of living for himself, and his family." This includes clothing, food, housing, and "the continuous improvement of living conditions." In addition, the American Convention on Human Rights Additional Protocol asserts a right to "adequate nutrition" that "guarantees the possibility of enjoying the highest level of physical, emotional and intellectual development." The **International Labor Organization (ILO)** Convention Concerning Basic Aims and Standards of Social Policy (No. 117) calls for the improvement in global standards of living but only a minority of states have ratified it, thereby mitigating its force.

International and regional agreements on **work** imply that people have a right to be free from poverty. The Universal Declaration asserts that remuneration for work should ensure "an existence worthy of human dignity." The Covenant on Economic, Social, and Cultural Rights indicates that remuneration for work should provide a "decent living." The **American Declaration of the Rights and Duties of Man** recognizes that remuneration should ensure a suitable standard of living. The **European Social Charter** emphasizes that remuneration should be "sufficient for a decent standard of living." The **African Charter on Human and Peoples' Rights** asserts that individuals have a "right to work under equitable and satisfactory condition." Furthermore, international agreements on **social security** can be inferred to provide the basis for a right to be free of poverty, asserting either that all persons or at least the elderly have a right to "social security." Added to these agreements are those related to the subject of **health** that recognize either a right to a standard of living adequate for health or a right to the "highest attainable standard of physical and mental health."

In 1988 the United Nations **Economic and Social Council (ECOSOC)** noted that a large percentage of the world's population lived in extreme poverty and that too little attention was being paid to this problem. Periodically, both ECOSOC and the **United Nations General Assembly** have called upon states to develop strategies to combat poverty. The connection between extreme poverty and denial of human rights has been the object of study by the **Commission on Human Rights (CHR)** and other human rights bodies.

Some human rights experts argue that poverty is a violation of human rights since it is "the cause and effect of the total or partial denial of human rights." This relationship is seen to exist especially where denial of civil, political, cultural, economic, and social rights is itself the cause of poverty, and too often the cause of rapidly degenerating and extreme poverty characteristic of emergency situations that are frequently associated with general conditions of conflict and abuse.

Like many other rights falling in the economic and social arena, international agreements recognize that economic and resource constraints limit the capacity of many governments to fully guarantee such rights as freedom from poverty. Moreover, poverty is a relative condition, subject to variable definition over time and place. The institutions grappling most directly with the condition are the **family** as well as churches and local communities, which require at times facilitative support from governments or even international bodies when the extremities of indigence threaten life. Poverty has been a persistent condition in human society throughout history. The development by individuals of a lively sense of charity and of direct and immediate alleviation of indigency through almsgiving has thus been a central feature of religious practice. Only in recent times have governmental and public bodies themselves been seen as the primary agents for poverty relief.

PRIVACY. The right to privacy is protected by five different declarations and conventions. The **Universal Declaration of Human Rights** states in Article 12 that "No one shall be subjected to arbitrary interference with his privacy, **family**, home or correspondence, nor to attacks upon his honor and reputation. Everyone has the right to protection of the law against such interference or attacks."

The **American Declaration of the Rights and Duties of Man**, in Article V, phrases the right in the following way: "Every person has the right to the protection of the law against abusive attacks upon his honor, his reputation, and his private and family life." The **Inter-American Convention on Human Rights** states that "No one may be the object of arbitrary or abusive interference with his private life, his family, his home, or his correspondence, or of unlawful attacks on his honor or reputation." Article 11 of this convention legally protects people from such infringements. Another regional instrument, the **European Convention on Human Rights**, similarly announces that "Everyone has the right to respect for his private and family life, his home and his correspondence." Yet the European Convention does allow "interference" with this right when it is "necessary" to prevent disorder or crime, or to protect economic well-being, national security, public **health** and morals, or the rights and freedoms of others, as well as for purposes of public safety.

At the global level, the **International Covenant on Civil and Political Rights** stipulates that "No one shall be subjected to arbitrary or unlawful interference with his privacy, family, home or correspondence, nor to unlawful attacks on his honor and reputation," and that everyone had a right to legal protection against such things.

The United Nations **Human Rights Committee (HRC)** has taken up the issue of privacy resulting from reports from states parties to the International Covenant on Civil and Political Rights. It asserts that the right of privacy is protected from actions of both governments and any other legal persons. It calls upon states to adopt measures to protect the right, observing that the state reports lacked adequate information on institutional mechanisms and authority for the protection of privacy. Complicating the observance of the right are the implications of modern computer technology, which requires appropriate domestic legislation.

PROCEDURAL RIGHTS. Procedural rights deal with those rights that set out the way rights may be enforced or exercised and provide for judicial safeguards to ensure recourse in case of violations of those rights.

Many international agreements protect procedural rights. Among these are the **Universal Declaration of Human Rights**, which provides that everyone has a right to recognition as a legal person, to fair and public trials, to presumption of innocence, and to freedom from ex post facto laws (articles 6, 10, and 11). **The European Convention on Human Rights** further provides that everyone is entitled to a fair and public trial, including having an impartial judge, being informed of charges, having adequate time to prepare a defense, having access to counsel and witnesses, and having an interpreter. A subsequent protocol to the convention added rights of appeal, compensation for wrongful punishment, and freedom from double jeopardy.

The **International Convention on the Elimination of All Forms of Racial Discrimination** guarantees the right of everyone, irrespective of race, color, or national or ethnic origin, to **equality** before the law, especially the right to equal treatment before all institutions of justice. The **International Covenant on Civil and Political Rights** states that all people are equal before the law. The range of procedural rights stipulated by the convention is similar to that outlined in the Universal Declaration and the European Convention.

Other conventions providing for procedural rights include the **Convention against Torture and Other Cruel, Inhuman, or Degrading Treatment or Punishment**, which provides for investigations of allegations and compensation for victims; the **Convention on the Elimination of All Forms of Discrimination against Women**, which calls for **women** to have a capacity equal to men before the law; and the **African Charter on Human and Peoples' Rights**, which acknowledges everyone's right to be a legal person.

In its review of reports of states parties to the International Covenant on Civil and Political Rights, the United Nations **Human Rights Committee (HRC)** has noted that governments need to show more solicitude in assuring the effectiveness of protection of procedural rights.

PROPERTY. The right to own property is expressed in many international agreements. The **Universal Declaration of Human Rights** recognizes the right of everyone to own property singly or jointly and not to be deprived of property arbitrarily. The **International Convention on the Elimination of All Forms of Racial Discrimination** states that all states parties to the convention pledge to prohibit and eliminate **racial discrimination** and to guarantee everyone, regardless of race, color, national or ethnic origin, to **equality** before the law, in particular the right to own property singly or jointly and the right to inherit. Although the declaration affirms the idea of a right to property, neither the **International Covenant on Civil and Political Rights** nor the **International Covenant on Economic, Social, and Cultural Rights** mentions such a right, owing to disagreements among governments over how to define property and what restrictions could legitimately be placed on property.

The **Inter-American Convention on Human Rights** states that everyone has the right to enjoy and use property but that this right might be legally subordinated in the interests of society. Further, no person is to be deprived of his property except legally, with compensation and for reasons of public or social interest. Usury is also prohibited. **The Convention on the Elimination of All Forms of Discrimination against Women** provides that all states parties to the convention would take measures to eliminate discrimination against **women** in socioeconomic life to ensure equal rights with men concerning the right to **family** benefits, bank loans, mortgages, participation in recreational activities, sports, and all aspects of cultural life. Also, states parties should provide "women equal rights to conclude contracts" and to administer property.

The **African Charter on Human and Peoples' Rights** guarantees the right of property but provides that it can be legally encroached upon in the interest of the community or public need. The Declaration on Social Progress and Development and the **Declaration on the Right to Development** both recognize that property has a role in protecting human rights. The **United Nations General Assembly** has acknowledged this point, and it has called upon the secretary-general to undertake studies on the issue. The **Commission on Human Rights (CHR)** has also noted the relationship between the ownership of property and the protection of human rights.

The U.S. Supreme Court sparked a major controversy in U.S. law with its decision in *Kelo versus New London, Connecticut* (2005), which allowed states and local governments broad eminent domain authority even if the "public use" was the transfer of real property from the government to a private company for the purposes of economic development. Many state governments swiftly initiated revisions of their eminent domain statutes to restrict such authority and thus insulate property owners from the potentially broad and adverse effects of the Court's ruling.

PROTOCOL RELATING TO THE STATUS OF REFUGEES. Done at New York on 31 January 1967 and entering into force on 4 October 1967, this agreement extends the protections found in the 1951 **Convention Relating to the Status of Refugees** to individuals who became **refugees** as a result of events occurring after 1 January 1951. The 1951 convention had limited the extension of refugee status only to those fleeing from events occurring prior to 1 January 1951. The protocol, which has been ratified by 143 countries, additionally stipulated that its terms would apply without geographic limitation. For a text of the protocol, see *United Nations Treaty Series* no. 8791, vol. 606, p. 267.

PUBLIC EMERGENCY. Several human rights instruments permit countries to derogate from their obligation to observe human rights during times of national exigency or public emergency. On the other hand, some rights are considered so important that their enforcement and protection must be observed during emergencies, such as the **right to life**; the right to be free from **torture**, inhuman, and degrading punishment; and from **slavery**. The **International Covenant on Civil and Political Rights** and the **European Convention on Human Rights** permit **derogation**, for example, but not from the rights just listed. Typically, a state must give notice to other states parties through the appropriate international bodies when declaring such public emergencies or terminating them.

PUGWASH CONFERENCES. *See* ROTBLAT, JOSEPH (1908–2005).

– R –

RACIAL DISCRIMINATION. A variety of international human rights instruments forbid the practice of racial discrimination and call upon states to eliminate this form of prejudicial treatment that violates the notion of the right of **equality**. Racial discrimination is forbidden implicitly or explicitly in the **United Nations Charter**, the **Universal Declaration of Human Rights**, the **International Covenant on Civil and Political Rights**, the **International Covenant on Economic, Social, and Cultural Rights**, the United Nations Educational, Scientific, and Cultural Organization (UNESCO), Declaration on Race and Racial Prejudice, the **International Convention on the Elimination of All Forms of Racial Discrimination**, as well as in a variety of regional human rights treaties. The Convention on the Elimination of Racial Discrimination establishes a **Committee on the Elimination of Racial Discrimination (CERD)**, which has some enforcement powers in terms of hearing complaints from states parties and individuals concerning failure of a state party to adhere to the provisions of the covenant. The Subcommission on Prevention of Discrimination and Protection of Minorities of the United Nations **Commission on Human Rights (CHR)** has been active in promoting international awareness of various issues surrounding racial discrimination. The **United Nations General Assembly** has also proclaimed on three occasions its intentions to combat racism and racial discrimination. The most successful international campaign against racial discrimination concerned the end of **apartheid** in South Africa, a by-product of decades of international pressure and internal opposition that eventually led to the historic reforms of the early 1990s, in which figures such as **Nelson Mandela**, among others, played such a visible role.

RED CROSS AND RED CRESCENT SOCIETY. *See* GENEVA RED CROSS CONVENTIONS (of 1929, 1949) AND PROTOCOLS; INTERNATIONAL COMMITTEE OF THE RED CROSS (ICRC); INTERNATIONAL FEDERATION OF RED CROSS AND RED CRESCENT SOCIETIES (IFRC).

REFUGEES. According to the 1951 **Convention Relating to the Status of Refugees**, a refugee is any person who, "owing to a well-founded fear of being persecuted for reasons of race, religion, **nationality**, membership of a particular social group or political opinion, is outside the country of his nationality and is unable or, owing to such fear, is unwilling to avail himself of the protection of that country, or who, not having a nationality and being outside the country of his former habitual residence, is unable or, owing to such fear is unwilling to return to it." Such persons are protected from forcible repatriation to their country of nationality or origin. They are entitled to seek **asylum** and to receive protection and assistance from the international community. The definition stipulates that two conditions must be met to achieve refugee status: refugees must have crossed national boundaries and thus be beyond the jurisdiction of their country of nationality or habitual residence; and they must have a well-founded fear of persecution if returned to that country.

More than 140 countries are parties to either the 1951 convention or the 1967 protocol that removed certain time and geographical restrictions to the application of the refugee definition. Other regional legal instruments, such as the Organization of African Unity (OAU) **Convention Governing the Specific Aspects of Refugee Problems in Africa**, expand the 1951 convention definition to include "every person who, owing to external aggression, occupation, foreign domination, or events seriously disturbing public order in either part or the whole of his country of origin or nationality, is compelled to leave his place of habitual residence in order to seek refuge in another place outside his country of origin or nationality." For purposes of their domestic legislation, governments are free to incorporate the legal definition of the term *refugee* most conducive to their interests, in keeping with the international treaties they have ratified. The United States, for instance, is party to the 1967 protocol to the 1951 Convention Relating to the Status of Refugees. The refugee definition found in this treaty has been incorporated into American law through its Refugee and Migration Act of 1980. The **United Nations High Commissioner for Refugees (UNHCR)** is the primary body providing oversight of international refugee conventions and working with governments to see that they are faithfully implemented.

Refugees have existed throughout human history, but the tumultuous events of the 20th century produced tens of millions of refugees and displaced persons, following the Balkan Wars, World War I, and World War II. International assistance and protection began during the period of the **League of Nations**, with the establishment of the League High Commissioner for Refugees Coming from Russia, an office held by Fridtjof Nansen, which rapidly expanded to address the needs of more than 10 million refugees, not only from Russia, but from the former territories of the Ottoman Empire in the Middle East and in the Balkans. This League office was succeeded by a series of ad hoc and temporary bodies that addressed refugee problems well beyond those caused by the Russian Revolution, later including the Jewish emigration from Nazi Germany.

World War II produced 30 million displaced persons and refugees, who were assisted by the **United Nations Relief and Rehabilitation Administration (UNRRA)** until the International Refugee Organization (IRO) was established in 1946. The IRO was an interim body as well, eventually giving way in 1951 to the UNHCR, which was also seen to be a stop-gap measure to deal with the European refugee problem. However, as the Cold War deepened and refugee problems emerged in Africa, Asia, and Central America, the UNHCR became a permanent feature of the **United Nations (UN)** system for response to global refugee needs. During the 1970s to the 1990s, the numbers of refugees neared the 20 million mark for some years. The collapse of communism in the 1990s produced refugee problems once again in the Balkans, but also in former republics of the Soviet Union. Today the number of refugees has fallen under the 10 million mark, but political and economic instabilities continue to plague parts of Africa, Asia, the Middle East, and Eastern Europe, suggesting that international organizations, such as the UNHCR, the **United Nations Relief and Works Agency for Palestine (UNRWA)**, the International Organization for Migration (IOM), and related assistance agencies of the UN system, as well as the growing number on nongovernmental organizations (NGOs) will be dealing with refugee assistance and protection issues for many years to come.

REPORTERS WITHOUT BORDERS. Reporters without Borders was founded in 1985 to defend the **freedom of the press**. It comes to the defense of reporters and journalists who have been imprisoned, and protests government actions against the formation and free functioning of the media and the promulgation of laws that restrict press freedom. Its permanent staff is headquartered in Paris. It engages in research activities in Africa, the Americas, Asia-Pacific, Europe, and the Middle East/North Africa, monitoring activities that might constitute breeches of press freedom. Once research confirms violations these are protested through letters and public statements. It finances its efforts through the sale of books and photographs as well as through private donations and grants from foundations and intergovernmental organizations. International Secretariat address: 5, rue Geoffroy-Marie, 75009 Paris, France. Website: www.rsf.org. *See also* FREEDOM OF OPINION AND EXPRESSION; INSTITUTE OF WAR AND PEACE REPORTING (IWPR).

RIGHT TO DEVELOPMENT. *See* DECLARATION ON THE RIGHT TO DEVELOPMENT.

RIGHT TO LEAVE AND RETURN TO A COUNTRY. *See* MOVEMENT AND RESIDENCE.

RIGHT TO LIFE. Ever since the formulation of the doctrine of natural rights in the 17th century, the most foundational right acknowledged by philosophers, politicians and lawyers, as reflected in fundamental **constitutions**, bills of right, and other human rights pronouncements is the right to life. Logically, all other rights flow from this right since without life, no other right is possible. The **Universal Declaration of Human Rights** asserts in Article 3 that "everyone has the right to life, liberty and the security of person." Similar pronouncements have been made in the **International Covenant on Civil and Political Rights**, the **Inter-American Convention on Human Rights**, and the **African Charter of Human and Peoples' Rights**. The **Human Rights Committee (HRC)** of the **United Nations (UN)**, in reviewing Article 6 in the International Covenant on Civil and Political Rights on two different occasions, has emphasized that the right to life is the "supreme right," from which no **derogation** is permissible even in times of emergency. Its commentary focuses on the issues of capital punishment and loss of life during war.

The subject gets more problematical when the issue of abortion is introduced, as it was in debates that took place during the drafting of the Universal Declaration of Human Rights by the United Nations **Commission on Human Rights (CHR)**. Proposals to include the phrase "from the moment of conception" after the words "right to life" were rejected since as a practical matter the existence of abortion legislation in several countries would have conflicted with the phrase. Disagreement existed among the drafters as to whether the phrase "from the moment of conception" was implicit in the notion of a right to life—some holding that it was, others that it need not be. When the debate over abortion was a matter of the potential clash of **women**'s right to life as opposed to that of the fetus, the issue was less controversial. When claims for abortion as an absolute right were advanced, the issue became more problematical. There is no international agreement on the subject as a matter for the **International Bill of Rights**, although advocacy groups at international women's conferences and population conferences have pressed for wider acceptance of abortion as a right, and thus by implication for a narrower definition of the right to life. Still, formal **United Nations (UN)** documents have dealt gingerly with the subject of abortion. It is currently not listed as a right in any major human rights instruments and national legislation on the legality of abortion varies considerably. *See also* DEATH PENALTY.

ROMERO, OSCAR (1917–1980). Oscar Arnulfo Romero y Galdamez was born in Ciudad Barrios in the department of San Miguel, El Salvador, on 15 August 1917. He attended the local school but around the age of 12 he was apprenticed to a carpenter. In 1931, Romero began his formal religious training under the Claretians. He completed his studies in Rome at the Gregorian University and was ordained a priest on 4 April 1942. Romero began a doctoral program in theology but did not complete it owing to the dislocations arising from World War II.

Back in El Salvador, Romero served as a parish priest for a short while until his bishop made him secretary of the diocese. Romero received the title of monsignor on 4 April 1967 and a few months later began his service as the secretary-general of the national bishops' conference. He took on additional duties in May 1968 as the executive secretary of the Central American Bishops' secretariat.

Romero was named auxiliary bishop in May 1970, and later as editor of the archdiocesan newspaper, *Orientacion*. Rome elevated him to the episcopacy in October 1974 and the new bishop was faced with the rising violence in his country. National Guardsmen raided the village of Tres Calles on 21 June 1975, killing five peasants and ransacking homes. Romero condemned the massacre, protested to the local guardian commander, and wrote a private letter to President Arturo Armando Molina protesting the atrocity. Romero succeeded Archbishop Luis Chavez in February 1977. Romero became archbishop just days after a fraud-riddled election awarded the presidency to General Carlos Humberto Romero, who was no relation to him. At the time, El Salvador faced a drastically distorted distribution of land and wealth, very low standard of living for the vast majority of the citizens, and rule by a series of repressive military governments, organized to support and sustain a small oligarchy's control of national wealth and deeply suspicious of any call for change. During his archbishopric, there was a significant increase in political violence committed mainly, though not exclusively, by the military, police, intelligence, and paramilitary forces such as the White Warriors Union and the Democratic Nationalist Organization.

Archbishop Romero consistently based his work and the work of the church in El Salvador on the teachings of Vatican II and various Latin American Bishops conferences. He publicly and consistently defended human rights through the use of news bulletins, Sunday homilies, interviews, the archdiocesan newspaper, funeral masses, radio broadcasts, and pastoral letters. Romero's homily of 14 May 1978 is a good example of Romero's very public defense of human rights. In it he enumerated human rights abuses in the country, including such acts as arrests without charge, **disappearances**, exiles not allowed to return, and prisoners subjected to **torture**. Similarly, Romero strongly supported human rights in his pastoral letters. In a pastoral letter of August 1978, he supported the right of workers to organize as did, he noted, the Salvadoran constitution, the **Universal Declaration of Human Rights**, **John XXIII's** *Pacem in Terris*, as well as the Second Vatican Council. Romero further denounced the "institutional violence" in the face of peaceful demands for an end to the injustice.

Romero hoped that the new junta that took power in the coup d'état of 15 October 1979 would be able to stop the violence and initiate meaningful socioeconomic reforms. Sadly, the new government was unable to control its own security forces and those of paramilitary organizations, and by the end of the first week of January 1980, all but one member of the junta resigned. Romero was disappointed at the end of the reform government and in his homilies of January,

February, and March 1980, condemned the new government's violent repression and called for power sharing and a redistribution of the national wealth. He also condemned the violence of the left and called for action to avert a civil war.

In his last homily, Romero explicitly called on the army, National Guard, and police to stop killing innocent people and end the repression. The next day, in the early evening of 24 March, as the archbishop was saying a funeral mass, Romero was shot and killed by a single bullet to the chest.

ROOSEVELT, ELEANOR (1884–1962). Anna Eleanor Roosevelt, politician, author, lecturer, and wife of Franklin D. Roosevelt, was born on 11 October 1884. Mrs. Roosevelt's mother died when she was eight and her father died only a year later. Thenceforth, she was raised by her maternal grandmother. Eleanor married Franklin D. Roosevelt in March 1905.

Mrs. Roosevelt developed a strong interest in **education** and in socioeconomic and political issues, and, when Franklin contracted polio in 1921, she helped him to fight the disease and to maintain his political life. In the 1920s, Mrs. Roosevelt joined the Women's Trade Union League and worked constantly on behalf of the Democratic Party. She strongly supported her husband for the New York State governorship and campaigned in his successful 1928 campaign.

While her husband transformed the office of the president during his administrations, Eleanor transformed the office of the First Lady. She took a high-profile position in dealing with social and economic issues, held a weekly press conference for **women** reporters, wrote a daily column that appeared in over a hundred newspapers, and hosted a radio program. She gave all of her earnings to the American Friends Service Committee. She traveled on average 40,000 miles annually during the New Deal and wartime years in support of various causes.

After the death of Franklin Roosevelt in 1945, President Harry S. Truman appointed Mrs. Roosevelt as a delegate to the **United Nations (UN)**. There she served as chair of the **Human Rights Commission (HRC)**, which drafted the **Universal Declaration of Human Rights** that was adopted by the **United Nations General Assembly** in December of 1948. She referred to the declaration as "a **Magna Carta** of mankind." She served on the U.S. delegation to the

UN until 1952 when she resigned. She spent her last decade keeping an extensive speaking schedule and devoting a good deal of time to writing. She died on 7 November 1962.

ROTBLAT, JOSEPH (1908–2005). Joseph Rotblat was born in Poland, then part of the Russian Empire, in November 1909. He earned his MA from the Free University of Poland in 1932 and a doctorate in physics in 1938 from the University of Warsaw, where he served as the assistant director of the Atomic Physics Institute. Rotblat fled Poland after his wife was killed in the **Holocaust**. In 1939, he won a fellowship to the University or Liverpool, England, where he studied with James Chadwick on the feasibility of an atomic bomb. Rotblat accompanied Chadwick to Los Alamos to work on the Manhattan Project. When the U.S. government confirmed in November 1944 that Germany was unable to build a nuclear explosive, Rotblat immediately resigned from the project, the only scientist to do so. For him, the only reason to develop the bomb was to deter Adolf Hitler from using a German-made bomb against the Allies.

Rotblat cofounded the Atomic Scientists Association in 1946 and organized the Atom Train in 1947, the first large exhibition on the peaceful uses of atomic energy, which also argued against the military use of nuclear energy. From 1950 to 1976, Rotblat was a professor of physics at Saint Bartholomew's Hospital Medical College at the University of London, where he continued to be affiliated as professor emeritus until his death.

In 1955, he was one of 11 signatories of a joint manifesto that urged all scientists to work to abolish war and nuclear armaments. The manifesto was initiated by Bertrand Russell and Albert Einstein. A series of scientific conferences known as the Pugwash Conferences later grew out of the manifesto.

The first Pugwash Conference was held in 1957 at Pugwash, Nova Scotia. It was attended by 22 scientists from Britain, France, the United States, China, Poland, and the Soviet Union. Scientists were admitted to the conference by invitation as individuals rather than as representatives of governments or institutions. Scientists from communist countries, however, attended with government support. Many times, Western scientists attended against the wishes of their governments. Rotblat was a founding member of the conference and he served as its secretary-general from 1957 to 1973, and later as its president.

At a Pugwash Conference in the early 1960s, a joint U.S.-Soviet proposal was developed that identified seismic monitoring as a way to detect nuclear tests. This proposal facilitated the negotiations for the Limited Nuclear Test Ban Treaty of 1963.

The Pugwash Conferences were only a part of Rotblat's activities on behalf of limiting nuclear weapons. He cofounded the U.K. Campaign for Nuclear Disarmament in 1958, initiated and served on the governing board of the Stockholm International Peace Research Institute, helped organize the Moscow Forum of Scientists, and participated in the UK and USSR Medical Exchange Program.

After the collapse of the Soviet Union, the conferences turned attention to such issues as the environment, population, and ways to control biological, chemical, and conventional weapons. Rotblat focused on nuclear disarmament as a main concern until his death in 2005. He was the author of more than 300 published works, including 20 books, on the control of nuclear weapons, disarmament, nuclear and medical physics, the Pugwash Conferences, radiation biology, and the social responsibility of the scientist. Rotblat and the Pugwash Conference jointly received the Nobel Peace Prize in 1995. Rotblat died on 2 September 2005 at the age of 96.

– S –

SAKHAROV, ANDREI (1921–1989). Andrei Sakharov was born on 21 May 1921 in Moscow. His father was a high school physics teacher and an author of both textbooks and science books for lay audiences. Sakharov graduated from high school with honors in 1938 and from Moscow University with honors in 1942. During his three years working in an arms factory, he invented several devices that improved the quality of the products. In 1945, Sakharov entered the Lebedev Physical Institute, and in 1948, he was assigned to a group working to develop a Soviet hydrogen bomb. In recognition for his work in developing the bomb, Sakharov was elected to the Soviet Academy of Sciences in 1953.

In the late 1950s, Sakharov began to lobby for limiting nuclear testing, and he helped promote the Limited Test Ban Treaty of 1963.

In 1964, he spoke out against Trofim Lysenko and political interference in scientific research. In 1968, Sakharov published an essay, "Thoughts on Progress, Peaceful Coexistence, and Intellectual Freedom." The essay called for peaceful coexistence between the superpowers, international cooperation to solve problems of hunger and ecological degradation, implementation of the **Universal Declaration of Human Rights**, and increased intellectual freedom and democratization in the Soviet Union. As a result of this publication, Sakharov was banned from secret scientific work and denied many benefits accorded to Soviet scientists. During the same year, he gave almost all of his savings to the Red Cross to build a cancer hospital.

In 1970, Sakharov sent a letter with other prominent Soviet dissidents to the Communist Party, the Council of Ministers, and the Presidium arguing for the need to democratize the USSR. Later in the year, he and others founded the Human Rights Committee. The committee appealed for an end to forcible psychiatric hospitalization and resettlement of individuals and ethnonationalistic groups.

Sakharov drafted an appeal to the Supreme Soviet to release political prisoners, and he protested the murder of Israeli athletes at the Munich Olympics. The government soon launched a press campaign against him and his wife, Elena Bonner, who was subjected to KGB interrogation on several occasions. People claiming to be members of Black September, a Palestinian resistance group, threatened to kill Sakharov and his family. Undaunted, Sakharov launched a hunger strike to demand the release of political prisoners during U.S. President Richard Nixon's visit to the USSR in 1974.

In 1975, Sakharov was awarded the Nobel Peace Prize, but the Soviet government would not allow him to travel to Sweden to receive it. The next year, Sakharov was elected vice president of the **International League for Human Rights**. After bombings in the Moscow subway system in 1977, Sakharov denied the government charges of dissident responsibility. The USSR Procurator's Office warned him to stop speaking on these issues and harassment of his family increased. Sakharov demanded publicly that political prisoners should be granted **amnesty**. In 1979, he denounced the conviction and jailing of members of Charter 77, a human rights group.

On 22 January 1980, Sakharov was arrested, deprived of all his government awards and prizes, and internally exiled to Gorky under constant guard by the police and the KGB. In 1981, his diary, letters, manuscripts, and notes were stolen from his residence. Sakharov and his wife began a hunger strike to protest the restrictions placed on their daughter-in-law's departure from the Soviet Union in November and they were forcibly hospitalized. When the Soviet Union allowed their daughter-in-law to leave, they discontinued the hunger strike.

The governments of Belgium, Denmark, the Federal Republic of Germany, France, Italy, Norway, Portugal, Sweden, Great Britain, and the Holy See expressed concern over the treatment of Sakharov. President François Mitterrand of France expressed the concern of Western Europe over the fate of Sakharov and others who had acted in the name of human rights during an official visit to Moscow in June 1984. Mikhail Gorbachev, as part of his policy of glasnost, released Sakharov from exile in December 1986. In 1987, he was elected to the Congress of People's Deputies and worked diligently on a draft of a new constitution. Sakharov died on 14 December 1989.

SALVATION ARMY. The Salvation Army was founded in 1865, dedicating itself to the principle of providing voluntary support in religious service to the needy. Its programs extend throughout the world. As a nongovernmental organization (NGO), it enjoys consultative status with the United Nations **Economic and Social Council (ECOSOC)** and the **United Nations Educational, Scientific, and Cultural Organization (UNESCO)**. Through dozens of national offices it maintains a range of community development, **food** production, public **health**, disaster relief, and social welfare programs, with a special emphasis on projects in developing countries. The Salvation Army World Service Office (SAWSO) is the international assistance branch of the Salvation Army, and was incorporated in August 1977. SAWSO has channeled $100 million in goods and services to developing countries throughout the world in both disaster response and development-related programs. It, in turn, works through tens of thousands of local Salvation Army personnel in the countries of assistance. Programs address a variety of sectors including **education**, health services, HIV/AIDS, relief and reconstruction, and income-generation initiatives. Salvation Army International Headquarters: 101 Queen Victoria Street, London EC4P 4EP, UK. SAWSO address:

615 Slaters Lane, P.O. Box 269, Alexandria, VA 22313, USA. International Website: www1.salvationarmy.org. SAWSO website: www.sawso.org.

SARO-WIWA, KEN (1941–1995). Kenule Beeson Saro-Wiwa was born on 10 October 1941 in Bori, Rivers State, Nigeria. His family was Ogoni, an ethnic **minority** in the Niger River Delta. Saro-Wiwa was an excellent student and received government scholarships to Government College in Umuahia and the University of Ibadan, (both in Nigeria), graduating from the latter in 1965. Saro-Wiwa taught high school and then university classes. During the Nigerian Civil War (1967–1970), Saro-Wiwa served as the Civilian Administrator for Bonny, a port in the Niger Delta. He then served as the regional commissioner for education in the Rivers State Cabinet in the early 1970s until he was dismissed in 1973 for supporting autonomy for the Ogoni.

Saro-Wiwa helped establish the Movement for the Survival of the Ogoni People (MOSOP), based on nonviolence, in 1990. The organization was founded to advocate increased autonomy for the Ogoni, an equitable distribution of oil revenues, and remediation of environmental damage caused by oil exploration and production. In 1992, Saro-Wiwa devoted himself to work for the Ogoni people practically full time. Nigeria's military government arrested him five times between 1992 and 1994, usually jailing him without a trial. He was arrested in June 1993 and imprisoned for a month.

In May 1994, a mob attacked a meeting of a faction of the MOSOP, killing four people. Saro-Wiwa was not present at the meeting but he was arrested, beaten, and imprisoned for eight months without charge. During his incarceration, he was in leg irons, subjected to **torture**, and not allowed to see either a doctor or a lawyer. In January 1995, he was charged with incitement to murder. Saro-Wiwa was found guilty by a military tribunal and sentenced to death. Saro-Wiwa and eight other leaders of MOSOP were hanged on 10 November 1995. British Prime Minister John Majors called the executions "judicial murder"; **Nelson Mandela** and **Desmond Tutu** denounced the killings; 18 countries recalled ambassadors, including the United States and Great Britain; the World Bank withheld a $100 million loan; and Nigeria was suspended from the Commonwealth of Nations.

SAVE THE CHILDREN ALLIANCE (SCA). The first Save the Children organization was founded in 1919 by Eglantyne Jebb and her sister, Dorothy Buxton, in London to advocate for the well-being of children; in the following year, the International Save the Children Union was founded and spread rapidly to about 20 countries. A group of American businessmen and philanthropists founded the Save the Children Fund in 1932 to address the problem of **poverty** in the Appalachian region during the Great Depression in the United States. The Save the Children Alliance was officially established in Geneva in 1977 when a number of Save the Children organizations decided to coordinate their activities and influence international policy toward children. In 1997 the International Save the Children Alliance was formed to enhance coordination between the national Save the Children organizations that now include 27 national agencies. The SCA serves as a coordinating body of these organizations in the provision of **education**, public **health**, nutrition, and community development programs. These programs on behalf of children reach 110 countries throughout the world. It maintains offices in New York and Geneva to lobby **United Nations (UN)** agencies and one in Brussels to influence the policies of the **European Union (EU)**.

The SCA and its constituent organizations fund programs dealing with the health and education of children, eradication of the exploitation and abuse of children, and the provision of assistance to children in situations of conflict, disasters, and emergency situations. It also advocates for **children's rights**, has supported the ratification and implementation of the **Convention on the Rights of the Child**, and is a member of the **Coalition to Stop the Use of Child Soldiers**. International Office Address: ISCA, Second Floor, Cambridge House, 100 Cambridge Grove, London W6 0LE, UK. Website: www .savethechildren.net.

SELF-DETERMINATION. Concern about the effects that a lack of self-determination had on international peace and security was reflected after World War I in the inclusion of the right of self-determination of peoples in U.S. President Woodrow Wilson's Fourteen Points. The notion was implicit in the formation of the **League of Nations** mandate system. Article 1, paragraph 2, of the **United Nations Charter** identifies as one of the purposes of the **United Nations (UN)** the development of "friendly relations among nations based on respect for the principle of equal rights and self-determination of peoples." In its Declaration on the Granting of Independence to Colonial Countries and Peoples, the **United Nations General Assembly** reiterated this right. In the first article of both the **International Covenant on Civil and Political Rights** and the **International Covenant on Economic, Social, and Cultural Rights**, the right to self-determination is stated thusly: "All peoples have the right of self-determination. By virtue of that right they freely determine their political status and freely pursue their economic, social, and cultural development." The right has been reaffirmed in countless other regional and international settings. Nevertheless, it is important to observe that the right of self-determination, especially as it may apply to indigenous populations or **minorities**, presents a conflict to the even more widely accepted norms under **international law** of the **sovereignty**, political independence, and territorial integrity of states. The widespread civil instability and turmoil present in the world suggests that the tensions existing between the rights of sovereignty of existing states and the rights of people who lack self-determination remain a major complicating factor in contemporary international relations.

SLAVERY. The practice of slavery can be traced back to the earliest times of antiquity. Although slavery as a publicly sanctioned institution largely disappeared in many parts of Western Europe during the Middle Ages under the humane influence of Christian teaching, it persisted vigorously in most of the rest of the world, and was reintroduced in European colonial areas during the age of exploration and European expansion, although persistently opposed by the Church. Only in the 19th and 20th centuries were determined efforts undertaken to abolish slavery and practices similar to slavery and to interdict the slave trade on a global scale. These efforts, though largely successful, have not completely eradicated the practice. Studies by various human rights bodies have identified pockets of slavery in North Africa, especially in Mali and the Sudan, and the Arabian Peninsula as well as in parts of Asia. Still, compared to the widespread practice of slavery from antiquity until just two centuries ago, remarkable progress has been made in the gradual elimination of a practice once thought to be ineradicable.

Although historically slavery was considered natural by many societies, Judeo-Christian teachings on the subject, as well as the writings of Greek political philosophers, recognized the dilemmas and injustice surrounding the notion of slavery. The Christian conception of human beings as equal before the sight of God reduced the distinction between master and slave, and although it did not explicitly call for the eradication of slavery, it did call for its mitigation as a necessary evil, and, as noted above, in many parts of Western Europe, the institution largely died out during the Middle Ages.

Aristotle, whose teachings on slavery are widely misinterpreted, made a distinction between natural and conventional slaves. The natural slave was a person whose rational faculty was severely impaired, and thus needed to be guided and led by others. Conventional slaves, on the other hand, were people whose rational capacity was completely intact, but who, because they had been captured in time of war, had become legally the property of the victors. Such people were not natural slaves, and the vast majority of slaves in the Greek world were slaves of the conventional variety. Aristotle pointed out the dilemma that existed for Greek cities that relied heavily on conventional slaves for labor. While he believed that slavery was essential to the economic health of many Greek poleis, on the other hand, he could not ignore the injustice associated with keeping those who were not natural slaves in a condition of slavery. Indeed, such people, naturally disposed to a life of freedom and independence, represent a potential threat to the stability of the state because of their resentment and their inclination to revolt. For both religion and philosophy, then, the institution of slavery posed dilemmas that did not go unnoticed over the centuries. Most of those who opposed slavery in principle, however, seemed resigned to the notion that it could not be rooted out, that it was a necessary evil, a by-product of the fallen state of humanity, a by-product of sin, or a consequence of war.

This notion changed in the early 19th century. Great Britain took the lead in abolishing slavery in the British realm in 1807. Then enjoying substantial sea power, Britain began to interdict the slave trade. In 1808, the U.S. Congress, which had been barred by the Constitution from prohibiting the importation of slaves until that year, enacted legislation barring the African slave trade, and later declared those engaging in the importation of slaves to be pirates. European states began to follow Britain's lead, and at the Congress of Vienna in 1815 a British proposal to enforce economic boycotts against states refusing to abolish slavery was considered. A watered-down version of this proposal was adopted by the Congress of Vienna, expressing condemnation of the Negro slave trade, but lacking clear-cut enforcement mechanisms. But the British persisted in the use of the naval power to interdict slave trade, often in cooperation with other states through bilateral agreements.

The actual emancipation of large slave populations, however, came only later, and in the United States, only in the context of a bloody civil war that to a great extent was fought over the issue of slavery. In 1863, during the height of the Civil War, President Abraham Lincoln asserted the Emancipation Proclamation. This marked a milestone in the gradual process of eradicating slavery in the United States. The emancipation of serfs in Russia, which occurred in 1861, represented another major step toward global abolition of slave practices.

Momentum toward abolition of slavery picked up in the early 20th century and culminated in the Convention of St. Germain-en-Laye of 1919. This treaty proclaimed the complete abolition of slavery and of the slave trade by land or sea. A related agreement concluded in 1926 at Geneva was the **Convention to Suppress Slave Trade and Slavery**, broadened the terms of the Convention of St. Germain-en-Laye. This convention was later amended by a **United Nations (UN)** protocol of 1953, and in 1956, it was further expanded and updated by the **Supplementary Convention on the Abolition of Slavery, the Slave Trade, and Institutions and Practices Similar to Slavery**, also done at Geneva. For an excellent intellectual history of the idea and practice of slavery, see Davis (1965). On the international legal aspects of slavery, see von Glahn (1995). *See also* FORCED LABOR.

SOCIAL SECURITY. The right to social security is stipulated in numerous international human rights instruments, including Article 25 of the **Universal Declaration of Human Rights** and Article 9 of the **International Covenant on Economic, Social, and Cultural Rights**. The declaration holds that "Everyone has a right to a standard of living adequate for the health and well-being of himself and of his **family**, including . . . the right to social security in the event of unemployment, sickness, disability, widowhood, old age or other lack of livelihood in circumstances beyond his control." The **International Labour Organization (ILO)** in a number of its conventions, including the Social Security Convention of 1952 and the Equality of Treatment Convention of 1962, also establishes standards for social security policy of ratifying states. The actual social security policies of nations vary considerably, however, even among signatories to the several agreements on the subject. The right is also upheld in the **European Convention on Social Security**.

SOLIDARITY. Solidarity is the principle whereby people, institutions, and organizations demonstrate their support and fellow feeling for one another. Solidarity is normally felt most keenly in the context of kinship relations in the **family**, clans, and other local religious, social, civic, or economic organizations. Solidarity at the national level may manifest itself in a sense of patriotism. At the international level, humanitarian assistance and promotion of human rights is an expression of solidarity. Solidarity is honored whenever people express and give support to one another, especially in time of need. When more familial, familiar, local, immediately effective, and accountable institutions have difficulty meeting their normal duties or carrying out their normal functions, support from more remote but also more comprehensive institutions may be needed, in a show of solidarity to step in to assist and facilitate in the restoration of the local capacities. In such demonstrations of solidarity, the intervening institutions need to respect the principle of **subsidiarity**.

SOLZHENITSYN, ALEXANDER (1918–). Alexander Solzhenitsyn—winner of the Nobel Prize in Literature in 1970 for his fictional but also quasi-autobiographical works exposing the excesses of the Soviet prison system—is both an icon for **freedom of opinion and expression** and an example of the personal hardship endured by millions living under authoritarian rule. Having served in the Red Army during World War II and attaining the rank of captain, Solzhenitsyn was arrested for criticism of Joseph Stalin in letters written to his brother-in-law. This led to eight years of detention and hard labor in a series of camps in the Soviet Gulag. His books *One Day in the Life of Ivan Denisovich* (1962) and *The First Circle* (1968), which would launch him into literary fame, were based upon his personal experience in the Soviet labor camp system. These and other works, such as the *Cancer Ward* (1968), were the basis of his Nobel award. His later more ambitious documentary work, *The Gulag Archipelago*, published in three volumes (1973–1978) in which he traced the development of the entire Soviet prison system, was a very influential book, appearing just at the time the superpowers were enjoying a period of détente.

Solzhenitsyn was expelled from the Soviet Union in 1974, as this critical work was reaching a wide readership. He was stripped of his citizenship and deported to West Germany, spending the next 20 years of his life in exile, at Zurich, Switzerland, and for a time, in Vermont. He returned to Russia in 1994, after the collapse of the communist system, meeting with Russian President Boris Yeltsin. Solzhenitsyn continued writing during his exile, producing several historical novels dealing with Russia, and after his return to his native land, took up more political themes in his writing, including Russian-Jewish relations in his *Two Hundred Years Together* (2002), an assessment of Russian-Jewish relations over two centuries—a book that raised once again charges of anti-Semitism, that from time to time had been voiced concerning Solzhenitsyn's views.

But caricatures of him as a reactionary, a tsarist, and even as a theocrat or an antidemocrat, fail to capture a more subtle political philosophy rooted in an effort to give due attention to both the moral and spiritual, as well as the political and social nature of human beings, and of the nature of moral and political freedom. Solzhenitsyn's synthesis may seem utopian in an age when moral matters are seen as being divorced from political action, but for him, this was precisely the problem in Soviet totalitarianism and, for that matter, in much of secular thought in the West, which seemed to him as having lost its soul.

SOUTH ASIA HUMAN RIGHTS DOCUMENTATION CENTRE (SAHRDC). SAHRDC is a network of individuals across Asia who promote human rights treaties and conventions and human rights education and dissemination, and who investigate, document, and disseminate information concerning human rights abuses in Asia. Its investigative work centers on violations of the rights of **refugees**, **freedom of the press**, and other **political rights**, as well as on incidences of

torture and forced **disappearances**. SAHRDC is an example of a small organization headquartered in New Delhi, India, that, owing to modern computer technology, has a large impact through its research and reports, its training programs, and its networking with other non-governmental organizations (NGOs) as well as international media and governments. It enjoys special consultative status with the United Nations **Economic and Social Council (ECOSOC)**. Website: www .hrdc.net.

SOUTHERN AFRICA DEVELOPMENT COMMUNITY (SADC). Originally founded in 1980 as the Southern African Development Coordination Conference, SADC sought from its inception to reduce the dependence of southern African states on South Africa by coordinating and enhancing development and humanitarian cooperation. In 1992, at Windhoek, Namibia, SADC member-states revised its focus from a coordinating body into a development community. It has focused on developing communication and transportation infrastructure, improving **food** security, promoting early warning of humanitarian emergencies, advancing freedom and social justice, creating a regional food reserve, and sponsoring research on indigenous drought-resistant grains. Most SADC projects are funded by external donors. It is now one of the regional economic commissions of the **African Union (AU)**. SADC restructured again in 2001, emphasizing such common principles as promotion of sustainable and equitable economic and social development, **subsidiarity**, market integration and development, promotion of trade and investment, and the promotion of common democratic political values. To advance this more ambitious agenda, SADC reorganized its structure, including the Integrated Committee of Ministers and SADC National Committees. Address: Private Bag 0095, Gaborone, Botswana. Website: www.sadcreview.com.

SOVEREIGNTY. This is the legal principle establishing the state as the highest legal authority in international relations. It implies that states are independent, legally equal, and in complete legal control of their foreign and domestic policies. It implies that within their own territory they enjoy complete legal jurisdiction and that they are free from external interference. States alone may qualify their sovereignty, and they often do through customary or treaty law. Progress in the area of human rights depends ultimately on decisions by states to incorporate human rights standards into their domestic legal orders and to permit international scrutiny of their human rights performance. In the area of human rights abuses, sovereignty has not infrequently been claimed by governments as an absolute protection from outside interference, but it is clear both from the **natural law** tradition out of which modern **international law** emerged, and from actual state practice that sovereignty does not offer absolute immunity from outside intervention or regulation. The principle of **subsidiarity** implies that governments do have the primary right, but also the primary duty, to promote and respect human rights, but when that duty has been flagrantly violated by the very government responsible for protection of human rights, international law and practice has tolerated intervention to protect and restore them.

STANTON, ELIZABETH CADY (1815–1902). A prominent American **women**'s rights advocate of the 19th century, Elizabeth Cady Stanton was born on 12 November 1815 in Johnstown, New York, to the Cady family. Her father was a prominent politician and her mother an advocate of the abolition of **slavery** and the promotion of women's rights. She studied at Johnstown Academy and attended the Troy Female Seminary prior to marrying Henry Stanton, an abolitionist, in 1840. In the same year, she attended the first World Antislavery Convention in London, where she met **Lucretia Mott** and **William Lloyd Garrison**. She developed a lifelong attachment with the former. Together with Mott and other feminists, she planned the Seneca Falls Convention in 1848. She drafted the main document for the convention, modeled on the **Declaration of Independence**. Among other things, it demanded voting rights for women. The convention passed the Declaration of Sentiments and other resolutions declaring the **equality** of the sexes and supporting the right of women to vote and to participate in trades, professions, and commerce.

In the years that followed, Stanton made periodic forays into public life. She met **Susan B. Anthony**, and together they served as officers of the Women's State Temperance Society in 1852. Stanton lobbied for liberalization of New York's divorce laws, marriage contracts, and women's access to professions. In 1863, she and Anthony formed the National Woman's Loyal League to lobby on behalf of an abolition amendment to the Constitution. She helped to form the National Woman Suffrage Association in 1869. Her later years were spent in writing and occasional service as an officer of the National American Women's Association. She died on 26 October 1902.

STATELESSNESS. People who do not possess a **nationality** are said to be stateless. In this condition, they do not enjoy the protection of a state especially when residing or traveling abroad. Stateless persons face a number of problems. Lacking a nationality, there is no state to issue them passports or visas, identity papers, travel permits, **work** cards, professional and marriage licenses, and so on. This can lead to interminable problems. *De jure* statelessness is potentially quite problematical. Although rare, such persons have no national connection, having been formally stripped of their nationality by their former country of citizenship. *De facto* statelessness is far more common and refers to the predicament of **refugees**, who though they have not been formally stripped of their citizenship in most instances, cannot effectively rely on their country of nationality to protect their interests abroad. Such persons fear persecution at the hands of their former government of nationality.

Apart from the 1951 **Convention Relating to the Status of Refugees** and various regional refugee instruments, efforts to address the problem of statelessness, especially for *de jure* stateless persons, have only been marginally successful. The earliest effort to cope with the problem came in 1930 with the adoption of the Special Protocol Concerning Statelessness at The Hague, but it only entered into force briefly in 1973. Still, one of the first **United Nations (UN)** conferences met to discuss both the problems of refugees and statelessness. That conference suggested that the two problems of refugees and stateless persons be taken up separately. A conference on refugees later produced the 1951 **Convention Relating to the Status of Refugees**. The UN Conference on the Status of Stateless Persons met in 1954. It produced the United Nations **Convention Relating to the Status of Stateless Persons**, which closely parallels the 1951 Convention Relating to the Status of Refugees. The former agreement came into force in June of 1960, although only a relatively small number of states are parties.

A further **Convention on the Reduction of Statelessness** was adopted at New York on 30 August 1961. It entered into force in December 1975. This treaty took the most ambitious steps to date in attempting to reduce the number of stateless persons. However, owing to the small number of ratifying states, its overall impact has been quite marginal. For a full text of the Convention Relating to the Status of Stateless Persons, see *United Nations Treaty Series*, no. 5158, vol. 360, p. 117; for a text of the Convention on the Reduction of Statelessness, see UN Document A/CONF.9/15, 1961, or UN General Assembly Official Records, Ninth Session, Supplement no. 21 (A2890), p. 49.

STATE OF EMERGENCY. *See* PUBLIC EMERGENCY.

STATE RESPONSIBILITY. The **international law** of state responsibility has long recognized the duty of governments to respect the fundamental rights of aliens who reside within, visit, or transit through their territories. In order to enhance international trade, commerce, travel, and other forms of mutually beneficial contact, governments reciprocally recognize that aliens must be given a degree of legal protection and individual rights at least equal to that provided the government's citizens. This includes the right to protection of the police system, preservation of their person from violence, protection of their **property** from unlawful seizure, and free access to the courts in order to seek redress for grievances or injuries committed against them. In cases where aliens have been denied due process of law or equal access to the courts through unfair or unjust treatment by the executive or judicial arms of the foreign government, or where by negligence or direct action of arms of the state they have suffered unredressed injuries, and where they have exhausted all local remedies, individuals have had the right to appeal to their country of **nationality** to press a suit against the offending government. Where an injury has occurred that is attributable to a lack of due diligence by the offending government or where state responsibility can be shown to exist as a basis for the injury, the injured alien's government may expect compensation for the negligence or injury to its citizen. At its discretion, the citizen's government may then pass any reparations on to its citizen.

These principles have a long tradition of observance as customary law among nations. In 1985, the **United Nations General Assembly** adopted the **Declaration on the Human Rights of Individuals Who Are Not Nationals of the Country in Which They Live**, which was an effort to reaffirm and clarify the existing customary law of state responsibility. Although nonbinding, it does provide a sense of the international consensus about the appropriate treatment of aliens, particularly those of minority status in their country of residence. *See also* ALIENS' RIGHTS.

SUBSIDIARITY. This principle of ethics and organization holds that those responsible persons or institutions most familiar and immediately accountable for particular human activities should exercise full and local responsibility for such activities. When institutions or individuals most capable of undertaking independent and effective activity at the personal or local level are unable or unwilling to assume their normal responsibilities, more distant and less familiar and immediate bodies may need to intervene in order to accomplish the lo cal tasks and facilitate the capacity of local institutions to resume their natural functions. The **family**, churches, and local civic and social organizations are the foundations of society that nurture individuals and give rise to effective local action. When these highly local, immediate, and more accountable bodies are dysfunctional or disrupted, more comprehensive political institutions, such as regional or national governments, may need to intervene as a demonstration of **solidarity**. When these are unable or unwilling to do so, international bodies may be called upon to demonstrate solidarity in restoring national and local capacities. The principle is an ancient one, often expressed in modern times by the concept of "grassroots" development, or in national constitutions by the political principle of federalism.

SUPPLEMENTARY CONVENTION ON THE ABOLITION OF SLAVERY, THE SLAVE TRADE, AND INSTITUTIONS AND PRACTICES SIMILAR TO SLAVERY. After the adoption in 1953 by the **United Nations (UN)** of the Protocol Amending the Slavery Convention, further studies showed that **slavery** or practices similar to it, together with the slave trade, continued to exist in parts of the world. In 1956, the United Nations **Economic and Social Council (ECOSOC)** convened a conference in Geneva to consider and adopt a supplementary convention dealing with the matter of slavery. The convention was adopted on 7 September 1956 and entered into force the following year, on 30 April 1957. The convention called upon the signatories to eradicate such practices as debt bondage, serfdom, forced marriage, the inheritance of persons, and forced child labor. It also stipulated that they were obliged to interdict the slave trade not only at sea but by air, and it granted automatic freedom to any slave taking refuge on board any vessel of a state party to the convention. *See also* FORCED LABOR.

SURVIVAL INTERNATIONAL. Survival International was established in 1969 to help tribal peoples protect their physical existence and cultures in face of indifferent or even hostile governments. Specifically, it has worked to support tribal peoples' rights to survival and **self-determination**, to ensure adequate presentation of tribal peoples' interests in all decision making affecting them, and to obtain tribal peoples' ownership and use of land and other resources.

Survival International's secretariat is located in London, with other national offices in France, Italy, and Spain, and it enjoys an individual membership roster of about 12,000 in 75 countries. Survival International's work in protection of **indigenous rights** focuses on field projects, public campaigns, educational outreach, and publications. For example, its three-year vigil at Brazilian embassies led to the recognition by Brazil of Yanomani land rights, while its lobbying efforts stopped a road project in the Central African Republic, thereby saving the land of 20,000 Aka Pygmies. As part of its educational work, Survival International participates in international conferences and produces films, photo exhibits, and educational packets. It publishes a newsletter, as well as books, reports, and Urgent Action Bulletins that alert its members and supporters to specific threats to tribal peoples. In 1989, it was the recipient of the Right Livelihood Award. Address: 6 Charterhouse Buildings, London EC1M 7ET, England. Website: www.survival-international.org. *See also* CULTURAL SURVIVAL; WORLD COUNCIL OF INDIGENOUS PEOPLES (WCIP).

– T –

TERESA, MOTHER (1910–1997). Born on 26 August 1910 in Skopjie, Serbia, in the predominantly Albanian province of Kosovo and baptized as Gonxha Agnes, the woman who would become a world-renowned figure as a diminutive nun and caregiver to tens of thousands of beggars in Calcutta began life in comfortable circumstances, but the death of her father in 1919 left the family in financial straits. In 1928 she left her family, joining the Institute of the Blessed Virgin Mary, also known as the Irish Sisters of Loreto, where she took the name of Sister Mary Teresa. She was sent to India, where she arrived in January 1929, to begin a lifelong journey of service to humanity. She made her first profession of vows in 1931 and was assigned to teaching at St. Mary's School for girls, whose clientele consisted of girls from well-to-do families. She professed final vows in 1937, continuing to pass happy and fruitful years.

However, on a train ride from Calcutta to Darjeeling for an annual retreat, she experienced a second conversion, or what she called a "call within a call" to devote herself more intensely to Jesus and to his presence in the form of the "distressing disguise of the poor." Over the next two years, her conviction grew that she needed to establish a new religious order devoted exclusively to the care of the poorest of the poor in Calcutta. She left Loreto in August 1948, wearing the characteristic garb of white, blue-bordered sari that eventually became the trademark of the Missionaries of Charity. Within a decade, Mother Teresa began sending the sisters who flocked to her order to other parts of India where they worked among the poor and the untouchables. A papal decree of praise in 1965 by Pope Paul VI encouraged her to venture forth into Latin America to establish a new foundation in Venezuela, an appeal she answered, even as new houses were established at Rome, in Tanzania, in her homeland of Albania, and eventually in every corner of the world.

As early as 1962, Mother Teresa's charitable work among the poor was acknowledged in India with the conferral of the Indian Padmashri Award. In 1979, she was awarded the Nobel Peace Prize. Her reputation was further enhanced by the publication of Malcolm Muggeridge's *Something Beautiful for God* (1977), in which the experienced British journalist chronicled the spiritual passion motivating

Mother Teresa's ministry and her recognition of the human dignity of every human person, including the unborn. She was a fearless advocate of the **right to life**, and to the dignity of all human life even among the poorest and those most subject to suffering and neglect. She advanced the basic human rights through direct action on her own part and on the part of her ever-expanding order, which came to include the Missionary Charity Brothers in 1963, contemplative branches of the Missionary Sisters in 1976 and of the Brothers in 1979, the Missionaries of Charity Fathers in 1984, and associated lay groups, including the Lay Missionaries of Charity in 1989. Before her death on 5 September 1997, her work had radiated out from Calcutta into more than 600 foundations in 123 countries.

India honored her passing with a state funeral, and her cause for canonization to sainthood was given the blessings of Pope **John Paul II**. She was beatified on 20 December 2002 and her cause for sainthood awaits final proclamation. In the meantime, her charitable work goes on in slums and ghettos throughout the world, as her sisters, brothers, and dedicatees work among the homeless, AIDS victims, and others in great distress. The Mother Teresa Society of Kosovo was a major actor in the successful provision of humanitarian assistance for **refugees** and returnees generated in the wake of the Kosovo war in the late 1990s.

TERRITORIAL ASYLUM. *See* ASYLUM.

TERRORISM. Modern multilateral efforts to cope with the emergence of terrorist acts against innocent civilian populations hearken back to the **League of Nations**, which adopted a Convention for the Prevention and Punishment of Terrorism. That instrument, however, failed to enter into force owing to insufficient ratifications. Further efforts to curb terrorism tended to focus on the more narrow problem of the safety of air travel in subsequent decades, as governments established the **International Civil Aviation Organization (ICAO)**, which, in turn, sponsored the negotiation of treaties aimed at curbing crimes aboard aircraft, and at deterring and punishment air piracy and other acts of violence against civil aviation. Several treaties entered into force to effect such goals, including the Tokyo Treaty of 1963, the Hague Convention of 1970, and the Montreal Convention of 1971.

In the wake of the Black September terrorist attacks on the Israeli delegation to the Munich Summer Olympics in 1972, the **United Nations General Assembly**, at the request of Secretary-General Kurt Waldheim, placed terrorism on its agenda for the first time. The title given to that agenda item suggests the political volatility of the topic in international relations at the time: "Measures to prevent international terrorism which endangers or takes innocent human lives or jeopardizes fundamental freedoms, and study of the underlying causes of those forms of terrorism and acts of violence which lie in misery, frustration, grievance and despair and which cause some people to sacrifice human lives, including their own, in an attempt to effect radical changes." Debate on the issue was highly contentious, with some Western governments seeking strong punishment of terrorists, while many governments from the developing world saw the new terrorism as being connected to the old terrorism of colonial domination and lack of **self-determination**. Given the preponderance of developing countries, their view about the importance of the underlying causes of terrorism prevailed, and an Ad Hoc Committee on International Terrorism was established to study the matter further. Disputes about how to define terrorism persisted, with the developing country majority insisting on a distinction between individual acts of terrorism worthy of condemnation and acts committed by groups in pursuit of "national liberation," which were seen as falling outside the definition of terrorism. Despite the definitional impasse, the General Assembly did pass the **United Nations (UN)** Convention for the Protection and Punishment of Crimes against International Protected Persons, Including Diplomatic Agents in 1973, and in 1979 it approved the Convention against the Taking of **Hostages**.

Real progress toward a more universal condemnation of terrorist acts, and efforts to concert international cooperation to deter and punish them came in the 1990s after the end of the Cold War. In 1994, the General Assembly adopted a Declaration on Measures to Eliminate International Terrorism, which encouraged states to strengthen **extradition** agreements and the sharing of information on terrorists, a process that was already largely underway through INTERPOL, an agency dedicated to encouraging cooperation between and among the domestic police enforcement agencies of governments. In the same year, the **International Law Commission**, acting on the urgent request of the General Assembly, approved the draft statute of the **International Criminal Court (ICC)**, which was formally adopted in 1998. This body was granted the power to prosecute individuals guilty of **war crimes**, **crimes against humanity**, taking of hostages, hijacking, and other acts of terrorism. Two further steps were taken by the UN General Assembly to promote interstate cooperation in suppressing terrorism, including the International Convention for the Suppression of Terrorist Bombings of 1997 and the International Convention for the Suppression of the Financing of Terrorism in 1999.

In 1997, the General Assembly for the first time declared unequivocally that terrorist acts were "criminal acts intended or calculated to provoke a state of terror in the general public, a group of persons or particular persons for political purposes." Furthermore, the assembly condemned all such acts "under any circumstances whatever the considerations of a political, philosophical, ideological, racial, ethnic, religious or any other nature that may be invoked to justify them." This represented a departure from the earlier tendency to soft pedal criticism of violence against innocent persons done in the name of national liberation. With this step, the UN was finally coming to terms with the intrinsically evil nature of all acts of violence aimed at innocent persons for the explicit purpose of engendering terror. The long-standing traditional notion that innocent civilians should be protected insofar as is possible, even during time of war, finally was reaffirmed by the international community. Terrorism, then, was a criminal activity, whether in time of war or peace, and it properly evoked the disgust and rejection of civilized nations.

Despite the growing awareness of and international determination to suppress terrorism, the events of 11 September 2001 illustrated the capacity of nonstate actors such as the terrorist group Al-Qaeda to flout the international consensus. The murder of innocent civilians by the terrorist acts of that day indicated how vulnerable the international community was to the execution of such wanton terrorist acts. The United States, in particular, whose homeland had hitherto been largely immune from terrorist activities, suddenly felt particularly vulnerable. Other countries with a past history of terrorist violence were less deeply affected. However, the spate of terrorist attacks both before and after 11 September in a variety of countries and continents continues to point out the vulnerability of the international community to the determined and radical animus of terrorist organizations.

Since the primary function of national governments is the safety and security of their territory and population, it is not surprising that various countries have embarked on a more determined "war on terrorism." During times of **public emergency**, governments are obliged in prudence to crack down of the capacity of illicit organizations to threaten public well-being. The **right to life** is the most basic human right, and governments have the obligation to ensure that their citizens are not subject to acts of terrorist violence. Under such conditions, states are bound to take more stringent security precautions, and the **procedural rights** of suspected terrorists can be expected to be curtailed. The general public may thus be subjected to the inconvenience of security checks and surveillance in public places, means of conveyance and transportation, and even in communications networks, in ways that constrain full freedom of movement and communication. The lines between public and private life are drawn more narrowly when public safety is threatened, with the zone of **privacy** being necessarily and, one hopes, appropriately curtailed. Governments must take prudent steps within the bounds of justice to achieve the goals of safety while not overstepping the bounds of liberty and justice.

There are, however, certain human rights that even terrorists enjoy, including the right not to be subjected to **torture**, the right to be treated humanely, and the right to judicial due process and a **fair trial**. How soon hearings or a trial must be held and by what judicial body in the case of detainees depends upon circumstances. So, for instance, a suspected terrorist detained within a country will be normally subject to the application of that country's statutory law and procedure. However, those captured and detained during time of war in zones of conflict may be held until the end of hostilities. This becomes especially problematical in the case of individuals detained during the war in Afghanistan, which remains, at a much-reduced level, subject to martial activity. When does such a war end? These are matters over which much disagreement exists in the interpretation and application of the **Geneva Red Cross Conventions**, to prisoners of war and other detainees who, though not prisoners of war by virtue of their own violations of the convention, must still be treated humanely and be given due process by appropriate judicial bodies, even on the fundamental matter of determining their status under relevant instruments of international humanitarian law.

A great deal of variation exists between and among governments on how aggressively the war on terror should be pursued and on how to handle individuals apprehended as terrorist suspects. Human rights advocacy organizations have been especially critical of the U.S. government's and other governments' handling of both. The role of such private bodies as advocates of human rights tends to focus on the rights of the individual. However, it must be observed that governments have a larger responsibility, which is that of protecting whole societies from the threat of violence. Moreover, it is the governments that are responsible and accountable for the preservation of the general welfare, a function that does not fall to human rights advocacy groups. The latter are not accountable morally, legally, or politically for this important function. Thus, it should be no surprise that they would view the problem of terrorism and the suppression of terrorism through different lenses than those of the governments who will be held accountable in the final analysis not by human rights agencies but by their own people. Democratic governments, in contrast to authoritarian ones, generally do a far better job of preserving and protecting human rights, including those of suspected terrorists. However, even democratic governments must take steps to protect innocent lives, and appropriately so, when threatened by individuals and groups having no respect for human rights and little regard for innocent human life. *See also* HOSTAGES.

TORTURE. The torture of detainees or prisoners is unfortunately still widely practiced or sanctioned by governments. However, customary **international law**, especially in the form of the law of war, forbids torture. Since World War II, facing the widespread practice of torture, the **United Nations (UN)** and a variety of regional bodies have undertaken steps to outlaw and prevent this practice. In 1975, the UN sponsored a Congress on Crime Prevention and Treatment of Offenders in Geneva. This conference produced a declaration banning torture, which was adopted by the **United Nations General Assembly** in the same year, in the form of a **Declaration on the Protection of All Persons from Being Subjected to Torture and Other Cruel,**

Inhuman, or Degrading Treatment or Punishment. This declaration did not create legally binding obligations on governments, but it did draw international attention to the question of torture, and it spurred further discussion and debate that eventually led to the drafting of a full-fledged convention on the subject in 1984.

The **Convention against Torture and Other Cruel, Inhuman, or Degrading Treatment or Punishment** entered into force on 26 June 1987, and most national governments are currently either full ratifying parties or signatories. This instrument defined torture and attempted to draw further international attention to the problem of torture by creating a **Committee against Torture (CAT)**, consisting of 10 experts. Governments party to the treaty are obliged to submit regular reports to this committee concerning steps taken by them to implement provisions of the convention. In December 2002, the UN General Assembly adopted the Optional Protocol to the Convention against Torture for the consideration of its member-states. This protocol would strengthen the torture treaty by establishing a system of regular visits by an independent international body under the supervision of the CAT, known as the Subcommittee on Prevention of Torture, and Other Cruel, Inhuman, or Degrading Treatment or Punishment, and by national bodies to locations where people are deprived of liberty to ensure that they are not subjected to torture. Each state party agrees to establish a national preventive mechanism composed of domestic visiting bodies, and to grant the international and national bodies access to detained persons. The optional protocol currently falls well short of the 20 ratifications necessary for entry into force, and only a fraction of national governments are to date signatories.

Regional efforts to combat the practice of torture are found in the provisions and practice of the **European Convention on Human Rights** and the **European Court of Human Rights (ECHR)**. The **Council of Europe (COE)** took steps in its **European Convention for the Prevention of Torture and Inhuman or Degrading Treatment or Punishment** to further interdict this practice. This agreement, which in less than a year secured ratifications from 15 European states, relies on the concept of investigation and publicity of acts of torture as a means of discouraging governments from sanctioning such practices. Among other things, the convention established the special committee consisting of 15 elected experts, which may visit prison and detention facilities of member-states and make recommendations concerning protection of inmates from practices forbidden by the convention.

In the Americas, the **Organization of American States (OAS)** adopted in 1985 the Inter-American Convention to Prevent and Punish Torture. This instrument declares torture ordered or performed by an agent of the state to be a crime.

Torture is unfortunately still widely practiced by the national and local police forces and militaries of many governments despite the existence of treaty norms and institutions meant to eradicate the practice. Terrorist organizations routinely disregard these norms, as do the members of rebel forces and guerrilla groups who often operate either in utter ignorance or utter disregard of humane values. The international war on such lawless groups, and on **terrorism** generally, presents a major dilemma for civilized nations seeking to eliminate torture from their interrogation methods.

Part of the dilemma centers on the definition of torture, which does not specifically identify each and every possible method of interrogation, which run the gamut from clearly impermissible practices such as the infliction of physical pain, bodily mutilation, threats of death, starvation, and the like, to highly questionable practices such as "water-boarding," which induces a fear of drowning in the victim, to other practices such as solitary confinement, sensory deprivation designed to confuse a person's sense of time and place, lengthy and aggressive questioning, and the like. When terrorist suspects are first brought into custody, the need for intelligence they may possess is often critical to the prevention of criminal acts and the saving of innocent lives. The temptation to use impermissible forms of torture or other inhumane and degrading techniques may be very strong, but the employment of clearly illegal or unethical methods degrades the abuser as well as the victim, and there is considerable evidence that information extracted by means of torture is usually highly unreliable. Military and police officials are normally warned in training against their usage for this reason. The torture treaty and proposed protocol are binding on states parties, and the use of reservations permits ratifying states to adopt a national definition of torture, as the United States has done by applying the U.S. constitutional standard of "no cruel or unusual punishment" under the Eighth Amendment and related domestic jurisprudence.

Numerous nongovernmental organizations (NGOs) with a focus on human rights monitor governmental practices in this arena. In addition to the well-known human rights agencies such as **Amnesty International (AI)** and **Human Rights Watch**, specialized advocacy and watchdog groups, such as the **Association for the Prevention of Torture (APT)** and the **World Organization against Torture**, have also emerged.

TRUSTEESHIP COUNCIL. One of the six main organs of the **United Nations (UN)**, the Trusteeship Council built on the practice of the **League of Nations** mandate system in providing an international means of overseeing the process of **self-determination** and eventual independence of non-self-governing territories. A total of 11 territories were placed under the supervision of the UN Trusteeship Council, which virtually worked itself out of a job in November 1994, as the island of Palau, the last part of the last trust territory, achieved independence. The council, during the period of its trust functions, received reports from the states serving as trustees concerning steps taken to prepare the territory for independence. It could also examine petitions from inhabitants of the territories. The overall objectives of the council's work, as stated in the **United Nations Charter**, included promoting the economic, political, social, and educational advancement of peoples inhabiting the trust territories, encouraging their progressive development toward freely chosen self-government, and encouraging respect for human rights and fundamental freedoms. The functions of the now inactive Trusteeship Council now reside with the five permanent members of the **United Nations** Security Council. Proposals for reviving the Trusteeship Council to address global common issues have yet to be successfully achieved.

TRUTH AND RECONCILIATION COMMISSION (TRC). On 19 July 1995, South African President **Nelson Mandela** signed the Promotion of National Unity and Reconciliation Act, which established the TRC. Although there had been at least 15 **truth commissions** established worldwide as of 1994, the TRC's origins were unique to South Africa. **Amnesty** for alleged violators of human rights active in the last years of **apartheid** was the most important issue blocking agreement on an interim democratic constitution for South Africa. According to most observers, there would have been no political settlement without the amnesty provision in the interim constitution of 1993. Importantly, while the National Party argued for a blanket amnesty, the African National Congress (ANC) successfully insisted on a conditional amnesty, which offered perpetrators on an individual basis an amnesty in exchange for fully disclosing their criminal actions.

Nongovernmental organizations (NGOs), churches, and political parties all forwarded nominees to the government, who then interviewed the nominees publicly and sent a short list of recommended nominees to the president and cabinet. President **Nelson Mandela**, in consultation with his cabinet, appointed 17 commissioners to the TRC on 29 November 1995. The commission was composed of seven blacks, two Coloureds, two Indians, and six whites. Seven commissioners were from the legal profession while four were ordained ministers. **Desmond Tutu** and Alex Boraine were the chair and vice-chair, respectively, of the TRC.

The mandate of the TRC was to compile a complete record of past human rights violations, permit victims to give testimony and make recommendations, and consider amnesty requests by those people who had violated human rights for political reasons and who gave a full public reckoning of their actions to the commission. The TRC established three committees: the Committee on Human Rights Violations, the Committee on Amnesty, and the Committee on Reparations and Rehabilitation.

The Committee on Human Rights Violations heard testimony from victims in order to determine if a gross human rights violation had occurred. A gross human rights violation was defined as the "violation of human rights through the killing, abduction, **torture**, or severe ill treatment of any person . . . which emanated from conflicts of the past . . . and the commission of which was advised, planned, directed, commanded or ordered by any person acting with a political motive." The Committee on Amnesty was appointed separately from the TRC. In the end, the committee had 19 members and received amnesty applications "for acts associated with political objectives." Important amnesty cases heard were former security policeman Dirk Coetzee's killing of human rights lawyer Griffiths Mxenge in 1981, the 1993 assassination of Chris Hani, and the former security policemen's killing of **Steven Biko** in 1977. The Reparation and Rehabilitation Committee decided on compensation for each victim so as "to restore the human and civil dignity" of the victim.

The amnesty provision was the most controversial part of the TRC. Critics have argued that the failure to work for retributive justice would lead to cycles of violence and counterviolence; that countries have a responsibility under **international law** to prosecute gross violations of human rights; that full disclosure overrode all other criteria for amnesty; that there was no requirement for remorse, repentance, or even community service; and that higher ranking officials, such as P. W. Botha and F. W. de Klerk, never acknowledged their roles in the violations of human rights in the 1980s and 1990s.

Supporters of the TRC have pointed out that amnesty was required to forestall a racial civil war; amnesty required individuals to disclose their crimes; its processes ensured greater respect for witnesses than would have been the case in the court system; findings were based on a balance of evidence, not evidence beyond a reasonable doubt as in a court of law; and the TRC covered a greater number of human rights violations in a shorter time period than could criminal trials.

The TRC held 140 hearings in 61 towns, took 22,000 victim statements dealing with 37,000 violations, and processed over 7,000 amnesty applications. The TRC submitted its final report in October 1998 but the Amnesty Committee continued convening until 31 May 2001, when it was dissolved by President Thabo Mbeki. At least, the TRC will make it more difficult for people in the future to weave a culture of lies that the apartheid system was not based on fundamental and gross violations of human rights.

TRUTH COMMISSIONS. In the wake of civil wars involving substantial violations of human rights and serious violations of international humanitarian law, an alternative approach to rebuilding civil society without pursuing expensive and potentially controversial **war crimes** trials, is for a country to establish a truth commission, whereby victims of criminal abuse can voice their grievances and restore a measure of their human dignity. Truth commissions can be undertaken in concert with trials with the commissions exposing abuses at lower echelons, while the trials focus on major perpetrators. Although truth commissions or national reconciliation commissions may shield perpetrators from criminal punishment, they nevertheless do expose those responsible for human rights abuses to public notice and opprobrium. Truth commissions afford a country a more detailed public record of abuses, and they can encourage speedier national reconciliation. **United Nations (UN)**–brokered truth commissions have been established in Burundi, East Timor, El Salvador, Guatemala, Liberia, and Sierra Leone. Twenty-two countries, including most notably South Africa, have established national truth or reconciliation commissions to investigate past wrong doing. *See also* TRUTH AND RECONCILIATION COMMISSION (TRC).

TUBMAN, HARRIET (ca. 1820–1913). The most famous conductor of the Underground Railroad was born Araminta Ross to a free black father and a slave mother near Buckhorn, in Dorchester County, on Maryland's Eastern Shore in 1820. Two events of her childhood marked Tubman for the rest of her life. First, two of her sisters were sold to a slave trader and never heard from again. This breakup of her **family**, in addition to the abuse she suffered as an enslaved worker, instilled in Tubman a deep conviction of the immorality of **slavery** and a desire to free her family from bondage. Second, Tubman was severely injured in her teens when she was hit in the head by a heavy object thrown by an overseer at another slave. This injury appears to have caused her "sleeping sickness." For the rest of her life, she experienced visions during her sleeping spells that deepened her Christian faith, her spirituality, and her conviction that she was being called to help her fellow slaves escape bondage.

In 1844, Araminta married a free black, John Tubman. They had no children and he refused to join her after she escaped to freedom, an event that was precipitated by a threat to sell her. In September 1849, she left her Maryland home and traveled through Delaware and Pennsylvania to Philadelphia. Upon reaching free soil, she chose the name Harriet Tubman as a new name for herself, and then she embarked on her remarkable career as a conductor of the Underground Railroad. Although there is disagreement as to the number of people she rescued from slavery from 1851–1860 (some putting the number at under 100, others at more than 300), Tubman's achievement is impressive by any standard. She was illiterate, the only **woman**, the only fugitive slave, and one of the few African Americans to have achieved such public acclaim in the North. Furthermore, Tubman achieved her success in the Underground Railroad without ever being caught and never losing a passenger, even after the Fugitive Slave Act of 1850 made such success more difficult.

Tubman's last major effort was to establish the John Brown Hall to care for old and indigent African Americans, which opened in 1908. Throughout her life she spoke in support of full civil rights for African Americans. After a long illness, she died in Auburn, New York, on 10 March 1913.

TUTU, DESMOND (1931–). Desmond Tutu was born on 19 February 1931 in Klerksdorp, west of Johannesburg. Tutu's childhood was happy but he later described the **racial discrimination** against blacks as a kind of brainwashing "filling you with self-disgust, self-contempt, and self-hatred, accepting a negative self-image."

Tutu, though raised as a Methodist, was educated at an Anglican institution. He contracted tuberculosis at 14 and was treated at a sanitarium, where he began a lifelong friendship with Father Trevor Huddleston, who Tutu acknowledges as being one of the strongest influences on his life. Tutu earned a teaching diploma from the Pretoria Bantu Normal College and a BA through the University of South Africa. He taught school for four years but left in 1958 when the government took control of the schools from the churches. Tutu was ordained a priest in 1961. He studied at King's College, London, where he earned his bachelor of divinity and his master of theology in 1965 and 1966 respectively.

Tutu returned to South Africa and taught at the Federal Theological Seminary in the Eastern Cape and then as a lecturer in Lesotho. In 1974, he became the dean of St. Mary's Cathedral in Johannesburg, the first black to hold that position, and he did what he could to console the parents whose children had been killed in the Soweto protests of 1976. At his speech at the funeral of **Steven Biko** in 1977, Tutu warned that "Nothing . . . not even the most brutally efficient police . . . will stop people once they are determined to achieve their freedom and their right to humanness."

Tutu was appointed general secretary of the South African Council of Churches (SACC) in 1978 and it was from this position that he waged his campaign against **apartheid**. In 1979, SACC approved a resolution advocating civil disobedience against racist laws. In the late 1970s and throughout the 1980s, Tutu supported sanctions and boycotts against South Africa. The government confiscated Tutu's passport many times, requiring him to ask permission every time he wanted to travel. Most times, the request was refused.

Tutu was awarded the 1984 Nobel Peace Prize in the same year he became bishop of Johannesburg. In a speech to the **United Nations General Assembly** in 1985 he likened apartheid to a monster. He harshly criticized Western leaders such as Ronald Reagan and Margaret Thatcher for refusing to implement sanctions against South Africa, saying that those leaders were saying effectively that blacks were "utterly dispensable." In 1988, Tutu became archbishop of Cape Town, and he continued to develop an antiapartheid theology. Tutu's rejection of apartheid rested on two Christian doctrines: all of mankind was made in the image of God, and human reconciliation was made possible by Jesus Christ. Tutu's theology also was the foundation of his advocacy of nonviolent methods to overthrow apartheid.

Tutu continued to lead demonstrations and protests until the government of F. W. de Klerk lifted the ban on a range of political parties and organizations and released **Nelson Mandela** from prison. Tutu became an important advisor to President Mandela and served as chair of the **Truth and Reconciliation Commission (TRC)**. The TRC's final report identified around 400 persons culpable in human rights violations and President Mandela lauded Tutu's work along with that of the TRC.

– U –

UNITED NATIONS (UN). Successor to the **League of Nations**, the UN was brought into being by the San Francisco Conference during the summer of 1945, as World War II neared its end. The UN's primary goals were to control conflicts among nations through principles of collective security and to eliminate the underlying causes of conflict through international cooperative endeavors. The **United Nations Charter** mentioned the importance of human rights in its preamble and in numerous of its articles, particularly in Article 1, where promotion of human rights is listed as one of the main purposes of the UN. All six organs of the UN somehow deal with human rights issues, although the primary locus of human rights activities was designed to rest in the United Nations **Economic and Social Council (ECOSOC)**, which in turn reports to the **United Nations General Assembly**. A United Nations **Commission on Human Rights (CHR)** was established reporting to ECOSOC on its work to advance human rights and fundamental freedoms. This body ceased to exist in 2006, when it was replaced by a reformed **Human Rights Council**. The General Assembly's Third Main Committee remained the primary focal point for its discussions on human rights questions. The United Nations **Trusteeship Council** dealt explicitly with the human right of self-determination, and it received reports from administering powers regarding progress toward independence and promotion of human rights in the administered territories. The **International Court of Justice (ICJ)**, which was established both as a constitutional court for interpretation of the UN Charter and as a venue for litigation of contentious claims between member governments, is not a body established primarily to hear human rights complaints, but over the years a number of its cases have dealt with the human rights practices of governments. The **United Nations Secretariat** staffs and funds the regular work of many human rights bodies established over the years, while the United Nations Security Council has on occasion justified peacekeeping or peacemaking operations on the basis of human rights considerations.

The UN's role in humanitarian issues was apparent from the outset, as the General Assembly took up questions concerning **refugees** and displaced persons and problems surrounding the emergency needs of children and **children's rights** in its first sessions. Growing out of the former concern were a series of refugee-related bodies and growing out of the latter discussions, was the formation of the **United Nations Children's Fund (UNICEF)**. Coping with poverty and its consequences eventually led the UN to develop ever more extensive machinery for promoting economic development. ECOSOC served as a major coordinating body for humanitarian and development activities.

The UN's human rights bodies have generated numerous draft declarations and treaties over the years, two of the earliest and most important being the **Universal Declaration of Human Rights** and the UN **Genocide** Convention, both adopted in 1948. A cascade of subsequent declarations, covenants, and conventions has followed. Thus, while bodies such as the League of Nations and the **International Labour Organization (ILO)** had been at work on human rights questions much earlier, the UN can be rightly seen as the primary institutional body marking the modern revolution in human rights legislation. However, given the UN's primary norm of state **sovereignty** and of noninterference into the domestic affairs of its members, a large part of the progress in human rights has been of a voluntary nature, with governments being generally reluctant to fashion truly effective international human rights treaties. Indeed, the protection and promotion of human rights remains a duty first and foremost of governments within their own domestic legal systems. International bodies serve as an additional means of cooperation and oversight, but governments themselves are in the most decisive position either to respect or abuse human rights.

After the 1993 **World Conference on Human Rights**, the **United Nations High Commissioner for Human Rights (UNHCHR)** was established in Geneva, and gradually much of the work of various human rights committees established by treaties has gravitated from New York to Geneva, including the work of the newly formed Human Rights Council, which does not report to ECOSOC, as its predecessor the United Nations Commission on Human Rights (CHR) did, but rather to the UNHCHR.

Major reforms and reorganization of the UN Secretariat occurred throughout the 1990s. Currently the UN is organized into five major departments dealing with peace and security, economic and social development, human rights, humanitarian affairs, and **international law**. Serving as the focal point for humanitarian efforts is the **United Nations Office for the Coordination of Humanitarian Affairs (UNOCHA)**, which in turn supervises an Interagency Standing Committee (IASC) composed of numerous UN specialized agencies dealing with humanitarian aid and emergency and disaster relief, including most prominently the **United Nations High Commissioner for Refugees (UNHCR)**, UNICEF, the **United Nations Development**

Programme (UNDP), and the **World Food Programme (WFP)**, among others.

The UN and its related agencies have increasingly relied on nongovernmental organizations (NGOs) for information and program implementation in the areas of human rights and humanitarian assistance. NGOs can gain official consultative status with the UN through ECOSOC, and many of them serve as active implementers of UN aid programs. The **International Committee of the Red Cross (ICRC)** is a major nongovernmental partner with the UN in both human rights and humanitarian aid, along with hundreds of other NGOs. UN Headquarters Address: United Nations, New York, NY 10017, USA. Website: www.un.org.

UNITED NATIONS ANGOLA VERIFICATION MISSIONS (UNAVEM I, II, III). UNAVEM actually came in three installments. The first mission was authorized by the **United Nations (UN)** Security Council in December 1988 to monitor Cuban troop withdrawal. The second mission was authorized in June 1991 to monitor the Angolan elections resulting from the Lisbon Accords. However, the second UNAVEM Mission ran into trouble as civil war erupted again in Angola following the elections. The UNAVEM II force soon found itself engaged in humanitarian activities, providing safe passage for **refugees**, and working with UN agencies in securing delivery of humanitarian aid. UNAVEM forces were substantially curtailed in 1993 with the resumption of violence and the breakdown of the Lisbon Accords. Further negotiations between the Angolan government and the opposition National Union for the Total Independence of Angola (UNITA) resulted in renewed hope for resolution of conflict in Angola as the parties signed the Protocol of Lusaka on 20 November 1994, at which time UNAVEM III was initiated. This agreement established the basis for the reestablishment of the cease-fire, the demilitarization of all UNITA forces, the disarming of civilians, the continuation of the electoral process, and the ongoing supervisory role of UNAVEM III forces, which was later expanded to perform its new roles under the protocol.

The Lusaka Accords also failed to resolve the dispute between the government and UNITA, and in 1997 UNAVEM III was terminated and replaced with the United Nations Observer Mission in Angola

(MONUA), which represented a last-ditch effort to retrieve a peaceful solution to the civil war. It also was terminated in February 1999, as the world gave up on resolving one of Africa's most inveterate civil wars. The death of UNITA's leader Jonas Savimbi in February 2002 paved the way for the resolution of the country's civil war on its own terms, largely without international intervention. Government forces and UNITA leaders signed a cease-fire in April 2002, and the country began the laborious effort of rehabilitation after nearly 30 years of continuous warfare. The oil-rich Cabinda province, an enclave separated from Angola by the Democratic Republic of the Congo, remains a haven for government opposition, and charges of human rights abuse by the government in an effort to pacify this strategic area have been made by advocacy organizations.

UNITED NATIONS CHARTER. References to fundamental human rights and freedoms are found throughout the United Nations Charter, which was signed by the representatives of 50 states at the San Francisco Conference of 1945. The preamble of the charter states that members of the **United Nations (UN)** are "determined . . . to reaffirm faith in fundamental human rights, in the dignity and worth of the human person, in the equal rights of men and **women**." Preambles are not considered legally binding parts of treaties. However, the UN Charter goes on to make several additional references to human rights. Paragraph 3 of Article 1, which lists the purposes of the United Nations, indicates that one of the main purposes of the charter is "to achieve international cooperation in solving international problems of an economic, social, cultural or humanitarian character, and in promoting and encouraging respect for human rights and for fundamental freedoms for all without distinction as to race, sex, language, or religion." The charter gives the **United Nations General Assembly** the capacity to initiate studies and make recommendations concerning the progressive development of **international law** and its codification, and to assist in the realization of human rights and fundamental freedoms. In Chapters IX and X of the charter, further institutional mechanisms are established to promote "universal respect for, and observance of, human rights and fundamental freedoms for all without distinction as to race, sex, language, or religion" (Article 55c). In the subsequent article, states pledge to take joint and separate action to cooperate with the United Nations in achieving this and related goals. The United Nations **Economic and Social Council (ECOSOC)**, members of which are elected by the General Assembly, is empowered by the charter to "make recommendations for the purpose of promoting respect for, and observance of, human rights and fundamental freedoms for all" (Article 62b). ECOSOC is permitted, under the terms of Article 68, to create commissions in the economic and social areas, as well as for the promotion of human rights. It has been very active in this regard, and served as the primary oversight body for various human rights committees established by member-states in connection with the entry into force of numerous human rights conventions. More recently, the **United Nations High Commissioner for Human Rights (UNHCHR)** has undertaken direct supervision of these bodies, including the newly reformed **Human Rights Council**, which succeeded the United Nations **Commission on Human Rights (CHR)**.

References to human rights in the charter are scattered and not well defined. No list of human rights is found in the charter, apart from the prohibition of discrimination. Still, the very fact that numerous references to human rights and fundamental freedoms are made reflected a belief by member-states that such matters were subject to international attention and discussion. Article 2(7), however, stipulates that the United Nations may not, except for collective security purposes, intervene in matters that are essentially within the domestic jurisdiction of any state. This underscores the **sovereignty** of the member-states and highlights the problematic character of discussions about human rights when such discussions move into the realm of action. Indeed, the United Nations has the authority to discuss human rights issues and to make recommendations regarding them, but such recommendations are not binding, unless they issue from the **United Nations** Security Council in connection with its authority under Chapter VII of the charter to make decisions regarding threats to the peace and acts of aggression. However, most human rights violations committed by states do not qualify as threats to international peace in such a way that would justify Security Council action, although there are notable exceptions, as illustrated by its actions concerning the Kurds in Iraq, the civil war in Somalia, and the situation in Haiti under the military junta.

UNITED NATIONS CHILDREN'S FUND (UNICEF). The **United Nations General Assembly** established UNICEF in 1946 with a view to mitigating the hardships faced by children in emergency situations. Its initial title was the United Nations International Children's Emergency Fund. In 1953 the agency's title was shortened and its mandate broadened. Although UNICEF provides water, sanitation, **health**, **food**, aid, and **education** in all parts of the developing world, it is still particularly active in assisting **refugees** and disaster victims. One of just a few **United Nations (UN)** agencies that has field operational capabilities, like the **United Nations High Commissioner for Refugees (UNHCR)**, UNICEF is called upon to respond to many humanitarian emergencies in order to ensure the availability of potable water supplies, to provide oral rehydration therapy that is essential to the survival of young children with diarrhea and waterborne infections, and to promote rapid responses to emergency situations. By providing such basic health services essential to survival, UNICEF directly addresses basic human needs and promotes the most fundamental rights of human beings.

UNICEF was one of the chief advocates of the promulgation and implementation of the **Convention on the Rights of the Child**. It also advocates strongly for **women**'s rights. It works actively not only to protect children from abuse in conflict situations but also to preserve them during times of emergency, which it estimates accounted for the deaths of two million children just in the last decade. It has become increasingly involved in the prevention of HIV/AIDS, which has not only killed countless children, but also left 14 million more as orphans, and in programs designed to advance the education of girls.

Although it is an intergovernmental organization, UNICEF enjoys financial support from funds raised by its numerous national committees. Voluntary contributions and other revenue reached nearly $2 billion in 2004, while $1.6 million were spent on program activities, nearly a third of which involved various forms of humanitarian assistance. UNICEF was a major actor in the tsunami emergency relief program during 2005. UNICEF is overseen by an executive board composed of member-states that meets annually and reports to the General Assembly through the **Economic and Social Council (ECOSOC)**. Address: United Nations, New York, NY 10017, USA. Website: www.unicef.org. *See also* CHILDREN'S RIGHTS.

UNITED NATIONS CONFERENCE ON ENVIRONMENT AND DEVELOPMENT (UNCED). Held in Rio de Janeiro from 3–14 June 1992, UNCED adopted two documents, Agenda 21 and the Rio Declaration on Environment and Development. The latter consists of 27 principles meant to guide state action in reference to human relations with the environment. The first principle notes that "human beings are at the center of concerns for sustainable development," and that they "are entitled to a healthy and productive life in harmony with nature." Principle 3 asserted that the "right to development must be fulfilled so as to equitably meet developmental and environmental needs." Other principles that relate to human rights or humanitarian issues include the immediate notification of natural disasters or other emergencies that are likely to adversely affect the environment of neighboring states, the acknowledgment of the vital role that **women** and indigenous peoples play in environmental management and development, and the need for states to avoid warfare, which inherently inhibits sustainable development. The declaration is nonbinding and certain governments have stipulated reservations on various principles, including that relating to the right to development. The Agenda 21 text deals with a range of economic and social rights, including alleviating **poverty**, providing adequate shelter for all, enhancing the economic development of women and indigenous people, and promoting human **health**. For a text of the Rio Declaration, see *UN Chronicle*, vol. 29, no. 3 (September 1992): 66–67.

UNITED NATIONS CONFERENCE ON HUMAN SETTLEMENTS. *See* VANCOUVER DECLARATION ON HUMAN SETTLEMENTS.

UNITED NATIONS COORDINATOR FOR HUMANITARIAN AND ECONOMIC ASSISTANCE PROGRAMS RELATING TO AFGHANISTAN (UNOCA). This **United Nations (UN)** humanitarian body was established by the **United Nations General Assembly** in 1988 in order to provide a focal point for emergency assistance and to coordinate appeals for the anticipated repatriation and rehabilitation needs of Afghan **refugees** and displaced populations, and for the economic rehabilitation of the country. Difficult years followed with ongoing civil war and the emergence of Taliban rule in the mid-1990s. In 1993, UNOCA's mandate was restricted to humanitarian assistance, and its acronym revised to UNOCHA to reflect this shift of emphasis. It was placed in that year under the purview of the United Nations **Department of Humanitarian Affairs (DHA)**. Even before the DHA was later replaced by the **United Nations Office for the Coordination of Humanitarian Affairs (UNOCHA)** in 1996, which assumed the acronym UNOCHA for its own work, the office for humanitarian work in Afghanistan was renamed first the Office of the Secretary-General for Afghanistan in 1995, and in July 1996 was renamed again as the United Nations Special Mission for Afghanistan (UNSMA).

UNSMA continued to respond to large ongoing displacements of people, and as abusive human rights situations persisted in Afghanistan, in 1999, the **United Nations** Security Council imposed sanctions on the Taliban regime owing to its support of drug trafficking, exportation of **terrorism**, and ongoing and grave human rights abuses. The situation in that country took a decisive turn on 11 September 2001, with the terrorist attacks against the United States and the U.S. government intervention that took place in subsequent months, during which the Taliban government was overthrown, the long process of rehabilitation and recovery in Afghanistan began, and humanitarian aid could again flow to much of the country. Eventually, Afghanistan elected its first democratic government, which could begin to interact directly with international aid-giving bodies to promote a more stable human rights climate.

UNITED NATIONS DEVELOPMENT PROGRAMME (UNDP). The UNDP performs the principal coordinating role among **United Nations (UN)** development-related agencies. It was established in 1971. UNDP country representatives are stationed in 166 countries. The UNDP resident representatives serve as the focal point for all UN development-related activities in developing countries. They assist the host government in devising country development plans and call upon UN technical support for development. UNDP is often involved in humanitarian and refugee activities. In countries where the **United Nations High Commissioner for Refugees (UNHCR)** does not have representation, the UNDP resident representative serves to protect and assist **refugees**. It has also collaborated extensively with UNHCR since the early 1980s in responding to the development-related assistance needs of countries hosting large refugee populations. UNDP was given official responsibility for follow-up activities to the Second International Conference on Assistance to Refugees in Africa (ICARA II) of 1984 and to the International Conference on Central American Refugees (CIREFCA) of 1989. In the latter case, UNDP was engaged with UNHCR in the innovative use of Quick Impact Projects intended to bridge the gap between emergency and development aid. UNDP is also a member of the Interagency Standing Committee (IASC) of the **United Nations Office for Coordination of Humanitarian Affairs (UNOCHA)**.

During the 1990s, UNDP explored new approaches for advancing development in the developing world, including a new awareness of the connection between environment and development and the need to encourage "sustainable development" in developing areas. UNDP operates through its resident representatives in 166 countries, and its programs and support now mirror the **Millennium Development Goals** issued in the Millennium Declaration, which identifies five priority areas for governmental action to promote development, including the promotion of democratic governance, **poverty** reduction, crisis prevention and recovery, energy and environment policies, and HIV/AIDS prevention, control, and reduction. Human rights concerns cut across these sectors.

UNDP publishes an annual *Human Development Report* as well as regional, national, and local human development reports. In the UN organizational reform of the late 1990s, UNDP was identified as the focal point of the establishment of UN Houses within host countries, so as to consolidate UN field activities under one roof, thus reducing costs. UNDP oversees the United Nations Capital Development Fund, which since 1999 has emphasized the expansion of microcredit programs and local development programs. UNDP also oversees the work of the United Nations Development Fund for **Women** or UNIFEM, and it supervises the United Nations Volunteer Program, which in 2004 alone mobilized 7,300 volunteers to work in 140 countries. Website: www.undp.org.

UNITED NATIONS EDUCATIONAL, SCIENTIFIC, AND CULTURAL ORGANIZATION (UNESCO). UNESCO was established on 16 November 1945 as a result of the **United Nations (UN)** London Conference. Its constitution authorizes UNESCO to promote and to seek international peace and security though **education** and cultural exchanges and promotion of respect for human rights. UNESCO is governed by its general conference consisting of representatives of member-states. The general conference elects an executive board of 58 members consisting of representatives of governments to the organization. The executive board prepares the agenda for the general conference, examines the work of the organization secretariat, and executes the decisions of the general conference. The secretariat of UNESCO consists of a director-general and his staff, who carry out the routine administration and activity of the organization. The director-general is nominated by the executive board and appointed by the general conference.

UNESCO engages in scientific activities regarding the collection of information on earthquakes and collaborates with UN disaster-relief mechanisms to this end. It has also sponsored numerous conferences and overseen the drafting of several international conventions, including the Convention against Discrimination in Education, the Convention for Protection of Cultural Property in Armed Conflict, and the Universal Copyright Convention. It has also issued numerous declarations on human rights issues, including race, racial prejudice, and international cultural cooperation, as well as recommendations on a host of related issues such as the preservation of cultural **property**, the status of teachers, and the promotion of human rights education, among many other subjects.

Like other UN bodies whose work touches on development, since 2000, UNESCO programs have been oriented toward the achievement of **Millennium Development Goals**. For UNESCO's special mission, this involves programs to help alleviate **poverty**, to achieve universal primary education, to eliminate gender disparity in primary and secondary education, and to enhance sustainable, environmentally friendly development. In light of the rise and globalization of **terrorism**, UNESCO is also responsible for promotion of a global dialogue based upon respect for shared values and the dignity of each civilization and culture. Address: 7 place de Fontenoy, F-75352, Paris 07 SP, France. Website: portal.unesco.org.

For copies of the texts and detailed descriptions of the UNESCO conventions, declarations, and recommendations, see the UNESCO website section devoted to them. Website: www.unesco.org.

UNITED NATIONS FUND FOR POPULATION ACTIVITIES (UNFPA). Supervised by the governing council of the **United Nations Development Programme (UNDP)**, UNFPA formally came into existence as a trust fund in 1969. UNFPA is engaged in a variety of population-related projects, studies, and conferences. It promotes studies on migration, on the effects of population growth on the environment, and on other social and economic issues related to population. UNFPA was actively engaged in the planning and preparation for the **International Conference on Population and Development** held in Cairo in 1989. UNFPA is a member of the Interagency Standing Committee (IASC) of the **United Nations Office for Coordination of Humanitarian Affairs**. It participates, with other **United Nations (UN)** agencies, in the advancement of the **Millennium Development Goals** aimed at the reduction of **poverty**, control of HIV/AIDS, and promoting gender **equality**, among others. Address: 220 East 42nd Street, New York, NY 10017, USA. Website: www.unfpa.org.

UNITED NATIONS GENERAL ASSEMBLY. Under the terms of Article 13 of the **United Nations Charter**, the United Nations General Assembly "shall initiate studies and make recommendations for the purpose of: a. promoting international cooperation in the political field and encouraging the progressive development of **international law** and its codification; b. promoting international cooperation in the economic, social, cultural, educational, and **health** fields, and assisting in the realization of human rights and fundamental freedoms for all without distinction as to race, sex, language, or religion."

The assembly is also empowered under Article 22 to establish such subsidiary organs as it deems necessary for the performance of its functions. The General Assembly's Third Committee, one of the seven main committees, is charged with handling questions relating to social and humanitarian questions, including those dealing with human rights. This committee, in turn, oversees the work of the United Nations **Economic and Social Council (ECOSOC)**, which is charged under Chapter X of the charter with initiating studies and reports on social and humanitarian questions, among others, and with "making recommendations for the purpose of promoting respect for, and observance of, human rights and fundamental freedoms for all."

It has the power to draft conventions for submission to the General Assembly and to call for international conferences on subjects within its competence, including the subject of human rights. ECOSOC, although an organ of the United Nations, reports to and acts under the direction of the General Assembly.

On 10 December 1948, the General Assembly approved the **Universal Declaration of Human Rights** without opposition, although eight abstentions were cast. Though not a legally binding document, this declaration did for the first time list specific personal, civil, political, and social rights as standards for aspiration and achievement for the peoples and nations, giving greater flesh to the hints about human rights referred to but not elaborated on in the UN Charter. By 1954, after several years of debate and drafting, the United Nations **Commission on Human Rights (CHR)** (now succeeded by the **Human Rights Council**) submitted drafts of two Human Rights Covenants and an Optional Protocol to the General Assembly and its Third Committee for further deliberation. Disputes over the terms of these drafts, especially relating to enforcement, delayed General Assembly action on them until 16 December 1966. Both the **International Covenant on Civil and Political Rights** and the **International Covenant on Economic, Social, and Cultural Rights** were adopted by the assembly unanimously. The **Optional Protocol to the International Covenant on Civil and Political Rights** was also adopted but with fewer positive votes and two negative ones. By 1966, then, the General Assembly had finally established the **International Bill of Human Rights** that had been anticipated in its earlier approval of the Universal Declaration. The covenants and protocol were then set forth for ratification.

The General Assembly has adopted numerous additional human rights instruments over the years, some in the form of nonbinding declarations, others in the form of draft conventions or conventions and treaties. These include, among others, the **International Convention on the Elimination of All Forms of Racial Discrimination** (1965), the **Declaration on the Elimination of Discrimination against Women** (1967), the **Declaration on Territorial Asylum** (1967), the Declaration on Elimination of All Forms of Intolerance and of Discrimination Based on Religion or Belief (1981), and the **Convention on the Elimination of All Forms of Discrimination**

against Women (1979). The assembly has also acted on the **Convention against Torture** (1984) and the **Convention on the Rights of the Child** (1989). It also acted on the practices of **genocide** and **apartheid**, as well as numerous other subjects such as **terrorism**, with the adoption of the Convention for the Suppression of Terrorist Bombing (1997) and the Convention for the Suppression of the Financing of Terrorism (1999).

Although many of the human rights instruments adopted by the General Assembly have entered into force, many states are reluctant to ratify them. The proliferation of such agreements, especially when they lack effective enforcement mechanisms, has raised considerable debate. Some see the very existence of such instruments and their proliferation as a positive step toward encouraging state participation. Others see them as creating only an illusion of progress. Many states that ratified such agreements continue to display substandard human rights records. If enforcement mechanisms in these agreements had been more effective many such states would surely have displayed greater reluctance in ratifying them. The dilemma is that the more effective an instrument is, the less likely it is to enjoy widespread ratification. The less effective instruments may enjoy wider participation, but they are not effectively enforced. Majorities to adopt human rights instruments are more easily found in the General Assembly votes than they are when it actually comes to governmental ratification that implies recognition of binding legal obligations.

Currently, the General Assembly, in addition to maintaining oversight of ECOSOC activities concerning human rights, also directly supervises, in some cases in cooperation with the secretary-general, a **Committee on the Elimination of Racial Discrimination (CERD)**, and a **Committee against Torture (CAT)**, as well and numerous other Committees, Ad-Hoc Committees, Special Committees and Working Groups dealing with human rights concerns.

UNITED NATIONS HIGH COMMISSIONER FOR HUMAN RIGHTS (UNHCHR). On 20 December 1993, the **United Nations General Assembly** established the **United Nations (UN)** High Commissioner for Human Rights to serve under the direction and authority of the secretary-general for the purpose of promoting and protecting the enjoyment of human rights by all peoples. The **World**

Conference on Human Rights, held in June 1993, had recommended the establishment of such a position within the United Nations in its program of action. The high commissioner's functions include improving, coordinating, and streamlining existing human rights mechanisms and human rights–related bodies of the UN system, promoting human rights **education** and public information programs, and drawing governments into discussion on human rights matters of concern to them. The UNHCHR's primary function is to mainstream and coordinate human rights throughout the UN system. It is thus the primary human rights coordinating mechanism within the **United Nations Secretariat** and under the direction of the secretary-general. It maintains offices both in New York and at the Palais Wilson in Geneva, Switzerland. The UNHCHR is funded by both the UN regular budget and by voluntary contributions. About a third of the budget is funded through the UN regular budget, with the rest taking the form of voluntary contributions from governments, foundations, nongovernmental organizations (NGOs), and individuals. Although the budgets are comparatively small in relation to those of other humanitarian organizations, the UNHCHR's revenue from voluntary contributions has quadrupled from $15 million at its inception in 1994 to $60 million in 2004.

Over the years, a large number of human rights treaties and treaty bodies have been established to protect and promote human rights. These include the **Committee on Economic, Social, and Cultural Rights (CESCR)**, the **Human Rights Committee (HRC)**, the **Committee against Torture (CAT)**, the **Committee on the Elimination of Racial Discrimination (CERD)**, the **Committee on the Elimination of Discrimination against Women (CEDAW)**, the **Committee on the Rights of the Child (CRC)**, and the **Committee on Migrant Workers (CMW)**. Added to these are various human rights commissions, such as the **Commission on Crime Prevention and Criminal Justice**, the **Commission on the Status of Women**, and the **Commission on Human Rights (CHR)** with is various working groups, which was succeeded by the United Nations **Human Rights Council** in 2006. While all of these bodies answer to the United Nations **Economic and Social Council (ECOSOC)** and the General Assembly, their work is integral to that of the UNHCHR, which also maintains an active field presence in many countries and offers technical support to governments in order to promote the establishment of national human rights bodies, and the enactment of national human rights law coupled with appropriate human rights practices. Thus the UNHCHR serves a very important integrative function within the UN system to focus attention on human rights issues, law and practice within the UN system itself, with member-states, with other international organizations, with NGOs, and even within countries as they attempt to develop civil society at local levels, including the promotion of human rights education. José Ayala Lasso, former ambassador of Ecuador, was named the first high commissioner on 14 February 1994. He was succeeded by Mary Robinson of Ireland in 1997. Sergio Vieira de Mello of Brazil served from 2002 until his untimely death in a terrorist bombing attack in Baghdad, Iraq, in 2003. The current high commissioner is Louise Arbour of Canada. Address: 8-14 Avenue de la Paix, 1211 Geneva 10, Switzerland. Website: www.unhchr.ch.

UNITED NATIONS HIGH COMMISSIONER FOR REFUGEES (UNHCR). Successor of the International Refugee Organization (IRO), the UNHCR was established by a **United Nations General Assembly** resolution of 14 December 1950, and it commenced operations on 1 January 1951. Originally conceived as a temporary body to resolve the post–World War II problem of **refugees** in Europe, the UNHCR's role gradually expanded. It was charged with monitoring and implementing the 1951 United Nations **Convention Relating to the Status of Refugees**. Its own statute permitted it to handle refugee situations arising in contexts outside of Europe and unrelated to the events of World War II. Limited by the United Nations General Assembly at first to administrative functions alone, the UNHCR was later granted the capacity to raise funds and to seek funding for durable solutions. The primary role of the UNHCR is to afford legal protection to refugees and to ensure that governments honor their commitments under international refugee instruments. Related to this protection function is its capacity to provide humanitarian assistance to populations that have been displaced across international boundaries. Over the years, the United Nations General Assembly has directed the UNHCR to provide assistance to people a refugee-like situations, such as disaster and **famine** victims who have fled across international boundaries seeking assistance. After the tumultuous decades of the Cold War and post–Cold War, during which upward of 20 million people in any given year fell under the protection and assistance mandates of the UNHCR, the world has gradually seen a reduction in the numbers of refugees, although they still hover in the range of 9–10 million.

The UNHCR works closely with nongovernmental organizations (NGOs), governments, and other United Nations (UN) agencies to coordinate assistance activities for refugees. It maintains offices in more than 80 countries and coordinates assistance activities for some 10 million refugees globally. The programs and budget of the UNHCR are overseen by an executive committee composed of member-states. The assistance activities of the UNHCR have grown in size and importance over the decades. What was once an organization of lawyers fulfilling the legal-protection function for refugees has become one of the largest field-assistance agencies in the UN system. In its protection function, the UNHCR promotes human rights considerations, protects refugees from discrimination and forcible repatriation, and promotes their legal interests. In its assistance functions, the UNHCR has become one of the most visible UN agencies in terms of humanitarian responses to emergencies and long-term refugee situations.

The UNHCR promotes the gradual development of regional and international instruments dealing with refugees and the gradual incorporation of such instruments into the national legal systems of member-states. By focusing on its humanitarian role, the UNHCR seeks to promote the interests of refugees and **asylum** seekers. It intercedes with immigration authorities and foreign ministries to encourage fair asylum determination procedures, to ensure the rights of refugees to **nonrefoulement**, to provide travel documents and **work** permits to refugees, to seek alternative solutions for refugees where settlement in the country of first asylum is not feasible, to encourage **family** reunification, and to promote respect for the refugees' economic and social rights and access to the courts of host countries. The Office of the High Commissioner for Refugees has gained significant prestige over the years as the locus of a voice of human rights and humanitarian concern. For a full text of the statute of the UNHCR, see the Annex to United Nations General Assembly Resolution 428 (V) of 14 December 1950. Address: CP 2500, CH 1211, Geneva 2 Depot,

Switzerland. Website. www.unhcr.ch. *See also* CONVENTION ON THE REDUCTION OF STATELESSNESS.

UNITED NATIONS INSTITUTE FOR TRAINING AND RESEARCH (UNITAR). The **United Nations General Assembly** established UNITAR in 1963 to serve as a means of enhancing the **United Nations's (UN)** overall functions in promotion of international peace and security and in the provision of economic and social development programs, along with other charter-related responsibilities. UNITAR conducts seminars, studies, and research on a broad range of issues of interest to the UN and offers training programs for UN and governmental officials. It has issued reports on rules for disaster relief operations and on such human rights–related topics as the elimination of racism. Its training programs include such topics as international migration policy, **women** and children in conflict and postconflict situations, and in support of UN personnel activities in a wide range of economic and social development sectors. In addition to its Geneva office, UNITAR maintains offices in New York and Hiroshima, Japan. Geneva Postal Address: UNITAR, Palais de Nations, CH-1211, Geneva 10, Switzerland. Website: www.unitar.org.

UNITED NATIONS INTERIM ADMINISTRATION MISSION IN KOSOVO (UNMIK). Following the North Atlantic Treaty Organization (NATO) bombing of Serbia in the spring of 1999, to punish Serbia for its refusal to abide by an ultimatum to permit the deployment of NATO forces in Kosovo, hundreds of thousands of Kosovar **refugees** fled into neighboring Macedonia and Albania, as Serbian forces unleashed an intense campaign of **ethnic cleansing** in its Kosovo province. Eventually the Serbian government buckled under the pressure, and just as quickly as Kosovar refugees had fled from Kosovo, they returned under the protection of an international force that included both NATO and Russian troops.

The **United Nations (UN)** Security Council, which had not been consulted formally by NATO countries and which had not authorized the NATO bombings, accepted the fait accompli and decided in June 1999 to establish UNMIK, which undertook one of the most comprehensive and complex missions ever undertaken by a UN force, which included nothing short of the full interim administration and establishment of self-government in Kosovo. The multidimensional tasks of this mandate included coordination of humanitarian and disaster relief, maintenance of civil law and order and administration, promotion of human rights, and the safe return of all refugees and displaced persons. The **United Nations High Commissioner for Refugees (UNHCR)** took charge of coordination of all humanitarian assistance. In time UNMIK divided its work into four pillars, including Pillar I on Police and Justice and Pillar II on Civil Administration, under the UN directly. Pillar III on Democratization and Institution Building was headed by the **Organization for Security and Cooperation in Europe (OSCE)**, and Pillar IV on Reconstruction and Economic Development was led by the **European Union (EU)**.

The situation in Kosovo, though markedly improved for Kosovar Albanians, is not hospitable for the Serbian minority, many of whom have fled their homes in Kosovo out of well-founded concerns of retaliation by their non-Serbian neighbors. In this respect, the human rights situation remained tentative. Nonetheless, the Serbs were encouraged to participate in the assembly election in Kosovo, even by the new president of Serbia. These elections were held in November 2001. Relations between the Serb minority and Kosovar Muslim majority remained tenuous in subsequent years, including as late as March 2004 when a nasty outburst of violence by Albanians aimed at driving out the Serb, Roma, and Ashkali communities produced numerous deaths and injuries and the flight of hundreds from their homes, and the destruction of ancient Serbian cultural sites.

However, recent developments have given Serbs greater confidence that the Kosovar-dominated government under general international supervision will respect Serbian minority rights. The resignation in early March 2005 of Kosovo's former prime minister Ramush Haradinaj and his surrender to authorities in connection with charges brought against him by the **International Criminal Tribunal for Yugoslavia (ICTY)** for murder, rape, and the forced deportation of Serbians during the Kosovar civil war gave credibility to international efforts to ensure that the new government would respect Serbian citizens rights. Within two weeks, a new government was elected, and the new Kosovar prime minister, Bajram Kosumi, pledged to reach out to the Serb opposition. Within days, an initiative was announced to rebuild Serbian religious sites destroyed by earlier violence, and Serbian leaders urged Serbs living in Kosovo to participate in the political process there. After seven years of UNMIK administration, ethnic suspicions continue to exist in Kosovo, but signs of greater cooperation are also coming into evidence, offering hope that the situation in that deeply troubled region might admit of eventual reconciliation. Address: UNMIK Press and Public Information Section, Belgrade Street 32, 38000 Pristina, Serbia and Montenegro. Website: www.unmikonline.org.

UNITED NATIONS MISSION IN LIBERIA (UNMIL). Established by the **United Nations** Security Council in September 2003, UNMIL is but the latest effort by the United Nations (UN) to involve itself in the resolution of Liberia's 16-year-old civil war, which began in 1989 and which took the lives of 150,000 people and displaced many more, including 850,000 **refugees**, into neighboring countries. Human rights abuses proliferated as law and order broke down for most of this period, which was punctuated between 1997 and 2003 by a period of greater calm, which permitted elections to be held. Charles Taylor, one of the prominent rebel leaders of the first phase of the civil war, was elected president, but opposition to his rule continued and eventually intensified in 2003, leading to a second period of broader conflict. A civil war in neighboring Sierra Leone complicated the situation in Liberia even during the period of less intense civil conflict. In 1993, the United Nations Security Council reacted to the first phase of the conflict by fielding the United Nations Observer Mission in Liberia (UNOMIL), which was established to support the Economic Council of West African States (ECOWAS) Military Observer Group that had been deployed in Liberia as a regional peacemaking group in 1990. UNOMIL's work ultimately met with success with the fashioning of a framework for peace and then elections in 1997, and its mandate ended in September of that year. Two months later, the UN established a peace-building support office in Liberia, under the supervision of a representative of the UN secretary-general, with one area of the representative's activity being the promotion of human rights.

In July 2003, Liberia descended into another short but intense period of civil war. The UN acted more promptly on this occasion, and by August a Comprehensive Peace Agreement was signed in Accra. President Taylor resigned and quit the country, seeking **asylum** in Nigeria. In April 2006, he was extradited to Sierra Leone to face charges of **crimes against humanity** committed during his tenure as president of Liberia. In the meantime, a national transition government was formed in Liberia and ECOWAS forces were once again deployed. This paved the way for UN Security Council authorization of the UNMIL in September. To expedite UN action, about 3,500 ECOWAS Military Observer Group forces were "rehatted" as UN peacekeepers in October 2003, and the council authorized the deployment of up to 15,000 personnel for the UNMIL operation, which was to be a multidimensional exercise to address the political, military, humanitarian, and human rights situations. Demobilization and reintegration of combatants, special assistance to child soldiers, repatriation of refugees, humanitarian assistance, and protection of refugees and internally displaced persons as they returned to their homes all fell within the mandate of UNMIL. Address: UNMIL, Tubman Boulevard, 1st Street, Monrovia, Liberia. Website: www.unmil .org.

UNITED NATIONS MISSION IN SIERRA LEONE (UNAMSIL). The civil war in Sierra Leone began in March 1991 when a rebel organization, the Revolutionary United Front (RUF), took up arms against the government from its stronghold along the eastern border with Liberia, a country also beset by civil war. The Economic Council of West African States (ECOWAS) responded to the war by coming to the support of the government, which was overthrown by an army coup in 1992. The civil war continued until 1995 as the **United Nations (UN)**, the Organization of African Unity (OAU)—later renamed the **African Union (AU)**—and ECOWAS attempted to mediate the dispute and successfully brokered an agreement for elections that would restore civilian rule. These elections were held in 1996 and Dr. Ahmed Kabbah won the presidency. RUF boycotted the elections and continued resistance and Kabbah was overthrown by another coup involving his own armed forces now in coalition with RUF. This disturbing event sent Kabbah fleeing into exile in neighboring Guinea. The United Nations Security Council imposed an arms and oil embargo on the new regime, but it was able to continue operations owing to its control over the diamond mines and revenue generated from illicit trade of them.

The Security Council also authorized the deployment of ECOWAS forces in October 1997. Under this pressure, the new coalition government agreed to cooperate with the ECOWAS forces, the UN, and the **United Nations High Commissioner for Refugees (UNHCR)**, which was to spearhead the provision of humanitarian assistance. The government failed to live up to its promises and in February 1998, ECOWAS forces toppled the junta, which fled from the capital of Freetown. The Security Council then established the United Nations Observer Mission in Sierra Leone (UNOMSIL) in June of 1998, which began the process of disarmament under protection of ECOWAS forces. At this point, fuller disclosure of the massive atrocities perpetrated by RUF came to light, as UNOMSIL teams documented RUF human rights abuses, including killings, rapes, amputations, and sexual abuse and forced abduction and impressments of children into the rebel army. However, RUF and its allies from the former government eventually overran Freetown, forcing UNOMSIL forces to evacuate.

In July 1999, all parties to the conflict signed the Lomé Agreement to end the conflict and establish a government of national unity, but the agreement was achieved at the price of legitimizing RUF's leader, Foday Sankoh, as interim vice president, and he also retained control over the diamond industry. UNAMSIL was established by the UN Security Council in October 1999, and the council terminated the UNOMSIL mandate. UNAMSIL's mandate was expanded in a series of UN Security Council actions, authorizing the deployment of up to 17,000 personnel and the addition of several new mandate components, including the facilitation of humanitarian assistance, an agreement to provide security for elections, and an offer of protection to agents promoting the development of civil society and human rights. After the breakdown of order in 2000, more decisive intervention by UNAMSIL forces led to the recapture of Freetown and later to elections in May 2002, in which Kabbah again decisively won the presidency. Still, Sankoh and RUF elements continued to plague the country, until Sankoh's capture in 2003. He died in government custody while awaiting a **war crimes** trial. UNAMSIL began the withdrawal of its 17,000 troops in subsequent months as order was gradually restored. As of May 2005, about 3,500 troops remained in Sierra Leone.

The UN also assisted in the establishment of a Special Court in Sierra Leone to try those persons charged for serious violations of international humanitarian law in Sierra Leone since 30 November 1996. This national war crimes tribunal could exercise jurisdiction for those charged with war crimes, **crimes against humanity**, as well as violations of international humanitarian law. The former Liberian president, Charles Taylor, was extradited by Nigeria in April 2006 to face charges before the Court. Among the more egregious crimes subject to the court's jurisdiction were murder, rape, extermination, enslavement, sexual slavery, and conscription of children into armed forces, as well as attacks on UN peacekeepers, about 500 of whom were captured by rebel forces in one incident during 2000. The civil war took the lives of about 50,000 people and displaced hundreds of thousands more, before the restoration of peace in 2003 and the gradual process of recovery and rehabilitation of a country torn apart by more than a decade of strife.

UNITED NATIONS MISSION IN SUDAN (UNMIS). The civil war in Sudan has a long history going back to the formation of the country at independence in 1956. It is rooted in the religious and cultural differences of the North, which is Arab and Muslim, and the South, which is black African and Christian or animist by tradition. Civil wars have plagued Sudan from the onset, interspersed with periods of greater calm. A major civil war emerged in the early 1980s, especially after the autonomy of the southern provinces was revoked with the imposition by Khartoum of the *sharia* throughout Sudan, even in non-Muslim areas. John Garang formed the Sudanese People's Liberation Movement to resist the government, but even the rebel opposition was divided, thus complicating the civil war.

Darfur province, which is known as the breadbasket of the Sudan, has been the recent focus of fighting, which has prompted flows of **refugees** into neighboring Chad, and the displacement of hundreds of thousands inside Sudan, where the local population has been subjected to acts of **genocide** and **ethnic cleansing** by local Arab/Muslim *janjaweed* forces with at least some complicity with the government in Khartoum. Ongoing disputes among the two main rebel groups, the Sudanese People's Liberation Army/Movement and the Justice and Equality Movement, have complicated the peace process, which was sponsored by the **African Union (AU)** at Abuja, Nigeria. The AU has attempted to mediate the dispute through its Peace and Security Council and, in October 2004, it established the African Union Mission in Sudan (AMIS), in order to monitor the Humanitarian Ceasefire Agreement signed in N'Djamena, Chad, in April 2004, to assist in further confidence building among the parties, to provide security for humanitarian relief efforts, and to create a climate for the resettlement and return of internationally displaced persons and refugees. AMIS personnel began to document evidence of atrocities in the area, leading to further concern that acts of **genocide** were continuing.

In this climate, the United Nations **Security Council** decided to establish a **United Nations (UN)** advance mission in June 2004 for the purpose of preparing a full-fledged UNMIS, which was finally established in March 2005. UNMIS will consist of up to 10,000 military personnel and more than 700 civilian police. UNMIS was directed to support implementation of the Comprehensive Peace Agreement signed in January 2005, and to liaise closely with the AU and the AMIS forces already deployed in Darfur. The United Nations Security Council felt an urgent need to deploy larger numbers of human rights monitors to the region to monitor human rights violations, and it called upon the **United Nations High Commissioner for Human Rights (UNHCHR)** to accelerate the human rights monitoring program. A formal UN investigation into the situation stopped short of declaring that the Sudanese government was engaged in genocide, although it did admit that acts consisting of genocide had been committed. The matter of intent to commit genocide, however, was more difficult to prove, although some governments, including that of the United States, did declare that genocide was being committed in Darfur by *janjaweed* forces with the complicity of the government. The **International Criminal Court (ICC)** initiated an investigation of the charges of genocide in 2005. This mounting political pressure is seen as a means of forcing the Sudanese government to move quickly toward resolution of the conflict and the repair of the resulting harm to millions of innocent civilians. In the meantime, UNMIS in cooperation with AMIS continues to support the full implementation of peace in this troubled region and the restoration and rehabilitation of the economic infrastructure, in a setting of recognition of the human rights of those so badly afflicted by many years of civil war. A fragile peace agreement was reached between the rebel groups and the Sudanese government in May 2006. Address: UNMIS, P. O. Box 5013, Grand Central Station, New York, NY 10163-5013, USA. Website: www.unmis.org.

UNITED NATIONS OFFICE FOR THE COORDINATION OF HUMANITARIAN AFFAIRS (UNOCHA). United Nations (UN) efforts to respond to humanitarian emergencies were coordinated, until 1991, by the office of the secretary-general and by the United Nations Disaster Relief Organization (UNDRO), with a number of other agencies, such as the **United Nations Children's Fund (UNICEF)**, the **United Nations High Commissioner for Refugees (UNHCR)**, or the **World Food Programme (WFP)** undertaking programming for aid to children, **refugees**, or **famine** victims, respectively. Other agencies were also involved in specialized areas of assistance and relief. In 1991, the UN decided to centralize these efforts by establishing the post of the Emergency Relief Coordinator (ERC). Shortly after the creation of this new post, the UN secretary-general established a new **Department of Humanitarian Affairs (DHA)**, and the ERC was elevated to the status of Under-Secretary General for Humanitarian Affairs.

The ERC, under the 1991 reform measures was given authority to head the Interagency Standing Committee (IASC), composed of full member organizations with long experience in emergency relief activities, including UNICEF, UNHCR, WFP, as well as the **United Nations Development Programme (UNDP)**, the **Food and Agriculture Organization (FAO)**, the **World Health Organization (WHO)**, and the **United Nations Fund for Population Activities (UNFPA)**. Other intergovernmental and nongovernmental agencies were included in the IASC process as standing invitees, including the **United Nations High Commissioner for Human Rights (UNHCHR)**, the **World Bank**, the **International Committee of the Red Cross (ICRC)**, the **International Federation of Red Cross and Red Crescent Societies (IFRC)**, the International Organization for Migration (IOM), the **International Council of Voluntary Agencies (ICVA)**, and **Interaction**.

In addition to the coordination of emergency relief efforts through the IASC, the ERC was tasked with administration of the Consolidated Appeals Process (CAP) and the Central Emergency Revolving Fund (CERF) as mechanisms to expedite and rationalize emergency funding of relief programs and international responses to complex emergencies.

The reorganization of the **United Nations Secretariat** in 1998 saw the UNOCHA replace the DHA as the primary organizational body for humanitarian activities, including needs assessments, facilitating the CAP, establishing field-coordination agreements, and fostering the promotion of humanitarian policies and programs. UNOCHA employs about 860 staff members serving in its two primary offices in New York and Geneva and in various field offices. The current ERC is Jan Egelund of Norway. UNOCHA programs serve nearly 50 million people throughout the world, many caught in the web of complex emergencies where civil war complicates emergency assistance and famine aid.

UNOCHA has recognized the need to work with armed groups, rebel organizations, and nonstate actors in such conflicts, as well as to recognize and prevent sexual exploitation and abuse. UNOCHA also serves as the focal point for the United Nations Disaster Assessment and Coordination (UNDAC), the International Search and Rescue Advisory Group (INSARAG), and the Geographic Information Support Teams (GIST), all of which serve as rapid-response tools for humanitarian relief. In addition to this UNOCHA maintains a relief web, which includes extensive documentation and reports on various humanitarian situations around the globe, as well as links to the various intergovernmental and nongovernmental organizations (NGOs) actively involved in the provision of such assistance. The tsunami disaster of December 2004 in the Indian Ocean highlighted the role of UNOCHA as a mechanism for promoting and coordinating humanitarian aid in connection with major and sudden disasters.

UNOCHA's humanitarian activities involve efforts to promote the most basic human rights, including the **right to life**, to security and safety, and to basic human dignity, and the provision of basic human needs, such as **food**, sanitation, **health** care, and shelter. UNOCHA activities are intended to serve as a bridge from emergency aid to long-term development. However, despite the necessity and urgency of its work, its CAP initiatives and other programs and activities are routinely underfunded. It receives above a tenth of its funding from the regular UN budget, but relies entirely on voluntary contributions for the lion's share of its programming activities, which are usually undersubscribed.

Moreover, UNOCHA continues to face difficulties in asserting effective coordination of the far-flung UN system of largely independent agencies, even a decade after the initial efforts to centralize coordination of UN emergency relief activities under the ERC. A culture of institutional independence among UN bodies and operational programs responsible for the actual implementation of emergency aid makes effective centralized coordination a difficult task. This is further complicated by governments that continue to look to one or another aid agency as major implementers of emergency aid and by NGOs that compete for program funding not directly from UNOCHA, as such, but through the relief agencies that do the lion's share of the program implementation in the field. Thus UNOCHA continues to face difficulty both in funding and in establishing a clear reputation and responsibility for centralized coordination of emergency assistance in an interagency climate that resists management and seeks to preserve agency autonomy and protect traditional mandates and authorities. New York address: UNOCHA, New York, NY 10014, USA. Geneva address: UNOCHA, Palais des Nations, 1211 Geneva, Switzerland. Websites: ochaonline.un.org and www.reliefweb.int.

UNITED NATIONS OPERATION IN BURUNDI (ONUB). Burundi has suffered from disputes between Tutsis and Hutus since the time of independence in 1962, with the Tutsi **minority** generally having control of the government. In 2000, at Arusha, Tanzania, an agreement was reached to seek national reconciliation. The **United Nations** Security Council decided in May 2004 to establish ONUB in order to support Burundian efforts to achieve national reconciliation, by assisting in the demobilization and reintegration of combatants, to monitor illegal weapons flows into Burundi, to provide security for the provision of humanitarian aid, to supply a peaceful and secure environment for the holding of elections, to protect civilian populations from acts of violence, and to promote and secure human rights and protection of vulnerable populations. The United Nations Security

Council provided that up to 5,650 personnel could be deployed to these ends in Burundi.

UNITED NATIONS OPERATION IN SOMALIA (UNOSOM). First established in April 1992 by the **United Nations** Security Council, UNOSOM I was deployed in order to provide security for the delivery of humanitarian aid to civil war ravaged Somalia. The operation met significant local opposition and failed to achieve its goals. In December 1992, the Security Council authorized the use of all necessary means by its members to restore order and provide a climate of security in which humanitarian assistance could reach the starving and in which political reconciliation could be facilitated. The United States led Operation Restore Hope, which was later bolstered by the Unified Task Force (UNITAF), which involved the military forces of several nations. The operation succeeded in rapidly addressing the **famine**, in quickly securing the roads, and in providing humanitarian aid. In May 1993, UNITAF handed over operations to a reconstituted UNOSOM II. Efforts by that force to disarm the factions and to punish Mohammed Farah Aideed and his forces for the deaths of UNOSOM forces in the fall of 1993 failed. With Somali opposition to UNOSOM growing, and with the withdrawal of U.S. forces from the UNOSOM contingents, efforts to resolve the political feuding among Somali factions grew increasingly complex. With the humanitarian side of the operation having largely succeeded, the efforts to facilitate a successful political resolution proved elusive. UNOSOM II forces were eventually withdrawn in 1995, leaving the ultimate political fate of the country to its own divided leaderships.

UNITED NATIONS ORGANIZATION MISSION IN THE DEMOCRATIC REPUBLIC OF THE CONGO (MONUC). The Congo has long been a concern of the **United Nations (UN)** from the earliest days of that country's independence. Responding to political violence and turmoil when the Congo received independence from Belgium, the United Nations Security Council established the United Nations Operation in the Congo (ONUC) in July 1960. Its principal role was to restore order to the Congo and to forestall the threat of secession in Katanga province, but it also provided security for the provision of humanitarian assistance. The operation remained in the field until June 1964. More than 30 years of dictatorship under Mobutu Sese Seko followed, during which the Congo (renamed Zaïre by Mobutu) experienced an uneasy stability under corrupt government with periods of regional uprising. However, with this large country having retrogressed into deeper **poverty**, and under the pressure of large inflows of **refugees** from the Rwandan civil war, opposition to Mobutu intensified. Laurent Kabila overthrew the Mobutu regime in 1997, and renamed the country the Democratic Republic of the Congo (DRC). But the civil war did not end as the new government provoked further civil war; determined rebel opposition led the DRC to become the site of Africa's first continental war as Uganda and Rwanda intervened on behalf of its allies while other neighbors of the DRC weighed in with support for the Kabila government.

Regional attempts to achieve a peace settlement continued throughout the late 1990s, and in February 2000, the UN Security Council established MONUC for the explicit purpose of monitoring human rights and facilitating humanitarian assistance "with particular attention to vulnerable groups including **women**, children, and demobilized child soldiers." MONUC has provided temporary shelter to victims of armed conflict, and facilitated the transport of nongovernmental organizations (NGOs) and UN staff as well as humanitarian assistance supplies to areas in most need of relief. It has identified and coordinated dozens of Quick Impact Projects (QIPs), that have assisted nearly two million people throughout the DRC. The QIPs have addressed a variety of sectors, including **education**, **health**, environment, agriculture, public infrastructure rehabilitation, erosion control, income-generating activities, support for vulnerable groups, and a seminar on human rights.

As part of the UN's recent effort to mainstream gender issues within all areas of its mandate, a Gender Office was established in March 2002 to promote gender awareness in hiring and policymaking. However, despite this, MONUC has been plagued with frequent reports on the part of its own staff of sexual abuse of local women and children. Such abuse by DRC troops and its opposition has been common, but the scandal widened in recent years to include peacekeeping forces and UN representatives, adding yet another sad charge of corruption to the UN's battered reputation at a time when reports of sexual harassment at UN headquarters in New York and the Oil for Food investigations were finding widespread evidence of corruption at the highest levels of the **United Nations Secretariat**.

Still, despite these glaring violations of human rights, the overall work of MONUC has been commendable in seeking access to refugees and displaced persons and attempting to promote secure access to humanitarian assistance. MONUC still faces the daunting task of integrating refugees and displaced persons back into their home areas once the conflict has been finally resolved, and of undertaking demining operations and rehabilitation of a country where an estimated 17 million people lack access to sufficient food. Field Address: MONUC Information Focal Point, Humanitarian Affairs Section, Kinshasa, DRC. Website: www.monuc.org.

UNITED NATIONS PROTECTION FORCE (UNPROFOR). Established by the **United Nations (UN)** Security Council on 21 February 1992, UNPROFOR was deployed to the new republics of the former Yugoslavia in order to monitor borders, cease-fire agreements, and bans on military flights, as well as to ensure security for civilians in protected areas and to facilitate the secure delivery of relief supplies to the millions of **refugees** and displaced persons who have been uprooted by the civil wars. The **United Nations High Commissioner for Refugees (UNHCR)** was named the lead UN agency in the provision of humanitarian assistance. The attainment of UNPROFOR goals was especially difficult and complex, given the ongoing and shifting nature of the conflicts in the region. The widespread abuses of human rights, **ethnic cleansing** activities by all parties, and brutal character of the war combined to make UNPROFOR efforts all the more necessary, if difficult. With active conflicts disrupting humanitarian supply routes and protected areas, with various local forces prohibiting movement of humanitarian aid convoys, and with occasional international bombing of Serbian military targets by North Atlantic Treaty Organization (NATO) air forces, the job of providing relief on the ground became exceedingly dangerous. However, the peace talks at Dayton, Ohio, of November 1995 offered the first tangible hopes for a settlement to this stubborn dispute and on 20 December 1995 UNPROFOR's mandate ceased and peacekeeping responsibilities were turned over to the NATO force.

**UNITED NATIONS RELIEF AND REHABILITATION ADMIN-
ISTRATION (UNRRA).** During World War II, the Allies who comprised the **United Nations (UN)** formed the UNRRA in order to provide for the humanitarian needs of persons displaced by the war.
UNRRA replaced the **Intergovernmental Committee for Refugees
(IGCR)** as the principal international body for protecting and assisting **refugees** during and after the war. Actual administration of the
displaced persons camps was undertaken by the Supreme Headquarters of the Allied Expeditionary Force until July 1945, when UNRRA
assumed this role. During the next two years, in war-torn areas of Europe, Africa, and the Far East, UNRRA supplied over a billion dollars worth of humanitarian assistance and promoted resettlement of
refugees and displaced persons. UNRRA was disbanded in June
1947, its assets were distributed to other humanitarian agencies, and
its refugee protection function was assumed by the International
Refugee Organization (IRO).

**UNITED NATIONS RELIEF AND WORKS AGENCY FOR
PALESTINE (UNRWA).** With the major relief commitments that existed in Europe after World War II, the Arab-Israeli War of 1948 over-
taxed the response capacity and mandate of the International Refugee
Organization (IRO). Thus, the **United Nations (UN)** temporarily created the United Nations Relief for Palestinian Refugees (UNRPR) to
meet the immediate relief needs of Palestinians and in December 1949
established the more permanent body known as UNWRA. UNWRA
initially engaged in emergency and development assistance activities
on behalf of Palestinian **refugees**, but it now engages primarily in educational activities, special programs for the disabled and basic community **health** services. After the **United Nations High Commissioner for Refugees (UNHCR)** was created in 1951, UNRWA
continued to serve as the main humanitarian assistance agency for
Palestinians. Formerly headquartered in Beirut, Lebanon (1950–1978),
and then Vienna, Austria (1978–1996), UNRWA moved its entire operation in 1996 into the Middle East, with a new headquarters in Gaza.
With budgets often in excess of $200 million, UNRWA is a major pres-
ence in areas occupied by Palestinian refugees in Syria, Jordan,
Lebanon, and the Gaza Strip, where it still supplies some humanitarian
aid in addition to its considerable educational activities, including

elementary and preparatory education, vocational and technical training, and teacher training.

UNRWA operates in a highly charged political environment and must work with the governments of the region to see that its humanitarian and development-related assistance is successfully delivered. Recent progress in peace talks between the Palestine Liberation Organization (PLO) and the government of Israel held out the prospect that UNRWA may be able at some future date to hand over its work to fully local agencies, but the rise of Hamas as the governing party again threw the political situation into turmoil in early 2006, even as Israel withdrew from the Gaza Strip and much of the West Bank. Address: Gamal Abdul Nasser Street, Gaza City. Postal Address: P.O. Box 140157, Amman 11814, Jordan. Website: www.un.org/unrwa.

UNITED NATIONS RESEARCH INSTITUTE FOR SOCIAL DEVELOPMENT (UNRISD). This **United Nations (UN)** body is responsible for conducting research on the social implications of the development process. It was established in 1963 during the first UN Development Decade. It sponsors conferences and publishes studies on a range of social development issues, including those dealing with **women**, the problems of migration and **refugees**, the effects of displacement, and the social impact of emergency and development assistance. UNRISD attempts to complement the work of other UN agencies in addressing the political and social dimensions of development. Its research activities have included extensive studies on refugee repatriation, ethnic conflict and development, the socioeconomic effects of the drug trade, and the effects of adjustment policies on the social and economic well-being of countries. Beyond this, it has sponsored research on civil society and corporate responsibility, on gender **equality**, **health**, and HIV/AIDS, on the role of nongovernmental organizations (NGOs), and on water supply issues. Since the year 2000 its research focus has emphasized civil society and social movements; identity politics and its affects on conflict and social cohesion, the role of technology in society, and democracy and human rights. All such work enhances understanding of issues related to humanitarian assistance and human rights. Address: Palais des Nations, CH-1211 Geneva 10, Switzerland. Website: www.unrisd.org.

UNITED NATIONS SECRETARIAT. The secretariat is one of the six main organs of the **United Nations (UN)**. Its main role is to carry out the routine administration of UN bodies in keeping with the mandates and directives of the member-states and to fulfill the duties assigned to it in the **United Nations Charter**. The secretary-general is the chief UN administrative officer, and together with the UN staff, comprises the secretariat. The secretary-general is required to present an annual report to the **United Nations General Assembly** on the work of the United Nations and he may apprise the United Nations Security Council of any matters that potentially threaten international peace and security. Indeed, in the wake of the collapse of the Soviet Union and the passing of the Cold War, the UN Security Council found itself increasingly engaged in peacekeeping and peacemaking deployments that involved provision of security for humanitarian assistance, monitoring of human rights, and demobilization and reintegration of former combatants into civil society. Thus, the peacemaking agenda of the council was frequently tied to humanitarian and human rights causes. These multidimensional operations became increasingly more common as the council addressed civil war situations that produced complex emergencies threatening international pace and security.

The secretariat supervises a number of humanitarian and human rights bodies. The Center for Human Rights, located in the UN Geneva office, and the **United Nations Office for the Coordination of Humanitarian Affairs (UNOCHA)**, located in New York, are direct branches of the secretariat. The former gives administrative support and supervision to the human rights activities of the **United Nations General Assembly**, the **Economic and Social Council (ECOSOC)**, and until 2006, the **Human Rights Commission (HRC)**, which was succeeded by the **Human Rights Council**, as well as a number of committees established under various international human rights instruments, such as the **Human Rights Committee (HRC)** established by the **International Covenant on Civil and Political Rights**, the **Committee on Economic, Social, and Cultural Rights (CESCR)**, the **Committee against Torture (CAT)**, and the **Committee on the Elimination of Racial Discrimination (CERD)**, among others. UNOCHA, formerly the **Department of Humanitarian Affairs (DHA)**, which existed from April 1992 until 1997, serves as the coordinating mechanism for several UN specialized and related agencies engaged in humanitarian assistance and protection. Prior to the DHA, the United Nations Disaster Relief Organization (UNDRO) had performed these functions, which are now under the supervision of the under-secretary-general for humanitarian affairs, who also serves as the chair of the Interagency Standing Committee (IASC) and as the UN's Emergency Relief Coordinator (ERC). Disaster prevention and mitigation is now undertaken by UNOCHA through the Interagency Task Force on Disaster Reduction, which meets twice annually in Geneva, where the permanent focal point for developing an International Strategy for Disaster Reduction is located. In 1997, the UN established a special representative of the secretary-general for Children and Armed Conflict as an advocate for **children's rights** in the setting of wars. The representative operates no programs as such, but serves as a facilitator and coordinator to advance awareness and promote the development of law and policy favorable to the welfare of children caught in situations of conflict. Among the UN agencies participating in the IASC are UNOCHA, the **Food and Agriculture Organization (FAO)**, the **United Nations Development Programme (UNDP)**, the **United Nations High Commissioner for Refugees (UNHCR)**, the **United Nations Children's Fund (UNICEF)**, the **World Food Programme (WFP)**, the **World Health Organization (WHO)**, and the **United Nations Fund for Population Activities (UNFPA)**. Other standing invitees include **Interaction**, the **International Committee of the Red Cross (ICRC)**, the **International Council of Voluntary Agencies (ICVA)**, the **International Federation of Red Cross and Red Crescent Societies (IFRC)**, the International Organization for Migration (IOM), the Office of the **United Nations High Commissioner for Human Rights (UNHCHR)**, and the **World Bank**, among others.

UNITED NATIONS SECURITY COUNCIL. *See* UNITED NATIONS (UN); UNITED NATIONS CHARTER; UNITED NATIONS SECRETARIAT.

UNITED NATIONS STABILIZATION MISSION IN HAITI (MINUSTAH). Established in April 2004 by the **United Nations** Security Council, MINUSTAH, is but the latest in a long series of United Nations (UN) interventions in Haiti to support the establishment of stable and democratic government, to organize an effective civilian peace force educated in the principles of human rights and proper criminal justice procedures, to establish a climate for free and fair elections, and to strengthen the capacity to promote and protect human rights, to bring violators of human rights to justice, and to protect the human rights of returned **refugees** and displaced persons. Haiti has been marked by unstable and undemocratic government since its independence in 1804. It is one of the world's poorest countries and has a long tradition of emigration.

In December 1990, Haiti held its first democratic elections, but the government of Bertrand Aristide was overthrown by the army in September 1991. The UN continued to recognize the Aristide government as the legitimate government, and great international pressure was eventually brought to bear on the ruling junta, led by Raul Cedras. The United Nations Security Council authorized the deployment of military forces to restore a democratic government to power in August 1993. The United Nations Mission in Haiti (UNMIH) was subsequently deployed, with difficulty, to supervise the transition back to democratic rule. In was withdrawn in June 1996, but replaced by a series of temporary UN bodies deployed to assist with the transition to democratic government and the training of police units. The last of these was terminated in 2001, after the reelection of Aristide in elections that garnered only about 10 percent of Haitian voters. Political instability gradually rose in this climate of suspicion.

International and regional efforts to mediate the dispute continued through 2003 and into 2004, as a determined insurgency gained strength, which eventually forced the flight of Aristide. At the request of the new government, the Security Council deployed a Multinational Interim Force to ensure stability and security in Haiti for the formation of a transitional government. In April 2004 the UN Security Council established MINUSTAH to perform a multidimensional role in preparing the way for yet another democratic election. Its mandate includes restoration of security, and implementation of Quick Impact Projects to support humanitarian goals. MINUSTAH is also tasked with the ongoing process of ensuring that the civilian police force is adequately trained in the knowledge and practice of human rights. Haiti continued to experience a dangerous security environment throughout 2004 and into 2005, a year in which it was hoped that new and democratic elections could be held. The election was delayed until 7 February 2006, when Rene Preval of the Lavalas movement defeated candidates of the interim government of Haiti with about 50 percent of the vote. Although his nearest competitor won only 12 percent, controversy over vote tabulations persisted as to whether Preval had met the 50 percent standard that would avoid a runoff election. The controversy was not welcome in a country where two of three previously democratically elected regimes failed to survive their first term. MINUSTAH force levels reached about 9,300 in January 2006 just in advance of the elections.

UNITED NATIONS TRANSITIONAL ADMINISTRATION IN EAST TIMOR (UNTAET). The **United Nations (UN)** Security Council established UNTAET in October 1999, after the people of East Timor voted in August 1999 in favor of seeking independence. The elections had been supported by the United Nations Mission in East Timor (UNAMET). However, the election was followed by widespread violence, which was precipitated by Indonesian-backed opponents of independence and involved countless violations of human rights, such as murder, rape, and involuntary displacement. Under these circumstances, UNAMET was forced to reduce its presence, and the United Nations Security Council authorized deployment of an international force led by Australia to restore order. UNAMET then facilitated subsequent humanitarian assistance. Once Indonesia formally recognized the results of the popular consultation, the UN Security Council established UNTAET to restore and maintain order as an effective administration was constructed. It also coordinated delivery of humanitarian aid, and promoted the development of a local capacity for provision of civil and social services and for self-government under conditions of sustainable development. UNTAET was terminated on 20 May 2002, when East Timor formally achieved independence. It was succeeded by the United Nations Mission of Support in East Timor, which was established by the United Nations Security Council to promote the stability of the new government, which, unfortunately, has continued to experience domestic instability, conflict, and consequent violations of the human rights of its population.

UNITED NATIONS TRANSITIONAL AUTHORITY IN CAMBODIA (UNTAC). UNTAC was established by the **United Nations** Security Council in March 1992 in order to verify the withdrawal of foreign forces from Cambodia, to clear mines in advance of the repatriation of **refugees**, to repatriate and resettle Cambodian refugees in cooperation with the **United Nations High Commissioner for Refugees (UNHCR)**, to rehabilitate economic infrastructure, and to prepare for free and fair elections. It also served as the interim administration of the country until elections could be successfully held. UNTAC's comprehensive mandate, then, included both the traditional security elements of UN peacekeeping and also political, humanitarian aid, and human rights supervision. Its work was brought to a largely successful conclusion in December 1993, with the new government of the country pledging to respect the principles of international humanitarian law and human rights, a pledge that has not always been scrupulously observed.

UNITED NATIONS UNIVERSITY (UNU). Established by the **United Nations General Assembly** in December 1972, the central location of UNU is Tokyo, Japan. A number of affiliated academic institutions, research, and training centers throughout the world are associated with UNU. Among the principal functions of UNU is the conduct of research aimed at resolution of practical political, economic, social, and humanitarian problems. Its research efforts extend to issues surrounding migration, ethnic **minorities**, and a variety of human rights and humanitarian concerns. Address: Toho Seimei Building, 15-1 Shibuya-ku, Tokyo 150, Japan. For a firsthand historical account of UNU, see Narasimhan (1994). Website: www.unu.edu.

UNIVERSAL DECLARATION OF HUMAN RIGHTS. Adopted by the **United Nations (UN) General Assembly** on 10 December 1948, the Universal Declaration of Human Rights, although not originally conceived as a legally binding document, represented the first occasion on which the international community articulated a comprehensive set of standards regarding human rights that would serve as goals or aspirations that governments declared they would endeavor to emulate. The declaration was adopted by a vote of 48 in favor and none opposed with eight abstentions (those being Byelorussia, Czechoslovakia, Poland, Saudi Arabia, Ukraine, Union of Soviet Socialist Republics, South Africa, and Yugoslavia). Despite the broad understanding that the declaration as a whole lacked the binding force of law, from the beginning it was viewed as a clarification of the **United Nations Charter** call for protection of human rights and fundamental freedoms. To the extent that the declaration further specified the character of these charter-protected rights, it served to underscore these charter-related obligations. Indeed, many of the declaration's provisions already constituted general principles of **international law** practiced by states, and even those in disparity with actual legal norms were asserted as moral principles worthy of future aspiration. In time, many governments incorporated portions of the declaration into their own **constitutions** or domestic statutes, thus making them at least potentially enforceable. Some legal scholars have argued that the declaration as a whole has become binding customary law, but this view has been disputed by jurists who admit that portions of the declaration, such as those dealing with **torture** and **slavery** or perhaps even with discrimination, are clearly binding customary norms, while many other provisions lack such a legal character.

The declaration served as the basis for further debate in the **Commission on Human Rights (CHR)** as well as in the United Nations **Economic and Social Council (ECOSOC)** and the United Nations General Assembly. Efforts to draft more complete, detailed, and potentially enforceable covenants of human rights continued until 1966, when the **International Covenant on Civil and Political Rights**, a protocol to this covenant, and the **International Covenant on Economic, Social, and Cultural Rights** were adopted by the General Assembly and put before states for ratification. Together with these covenants, the declaration comprises what is known as the **International Bill of Human Rights**.

Consisting of 30 articles, the declaration starts out by proclaiming the freedom and **equality** of human beings on the basis of nondiscrimination. The rights of human beings include the **right to life**, liberty, security of person; freedom from slavery and torture; the right to a legal personality; freedom from **arbitrary arrest**, detention, and exile; the right to due process, legal defense, and a **fair trial**; and the rights to freedom of movement and to seek **asylum** from persecution. The declaration affirms that all persons have a right to a **nationality**, the right to marry and enjoy a **family**, and the right to own **property** and not to be deprived of it except by due process of law. Persons have a right to **freedom of religion**, to **freedom of opinion and expression**, to **freedom of assembly**, and **freedom of association** and political participation. Having identified the personal, civic, and **political rights** of persons, the declaration then spells out the **economic, social, and cultural rights** that all people should enjoy. In Article 22, however, the declaration acknowledges that attainment of such rights depends on the resources and organization of each country. Still, governments stipulated that all persons should have a right to **work**, to choose their employment, to equal pay for equal work, to a just wage, and to supplemental **social security** to ensure fundamental dignity, as well as a right to participate in unions. Further, persons have a right to rest and leisure, to an adequate standard of living, and to an **education**. The declaration also stipulates that individuals have duties to the communities of which they are a part. Many of the rights listed in the declaration remained somewhat vague, and clearly some rights might conflict with others. Still, the declaration served as a spur to further international discussion on human rights and fundamental freedoms, which in the following years mushroomed into numerous further treaties, declarations, and agreements. For a full text of the Universal Declaration, see appendix A.

UNIVERSAL DECLARATION ON THE ERADICATION OF HUNGER AND MALNUTRITION. This declaration was adopted by the World Food Conference held at Rome in November 1974 and endorsed by the **United Nations General Assembly** on 17 December 1974. In the opening paragraph of its preamble, the declaration recognized that the world's grave **food** crisis, "acutely jeopardizes the most fundamental principles and values associated with the **right to life** and human dignity as enshrined in the **Universal Declaration of Human Rights**." Again, in the first operative paragraph of the declaration, the World Food Conference proclaimed that "Every man, woman and child has the inalienable right to be free from hunger and malnutrition in order to develop fully and maintain their physical and mental faculties." The conference sought to place the world hunger problem squarely in the context of its human rights dimension. The declaration emphasizes that every government has a responsibility to increase food production and to cooperate with other governments to ensure an equitable and efficient distribution of food between and within countries. This includes providing incentives to farmers to increase production, removing obstacles to food production, providing technical support and assistance, improving technology, promoting conservation, and reducing food wastage. The declaration also called for the establishment of a Global Information and Early Warning System on Food and Agriculture designed to ensure better responses to emergency situations. *See also* FAMINE; FOOD; FOOD AND AGRICULTURE ORGANIZATION (FAO); WORLD FOOD PROGRAMME (WFP).

U.S. CONSTITUTION. *See* CONSTITUTION OF THE UNITED STATES.

– V –

VANCOUVER DECLARATION ON HUMAN SETTLEMENTS. Adopted by the **United Nations (UN)** Conference on Human Settlements, known as HABITAT, on 11 June 1976, this declaration sought to promote national development policies, which take into account the need for the progressive improvement in the provision of shelter. The declaration reaffirmed the right of freedom of movement of people and their right to choose a place of settlement. It acknowledged the right of governments to regulate the use of land, and it called upon states to give a high priority to the shelter needs of those displaced by natural or man-made catastrophes. It asserts that adequate shelter and services are a basic human right. The declaration is not a binding international instrument, but on 16 December 1976 the **United Nations General Assembly** did call upon governments to take its recommendations and guidelines for action into account in formulating their national settlement policies. A second Conference on Human Settlements (HABITAT II) was held in June 1996 in Istanbul, Turkey. Known as the "City Summit," it produced a lengthy and detailed Habitat agenda. Housing and urban settlement issues continue to be very relevant in UN discussions concerning **Millennium Development Goals**, including urban **poverty** reduction and reduction of vulnerability to disaster.

VATICAN. The Vatican, or Vatican City, is the site of the papal residence and the Curia, which govern the internal and external affairs of the Roman Catholic Church. Its diplomatic arm is the Holy See, which is accredited to the **United Nations (UN)** as an observer state, and enjoys the recognition of 174 governments. The Holy See participates in more than 30 international organizations and 10 regional organizations. The Vatican is a unique political entity, insofar as it is the center of one of the world's great historical religions, and its influence is more genuinely global than perhaps that of any secular state, insofar as the Roman Catholic Church's diocesan system of governance embraces every part of the globe.

For purposes of human rights, the Vatican teaches and advances principles consistent with Christianity, including the essential dignity of the human person, and the right of persons to enjoy the broad range of human rights, including **political rights** and **economic, social, and cultural rights**. It takes a keen interest in advancing the **freedom of religion**, and in the rights of the **family** as the natural basis of human society. Through the writings of the popes, including most recently those of Benedict XI, **John Paul II**, Paul VI, and **John XXIII**, the Vatican addresses a range of moral and ethical questions bearing on human rights, including the **right to life**, the right to **property**, the right to freedom of **movement and residence**, and the right to **work**, among many others. The Vatican has spoken out on the rights of **refugees**, of **women**, of **asylum** seekers, and of **minorities**. Apart from the official teachings of the popes enunciated in encyclicals and apostolic letters, the Vatican addresses matters of human rights both by Vatican Radio and its newspaper, *L'Osservatore Romano*, as well as an extensive website.

The Vatican also advances policies intended to reduce the scourge of **poverty** and to enhance the development of peoples and nations. It encourages the principle of **solidarity** in matters of peace, justice, and economic development, in keeping with the prudential norm of **subsidiarity**, the right of local bodies and institutions to advance the human good. It advances a wide range of humanitarian policies, and encourages the active participation of local Catholic churches and charitable associations to advance the corporal works of mercy, by tending to the needs of the poor, sick, homeless, imprisoned, handicapped, and stranger. These bodies include hundreds of local entities and Catholic nongovernmental organizations (NGOs), such as **Caritas Internationalis (CI)**, Catholic Relief Services, and many others. Website: www.vatican.va.

– W –

WALESA, LECH (1943–). Best known as the leader of Solidarity, the noncommunist trade union that courageously demanded worker's rights in the face of communist oppression, Lech Walesa rose from a humble background to the international spotlight as a human rights activist. He worked as a mechanic, did a tour in the Polish army, and then took employment as an electrician at the Gdansk shipyards. Shortly after his marriage to Danuta Golos, Walesa participated as a leader of workers who clashed with the government in 1970, for which he was briefly detained. In 1976, he was fired, owing to his ongoing agitation against government labor policies and political repression, and it was not long before he was involved in the organization of noncommunist trade unions. In August 1980, he led the famous Gdansk shipyard strike until the government eventually capitulated to worker demands and granted them the right to strike and to form their own union, a bitter concession on the part of the Polish Communist Party and government, which by its own definition and self-understanding operated a worker's paradise.

The ascendancy of **John Paul II** to the papacy added momentum to the formation of Solidarity, which the pope encouraged, while urging nonviolent and peaceful action against government repression. **Freedom of religion** played a major role in the labor movement in a country that is overwhelmingly Catholic. Workers had been denied the right to build a church or celebrate Mass, but the government was helpless in resisting the pope's influence and the yearnings of millions of Poles for their religious and political liberty. The government made concessions on the former while attempting to keep political control, signified by its crackdown against Solidarity in December 1981, which suspended the labor movement and led to the incarceration of its leaders, including Walesa, who was interned far to the south of Poland.

Walesa was released in November 1982 and permitted to **work** at the Gdansk Shipyards, although kept under tight surveillance. In

1983, he won the Nobel Peace Prize, much to the chagrin of Prime Minister Wojciech Jaruzelski's communist government. He sent his wife, Danuta, to receive the prize, fearing that the government might bar his return. In 1987, he formed a Temporary Executive Committee of Solidarity, which had a dubious legal status, and he agitated for the full relegalization of Solidarity. As a result of talks with the communist government, quasi-free elections were agreed to in which the communists were guaranteed in advance 51 percent of the seats. Virtually all of the free seats were won by the opposition, indicating the wide unpopularity of communist rule. The demise of the communists then quickly ensued, with the formation of a noncommunist majority coalition government that began instituting free enterprise reforms in the decrepit Polish economy.

In December 1990, Walesa was elected president of Poland. He served a five-year term, and he presided over the rapid transition of the country toward liberalization of the economy and democratization of political life. Nonetheless, Walesa lost his bid for reelection, and subsequent efforts to reenter political life failed, including a bid for the presidency in 2000, in which he received less than 1 percent of the vote. Still, Walesa's role in the downfall of communism cannot be disputed. He personified the Polish yearning for religious and political freedom, and his bold and brave efforts in favor of worker's rights constituted the spark that led not just to the fall of communism in Poland but eventually to the collapse of the entire communist colossus built up by Moscow over decades. *See also* FREEDOM OF RELIGION.

WAR CRIMES. Rooted in a long tradition of customary law, modern efforts to codify war crimes in army manuals and treaties began in the late 19th century. One of the most influential attempts to codify the customs of war and to identify war crimes was Francis Lieber's *Instructions for the Government of the Armies of the United States in the Field*, which were commissioned by President Abraham Lincoln and issued by him as General Orders No. 100 to the Union Army in 1863. Lieber's work was quite influential and later served as a model for military manuals in a number of countries. Although only tangentially related to Lieber's Manual, the trial after the Civil War of Henri Wirz, Confederate commander of the Andersonville prison, served as one of the first war-crimes trials and a harbinger of later developments in the 20th century.

Subsequent to the American Civil War, private and public efforts to codify the laws of warfare on land culminated in The Hague Peace Conferences of 1899 and 1907, and with the drafting of the Fourth Convention Respecting the Laws and Customs of War on Land in 1907. This treaty, though failing to gain sufficient ratifications to enter into force, was declaratory of much existing customary law, and the rest of its provisions are now regarded as universally binding customary law. Its provisions concerning prisoners of war have been amended and updated by the **Geneva Red Cross Conventions** of 1949 and protocols of 1977, but states not party to these conventions are still bound by the older customs pertaining to prisoners found in the 1907 agreement. Among the war crimes listed in the 1907 treaty are the use of poison or poisoned weapons, the killing or wounding of unarmed enemy who have surrendered, the employment of arms or projectiles calculated to cause unnecessary suffering, the attack or bombardment of undefended enemy towns, and the wanton and indiscriminate bombardment of hospitals, religious sites, and places where the sick and wounded are gathered. Other acts, such as pillaging, willful **torture**, and inhuman treatment of civilians or prisoners, misuse of Red Cross emblems or flags of surrender or truce, the wearing of enemy uniforms, and other acts of treachery are also forbidden.

Until World War II, and the formation of the United Nations War Crimes Commission (UNWCC) in 1943, which prepared the groundwork for the Nuremburg trials and judgment after World War II, responsibility for war crimes rested with the offending government. However, even before Nuremburg, individual commanders who ordered war crimes were considered answerable to the enemy governments and could be tried and punished for war crimes if they fell under the enemy government's control during or after the war. The key was to determine which officers gave the orders constituting war crimes or to assess whether junior officers or soldiers exceeded legal orders in a way that constituted war crimes. In general, under the notion of *respondeat superior*, soldiers were viewed as having a duty to obey orders, and thus they were not liable to punishment if following the illegal orders of superiors. The latter, rather, were viewed as the culpable party. The Nuremburg judgment changed this by holding all soldiers responsible for the commission of acts constituting war crimes even when following orders. However, several factors may be taken into account in mitigating the punishment of soldiers who merely followed illegal orders constituting war crimes. These include recognition that in the heat of battle little time may exist to reflect on the legality of an order, that many war crimes remain controversial, that war crimes may be permitted in certain circumstances as reprisals against prior wrongs by the enemy (a fact not so easily discerned by soldiers in the field), and that soldiers may place themselves in physical danger by refusing to execute the orders of their superiors.

The contemporary laws and customs of war, then, recognize that even during hostilities both soldiers and civilians are bound to abide by certain human rights and humanitarian principles. A large body of humanitarian law has emerged, much of it under the supervision of the **International Committee of the Red Cross (ICRC)**, which is intended to mitigate the horrors of war and to lend a degree of humanity to what is otherwise a brutal and destructive business. Still, especially in regard to the punishment of wrongdoers and war criminals, enforcement is much wanting in international affairs. During war, crimes often are committed by forces on both sides. The normal practice is for the vanquished party's forces to be tried and the victor's forces to go free. Even when a government finds a member of its own armed forces guilty of war crimes, the tendency is to be lenient. The special circumstances prevailing at the end of World War II, with the victorious Allies bent on investigating, trying, and punishing the egregious violations of customary law and of the common decency of humanity committed by the vanquished militaries of the Nazi German regime and the Japanese forces in the Pacific, led to the Nuremburg trials in Europe and the Tokyo trials in the Pacific. These trials marked the first time under international action that violators of the laws of war were punished for their misdeeds, and that **crimes against humanity** and crimes against peace were litigated. Still, there can be little doubt that many other violations of the laws of war by all sides in World War II remained unpunished.

Although the Nuremburg and Tokyo trials established new precedents in the **international law** of war, which governments incorporated into their military training manuals and practice, no formal mechanism, such as an international criminal court, existed to monitor or prosecute war criminals. Governments were largely left to undertake this task within their own domestic legal settings. Thus, although a much longer and clearer list of war crimes now exists than ever before, full accountability for the commission of such acts is rarely achieved. These were some of the motivations that led to the reopening of discussions in 1989 at the **United Nations (UN)** for establishing a permanent **International Criminal Court (ICC)**, rather than to rely simply on governmental action or on ad hoc tribunals. With the widespread violations of the laws of war in the former Yugoslavia, the United Nations Security Council in May 1994 created the **International Criminal Tribunal for the Former Yugoslavia (ICTY)** to hear cases concerning war crimes in that region. Headquartered in The Hague, this body was created pursuant to the UN Security Council's authority under Chapter VII of the **United Nations Charter** to make decisions in connection with threats to the peace and acts of aggression. This, together with the establishment of an **International Criminal Tribunal for Rwanda (ICTR)** in 1994, represented the first step since Nuremburg by the international community to call war criminals to account for gross breaches of the laws of war and of the human rights of victimized populations. Meanwhile, momentum gathered in the drafting of a statute for the ICC, which was eventually accomplished under the Rome Statute of July 1998. The ICC was intended to promote wider justice, to end impunity for international crimes, to help end conflicts, to remedy the deficiencies of ad hoc tribunal approaches, to assume jurisdiction over war criminals when national governments are unwilling or unable to do so, and to more effectively deter future war criminals. Ultimately, however, the trial and punishment of war crimes remains the primary duty of national governments, under the principle of **subsidiarity**, which is identified in the ICC statute with the term "complementarity." A recent example of a government effort to punish war crimes is that of Sierra Leone where the UN has facilitated creation of a Special Court in Sierra Leone to try and punish serious violations of international humanitarian law committed during the course of that country's civil war. *See* UNITED NATIONS MISSION IN SIERRA LEONE (UNAMSIL).

WIDOWS' RIGHTS INTERNATIONAL (WRI). Founded by Margaret Owen in 1996, WRI is a nongovernmental organization (NGO) dedicated to advancing the welfare and rights of widows. Its primary objectives include raising international awareness to the plight of widows in developing countries and in postconflict situations, earning a place for widows' rights in the international human rights arena, and assisting groups in developing areas to promote and defend widows' rights. At its founding after the Beijing **Women**'s Conference, WRI worked under the name of Empowering Widows in Development, but changed its name to reflect its human rights orientation, specifically its work on promoting social justice for widows and combating discrimination against them. Specific rights advocated for widows include the right to keep their **family**, the right to own and inherit **property**, and the right to **work** outside the home. Address: 1-3 Berry Street, London, EC1V 0AA, UK. Website: www.widowsrights.org.

WIESEL, ELIE (1928–). Elie Wiesel was born in Sighet, Hungary, on 30 September 1928. As a young man Wiesel was deeply religious. He and his family were deported to Auschwitz in 1944. The prisoners were separated by gender at Auschwitz, and Wiesel never again saw his mother. He and his father were transferred in early 1945 to Buchenwald, where Wiesel's father died only months before American forces liberated the camp.

After the war, Wiesel was sent to Paris where he learned French and studied at the Sorbonne. He read and was deeply moved by the writings of Albert Camus. He later worked as a news correspondent. Although others had written on the **Holocaust**, Wiesel's *Night*, published in 1958, was widely regarded as the most powerful piece of literature on the subject. He is often regarded as having inaugurated Holocaust studies. Wiesel has written many books and novels, including *Dawn*, *The Accident*, *The Town beyond the Wall*, and *The Gates of the Forest*. Wiesel's works *The Jews of Silence* and *Zalmen or the Madness of God* helped initiate the Soviet Jewry movement. Wiesel's later works include *Beggar in Jerusalem*, *Souls on Ice*, and *The Oath*.

Since 1976, Wiesel has been the Andrew W. Mellon Professor in the Humanities at Boston University. Wiesel also has served as the first Henry Luce Visiting Scholar in Humanities and Social Thought at Yale University and as Distinguished Professor of Judaic Studies at the City University of New York. Wiesel served as chair of the U.S. President's Commission on the Holocaust in 1979, which recommended that a museum and study center be built and annual days of remembrance held to honor those who lost their lives in the Holocaust. Wiesel also chaired the Holocaust Memorial Council in the United States, which oversaw the construction of the Holocaust Memorial in Washington, DC.

Wiesel has won such literary awards as the Prix Rivard, National Jewish Book Council Award, and the Jewish Heritage Award for Excellence in Literature. Wiesel won the Nobel Peace Prize in 1986. Over the decades, he has spoken out against repression and defended the plight of such disparate groups as Nicaragua's Miskito Indians, the victims of **disappearances** in Argentina, Soviet Jews, Cambodian **refugees**, African victims of **genocide**, war victims in Bosnia, and those suffering under **apartheid** in South Africa. Soon after receiving the Nobel Prize, Wiesel and his wife, Marion, established the Elie Wiesel Foundation for Humanity. In all his writings and activities, Wiesel has attempted to serve as a witness to the victims of the Holocaust and of oppression everywhere.

WOMEN. The rights of women throughout human history have been defined and variously protected within the contexts of cultural and religious norms rooted in customary law and local practice. Although at various times and places women are known to have enjoyed and practiced certain public and political rights, as a general rule their status in society has been a function of their role in the **family** and households, with but limited access to public expression. In the Middle Ages, for instance, it is known that in various parts of Europe women voted in local elections, that they ran businesses, owned property, paid taxes, received education and, as in the case of abbesses, ruled within monastic communities. But throughout most of the world for most of human history, including fairly recent times, women enjoyed fewer and less extensive rights than men, although an intervening factor has always been that of economic class. Moreover, until recent times, widespread political participation even for men was rare.

With the rise of modern democracies, and the gradual extension of **political rights** to those classes without property, the franchise eventually embraced more classes of men and, after concerted political action, eventually of women and various minority communities. The story of the women's rights movement is told in the lives of numerous suffragettes, including **Jane Addams, Susan B. Anthony, Lucretia Mott**, and **Elizabeth Cady Stanton**, among many others. Acting within countries, constitutional and statutory action was gradually taken by many nations to grant the right to vote to women. Limited suffrage was granted to women in local elections in Britain and Sweden during the 1860s. New Zealand was the first country to introduce universal voting rights to women in 1893. Australia extended the national franchise to women 1901, followed by Finland in 1906, and then by a host of other countries, mostly with democratic and parliamentary forms of government, although the Bolshevik government of the Soviet Union also recognized women's suffrage, as did other countries where the lack of full-blown democracy vitiated the extension of suffrage to a large extent. Women's rights organizations were at first national in scope, but as early as 1888 the **International Council of Women (ICW)** was founded in Washington, DC, and, in 1903, the **International Alliance of Women (IAW)** was established in Berlin as the International Women Suffrage Alliance.

During the period of the **League of Nations**, many more countries recognized women's suffrage, and the organization itself addressed a number of concerns related to women's rights, often at the urging of the ICW and other women's organizations. Among the major technical committees of the League was one attempting to eradicate the trafficking of women and children, a subject that occupied the League from the very outset in 1921 when it drafted the first international agreement on the Suppression of Trafficking in Women and Children, a subject that continued to occupy its attention into the 1930s. Its work was completed by the **United Nations General Assembly**, in 1949, with the promulgation of the **Convention for the Suppression of the Traffic in Persons and of the Exploitation of the Prostitution of Others**. The **International Labour Organization (ILO)** addressed issues concerning the occupation and social status of women, promulgating conventions on such subjects, commencing with its first conventions in 1919 and throughout subsequent years. Other efforts undertaken on behalf of women emerged in the Americas as countries attempted to establish rules that would permit women to obtain citizenship by an act of personal choice rather than automatically acquiring the citizenship of their husband upon marriage. To this end, governments of the Western Hemisphere adopted the Montevideo Convention on the **Nationality** of Women in 1933, but few countries ratified it, although later work by the **United Nations (UN)** reached fruition with the adoption of the Convention on the Status of Married Women in 1955.

The modern story of the expansion of the rights of women is rooted first and foremost in the **United Nations Charter**, which contained in Article 1 as one of its primary purposes the promotion of human rights and fundamental freedoms to all. The United Nations **Economic and Social Council (ECOSOC)** established a Commission on Women in 1946, which began to make recommendations in regard to the advancement of women's rights. The first and most important effort to identify human rights took the form of the **Universal Declaration of Human Rights** of 1948. The declaration (see appendix A) in its preamble and in Article 2 acknowledges the equal rights of men and women. Moreover, in Article 16, the declaration acknowledges the family as the natural and fundamental group in society deserving of protection by the state, and in Article 22 identifies motherhood and childhood as being entitled to special care and assistance. Women's rights as parents are acknowledged in Article 26 in terms of parental rights to determine the kind of **education** to be given to their children. The entire panoply of rights listed in the declaration are extended to everyone regardless of gender. Similar recognition and extension of women's rights are found in the **International Covenant on Economic, Social, and Cultural Rights** (see appendix B) and the **International Covenant on Civil and Political Rights** (see appendix C), both of which were promulgated by the UN in 1966. The UN had taken action in 1953, in advance of the drafting of the Covenant on Civil and Political Rights to adopt the **Convention on the Political Rights of Women**.

Special action to prevent discrimination against women was asserted by the UN General Assembly in 1967 with the **Declaration on the Elimination of Discrimination against Women**, which was followed in 1979 by the adoption of the **Convention on the Elimination of All Forms of Discrimination against Women**, which in turn established the United Nations **Committee on the Elimination of Discrimination against Women (CEDAW)**. In the aftermath of the World Conference on Women held in Mexico City in 1975, the UN established the **International Research and Training Institute for the Advancement of Women (INSTRAW)**. The Mexico Conference was followed by women's conferences in five-year intervals at Copenhagen, Nairobi, Beijing, and subsequently in New York, at which women's rights issues continue to be reviewed.

Advancement of women's rights at the local and national as well as the international levels are increasingly the work not only of governmental bodies but also of nongovernmental organizations (NGOs). Women have been important participants in the establishment of both human rights and humanitarian agencies. For example, Eglantyne Jebb was the initial founder of **Save the Children** in 1919 while Alexandra Tolstoy, Leo Tolstoy's youngest daughter, established the Tolstoy Foundation in 1939. More recently, the work of **Mother Teresa** through the various orders she founded has reached millions of victims of starvation, AIDS, and other illnesses. Women's NGOs continue to be established with lively frequency to address a range of issues, including trafficking in women. The **Coalition against Trafficking of Women**, for instance, was founded in 1988, while even more recently **FAIR Fund** was established in 2002 to provide grassroots support to women in Eastern Europe subjected to various forms of trafficking. Most international NGOs have specialized programs for assistance to women in order to promote development and to address their needs as especially vulnerable populations such as **refugees** and displaced persons during **famine** emergencies and other disasters. Moreover, the range of humanitarian agencies with special programs for assistance to women includes the whole spectrum of UN emergency and development assistance agencies, including especially the **United Nations Children's Fund (UNICEF)**, the **United Nations High Commissioner for Refugees (UNHCR)**, and the **World Food Programme (WFP)**, among others. The various components of the Red Cross system are similarly engaged in promoting both the human rights and humanitarian needs of women. One would be hard-pressed today to find an international agency or intergovernmental organization that is not in some fashion, measure, or degree involved in the improvement of women's lives. *See also* CHILDREN'S RIGHTS; WIDOWS' RIGHTS INTERNATIONAL (WRI).

WORK. The right to work is upheld in a variety of human rights instruments. Article 23 of the **Universal Declaration of Human Rights** asserts the right to work, to free choice of employment, to just and favorable conditions of work, to **equal** pay for equal work, to adequate remuneration, to protection against unemployment, and to join unions. The **International Covenant on Economic, Social, and Cultural Rights** reaffirms these rights and adds to them the rights to rest, leisure, and reasonable working hours. The **International Labour Organization (ILO)** is the principal body within the system of UN specialized agencies that addresses most explicitly the content of the right to work, which it has done through a variety of its conventions. *See also* FORCED LABOR.

WORLD ALLIANCE OF REFORMED CHURCHES (WARC). Embracing a population of 75 million Reformed Christians in 208 churches in 107 countries, WARC promotes fellowship among Congregational, Presbyterian, Reformed, and United Churches in the Calvinist tradition, as well as ecumenical dialogue with other religious traditions. WARC is headquartered in Geneva, where its secretariat maintains a Department of Partnership of **Women** and Men, which promotes gender **equality**. Its Department of Cooperation and Witness promotes a range of human rights concerns, including **political rights**, **economic rights**, and the fostering of democracy and civil society. It promotes an end to hunger and the right of all persons to an adequate standard of living. To these ends, it examines the impact of globalization on the welfare of peoples in developing countries and on the prospects for attaining sustainable development consistent with environmental well-being. WARC seeks to promote peace and justice as a means for stable promotion of human rights. It works to end **racial discrimination**, as it did in opposing **apartheid** in South Africa. It also promotes the spread of democracy in the countries of Southern Africa. Address: 150, route de Ferney, 1211 Geneva 2, Switzerland. Website: www.warc.ch.

WORLD BANK. The World Bank includes four organizational elements, namely the International Bank for Reconstruction and Development (IBRD), the International Development Association (IDA), the International Finance Corporation (IFC), and the Multilateral Investment Guarantee Agency (MIGA). Officially known as the IBRD at its creation in 1944 as a result of the Bretton Woods Conference, the World Bank was initially conceived of as a mechanism for provision of long-term reconstruction assistance to the war-ravaged countries of Europe. Within a matter of decades, the European countries had recovered and the bank shifted its focus to long-term development lending in the developing world.

Decisions by the World Bank, coupled with those of the International Monetary Fund (IMF), have a significant impact on developing country economies. Efforts by these bodies to emphasize restructuring and privatization of national economic policies during the 1980s and 1990s and the ending of counterproductive subsidies and inefficient governmental programs has led to a decline in social programs for the poorest in poor countries, raising criticism concerning the adverse effects of structural adjustment policies on the well-being of the very poorest, as the **Khartoum Declaration** illustrates. Although World Bank programs have been widely criticized, most governments of developing countries continue to rely on them for development-related resources. Between the IBRD, which aims assistance at middle-income and creditworthy poor countries, and the IDA, which addresses the needs of the poorest countries, some 184 member-states participate in the loan programs as donors or recipients. The World Bank issues grants and loans of about $18–20 billion annually, making it the largest multilateral assistance organization in the world. Address: 1818 H Street NW, Washington, DC 20433, USA. Website: www.worldbank.org. *See also* POVERTY.

WORLD CONFEDERATION OF LABOR (WCL). A well-established international nongovernmental organization (NGO), WCL was founded at The Hague in 1920. Initially known as the International Federation of Christian Trade Unions, it changed its name to its current title in 1968. Like other labor-related organizations, WCL is concerned with the promotion of the right to **work** and of workers' rights, but also with the equitable distribution of income and the dignity of the human person. It enjoys consultative status with the United Nations **Economic**

and Social Council (ECOSOC) as well as with other **United Nations (UN)** specialized agencies, such as the **International Labor Organization (ILO)**. It serves as a coordinating body for 144 trade unions from 116 countries, with a membership of more than 26 million. Address: rue de Treves 33, B-1040 Brussels, Belgium. Website: www.cmt-wcl.org. *See also* INTERNATIONAL CONFEDERATION OF FREE TRADE UNIONS (ICFTU); WORLD FEDERATION OF TRADE UNIONS (WFTU).

WORLD CONFERENCE ON HUMAN RIGHTS. Held from 14–25 June 1993 in Vienna, this conference was initially proposed by the **United Nations General Assembly** on 18 December 1990. A total of 171 governments and over 800 nongovernmental organizations (NGOs) participated in this global conference on human rights. Prior to the conference, as part of the preparatory process, governments were encouraged to convene regional meetings on human rights issues of special concern to them. The African states met at Tunis in November 1992. Latin American and Caribbean states met at San José, Costa Rica, in January 1993, and Asian governments met in Bangkok in later March and early April of 1993. Each of these regional conferences produced a declaration on the subject of human rights. The World Conference itself was the first of its sort held since the Conference of Teheran of 1968.

The conference called upon **United Nations (UN)** bodies to treat human rights as a priority in their actions worldwide. It adopted language on a right to development in keeping with the **Declaration on the Right to Development** of 1986. It called upon the UN General Assembly to establish a **United Nations High Commissioner for Human Rights (UNHCHR)** and it called for the creation of the **International Criminal Court (ICC)** to deal with gross violations of international humanitarian law in the former Yugoslavia. The declaration of the conference, after considerable debate and controversy, reaffirmed the universal and indivisible nature of human rights and called upon governments to promote and protect human rights as their "first responsibility." The program of action of the conference called for improved coordination of UN human rights bodies, the development of human rights education programs, the establishment of effective measures to protect **children's rights**, particularly to be free from abuse and exploitation, and further promotion of elimination of discrimination and violence against **women**. China offered a dissenting voice concerning the principle of the universality of human rights, arguing from a position of cultural relativism, at a time when multicultural sentiments were growing even in the Western world, launching a debate that has continued in subsequent years.

WORLD COUNCIL OF CHURCHES (WCC). The WCC serves as the principal human rights, development, and relief assistance coordinating body of more than 340 Protestant churches in more than 100 countries throughout the world. Headquartered in Geneva, it serves as a human rights advocacy group; provides refugee resettlement and integration services; engages in community development, training, and educational activities; and provides a liaison mechanism for its constituent church organizations for contact with the international human rights advocacy groups and with the humanitarian and development assistance agency network located in Geneva. About a quarter of WCC's budget is spent on assistance activities. In addition to its assistance programs, WCC also functions as an advocacy organization for peace and justice and for the promotion of human rights, all of which it attempts to advance through its consultative status at the **United Nations (UN)**. An example of its human rights initiatives is the Ecumenical Accompaniment Programme in Palestine and Israel, launched in 2002 to monitor and report on violations of human rights and humanitarian law in occupied areas of Palestine. WCC has also launched a Decade to Overcome Violence (2001–2010), in an effort to promote local and international reconciliation and peace with justice. It also has a long track record in opposition to **racial discrimination**, as evidenced in its past work against **apartheid** in South Africa, and in its ongoing efforts against discrimination toward **minorities** and in its promotion of **indigenous rights**. About 13 percent of its budget is spent on advocacy activities. Address: P.O. Box 2100, 150 route de Ferney, CH-1211 Geneva 2, Switzerland. Website: www.wcc-coe.org.

WORLD COUNCIL OF INDIGENOUS PEOPLES (WCIP). Founded and headquartered in Canada, WCIP was established in 1975 in conjunction with the International Conference on Indian Peoples. It seeks to protect the human rights, cultural integrity, and survival of indigenous peoples. It sponsors international deliberations and research activities concerning, among others, **health** issues and the extension of self-government to indigenous people. It has consultative status with the United Nations **Economic and Social Council (ECOSOC)** and the **United Nations Educational, Scientific, and Cultural Organization (UNESCO)**. Address: 100 Argyle Ave., Ottawa, Canada K2P 1B6. Website: www.cwis.org/wcip. *See also* CULTURAL SURVIVAL; INDIGENOUS RIGHTS; MINORITIES; SURVIVAL INTERNATIONAL.

WORLD FEDERATION OF TRADE UNIONS (WFTU). WFTU was established in Paris in October 1945 to serve as the coordinating body for national trade union organizations. It seeks to promote universal human rights, with special reference to the rights and freedoms of workers. These basic rights include the right to organize, to be free of all forms of discrimination, the right to **work**, at adequate rates of pay and with **social security** protections. It supported the right to **self-determination** of peoples in its early years, and for better opportunities for workers in both developed and developing countries. It enjoys consultative status with the United Nations **Economic and Social Council (ECOSOC)** and the **International Labor Organization (ILO)**, as well as with other specialized **United Nations (UN)** agencies. Address: Branicka 112, CZ-14701, Prague 4, Czech Republic. Website: www.wftu.cz. *See also* INTERNATIONAL CONFEDERATION OF FREE TRADE UNIONS (ICFTU); WORLD CONFEDERATION OF LABOR (WCL).

WORLD FOOD PROGRAMME (WFP). Established in 1961 by combined **United Nations General Assembly** and **Food and Agriculture Organization (FAO)** resolutions, the WFP became operational in 1963, under the direction of the Committee on Food Aid policies and programs (CFA), which is composed of representatives of 30 member-states of the WFP. The WFP was created as a distinct entity in cooperation with the FAO in order to coordinate emergency **food** aid in disaster situations. In 1966, after a three-year trial period, the WFP became a permanent fixture in the **United Nations (UN)** efforts to provide humanitarian food aid. The vast majority of its assistance is provided in emergency contexts, but the WFP has undertaken hundreds of longer-term development-oriented projects designed to alleviate hunger as well. The WFP maintains a substantial food transportation capability, and provides technical assistance to improve food production, storage, and distribution capabilities.

As a member of the Interagency Steering Committee of the **United Nations Office for Coordination of Humanitarian Affairs (UN-OCHA)**, the WFP works very closely with the **International Committee of the Red Cross (ICRC)**, and the **United Nations High Commissioner for Refugees (UNHCR)**, as well as with other UN specialized agencies in providing food aid to **refugees** and displaced persons. Its food-for-work programs are designed not only to alleviate hunger but also to provide job opportunities in creating needed infrastructure in emergency-affected areas. The WFP works with more than 1,100 nongovernmental organizations (NGOs) in providing food assistance, including major NGOs such as Catholic Relief Services, **Save the Children (SCA)**, **World Vision**, **CARE**, **Caritas Internationalis (CI)**, and the **Lutheran World Federation (LWF)**. WFP also has ties to private foundations and corporate partners. The largest percentage of its resources, however, are provided by donor governments such as the United States, which has supplied $1 billion in 2004, followed by the European Commission at $200 million and Japan at $136 million. Italy assists WFP with the funding of the UN's comprehensive humanitarian rapid-response base in Brindisi, Italy. About 60 countries contribute on a strictly voluntary basis to WFP operations, which total nearly $3 billion annually. A high percentage of WFP expenditures take the form of purchasing food and other services in the developing world itself.

The WFP as a major player in response to the Ethiopian **famine** of 1983, where it supplied 400 trucks to deliver its food, and where it also invested in upgrading ports and road improvement. In 1989, WFP was the central food aid agency in Operation Lifeline Sudan, which initiated to provide food to millions in the midst of civil war. WFP assistance in Southern Africa during the early 1990s helped avert famine there and, in 1995, began work in North Korea to avert a worsening of famine. Its food assistance and famine abatement strategies have persisted in the Horn of Africa throughout the past decade. In 2004, WFP food aid reached more than 110 million people in 80 countries.

A major focus of its assistance in 2005 was delivery of food to 1.75 million tsunami survivors in the Indian Ocean Region, many of which were reached by air and sea as well as by overland operations. Address: via C.G. Viola 68, Parco dei Medici, 00148 Rome, Italy. Website: www.wfp.org.

WORLD HEALTH ORGANIZATION (WHO). The preamble of the WHO Constitution affirms that "the enjoyment of the highest attainable standard of **health** is one of the fundamental rights of every human being without distinction of race, religion, political belief, economic or social condition." In this sense, the WHO works to provide one of the rudimentary human needs. By fostering cooperative efforts among nations to study, control, and eradicate disease and the spread of disease, it has spared millions of people from the scourge of deadly and debilitating illness. The WHO was officially established in 1948 as an autonomous specialized agency in cooperation with the **United Nations (UN)**.

Its World Health Assembly, consisting of its 192 member states, meets annually and its routine administration is undertaken by a secretariat headed by the director-general headquartered in Geneva. Much of the actual work of the organization, however, is undertaken by six regional offices in various parts of the world. The WHO provides technical assistance on health matters not only to governments but also to other international agencies. It has special assistance accounts to fund programs to alleviate heath menaces in the context of disasters and catastrophes. The WHO takes a broad view of human health, which consists not just in the absence of disease or infirmity but also a "state of complete physical, mental and social well-being." Defined in this way, the WHO's work is allied with the general thrust of human rights, which is the promotion of the well-being and dignity of the human person. The WHO works closely with the **United Nations Children's Fund (UNICEF)** and with the **United Nations High Commissioner for Refugees (UNHCR)** in providing health assistance to the needy and **refugees**. It also works closely with nongovernmental organizations (NGOs) at the national level, who also sometimes serve as implementers of WHO programs as well as collaborators in the advancement of good health initiatives. Address: Avenue Appia 20, 1211 Geneva 27, Switzerland. Website: www.who.int.

WORLD ORGANIZATION AGAINST TORTURE (OMCT). Founded in 1986 as the Organisation Mondiale Contre la Torture, this coalition of nongovernmental organizations (NGOs) originally consisted of 48 human rights agencies dedicated to the prevention of **torture** and to provision of assistance to victims of torture. The OMCT is comprised of many organizations operating at the grassroots level. The secretariat of the organization is located in Geneva, Switzerland, and OMCT Europe maintains an office in Brussels to work with **European Union (EU)** bodies. OMCT lobbies the **United Nations (UN)**, seeking to provide information to the **Committee against Torture** and other UN human rights bodies in order to advance the eradication of torture. Secretariat address: OMCT International Secretariat, P.O. Box 21, 8, rue du vieux-Billard, CH-1211 Geneva 8, Switzerland. OMCT-Europe address: Rue du Marteau 19, B-1000 Brussels, Belgium. Website: www.omct.org.

WORLD VISION. Established in 1950 to address the needs of Korean War orphans, World Vision is a Christian nongovernmental organization (NGO) dedicated to provision of both long-term development aid, the human rights of children, and humanitarian assistance. Its assistance and child sponsorship programs reach nearly 20 million people throughout the world. This large agency has annual budgets exceeding $1.5 billion, mostly derived from privately generated sources, although substantial amounts also come from government grants and in-kind contributions. World Vision is heavily involved in emergency assistance activities, development **education**, natural resource management, international **health**, **food**, security, and conservation programs. It is one of the largest international nongovernmental organizations, reaching 100 million people in 96 countries. Like many other large NGOs such as **CARE**, World Vision has grown from its American national origins to become an international partnership of agencies with offices in Geneva, Bangkok, Nairobi, Cyprus, Los Angeles, and San José, Costa Rica. National boards make most operational decisions, while the international board of directors oversees the World Vision International Partnership.

World Vision's human rights activities target primarily the well-being of children with programs throughout the world aimed at children's education, health care, vocational training, counseling, and

family reunification. It conducts workshops on the rights of children and promotes programs intended to reduce domestic violence and child abuse. Ultimately, its emphasis on **poverty** reduction is aimed at promoting a world where children can live in economic security and health. Its publications and reports include a number of titles dealing with **children's rights**, the special situation of girls, and on the problems for children living in conflict zones. World Vision's publication list includes reports on the impact of World Bank programs on people in poverty-stricken areas, and on a range of peace and justice issues. It is also a member of the **Coalition to Stop the Use of Child Soldiers**.

In the humanitarian assistance arena, World Vision programs currently focus on tsunami relief in the Indian Ocean and on the African food crisis. In tsunami-ravaged areas, World Vision's work is comprehensive, helping fisherman to buy new boats and nets, supplying temporary **housing**, repairing roads, schools, hospitals, water supply systems and other infrastructure programs, and providing seed money to initiate small businesses, It also supports child protection programs there. World Vision's food programs have centered on the Darfur region of Sudan, in southern Africa, and in the Sahel region in such countries as Mauritania and Niger. It has also distributed millions of dollars worth of food aid in Afghanistan, where it also runs health and nutrition education and maternal and child health care programs. Address: 919 West Huntington Drive, Monrovia, CA 91016, USA. For further information, see Interaction (www.interaction.org) member profiles. Website: www.worldvision.org. *See also* INTERACTION.

– X –

XENOPHOBIA. Xenophobia is the exaggerated fear of strangers. It is not the direct subject of any human rights instruments, but international efforts on behalf of the protection and assistance of **refugees** and **aliens' rights** do have a bearing on this phenomenon, as does the **International Convention on the Protection of the Rights of All Migrant Workers and Members of Their Families** and the **International Convention on the Elimination of All Forms of Racial**

Discrimination. United Nations (UN) committees also deal with the question through committees established by the just mentioned treaties, including the **Committee on Migrant Workers (CMW)** and the **Committee on the Elimination of Racial Discrimination (CERD).** In addition, the **United Nations High Commissioner for Refugees (UNHCR)** is directly charged with fostering a climate of receptivity toward and protection of individuals who are forced to seek haven outside their countries of origin owing to a well-founded fear of persecution. Working with host governments, other international agencies, and nongovernmental organizations (NGOs), the UNHCR seeks to encourage varieties of assistance to refugee populations, which will benefit local populations and avoid the growth of resentment toward displaced populations. Xenophobia is often accompanied by restrictive immigration and **asylum** policies of governments, which can be highly detrimental to the human rights of refugees, asylum seekers, and immigrant populations.

Appendix A: Universal Declaration of Human Rights

PREAMBLE

Whereas recognition of the inherent dignity and of the equal and inalienable rights of all members of the human family is the foundation of freedom, justice and peace in the world,

Whereas disregard and contempt for human rights have resulted in barbarous acts which have outraged the conscience of mankind, and the advent of a world in which human beings shall enjoy freedom of speech and belief and freedom from fear and want has been proclaimed as the highest aspiration of the common people,

Whereas it is essential, if man is not to be compelled to have recourse, as a last resort, to rebellion against tyranny and oppression, that human rights should be protected by the rule of law,

Whereas it is essential to promote the development of friendly relations between nations,

Whereas the peoples of the United Nations have in the Charter reaffirmed their faith in fundamental human rights, in the dignity and worth of the human person and in the equal rights of men and women and have determined to promote social progress and better standards of life in larger freedom,

Whereas Member States have pledged themselves to achieve, in cooperation with the United Nations, the promotion of universal respect for and observance of human rights and fundamental freedoms,

Whereas a common understanding of these rights and freedoms is of the greatest importance for the full realization of this pledge.

Now, Therefore,
THE GENERAL ASSEMBLY
proclaims
This universal declaration of human rights as a common standard of achievement for all peoples and all nations, to the end that every individual and every organ of society, in keeping this Declaration constantly in mind, shall strive by teaching and education to promote respect for these rights and freedoms and by progressive measures, national and international, to secure their universal and effective recognition and observance, both among the peoples of Member States themselves and among the peoples of territories under their jurisdiction.

Article 1

All human beings are born free and equal in dignity and rights. They are endowed with reason and conscience and should act towards one another in a spirit of brotherhood.

Article 2

Everyone is entitled to all the rights and freedoms set forth in this Declaration, without distinction of any kind, such as race, color, sex, language, religion, political or other opinion, national or social origin, property, birth or other status.

Furthermore, no distinction shall be made on the basis of the political, jurisdictional or international status of the country or territory to which a person belongs, whether it be independent, trust, non-self-governing or under any other limitation of sovereignty.

Article 3

Everyone has the right to life, liberty and security of person.

Article 4

No one shall be held in slavery or servitude; slavery and the slave trade shall be prohibited in all their forms.

Article 5

No one shall be subjected to torture or to cruel, inhuman or degrading treatment or punishment.

Article 6

Everyone has the right to recognition everywhere as a person before the law.

Article 7

All are equal before the law and are entitled without any discrimination to equal protection of the law. All are entitled to equal protection against any discrimination in violation of this Declaration and against any incitement to such discrimination.

Article 8

Everyone has the right to an effective remedy by the competent national tribunals for acts violating the fundamental rights granted him by the constitution or by law.

Article 9

No one shall be subjected to arbitrary arrest, detention or exile.

Article 10

Everyone is entitled in full equality to a fair and public hearing by an independent and impartial tribunal, in the determination of his rights and obligations and of any criminal charge against him.

Article 11

1. Everyone charged with a penal offense has the right to be presumed innocent until proved guilty according to law in a public trial at which he has had all the guarantees necessary for his defense.

2. No one shall be held guilty of any penal offense on account of any act or omission which did not constitute a penal offense, under national or international law, at the time when it was committed. Nor shall a heavier penalty be imposed than the one that was applicable at the time the penal offense was committed.

Article 12

No one shall be subjected to arbitrary interference with his privacy, family, home or correspondence, nor to attacks upon his honor or reputation. Everyone has the right to the protection of the law against such interference or attacks.

Article 13

1. Everyone has the right to freedom of movement and residence within the borders of each state.
2. Everyone has the right to leave any country, including his own, and to return to his country.

Article 14

1. Everyone has the right to seek and to enjoy in other countries asylum from persecution.
2. This right may not be invoked in the case of prosecutions genuinely arising from non-political crimes or from acts contrary to the purposes and principles of the United Nations.

Article 15

1. Everyone has the right to a nationality.
2. No one shall be arbitrarily deprived of his nationality nor denied the right to change his nationality.

Article 16

1. Men and women of full age, without any limitation due to race, nationality or religion, have the right to marry and to found a fam-

ily. They are entitled to equal rights as to marriage, during marriage and at its dissolution.

2. Marriage shall be entered into only with the free and full consent of the intending spouses.
3. The family is the natural and fundamental group unit of society and is entitled to protection by society and the State.

Article 17

1. Everyone has the right to own property alone as well as in association with others.
2. No one shall be arbitrarily deprived of his property.

Article 18

Everyone has the right to freedom of thought, conscience and religion; this right includes freedom to change his religion or belief, and freedom, either alone or in community with others and in public or private, to manifest his religion or belief in teaching, practice, worship and observance.

Article 19

Everyone has the right to freedom of opinion and expression; the right includes freedom to hold opinions without interference and to see, receive and impart information and ideas through any media and regardless of frontiers.

Article 20

1. Everyone has the right to freedom of peaceful assembly and association.
2. No one may be compelled to belong to an association.

Article 21

1. Everyone has the right to take part in the government of his country, directly or through freely chosen representatives.

2. Everyone has the right of equal access to public service in his country.
3. The will of the people shall be the basis of the authority of government; this will shall be expressed in periodic and genuine elections which shall be by universal and equal suffrage and shall be held by secret vote or by equivalent free voting procedures.

Article 22

Everyone, as a member of society, has the right to social security and is entitled to realization, through national effort and international cooperation and in accordance with the organization and resources of each State, of the economic, social and cultural rights indispensable for his dignity and the free development of his personality.

Article 23

1. Everyone has the right to work, to free choice of employment, to just and favorable conditions of work and to protection against unemployment.
2. Everyone, without any discrimination, has the right to equal pay for equal work.
3. Everyone who works has the right to just and favorable remuneration ensuring for himself and his family an existence worthy of human dignity, and supplemented, if necessary, by other means of social protection.
4. Everyone has the right to form and to join trade unions for the protection of his interests.

Article 24

Everyone has the right to rest and leisure, including reasonable limitation of working hours and periodic holidays with pay.

Article 25

1. Everyone has the right to a standard of living adequate for the health and well-being of himself and of his family, including food,

clothing, housing and medical care and necessary social services, and the right to security in the event of unemployment, sickness, disability, widow-hood, old age or other lack of livelihood in circumstances beyond his control.

2. Motherhood and childhood are entitled to special care and assistance. All children, whether born in or out of wedlock, shall enjoy the same social protection.

Article 26

1. Everyone has the right to education. Education shall be free, at least in the elementary and fundamental stages. Elementary education shall be compulsory. Technical and professional education shall be made generally available and higher education shall be equally accessible to all on the basis of merit.

2. Education shall be directed to the full development of the human personality and to the strengthening of respect for human rights and fundamental freedoms. It shall promote understanding, tolerance and friendship among all nations, racial or religious groups, and shall further the activities of the United Nations for the maintenance of peace.

3. Parents have a prior right to choose the kind of education that shall be given to their children.

Article 27

1. Everyone has the right freely to participate in the cultural life of the community, to enjoy the arts and to share in scientific advancement and its benefits.

2. Everyone has the right to the protection of the moral and material interests resulting from any scientific, literary or artistic production of which he is the author.

Article 28

Everyone is entitled to a social and international order in which the rights and freedoms set forth in this Declaration can be fully realized.

Article 29

1. Everyone has duties to the community in which alone the free and full development of his personality is possible.
2. In the exercise of his rights and freedoms, everyone shall be subject only to such limitations as are determined by law solely for the purpose of securing due recognition and respect for the rights and freedoms of others and of meeting the just requirements of morality, public order and the general welfare in a democratic society.
3. These rights and freedoms may in no case be exercised contrary to the purposes and principles of the United Nations.

Article 30

Nothing in this Declaration may be interpreted as implying for any State, group or person any right to engage in any activity or to perform any act aimed at the destruction of any of the rights and freedoms set forth herein.

Appendix B: International Covenant on Economic, Social, and Cultural Rights

PREAMBLE

The States Parties to the present Covenant,
Considering that, in accordance with the principles proclaimed in the Charter of the United Nations, recognition of the inherent dignity and of the equal and inalienable rights of all members of the human family is the foundation of freedom, justice and peace in the world,

Recognizing that these rights derive from the inherent dignity of the human person,

Recognizing that, in accordance with the Universal Declaration of Human Rights, the ideal of free human beings enjoying freedom from fear and want can only be achieved if conditions are created whereby everyone may enjoy his economic, social and cultural rights, as well as his civil and political rights,

Considering the obligation of States under the Charter of the United Nations to promote universal respect for, and observance of, human rights and freedoms,

Realizing that the individual, having duties to other individuals and to the community to which he belongs, is under a responsibility to strive for the promotion and observance of the rights recognized in the present Covenant,

Agree upon the following articles:

PART 1

Article 1

1. All peoples have the right of self-determination. By virtue of that right they freely determine their political status and freely pursue their economic, social and cultural development.
2. All peoples may, for their own ends, freely dispose of their natural wealth and resources without prejudice to any obligations arising out of international economic co-operation, based upon the principle of mutual benefit, and international law. In no case may a people be deprived of its own means of subsistence.
3. The States Parties to the present Covenant, including having responsibility for the administration of Non-Self-Governing and Trust Territories, shall promote the realization of the right of self-determination, and shall respect that right, in conformity with the provisions of the Charter of the United Nations.

PART II

Article 2

1. Each State Party to the present Covenant undertakes to take steps, individually and through international assistance and co-operation, especially economic and technical, to the maximum of its available resources, with a view to achieving progressively the full realization of the rights recognized in the present Covenant by all appropriate means, including particularly the adoption of legislative measures.
2. The States Parties to the present Covenant undertake to guarantee that the rights enunciated in the present Covenant will be exercised without discrimination of any kind as to race, colour, sex, language, religion, political or other opinion, national or social origin, property, birth or other status.
3. Developing countries, with due regard to human rights and their national economy, may determine to what extent they would guar-

antee the economic rights recognized in the present Covenant to non-nationals.

Article 3

The States Parties to the present Covenant undertake to ensure the equal right of men and women to the enjoyment of all economic, social and cultural rights set forth in the present Covenant.

Article 4

The States Parties to the present Covenant recognize that, in the enjoyment of those rights provided by the State in conformity with the present Covenant, the State may subject such rights only to such limitations as are determined by law only in so far as this may be compatible with the nature of these rights and solely for the purpose of promoting the general welfare in a democratic society.

Article 5

1. Nothing in the present Covenant may be interpreted as implying for any State, group or person any right to engage in any activity or to perform any act aimed at the destruction of any of the rights or freedoms recognized herein, or at their limitation to a greater extent than is provided for in the present Covenant.
2. No restriction upon or derogation from any of the fundamental human rights recognized or existing in any country in virtue of law, conventions, regulations or custom shall be admitted on the pretext that the present Covenant does not recognize such rights or that it recognizes them to a lesser extent.

PART III

Article 6

1. The States Parties to the present Covenant recognize the right to work, which includes the right of everyone to the opportunity to gain his living by work which he freely chooses or accepts, and will take appropriate steps to safeguard this right.

2. The steps to be taken by a State Party to the present Covenant to achieve the full realization of this right shall include technical and vocational guidance and training programmes, policies and techniques to achieve steady economic, social and cultural development and full and productive employment under conditions safeguarding fundamental political and economic freedoms to the individual.

Article 7

The States Parties to the present Covenant recognize the right of everyone to the enjoyment of just and favourable conditions of work, which ensure, in particular:

a. Remuneration which provides all workers, as a minimum with:
   i. Fair wages and equal remuneration for work of equal value without distinction of any kind, in particular women being guaranteed conditions of work not inferior to those enjoyed by men, with equal pay for equal work;
   ii. A decent living for themselves and their families in accordance with the provisions of the present Covenant;
b. Safe and healthy working conditions;
c. Equal opportunity for everyone to be promoted in his employment to an appropriate higher level, subject to no considerations other than those of seniority and competence;
d. Rest, leisure and reasonable limitation of working hours and periodic holidays with pay, as well as remuneration for public holidays.

Article 8

1. The States Parties to the present Covenant undertake to ensure:
   a. The right of everyone to form trade unions and join the trade union of his choice, subject only to the rules of the organization concerned, for the promotion and protection of his economic and social interests. No restrictions may be placed on the exercise of this right other than those prescribed by law and which are necessary in a democratic society in the interests of national security or public order or for the protection of the rights and freedoms of others;

b. The right of trade unions to establish national federations or confederations and the right of the latter to form or join international trade-union organizations;

c. The right of trade unions to function freely subject to no limitations other than those prescribed by law and which are necessary in a democratic society in the interests of national security or public order or for the protection of the rights and freedoms of others;

d. The right to strike, provided that it is exercised in conformity with the laws of the particular country.

2. This article shall not prevent the imposition of lawful restrictions on the exercise of these rights by members of the armed forces or of the police or of the administration of the State.

3. Nothing in this article shall authorize States Parties to the International Labour Organization Convention of 1948 concerning Freedom of Association and Protection of the Right to Organize to take legislative measures which would prejudice, or apply the law in such a manner as would prejudice, the guarantees provided for in that Convention.

Article 9

The States Parties to the present Covenant recognize the right of everyone to social security, including social insurance.

Article 10

The States Parties to the present Covenant recognize that:

1. The widest possible protection and assistance should be accorded to the family, which is the natural and fundamental group unit of society, particularly for its establishment and while it is responsible for the care and education of dependent children. Marriage must be entered into with the free consent of the intending spouses.

2. Special protection should be accorded to mothers during a reasonable period before and after childbirth. During such period working mothers should be accorded paid leave or leave with adequate social security benefits.

3. Special measures of protection and assistance should be taken on behalf of all children and young persons without any discrimination for reasons of parentage or other conditions. Children and young persons should be protected from economic and social exploitation. Their employment in work harmful to their morals or health or dangerous to life or likely to hamper their normal development should be punishable by law. States should also set age limits below which the paid employment of child labour should be prohibited and punishable by law.

Article 11

1. The States Parties to the present Covenant recognize the right of everyone to an adequate standard of living for himself and his family, including adequate food, clothing and housing, and to the continuous improvement of living conditions. The States Parties will take appropriate steps to ensure the realization of this right, recognizing to this effect the essential importance of international co-operation based on free consent.

2. The States Parties to the present Covenant, recognizing the fundamental right of everyone to be free from hunger, shall take, individually and through international co-operation the measures including specific programmes, which are needed:
   a. To improve methods of production, conservation and distribution of food by making full use of technical and scientific knowledge by disseminating knowledge of the principles of nutrition and by developing or reforming agrarian systems in such a way as to achieve the most efficient development and utilization of natural resources;
   b. Taking into account the problems of both food-importing and food-exporting countries, to ensure an equitable distribution of world food supplies in relation to need.

Article 12

1. The States Parties to the present Covenant recognize the right of everyone to the enjoyment of the highest attainable standard of physical and mental health.

2. The steps to be taken by the States Parties to the present Covenant to achieve the full realization of this right shall include those necessary for:
   a. The provision for the reduction of the stillbirth-rate and of infant mortality and for the healthy development of the child;
   b. The improvement of all aspects of environmental and industrial hygiene;
   c. The prevention, treatment and control of epidemic, endemic, occupational and other diseases;
   d. The creation of conditions which would assure to all medical service and medical attention in the event of sickness.

Article 13

1. The States Parties to the present Covenant recognize the right of everyone to education. They agree that education shall be directed to the full development of the human personality and the sense of its dignity, and shall strengthen the respect for human rights and fundamental freedoms. They further agree that education shall enable all persons to participate effectively in a free society, promote understanding, tolerance and friendship among all nations and all racial, ethnic or religious groups, and further the activities of the United Nations for the maintenance of peace.
2. The States Parties to the present Covenant recognize that, with a view to achieving the full realization of this right:
   a. Primary education shall be compulsory and available free to all;
   b. Secondary education in its different forms, including technical and vocational secondary education, shall be made generally available and accessible to all by every appropriate means, and in particular by the progressive introduction of free education;
   c. Higher education shall be made equally accessible to all, on the basis of capacity, by every appropriate means, and in particular by the progressive introduction of free education;
   d. Fundamental education shall be encouraged or intensified as far as possible for those persons who have not received or completed the whole period of their primary education;
   e. The development of a system of schools at all levels shall be actively pursued, an adequate fellowship system shall be

established, and the material conditions of teaching staff shall be continuously improved.

3. The States Parties to the present Covenant undertake to have respect for the liberty of parents and, when applicable, legal guardians, to choose for their children schools, other than those established by the public authorities, which conform to such minimum educational standards as may be laid down or approved by the State and to ensure the religious and moral education of their children in conformity with their own convictions.

4. No part of this article shall be construed so as to interfere with the liberty of individuals and bodies to establish and direct educational institutions, subject always to the observance of the principles set forth in paragraph 1 of this article and to the requirement that the education given in such institutions shall conform to such minimum standards as may be laid down by the State.

Article 14

Each State Party to the present Covenant which, at the time of becoming a Party, has not been able to secure in its metropolitan territory or other territories under its jurisdiction compulsory primary education, free of charge, undertakes, within two years, to work out and adopt a detailed plan of action for the progressive implementation, within a reasonable number of years, to be fixed in the plan, of the principle of compulsory education free of charge for all.

Article 15

1. The States Parties to the present Covenant recognize the right of everyone:
   a. To take part in cultural life;
   b. To enjoy the benefits of scientific progress and its applications;
   c. To benefit from the protection of the moral and material interests resulting from any scientific, literary or artistic production of which he is the author.

2. The steps to be taken by the States Parties to the present Covenant to achieve the full realization of this right shall include those nec-

essary for the conservation, the development and the diffusion of science and culture.

3. The States Parties to the present Covenant undertake to respect the freedom indispensable for scientific research and creative activity.

4. The States Parties to the present Covenant recognize the benefits to be derived from the encouragement and development of international contacts and cooperation in the scientific and cultural fields.

PART IV

Article 16

1. The States Parties to the present Covenant undertake to submit in conformity with this part of the Covenant reports on the measures which they have adopted and the progress made in achieving the observance of the rights recognized herein.

2. a. All reports shall be submitted to the Secretary-General of the United Nations, who shall transmit copies to the Economic and Social Council for consideration in accordance with the provisions of the present Covenant.

   b. The Secretary-General of the United Nations shall also transmit to the specialized agencies copies of the reports, or any relevant parts therefrom, from States Parties to the present Covenant which are also members of these specialized agencies in so far as these reports, or parts therefrom, relate to any matters which fall within the responsibilities of the said agencies in accordance with their constitutional instruments.

Article 17

1. The States Parties to the present Covenant shall furnish their reports in stages, in accordance with a programme to be established by the Economic and Social Council within one year of the entry into force of the present Covenant after consultation with the States Parties and the specialized agencies concerned.

2. Reports may indicate factors and difficulties affecting the degree of fulfillment of obligations under the present Covenant.

3. Where relevant information has previously been furnished to the United Nations or to any specialized agency by any State Party to the present Covenant, it will not be necessary to reproduce that information, but a precise reference to the information so furnished will suffice.

Article 18

Pursuant to its responsibilities under the Charter of the United Nations in the field of human rights and fundamental freedoms, the Economic and Social Council may make arrangements with the specialized agencies in respect of their reporting to it on the progress made in achieving the observance of the provisions of the present Covenant falling within the scope of their activities. These reports may include particulars of decisions and recommendations on such implementation adopted by their competent organs.

Article 19

The Economic and Social Council may transmit to the Commission on Human Rights for study and general recommendation or as appropriate for information the reports concerning human rights submitted by States in accordance with Articles 16 and 17, and those concerning human rights submitted by the specialized agencies in accordance with Article 18.

Article 20

The States Parties to the present Covenant and the specialized agencies concerned may submit comments to the Economic and Social Council on any general recommendation under Article 19 or reference to such general recommendation in any report of the Commission on Human Rights or any documentation referred to therein.

Article 21

The Economic and Social Council may submit from time to time to the General Assembly reports with recommendations of a general nature and a summary of the information received from the States Parties to the present Covenant and the specialized agencies on the measures taken and the progress made in achieving general observance of the rights recognized in the present Covenant.

Article 22

The Economic and Social Council may bring to the attention of the other organs of the United Nations, their subsidiary organs and specialized agencies concerned with furnishing technical assistance any matters arising out of the reports referred to in this part of the present Covenant which may assist such bodies in deciding, each within its field of competence, on the advisability of international measures likely to contribute to the effective progress implementation of the present Covenant.

Article 23

The States Parties to the present Covenant agree that international action for the achievement of the rights recognized in the present Covenant includes such methods as the conclusion of conventions, the adoption of recommendations, the furnishing of technical assistance and the holding of regional meetings and technical meetings for the purpose of consultation and study organized in conjunction with the Governments concerned.

Article 24

Nothing in the present Covenant shall be interpreted as impairing the provisions of the Charter of the United Nations and of the constitutions of the specialized agencies which define the respective responsibilities of the various organs of the United Nations and of the specialized agencies in regard to the matters dealt with in the present Covenant.

Article 25

Nothing in the present Covenant shall be interpreted as impairing the inherent right of all peoples to enjoy and utilize fully and freely their natural wealth and resources.

PART V

Article 26

1. The present Covenant is open for signature by any State Member of the United Nations or member of any of its specialized agencies, by any State Party to the Statute of the International Court of Justice, and by any other State which has been invited by the General Assembly of the United Nations to become a party to the present Covenant.
2. The present Covenant is subject to ratification. Instruments of ratification shall be deposited with the Secretary-General of the United Nations.
3. The present Covenant shall be open to accession by any State referred to in paragraph 1 of this Article.
4. Accession shall be effected by the deposit of an instrument of accession with the Secretary-General of the United Nations.
5. The Secretary-General of the United Nations shall inform all States which have signed the present Covenant or acceded to it of the deposit of each instrument of ratification or accession.

Article 27

1. The present Covenant shall enter into force three months after the date of the deposit with the Secretary-General of the United Nations of the thirty-fifth instrument of ratification or instrument of accession.
2. For each State ratifying the present Covenant or acceding to it after the deposit of the thirty-fifth instrument of ratification or instrument of accession, the present Covenant shall enter into force three months after the date of the deposit of its own instrument of ratification or instrument of accession.

Article 28

The provisions of the present Covenant shall extend to all parts of federal States without any limitations or exceptions.

Article 29

1. Any State Party to the present Covenant may propose an amendment and file it with the Secretary-General of the United Nations. The Secretary-General shall thereupon communicate any proposed amendments to the States Parties to the present Covenant with a request that they notify him whether they favour a conference of States Parties for the purpose of considering and voting upon the proposals. In the event that at least one third of the States Parties favours such a conference, the Secretary-General shall convene the conference under the auspices of the United Nations. Any amendment adopted by a majority of the States Parties present and voting at the conference shall be submitted to the General Assembly of the United Nations for approval.

Article 30

Irrespective of the notifications made under Article 26, paragraph 5, the Secretary-General of the United Nations shall inform all States referred to in paragraph 1 of the same article of the following particulars:

a. Signatures, ratifications and accessions under Article 26;
b. The date of the entry into force of the present Covenant under Article 27 and the date of the entry into force of any amendments under Article 29.

Article 31

1. The present Covenant, of which the Chinese, English, French, Russian and Spanish texts are equally authentic, shall be deposited in the archives of the United Nations.
2. The Secretary-General of the United Nations shall transmit certified copies of the present Covenant to all States referred to in Article 26.

Appendix C: International Covenant on Civil and Political Rights

PREAMBLE

The States Parties to the present Covenant,
Considering that, in accordance with the principles proclaimed in the Charter of the United Nations, recognition of the inherent dignity and of the equal and inalienable rights of all members of the human family is the foundation of freedom, justice and peace in the world,

Recognizing that these rights derive from the inherent dignity of the human person,

Recognizing that, in accordance with the Universal Declaration of Human Rights, the ideal of free human beings enjoying civil and political freedom and freedom from fear and want can only be achieved if conditions are created whereby everyone may enjoy his civil and political rights, as well as his economic, social and cultural rights,

Considering the obligation of States under the Charter of the United Nations to promote universal respect for, and the observance of, human rights and freedoms,

Realizing that the individual, having duties to other individuals and to the community to which he belongs, is under a responsibility to strive for the promotion and observance of the rights recognized in the present Covenant.

Agree upon the following articles:

PART I

Article 1

1. All peoples have the right of self-determination. By virtue of that right they freely determine their political status and freely pursue their economic, social and cultural development.
2. All peoples may, for their own ends, freely dispose of their natural wealth and resources without prejudice to any obligations arising out of international economic co-operation, based upon the principle of mutual benefit, and international law. In no case may a people be deprived of its own means of subsistence.
3. The States Parties to the present Covenant, including those having responsibility for the administration of Non-Self-Governing and Trust Territories, shall respect that right, in conformity with the provisions of the Charter of the United Nations.

PART II

Article 2

1. Each State Party to the present Covenant undertakes to respect and to ensure to all individuals within its territory and subject to its jurisdiction the rights recognized in the present Covenant, without distinction of any kind, such as race, colour, sex, language, religion, political or other opinion, national or social origin, property, birth or other status.
2. Where not already provided for by existing legislative or other measures, each State Party to the present Covenant undertakes to take the necessary steps, in accordance with its constitutional processes and with the provisions of the present Covenant, to adopt such legislative or other measures as may be necessary to give effect to the rights recognized in the present Covenant.

3. Each State Party to the present Covenant undertakes:
   a. To ensure that any person whose rights or freedoms as herein recognized are violated shall have an effective remedy, notwithstanding that the violation has been committed by persons acting in an official capacity;
   b. To ensure that any person claiming such a remedy shall have his right thereto determined by competent judicial, administrative or legislative authorities, or by any other competent authority provided for by the legal system of the State, and to develop the possibilities of judicial remedy;
   c. To ensure that the competent authorities shall enforce such remedies when granted.

Article 3

The States Parties to the present Covenant undertake to ensure the equal right of men and women to the enjoyment of all civil and political rights set forth in the present Covenant.

Article 4

1. In time of public emergency with threatens the life of the nation and the existence of which is officially proclaimed, the States Parties to the present Covenant may take measures derogating from their obligations under the present Covenant to the extent strictly required by the exigencies of the situation, provided that such measures are not inconsistent with their other obligations under international law and do not involve discrimination solely on the ground of race, colour, sex, language, religion or social origin.
2. No derogation from Articles 6, 7, 8 (paragraphs 1 and 2) 11, 15, 16 and 18 may be made under this provision.
3. Any State Party to the present Covenant availing itself of the right of derogation shall immediately inform the other States Parties to the present Covenant, through the intermediary of the Secretary-General of the United Nations of the provisions from which it has derogated and of the reasons by which it was actuated. A further communication shall be made, through the same intermediary on the date on which it terminates such derogation.

Article 5

1. Nothing in the present Covenant may be interpreted as implying for any State, group or person any right to engage in any activity or perform any act aimed at the destruction of any of the rights and freedoms recognized herein or at their limitation to a greater extent than is provided for in the present Convention.

2. There shall be no restriction upon or derogation from any of the fundamental human rights recognized or existing in any State Party to the present Covenant pursuant to law, conventions, regulations or custom on the pretext that the present Covenant does not recognize such rights or that it recognizes them to a lesser extent.

PART III

Article 6

1. Every human being has the inherent right to life. This right shall be protected by law. No one shall be arbitrarily deprived of his life.

2. In countries which have not abolished the death penalty, sentence of death may be imposed only for the most serious crimes in accordance with the law in force at the time of the commission of the crime and not contrary to the provisions of the present Covenant and to the Convention on the Prevention and Punishment of the Crime of Genocide. This penalty can only be carried out pursuant to a final judgment rendered by a competent court.

3. When deprivation of life constitutes the crime of genocide, it is understood that nothing in this article shall authorize any State Party to the present Covenant to derogate in any way from any obligation assumed under the provisions of the Convention on Prevention and Punishment of the Crime of Genocide.

4. Anyone sentenced to death shall have the right to seek pardon or commutation of the sentence. Amnesty, pardon or commutation of the sentence of death may be granted in all cases.

5. Sentence of death shall not be imposed for crimes committed by persons below eighteen years of age and shall not be carried out on pregnant women.

6. Nothing in this article shall be invoked to delay or to prevent the abolition of capital punishment by any State Party to the present Covenant.

Article 7

No one shall be subjected to torture or to cruel, inhuman or degrading treatment or punishment. In particular, no one shall be subjected without his free consent to medical or scientific experimentation.

Article 8

1. No one shall be held in slavery; slavery and the slave-trade in all their forms shall be prohibited.
2. No one shall be held in servitude.
3. a. No one shall be required to perform forced or compulsory labour;
   b. Paragraph 3 (a) shall not be held to preclude, in countries where imprisonment with hard labour may be imposed as a punishment for a crime, the performance of hard labour in pursuance of a sentence to such punishment by a competent court;
   c. For the purpose of this paragraph the term 'forced or compulsory labour' shall not include:
      i. Any work or service, not referred to in sub-paragraph (b), normally required of a person who is under detention in consequence of a lawful order of a court, or of a person during conditional release from such detention;
      ii. Any service of a military character and, in countries where conscientious objection is recognized, any national service required by law of conscientious objectors;
      iii. Any service exacted in cases of emergency or calamity threatening the life and well-being of the community;
      iv. Any work or service which forms part of normal civil obligations.

Article 9

1. Everyone has the right to liberty and security of person. No one shall be subjected to arbitrary arrest or detention. No one shall be

deprived of his liberty except on such grounds and in accordance with such procedure as are established by law.

2. Anyone who is arrested shall be informed, at the time or arrest, of the reasons for his arrest and shall be promptly informed of any charges against him.

3. Anyone arrested or detained on a criminal charge shall be brought promptly before a judge or other officer authorized by law to exercise judicial power and shall be entitled to trial within a reasonable time or to release. It shall not be the general rule that persons awaiting trial shall be detained in custody, but release may be subject to guarantees to appear for trial, at any other stage of the judicial proceedings, and, should occasion arise, for execution of the judgment.

4. Anyone who is deprived of his liberty by arrest or detention shall be entitled to take proceedings before a court, in order that that court may decide without delay on the lawfulness of his detention and order his release if the detention is not lawful.

5. Anyone who has been the victim of unlawful arrest or detention shall have an enforceable right to compensation.

Article 10

1. All persons deprived of their liberty shall be treated with humanity and with respect for the inherent dignity of the human person.

2. a. Accused persons shall, save in exceptional circumstance, be segregated from convicted persons and shall be subject to separate treatment appropriate to their status as unconvicted persons;

   b. Accused juvenile persons shall be separated from adults and brought as speedily as possible for adjudication.

3. The penitentiary system shall comprise treatment of prisoners the essential aim of which shall be their reformation and social rehabilitation. Juvenile offenders shall be segregated from adults and be accorded treatment appropriate to their age and legal status.

Article 11

No one shall be imprisoned merely on the ground of inability to fulfill a contractual obligation.

Article 12

1. Everyone lawfully within the territory of a State shall, within that territory, have the right to liberty of movement and freedom to choose his residence.
2. Everyone shall be free to leave any country, including his own.
3. The above-mentioned rights shall not be subject to any restrictions except those which are provided by law, are necessary to protect national security, public order (*ordre public*), public health or morals or the rights and freedoms of others, and are consistent with the other rights recognized in the present Covenant.
4. No one shall be arbitrarily deprived of the right to enter his own country.

Article 13

An alien lawfully in the territory of a State Party to the present Covenant may be expelled therefrom only in pursuance of a decision reached in accordance with law and shall, except where compelling reasons of national security otherwise require, be allowed to submit the reasons against his expulsion and to have his case reviewed by, and be represented for the purpose before, the competent authority or person or persons especially designated by the competent authority.

Article 14

1. All persons shall be equal before the courts and tribunals. In the determination of any criminal charge against him, or of his rights and obligations in a suit at law, everyone shall be entitled to a fair and public hearing by a competent, independent and impartial tribunal established by law. The Press and the public may be excluded from all or part of a trial for reasons of morals, public order (*ordre public*) or national security in a democratic society, or when the interest of the private lives of the parties so requires, or to the extent strictly necessary in the opinion of the court in special circumstances where publicity would prejudice the interests of justice; but any judgement rendered in a criminal case or in a suit at law shall be made public except where the interest of juvenile

persons otherwise requires or the proceedings concern matrimonial disputes or the guardianship of children.

2. Everyone charged with a criminal offence shall have the right to be presumed innocent until proved guilty according to law.

3. In the determination of any criminal charge against him, everyone shall be entitled to the following minimum guarantees, in full equality:

    a. To be informed promptly and in detail in a language which he understands of the nature and cause of the charge against him;

    b. To have adequate time and facilities for the preparation of his defence and to communicate with counsel of his own choosing;

    c. To be tried without undue delay;

    d. To be tried in his presence, and to defend himself in persons or through legal assistance of his own choosing; to be informed, if he does not have legal assistance, of this right; and to have legal assistance assigned to him, in any case the interests of justice so require, and without payment by him in any such case if he does not have sufficient means to pay for it;

    e. To examine, or have examined, the witnesses against him and to obtain the attendance and examination of witnesses on his behalf under the same conditions as witnesses against him;

    f. To have the free assistance of an interpreter if he cannot understand or speak the language used in court;

    g. Not to be compelled to testify against himself or to confess guilt.

4. In the case of juvenile persons, the procedure shall be such as will take account of their age and the desirability of promoting their rehabilitation.

5. Everyone convicted of a crime shall have the right to his conviction and sentence being reviewed by a higher tribunal according to law.

6. When a person has by a final decision been convicted of a criminal offence and when subsequently his conviction has been reversed or he has been pardoned on the ground that a new or newly discovered fact shows conclusively that there has been a miscarriage of justice, the person who has suffered punishment as a result of such conviction shall be compensated according to law, un-

less it is proved that the non-disclosure of the unknown fact in time is wholly or partly attributable to him.

7. No one shall be liable to be tried or punished again for an offence for which he has already been finally convicted or acquitted in accordance with the law and penal procedure of each country.

Article 15

1. No one shall be held guilty of any criminal offence on account of any act or omission which did not constitute a criminal offence, under national or international law, at the time when it was committed. Nor shall a heavier penalty be imposed than the one that was applicable at the time when the criminal offence was committed. If, subsequent to the commission of the offence, provision is made by law for the imposition of a lighter penalty, the offender shall benefit thereby.
2. Nothing in this article shall prejudice the trial and punishment of any person for any act or omission which, at the time when it was committed, was criminal according to the general principles of law recognized by the community of nations.

Article 16

Everyone shall have the right to recognition everywhere as a person before the law.

Article 17

1. No one shall be subjected to arbitrary or unlawful interference with his privacy, family, home or correspondence, nor to unlawful attacks on his honour or reputation.
2. Everyone has the right to the protection of the law against such interference or attacks.

Article 18

1. Everyone shall have the right to freedom of thought, conscience and religion. This right shall include freedom to have or to adopt

a religion or belief of his choice, and freedom, either individually or in community with others and in public or private, to manifest his religion or belief in worship, observance, practice and teaching.

2. No one shall be subject to coercion which would impair his freedom to have or to adopt a religion or belief of his choice.

3. Freedom to manifest one's religion or beliefs may be subject only to such limitations as are prescribed by law and are necessary to protect public safety, order, health, or morals or the fundamental rights and freedoms of others.

4. The States Parties to the present Covenant undertake to have respect for the liberty of parents and, when applicable, legal guardians to ensure the religious and moral education of their children in conformity with their own convictions.

Article 19

1. Everyone shall have the right to hold opinions without interference.

2. Everyone shall have the right to freedom of expression; this right shall include freedom to seek, receive and impart information and ideas of all kinds, regardless of frontiers, either orally, in writing or in print, in the form of art, or through any other media of his choice.

3. The exercise of the rights provided for in paragraph 2 of this Article carries with it special duties and responsibilities. It may therefore be subject to certain restrictions, but these shall only be such as are provided by law and are necessary:

   a. For respect of the rights or reputations of others;

   b For the protection of national security or of public order (*ordre public*), or of public health or morals.

Article 20

1. Any propaganda for war shall be prohibited by law.

2. Any advocacy of national, racial or religious hatred that constitutes incitement to discrimination, hostility or violence shall be prohibited by law.

Article 21

The right of peaceful assembly shall be recognized. No restrictions may be placed on the exercise of this right other than those imposed in conformity with the law and which are necessary in a democratic society in the interests of national security or public safety, public order *(ordre public)*, the protection of public health or morals or the protection of the rights and freedoms of others.

Article 22

1. Everyone shall have the right to freedom of association with others, including the right to form and join trade unions for the protection of his interests.
2. No restrictions may be placed on the exercise of this right other than those which are prescribed by law and which are necessary in a democratic society in the interests of national security or public safety, public order *(ordre public)*, the protection of public health or morals or the protection of the rights and freedoms of others. This Article shall not prevent the imposition of lawful restrictions on members of the armed forces and of the police in their exercise of this right.
3. Nothing in this article shall authorize States Parties to the International Labour Organization Convention of 1948 concerning Freedom of Association and Protection of the Right to Organize to take legislative measures which would prejudice, or to apply the law in such a manner as to prejudice, the guarantees provided for in that Convention.

Article 23

1. The family is the natural and fundamental group unit of society and is entitled to protection by society and the State.
2. The right of men and women of marriageable age to marry and to found a family shall be recognized.
3. No marriage shall be entered into without the free and full consent of the intending spouses.
4. States Parties to the present Covenant shall take appropriate steps to ensure equality of rights and responsibilities of spouses as to

marriage, during marriage and at its dissolution. In the case of dissolution, provision shall be made for the necessary protection of any children.

Article 24

1. Every child shall have, without any discrimination as to race, colour, sex, language, religion, national or social origin, property or birth, the right to such measures of protection as are required by his status as a minor, on the part of his family, society and the State.
2. Every child shall be registered immediately after birth and shall have a name.
3. Every child has the right to acquire a nationality.

Article 25

Every citizen shall have the right and the opportunity, without any of the distinctions mentioned in Article 2 and without unreasonable restrictions:

a. To take part in the conduct of public affairs, directly or through freely chosen representatives;
b. To vote and to be elected at genuine periodic elections which shall be by universal and equal suffrage and shall be held by secret ballot, guaranteeing the free expression of the will of the electors;
c. To have access, on general terms of equality, to public service in his country.

Article 26

All persons are equal before the law and are entitled without any discrimination to the equal protection of the law. In this respect, the law shall prohibit any discrimination and guarantee to all persons equal and effective protection against discrimination on any ground such as race, colour, sex, language, religion, political or other opinion, national or social origin, property, birth or other status.

Article 27

In those States in which ethnic, religious or linguistic minorities exist, persons belonging to such minorities shall not be denied the right, in community with the other members of their group, to enjoy their own culture, to profess and practice their own religion, or to use their own language.

PART IV

Article 28

1. There shall be established a Human Rights Committee (hereafter referred to in the present Covenant as the Committee). It shall consist of eighteen members and shall carry out the functions hereinafter provided.
2. The Committee shall be composed of nationals of the States Parties to the present Covenant who shall be persons of high moral character and recognized competence in the field of human rights, consideration being given to the usefulness of the participation of some persons having legal experience.
3. The members of the Committee shall be elected and shall serve in their personal capacity.

Article 29

1. The members of the Committee shall be elected by secret ballot from a list of persons possessing the qualifications prescribed in Article 28 and nominated for the purpose by the States Parties to the present Covenant.
2. Each State Party to the present Covenant may nominate not more than two persons. These persons shall be nationals of the nominating State.
3. A person shall be eligible for renomination.

Article 30

1. The initial election shall be held no later than six months after the date of the entry into force of the present Covenant.

2. At least four months before the date of each election to the Committee, other than an election to fill a vacancy declared in accordance with Article 34, the Secretary-General of the United Nations shall address a written invitation to the States Parties to the Present Covenant to submit their nominations for membership of the Committee within three months.

3. The Secretary-General of the United Nations shall prepare a list in alphabetical order of all the persons thus nominated, with an indication of the States Parties which have nominated them, and shall submit it to the States Parties to the present Covenant no later than one month before the date of each election.

4. Elections of the members of the Committee shall be held at a meeting of the States Parties to the present Covenant convened by the Secretary-General of the United Nations at the Headquarters of the United Nations. At the meeting, for which two-thirds of the States Parties to the present Covenant shall constitute a quorum, the persons elected to the Committee shall be those nominees who obtain the largest number of votes and an absolute majority of the votes of the representatives of States Parties present and voting.

Article 31

1. The Committee may not include more than one national of the same State.

2. In the election of the Committee, consideration shall be given to equitable geographical distribution of membership and to the representation of the different forms of civilization and of the principal legal systems.

Article 32

1. The members of the Committee shall be elected for a term of four years. They shall be eligible for re-election if renominated. However, the terms of nine of the members elected at the first election shall expire at the end of two years; immediately after the first election, the names of these nine members shall be chosen by lot by the Chairman of the meeting referred to in Article 30, paragraph 4.

2. Elections at the expiry of office shall be held in accordance with the preceding articles of this part of the present Covenant.

Article 33

1. If, in the unanimous opinion of the other members, a member of the Committee has ceased to carry out his functions for any cause other than absence of a temporary character, the Chairman of the Committee shall notify the Secretary-General of the United Nations, who shall then declare the seat of that member to be vacant.
2. In the event of the death or the resignation of a member of the Committee, the Chairman shall immediately notify the Secretary-General of the United Nations, who shall declare the seat vacant from the date of death or the date on which the resignation takes effect.

Article 34

1. When a vacancy is declared in accordance with Article 33 and if the term of office of the member to be replaced does not expire within six months of the declaration of the vacancy, the Secretary-General of the United Nations shall notify each of the States Parties to the present Covenant, which may within two months submit nominations in accordance with Article 29 for the purpose of filling the vacancy.
2. The Secretary-General of the United Nations shall prepare a list in alphabetical order of the persons thus nominated and shall submit it to the States Parties to the present Covenant. The election to fill the vacancy shall then take place in accordance with the relevant provisions of this part of the present Covenant.
3. A member of the Committee elected to fill a vacancy declared in accordance with Article 33 shall hold office for the remainder of the term of the member who vacated the seat on the Committee under the provisions of that Article.

Article 35

The members of the Committee shall, with the approval of the General Assembly of the United Nations, receive emoluments from United

Nations resources on such terms and conditions as the General Assembly may decide, having regard to the importance of the Committee's responsibilities.

Article 36

The Secretary-General of the United Nations shall provide the necessary staff and facilities for the effective performance of the functions of the Committee under the present Covenant.

Article 37

1. The Secretary-General of the United Nations shall convene the initial meeting of the Committee at the Headquarters of the United Nations.
2. After its initial meeting, the Committee shall meet at such times as shall be provided in its rules of procedure.
3. The Committee shall normally meet at the Headquarters of the United Nations or at the United Nations Office at Geneva.

Article 38

Every member of the Committee shall, before taking up his duties, make a solemn declaration in open committee that he will perform his functions impartially and conscientiously.

Article 39

1. The Committee shall elect its officers for a term of two years. They may be re-elected.
2. The Committee shall establish its own rules of procedure, but these rules shall provide, *inter alia*, that:
   a. Twelve members shall constitute a quorum;
   b. Decisions of the Committee shall be made by a majority vote of the members present.

Article 40

1. The States Parties to the present Covenant undertake to submit reports on the measures they have adopted which give effect to the

rights recognized herein and on the progress made in the enjoyment of those rights:

   a. Within one year of the entry into force of the present Covenant for the States Parties concerned;

   b. Thereafter whenever the Committee so requests.

2. All reports shall be submitted to the Secretary-General of the United Nations, who shall transmit them to the Committee for consideration. Reports shall indicate the factors and difficulties, if any, affecting the implementation of the present Covenant.

3. The Secretary-General of the United Nations may, after consultation with the Committee, transmit to the specialized agencies concerned copies of such parts of the reports as may fall within their field of competence.

4. The Committee shall study the reports submitted by the States Parties to the present Covenant. It shall transmit its reports, and such general comments as it may consider appropriate, to the States Parties. The Committee may also transmit to the Economic and Social Council these comments along with the copies of the reports it has received from States Parties to the present Covenant.

5. The States Parties to the present Covenant may submit to the Committee observations on any comments that may be made in accordance with paragraph 4 of this Article.

Article 41

1. A State Party to the present Covenant may at any time declare under this article that it recognizes the competence of the Committee to receive and consider communications to the effect that a State Party claims that another State Party is not fulfilling its obligations under the present Covenant. Communications under this Article may be received and considered only if submitted by a State Party which has made a declaration recognizing in regard to itself the competence of the Committee. No communication shall be received by the Committee if it concerns a State Party which has not made such a declaration. Communications received under this article shall be dealt with in accordance with the following procedure:

   a. If a State Party to the present Covenant considers that another State Party is not giving effect to the provisions of the present

Covenant, it may, by written communication, bring the matter to the attention of that State Party. Within three months after the receipt of the communication, the receiving State shall afford the State which sent the communication an explanation or any other statement in writing clarifying the matter, which should include, to the extent possible and pertinent, reference to domestic procedures and remedies taken, pending, or available in the matter.

b. If the matter is not adjusted to the satisfaction of both States Parties concerned within six months after the receipt by the receiving State of the initial communication, either State shall have the right to refer the matter to the Committee, by notice given to the Committee and to the other State.

c. The Committee shall deal with a matter referred to it only after it has ascertained that all available domestic remedies have been invoked and exhausted in the matter, in conformity with the generally recognized principles of international law. This shall not be the rule where the application of the remedies is unreasonably prolonged.

d. The Committee shall hold closed meetings when examining communications under this Article.

e. Subject to the provisions of sub-paragraph (c), the Committee shall make available its good offices to the States Parties concerned with a view to a friendly solution of the matter on the basis of respect for human rights and fundamental freedoms as recognized in the present Covenant.

f. In any matter referred to it, the Committee may call upon the States Parties concerned, referred to in sub-paragraph (b), to supply any relevant information.

g. The States Parties concerned, referred to in sub-paragraph (b), shall have the right to be represented when the matter is being considered in the Committee and to make submissions orally and/or in writing.

h. The Committee shall, within twelve months after the date of receipt of notice under sub-paragraph (b), submit a report:

　i. If a solution within the terms of sub-paragraph (e) is reached, the Committee shall confine its report to a brief statement of the facts and of the solution reached;

ii. If a solution within the terms of sub-paragraph (e) is not reached, the Committee shall confine its report to a brief statement of the facts; the written submissions and record of the oral submissions made by the States Parties concerned shall be attached to the report.

In every matter the report shall be communicated to the States Parties concerned.

2. The provisions of this Article shall come into force when ten States Parties to the present Covenant have made declarations under paragraph 1 of this Article. Such declarations shall be deposited by the States Parties with the Secretary-General of the United Nations, who shall transmit copies thereof to the other States Parties. A declaration may be withdrawn at any time by notification to the Secretary-General. Such a withdrawal shall not prejudice the consideration of any matter which is the subject of a communication already transmitted under this Article; no further communication by any State Party shall be received after the notification of withdrawal of the declaration has been received by the Secretary-General, unless the State Party concerned has made a new declaration.

Article 42

1. a. If a matter referred to the Committee in accordance with Article 41 is not resolved to the satisfaction of the States Parties concerned, the Committee may, with the prior consent of the States Parties concerned, appoint an *ad hoc* Conciliation Commission (hereinafter referred to as the Commission). The good offices of the Commission shall be made available to the States Parties concerned with a view to an amicable solution of the matter on the basis of respect for the present Covenant;

   b. The Commission shall consist of five persons acceptable to the States Parties concerned. If the States Parties concerned fail to reach agreement within three months on all or part of the composition of the Commission the members of the Commission concerning whom no agreement has been reached shall be elected by secret ballot by a two-thirds majority vote of the Committee from among its members.

2. The members of the Commission shall serve in their personal capacity. They shall not be nationals of the States Parties concerned, or of a State not party to the present Covenant, or of a State Party which has not made a declaration under Article 41.
3. The Commission shall elect its own Chairman and adopt its own rules of procedure.
4. The meetings of the Commission shall normally be held at the Headquarters of the United Nations or at the United Nations Office at Geneva. However, they may be held at such other convenient places as the Commission may determine in consultation with the Secretary-General of the United Nations and the States Parties concerned.
5. The secretariat provided in accordance with Article 36 shall also service the commissions appointed under this Article.
6. The information received and collated by the Committee shall be made available to the Commission and the Commission may call upon the States Parties concerned to supply any other relevant information.
7. When the Commission has fully considered the matter, but in any event not later than twelve months after having been seized of the matter, it shall submit to the Chairman of the Committee a report for communication to the States Parties concerned.
   a. If the Commission is unable to complete its consideration of the matter within twelve months, it shall confine its report to a brief statement of the status of its consideration of the matter.
   b. If an amicable solution to the matter on the basis of respect for human rights as recognized in the present Covenant is reached, the Commission shall confine its report to a brief statement of the facts and of the solution reached.
   c. If a solution within the terms of sub-paragraph (b) is not reached, the Commission's report shall embody its findings on all questions of fact relevant to the issues between the States Parties concerned, and its views on the possibilities of an amicable solution of the matter. This report shall also contain the written submissions and a record of the oral submissions made by the States Parties concerned.
   d. If the Commission's report is submitted under sub-paragraph (c), the States Parties concerned shall, within three months of

the receipt of the report, notify the Chairman of the Committee whether or not they accept the contents of the report of the Commission.

8. The provisions of this Article are without prejudice to the responsibilities of the Committee under Article 41.

9. The States Parties concerned shall share equally all the expenses of the members of the Commission in accordance with estimates to be provided by the Secretary-General of the United Nations.

10. The Secretary-General of the United Nations shall be empowered to pay the expenses of the members of the Commission, if necessary, before reimbursement by the States Parties concerned, in accordance with paragraph 9 of this Article.

Article 43

The members of the Committee, and of the *ad hoc* conciliation commissions which may be appointed under Article 42, shall be entitled to the facilities, privileges and immunities of experts on mission for the United Nations as laid down in the relevant sections of the Convention on the Privileges and Immunities of the United Nations.

Article 44

The provisions for the implementation of the present Covenant shall apply without prejudice to the procedures prescribed in the field of human rights by or under the constituent instruments and the conventions of the United Nations and of the specialized agencies and shall not prevent the States Parties to the present Covenant from having recourse to other procedures for settling a dispute in accordance with general or special international agreements in force between them.

Article 45

The Committee shall submit to the General Assembly of the United Nations through the Economic and Social Council, an annual report on its activities.

PART V

Article 46

Nothing in the present Covenant shall be interpreted as impairing the provisions of the Charter of the United Nations and of the constitutions of the specialized agencies which define the respective responsibilities of the various organs of the United Nations and of the specialized agencies in regard to the matters dealt with in the present Covenant.

Article 47

Nothing in the present Covenant shall be interpreted as impairing the inherent right of all peoples to enjoy and utilize fully and freely their natural wealth and resources.

PART VI

Article 48

1. The present Covenant is open for signature by any State Member of the United Nations or members of any of its specialized agencies, by any State Party to the Statute of the International Court of Justice, and by any other State which has been invited by the General Assembly of the United Nations to become a party to the present Covenant.
2. The present Covenant is subject to ratification. Instruments of ratification shall be deposited with the Secretary-General of the United Nations.
3. The present Covenant shall be open to accession by any State referred to in paragraph 1 of this Article.
4. Accession shall be effected by the deposit of an instrument of accession with the Secretary-General of the United Nations.
5. The Secretary-General of the United Nations shall inform all states which have signed this Covenant or acceded to it of the deposit of each instrument of ratification or accession.

Article 49

1. The present Covenant shall enter into force three months after the date of the deposit with the Secretary-General of the United Nations of the thirty-fifth instrument of ratification or instrument of accession.
2. For each State ratifying the present Covenant or acceding to it after the deposit of the thirty-fifth instrument of ratification or instrument of accession, the present Covenant shall enter into force three months after the date of the deposit of its own instrument of ratification or instrument of accession.

Article 50

The provisions of the present Covenant shall extend to all parts of federal States without any limitations or exceptions.

Article 51

1. Any State Party to the present Covenant may propose an amendment and file it with the Secretary-General of the United Nations. The Secretary-General of the United Nations shall thereupon communicate any proposed amendments to the States Parties to the present Covenant with a request that they notify him whether they favour a conference of States Parties for the purpose of considering and voting upon the proposals. In the event that at least one third of the States Parties favours such a conference, the Secretary-General shall convene the conference under the auspices of the United Nations. Any amendment adopted by a majority of the States Parties present and voting at the conference shall be submitted to the General Assembly of the United Nations for approval.
2. Amendments shall come into force when they have been approved by the General Assembly of the United Nations and accepted by a two-thirds majority of the States Parties to the present Covenant in accordance with their respective constitutional processes.
3. When amendments come into force, they shall be binding on those States Parties which have accepted them, other States Parties still

being bound by the provisions of the present Covenant and any earlier amendment which they have accepted.

Article 52

Irrespective of the notifications made under Article 48, paragraph 5, the Secretary-General of the United Nations shall inform all States referred to in paragraph 1 of the same Article of the following particulars:

a. Signatures, ratifications and accessions under Article 48;
b. The date of the entry into force of the present Covenant under Article 49 and the date of the entry into force of any amendments under Article 51.

Article 53

1. The present Covenant, of which the Chinese, English, French, Russian and Spanish texts are equally authentic, shall be deposited in the archives of the United Nations.
2. The Secretary-General of the United Nations shall transmit certified copies of the present Covenant to all States referred to in Article 48.

Appendix D: Optional Protocol to the International Covenant on Civil and Political Rights

The States Parties to the present Protocol,
Considering that in order further to achieve the purposes of the Covenant on Civil and Political Rights (hereinafter referred to as the Covenant) and the implementation of its provisions it would be appropriate to enable the Human Rights Committee set up in part IV of the Covenant (hereinafter referred to as the Committee) to receive and consider, as provided in the present Protocol, communications from individuals claiming to be victims of any of the rights set forth in the Covenant.

Have agreed as follows:

Article 1

A State Party to the Covenant that becomes a party to the present Protocol recognizes the competence of the Committee to receive and consider communications from individuals subject to its jurisdiction who claim to be victims of a violation by that State Party of any of the rights set forth in the Covenant. No communication shall be received by the Committee if it concerns a State Party to the Covenant which is not a party to the present Protocol.

Article 2

Subject to the provisions of Article 1, individuals who claim that any of their rights enumerated in the Covenant have been violated and who have exhausted all available domestic remedies may submit a written communication to the Committee for consideration.

Article 3

The Committee shall consider inadmissible any communication under the present Protocol which is anonymous, or which it considers to be an abuse of the right of submission of such communications or to be incompatible with the provisions of the Covenant.

Article 4

1. Subject to the provisions of Article 3, the Committee shall bring any communications submitted to it under the present Protocol to the attention of the State Party to the present Protocol alleged to be violating any provision of the Covenant.
2. Within six months, the receiving State shall submit to the Committee written explanations or statements clarifying the matter and the remedy, if any, that may have been taken by that State.

Article 5

1. The Committee shall consider communications received under the present Protocol in the light of all written information made available to it by the individual and by the State Party concerned.
2. The Committee shall not consider any communication from an individual unless it has ascertained that:
   a. The same matter is not being examined under another procedure of international investigation or settlement;
   b. The individual has exhausted all available domestic remedies. This shall not be the rule where the application of remedies is unreasonably prolonged.

Article 6

The Committee shall include in its annual report under Article 45 of the Covenant a summary of its activities under the present Protocol.

Article 7

Pending the achievement of the objectives of resolution 1514 (XV) adopted by the General Assembly of the United Nations on 14 December 1960 concerning the Declaration on the Granting of Independence to Colonial Countries and Peoples, the provisions of the present Protocol shall in no way limit the right of petition granted to these peoples by the Charter of the United Nations and other international conventions and instruments under the United Nations and its specialized agencies.

Article 8

1. The present Protocol is open for signature by any State which has signed the Covenant.
2. The present Protocol is subject to ratification by any State which has ratified or acceded to the Covenant. Instruments of ratification shall be deposited with the Secretary-General of the United Nations.
3. The present Protocol shall be open to accession by any State which has ratified or acceded to the Covenant.
4. Accession shall be effected by the deposit of an instrument of accession with the Secretary-General of the United Nations.
5. The Secretary-General of the United Nations shall inform all States which have signed the present Protocol or acceded to it of the deposit of each instrument of ratification or accession.

Article 9

1. Subject to the entry into force of the Covenant, the present Protocol shall enter into force three months after the date of the deposit with the Secretary-General of the United Nations of the tenth instrument of ratification or instrument of accession.
2. For each State ratifying the present Protocol or acceding to it after the deposit of the tenth instrument of ratification or instrument of accession, the present Protocol shall enter into force three months after the date of the deposit of its own instrument of ratification or instrument of accession.

Article 10

The provisions of the present Protocol shall extend to all parts of federal States without any limitations or exceptions.

Article 11

1. Any State Party to the present Protocol may propose an amendment and file it with the Secretary-General of the United Nations. The Secretary-General shall thereupon communicate any proposed amendments to the States Parties to the present Protocol with a request that they notify him whether they favour a conference of States Parties for the purpose of considering and voting upon the proposal. In the event that at least one-third of the States Parties favours such a conference, the Secretary-General shall convene the conference under the auspices of the United Nations. Any amendment adopted by a majority of the States Parties present and voting at the conference shall be submitted to the General Assembly of the United Nations for approval.

2. Amendments shall come into force when they have been approved by the General Assembly of the United Nations and accepted by a two-thirds majority of the States Parties to the present Protocol in accordance with their respective constitutional processes.

3. When amendments come into force, they shall be binding on those States Parties which have accepted them, other States Parties still being bound by the provisions of the present Protocol and any earlier amendment which they have accepted.

Article 12

1. Any State Party may denounce the present Protocol at any time by written notification addressed to the Secretary-General of the United Nations. Denunciation shall take effect three months after the date of receipt of the notification by the Secretary-General.

2. Denunciation shall be without prejudice to the continued application of the provisions of the present Protocol to any communication submitted under Article 2 before the effective date of denunciation.

Article 13

Irrespective of the notifications made under Article 8, paragraph 5, of the present Protocol, the Secretary-General of the United Nations shall inform all States referred to in Article 48, paragraph 1, of the Covenant of the following particulars:

  a. Signatures, ratifications and accessions under Article 8;
  b. The date of the entry into force of the present Protocol under Article 9 and the date of the entry into force of any amendments under Article 11;
  c. Denunciations under Article 12.

Article 14

  1. The present Protocol, of which the Chinese, English, French, Russian and Spanish texts are equally authentic, shall be deposited in the archives of the United Nations.
  2. The Secretary-General of the United Nations shall transmit certified copies of the present Protocol to all States referred to in Article 48 of the Covenant.

Bibliography

I. INTRODUCTION

The literature on both human rights and humanitarian affairs is extensive. The following bibliography, then, is not meant to be exhaustive.
Rather it is intended to offer a taste of representative works on a variety
of human rights and humanitarian topics. The phenomenal growth of
both private and intergovernmental organizations dealing with these
subjects has not only excited substantial scholarly attention but also
generated a wealth of information, reports, studies, and publications by
the organizations themselves, much of which can be obtained directly
from the agencies either by writing to the agencies or by consulting
their websites, which, where appropriate, have been cited in the individual entries of the dictionary.

In terms of the scholarly literature, which is more prominently represented in the following bibliography, a great deal of attention has focused on the activities of United Nations (UN)–related human rights
agencies and a variety of regional human rights organizations, especially those found in Europe. Very useful scholarly and reference works
on the range of regional and international human rights agencies include
Thomas Buergenthal's *International Human Rights: In a Nutshell*, 3rd
edition; Peter R. Baehr, *Human Rights: Universality in Practice*; David
Forsythe, *Human Rights in International Relations*; Paul Gordon Lauren, *The Evolution of International Human Rights: Visions Seen*, and
Patrick James Flood, *The Effectiveness of UN Human Rights Institutions*. Two extensive compendiums that directly cite treaties and important human rights texts are Edward Lawson and Mary Lou Bertucci,
eds., *Encyclopedia of Human Rights* and Henry Steiner and Philip Alston, *International Human Rights in Context: Law, Politics and Morals*.
The latter includes extensive commentaries and excerpts of vital human
rights instruments, and the former includes full texts of important
treaties and resolutions.

On the history and philosophical development of human rights, several recent works may be recommended as general background including Patrick Hayden, *The Philosophy of Human Rights*, which is a collection of key writings of philosophers with introductory comments,
and Micheline Ishay, *The History of Human Rights: From Ancient
Times to the Globalization Era*, as well as the classic by Jack Donnelly,
Universal Human Rights in Theory and Practice, 2nd edition. Other

useful and recent works on the enduring problem of the application of universal norms to particular contexts include Tim Dunne, *Human Rights in Global Politics*; Christian Tomuschat, *Human Rights: Between Idealism and Realism*; and Rachel Seider, *Multiculturalism in Latin America: Indigenous Rights, Diversity, and Democracy*. Another recent work examining new challenges to human rights in light of modern developments is Alyson Brysk, ed., *Globalization and Human Rights*. An important recent work on the similarities and discontinuities between human rights and humanitarian law is René Provost, *International Human Rights and Humanitarian Law*. Finally, a very provocative critique of the human rights movement and the difficulty it faces in achieving universal respect in a world of deeply divided regional and ethnic settings is Michael Ignatieff, *Human Rights as Politics and Idolatry*. This work includes provocative analysis by Ignatieff with commentaries and critiques of his argument by other noted human rights specialists.

A number of the human rights agencies cited in this dictionary are also treated in a variety of ways in other historical dictionaries published by Scarecrow Press (Lanham, Maryland) as part of its International Organizations Series, edited by Jon Woronoff. Among the most important of these are Guy Arnold, *Historical Dictionary of Aid and Development Organizations* (1996); Jacques Fomerand, *Historical Dictionary of the United Nations* (2006); A. H. M. van Ginneken, *Historical Dictionary of the League of Nations* (2006); Joaquin Roy and Aimee Kanner, *Historical Dictionary of the European Union* (2006); Kelley Lee, *Historical Dictionary of the World Health Organization* (1998); Terry M. Mays and Mark W. DeLancey, *Historical Dictionary of International Organizations in Sub-Saharan Africa* (2002); Terry M. Mays, *Historical Dictionary of Multinational Peacekeeping* (2003); Boleslaw A. Boczek, *Historical Dictionary of International Tribunals* (1994); Ross B. Talbot, *Historical Dictionary of the International Food Agencies* (2005); Anne C. Salda, *Historical Dictionary of the World Bank* (2007) and, closely related to the humanitarian agencies dealt with in this dictionary, Robert F. Gorman, 2nd edition, *Historical Dictionary of Refugee and Disaster Relief Organizations* (2000). Other useful historical dictionaries dealing with the situations involving violations of human rights include Ludwig W. Adamec, *Historical Dictionary of Afghan Wars, Revolutions, and Insurgencies* (2005); Guy

Arnold, *Historical Dictionary of Civil Wars in Africa* (1999); David Kohut, Olga Vilella, and Beatrice Julian, *Historical Dictionary of the "Dirty Wars"* (2003); Martin Klein, *Historical Dictionary of Slavery and Abolition* (2002); and Sean K. Anderson and Stephen Sloan, *Historical Dictionary of Terrorism* (2002). Apart from these useful historical dictionaries, Scarecrow Press has published important reference works on international law, including John S. Gibson, *Dictionary of International Human Rights Law* (1996) and more recently, Boleslaw A. Boczek, *International Law: A Dictionary* (2005).

In addition to voluminous literature on human rights in the UN system, world politics, and global foreign policy, there has been tremendous growth in studies of human rights in various regional contexts. A sample of these is provided in the following bibliography. The European human rights system, for instance, has existed since the early 1950s. As the oldest regionally established human rights regime, it has provoked substantial scholarly interest, including an older classic, Arthur H. Robertson's, *Human Rights in Europe*. Robertson's more recent work with J. G. Merrills, *Human Rights: A Study of the European Convention on Human Rights*, is also a valuable contribution. Other more recent works on the development and practice of human rights law in Europe include Andrew Williams, *EU Human Rights Policies: A Study in Irony* and Conor A. Gearty, *Principles of Human Rights Adjudication*. Although the European system has dominated scholarship on human rights for many years, literature on human rights in Africa and Latin America has proliferated, and growing bodies of research that deal with the Middle East and Asia as well are evident. A sample of this literature is included in the regional section of the following bibliography.

The literature on humanitarian agencies has also grown substantially, especially in recent years. For readers who want a basic introduction to the refugee assistance and protection network in layman's terms, see Robert F. Gorman, *Mitigating Misery: An Inquiry into the Political and Humanitarian Aspects of U.S. and Global Refugee Policy*, or for critiques of the contemporary international refugee regime, see Arthur Helton, *The Price of Indifference: Refugees and Humanitarian Action in the New Century*; Nicholas Steiner et al., *Problems of Protection: The UNHCR, Refugees and Human Rights*; or the works of Gil Loescher, *The UNHCR and World Politics: A Perilous Path* and *Beyond Charity:*

International Cooperation and the Global Refugee Crisis. For a vintage classic on the root causes of refugee and humanitarian emergencies, see Aristide Zolberg, Astri Suhrke, and Sergio Aguayo, *Escape from Violence: Conflict and the Refugee Crisis in the Developing World*. A number of works deal with the activities of nongovernmental organizations (NGOs) in providing humanitarian relief and protection, including Elizabeth Ferris, *Beyond Borders: Refugees, Migrants and Human Rights in the Post–Cold War Era* and Thomas G. Weiss and Leon Gordenker, eds., *NGOs, the UN, and Global Governance*, the latter being a very useful collection of articles including several with human rights and humanitarian implications. An excellent work on the role of NGOs in human rights is that of Claude E. Welch Jr., ed., *NGOs and Human Rights: Promise and Performance*. Those interested in consulting other works on refugees and human rights could begin with the representative sample of works listed in this bibliography, or they could consult the more extensive bibliography found in Robert F. Gorman, *Historical Dictionary of Refugee and Disaster Relief Organizations*, 2nd edition (2000). As in the area of human rights, NGOs and international agencies publish a huge variety of reports, studies, and commentaries on refugee protection and assistance, humanitarian aid to the displaced, and disaster assistance programs.

This bibliography, then, is designed to provide the reader with a sample of some of the most widely available and notable works on human rights and humanitarian affairs. Because much of the literature on human rights is thematic in nature, we include a number of topical headings dealing with human rights and children, ethnic conflict, minorities, civil and political rights, and so on. Some titles are found under more than one heading if they deal with more than one subject area, region of the world, or topic. Most of the works cited are published books or articles in scholarly journals or monographs. Some articles from NGO publications are cited, but the number of NGO publications, as noted above, is far too extensive to completely document here. Similarly, vast numbers of UN and governmental documents and reports on human rights also exist. Because they are so numerous and because most are not readily available to a general readership, we have refrained from citing these as well. Readers interested in accessing such information should consult the websites listed at the end of individual entries.

II. GENERAL INTEREST

Aldridge, Alfred O. *Man of Reason: The Life of Thomas Paine*. New York: Lippincott, 1959.

Alston, Philip, and James Crawford. *The Future of UN Human Rights Treaty Monitoring*. Cambridge: Cambridge University Press, 2000.

Blaustein, Albert P., Roger S. Clark, and Jay A. Sigler, eds. *Human Rights Sourcebook*. New York: Paragon House, 1987.

Borneman, John. *Settling Accounts*. Princeton, NJ: Princeton University Press, 1997.

Brinkley, Douglas, and David Facey-Crowther. *The Atlantic Charter*. New York: St. Martin's, 1994.

Brownlie, Ian, and Guy Goodwin-Gill, eds. *Basic Documents on Human Rights*. Oxford: Oxford University Press, 2002.

Claude, Richard P., ed. *Comparative Human Rights*. Baltimore, MD: Johns Hopkins University Press, 1976.

Claude, Richard P., and Burns H. Weston. *Human Rights in the World Community: Issues and Action*. Philadelphia: University of Pennsylvania Press, 1992.

Davis, David B. *The Problem of Slavery in Western Culture*. Ithaca, NY: Cornell University Press, 1965.

Dominguez, Jorge I. *Enhancing Global Human Rights*. New York: McGraw-Hill, 1979.

Donnelly, Jack. *International Human Rights: Dilemmas in World Politics*. Boulder, CO: Westview Press, 1998.

——. *Universal Human Rights in Theory and Practice*. Ithaca, NY: Cornell University Press, 2002.

Donnelly, Jack, and Rhoda Howard, eds. *International Handbook of Human Rights*. Westport, CT: Greenwood Press, 1987.

Dunne, Tim. *Human Rights in Global Politics*. Cambridge: Cambridge University Press, 1999.

Flood, Patrick James. *The Effectiveness of UN Human Rights Institutions*. Westport, CT: Praeger, 1998.

Forsythe, David. P. *Human Rights in International Relations*. Cambridge: Cambridge University Press, 2000.

——. *The Internationalization of Human Rights*. Lexington, MA: Lexington Books, 1990.

Friedman, Julian R., and Marc I. Sherman, eds. *Human Rights: An International and Comparative Law Bibliography*. Westport, CT: Greenwood Press, 1985.

Gewirth, Alan. *Human Rights: Essays on Justification and Application*. Chicago: University of Chicago Press, 1984.

Glaser, Kurt, and Stefan T. Possony. *Victims of Politics: The State of Human Rights.* New York: Columbia, 1979.

Glendon, Mary Ann. *The World Made New: Eleanor Roosevelt and the Universal Declaration of Human Rights.* New York: Random House, 2001.

Gormley, W. Paul. *Human Rights and Environment: The Need for International Cooperation.* Leyden, Netherlands: A. W. Sijthoff, 1976.

Haas, Michael. *Improving Human Rights.* Westport, CT: Praeger, 1994.

Henkin, Louis, et al. *Human Rights.* New York: Foundation Press, 1999.

Ishay, Micheline. *The History of Human Rights: From Ancient Times to the Globalization Era.* Berkeley: University of California Press, 2004.

Jayawickrama, Nihal. *The Judicial Application of Human Rights Law.* Cambridge: Cambridge University Press, 2002.

Joyce, James A. *The New Politics of Human Rights.* London: Macmillan, 1978.

Laquer, Walter, and Barry N. Rubin, eds. *The Human Rights Reader.* New York: New American Library, 1979.

Lauren, Paul Gordon. *The Evolution of International Human Rights: Visions Seen.* Philadelphia: University of Pennsylvania Press, 2003.

Lutz, Ellen, Hurst Hannum, and Kathryn Burke, eds. *New Directions in Human Rights.* Philadelphia: University of Pennsylvania Press, 1989.

Marks, Stephen P. "Emerging Human Rights: A New Generation for the 1980s?" *Rutgers Law Review* 33 (Winter 1981): 435–52.

Meron, Theodor, ed. *Human Rights in International Law.* 2 vols. Oxford: Clarendon Press, 1984.

Morsink, Johannes. *The Universal Declaration of Human Rights: Origins, Drafting, and Intent.* Philadelphia: University of Pennsylvania Press, 1999.

Nelson, Jack L., and Vera M. Green, eds. *International Human Rights: Contemporary Issues.* New Brunswick, NJ: Human Rights Publishing, 1980.

Patrnogic, J., and Z. Meriboute. *Terrorism and International Law.* San Remo, Italy: International Institute of Humanitarian Law, 1987.

Pennock, F. Roland, and John W. Chapman. *Human Rights.* New York: New York University Press, 1981.

Plattner, Marc F. *Human Rights in Our Time: Essays in Memory of Victor Baras.* Boulder, CO: Westview Press, 1984.

Pollis, Adamantia, and Peter Schwab, eds. *Human Rights: Cultural and Ideological Perspectives.* New York: Praeger, 1979.

Ramcharan, G. G. *Human Rights Thirty Years after the Universal Declaration.* The Hague, Netherlands: Martinus Nijhoff, 1979.

Reiter, Randy B., M. V. Zunzunegui, and José Quiroga. "Guidelines for Field Reporting of Basic Human Rights Violations." *Human Rights Quarterly* 8 (November 1986): 628–53.

Robertson, A. H., and J. G. Merrills. *Human Rights in the World: An Introduction to the Study of the International Protection of Human Rights.* 4th ed. Manchester: Manchester University Press, 1996.

Schwab, Peter, and Adamantia Pollis, eds. *Toward a Human Rights Framework.* New York: Praeger, 1982.

Stanley, David T. *Prisoners among Us: The Problem of Parole.* Washington, DC: Brookings, 1976.

Tabendeh, Sulanhussein. *A Muslim Commentary on the Universal Declaration of Human Rights.* London: F. T. Goulding, 1970.

Thompson, Kenneth W., ed. *The Moral Imperatives of Human Rights: A World Survey.* Washington, DC: University Press of America, 1980.

UN Department of International Economic and Social Affairs. *Population and Human Rights.* New York: United Nations, 1990.

Vincent, R. J. *Human Rights and International Relations.* Cambridge: Cambridge University Press, 1986.

Wiltshire, Susan Ford. *Greece, Rome, and the Bill of Rights.* Norman: University of Oklahoma Press, 1992.

III. HUMAN RIGHTS THEORY

Alston, Philip. "Conjuring up New Human Rights: A Proposal for Quality Control." *American Journal of International Law* 78 (July 1984): 607–21.

Bay, Christian. "Self-Respect as a Human Right: Thoughts on the Dialectics of Wants and Needs in the Struggle for Human Community." *Human Rights Quarterly* 4 (February 1982): 53–75.

———. *Strategies of Political Emancipation.* Notre Dame, IN: University of Notre Dame Press, 1981.

Beitz, Charles. "Economic Rights and Distributive Justice in Developing Societies." *World Politics* 33 (April 1981): 321–46.

Bilder, R. R. "Rethinking International Human Rights: Some Basic Questions." *Wisconsin Law Review* 44 (1969): 171–217.

Bossuyt, M. "Human Rights and Non-Intervention in Domestic Matters." *Review of the International Commission of Jurists*, no. 35 (1985): 45–52.

Buergenthal, Thomas. "The Normative and Institutional Evolution of International Human Rights." *Human Rights Quarterly* 19, no. 4 (November 1998): 703–23.

Coomaraswamy, Radhika. "A Third-World View of Human Rights." *UNESCO Courier* 35 (August–September 1982): 49–52.

Cranston, Maurice. *What Are Human Rights?* New York: Basic Books, 1962.

Donnelly, Jack. *The Concept of Human Rights.* New York: St. Martin's Press, 1985.

———. "How Are Rights and Duties Correlative?" *Journal of Value Inquiry* 16 (1982): 287–97.

———. "Human Rights and Dignity: An Analytical Critique of Non-Western Conceptions of Human Rights." *American Political Science Review* 76, no. 2 (1982): 303–16.

———. "International Human Rights: A Regime Analysis." *International Organization* 40 (Summer 1986): 599–642.

———. *Universal Human Rights in Theory and Practice*. Ithaca, NY: Cornell University Press, 2002.

Falk, Richard. *Human Rights and State Sovereignty*. New York: Holmes and Meier, 1981.

Freeman, Michael D. A. "The Problem of Secularism in Human Rights Theory," *Human Rights Quarterly* 26, no. 2 (May 2004): 375–400.

Hayden, Patrick. *The Philosophy of Human Rights*. St. Paul, MN: Paragon House, 2001.

Henkin, Louis. *The Age of Rights*. New York: Columbia University Press, 1990.

Hoffman, Stanley. *Duties beyond Borders: On the Limits and Possibilities of Ethical International Politics*. Syracuse, NY: Syracuse University Press, 1981.

Howard, Rhoda E. "The Full-Belly Thesis: Should Economic Rights Take Priority over Civil and Political Rights?" *Human Rights Quarterly* 5 (November 1983): 467–90.

Ignatieff, Michael. *Human Rights as Politics and Idolatry*. Princeton, NJ: Princeton University Press, 2003.

Jochnick, Chris. "Confronting the Impunity of Non-State Actors: New Fields for the Promotion of Human Rights." *Human Rights Quarterly* 21, no. 1 (February 1999): 56–79.

Meron, Theodor. "On a Hierarchy of International Human Rights." *American Journal of International Law* 80 (1986): 1–23.

Milne, Alan J. *Human Rights and Human Diversity: An Essay in the Philosophy of Human Rights*. London: Macmillan, 1986.

Nickel, James W. *Making Sense of Human Rights: Philosophical Reflections on the Universal Declaration of Human Rights*. Berkeley: University of California Press, 1987.

Panikkar Raimundo. "Is the Notion of Human Rights a Western Concept?" *Diogenes* 27, no. 1 (1982): 28–43.

Pollis, Adamantia, and Peter Schwab, eds. *Human Rights: Cultural and Ideological Perspectives*. New York: Praeger, 1980.

Renteln, Alison Dundes. "The Unanswered Challenge of Relativism and the Consequences for Human Rights." *Human Rights Quarterly* 7 (November 1985): 514–40.

Roht-Arriaza, Naomi, ed., *Impunity and Human Rights in International Law and Practice*. Oxford: Oxford University Press, 1995.

Shapiro, Ian. *The Evolution of Rights in Liberal Theory.* Cambridge: Cambridge University Press, 1986.

Wellman, Carl. "Solidarity, the Individual and Human Rights." *Human Rights Quarterly* 22, no. 3 (August 2000): 639–57.

IV. HUMAN RIGHTS AND FOREIGN POLICY

Baehr, Peter. *The Role of Human Rights in Foreign Policy.* New York: St. Martin's 1994.

Brown, Peter G., and Douglas MacLean, eds. *Human Rights and U.S. Foreign Policy: Principles and Applications.* Lexington, MA: Lexington Books, 1979.

Buckley, William F., Jr. "Human Rights and Foreign Policy: A Proposal." *Foreign Affairs* 58 (Spring 1980): 775–96.

Cohen, Roberta. "Human Rights Diplomacy: The Carter Administration and the Southern Cone." *Human Rights Quarterly* 4 (May 1982): 212–42.

Cohen, Stephen B. "Conditioning U.S. Security Assistance on Human Rights Practices." *American Journal of International Law* 76 (April 1982): 246–79.

Forsythe, David P. *Human Rights and World Politics.* Lincoln: University of Nebraska Press, 1981.

Kirkpatrick, Jeane J. "Establishing a Viable Human Rights Policy." *World Affairs* 143 (Spring 1981): 323–34.

Kommers, Donald, and Gil Loescher. *Human Rights and American Foreign Policy.* Notre Dame, IN: University of Notre Dame Press, 1979.

Korey, William. *The Promises We Keep: Human Rights, the Helsinki Process and American Foreign Policy.* New York: St. Martin's, 1994.

Liang-Fenton, Debra, ed. *Implementing U.S. Human Rights Policy: Agendas, Policies, and Practices.* Washington, DC: United States Institute of Peace, 2004.

Luard, Evan. *Human Rights and Foreign Policy.* Oxford: Pergamon Press, 1981.

Matthews, Robert, and Cranford Pratt. "Human Rights and Foreign Policy: Principles and Canadian Practice." *Human Rights Quarterly* 7 (May 1985): 159–88.

Matthews, Robert, and Cranford Pratt, eds. *Canadian Foreign Policy and Human Rights.* Montreal: McGill-Queens University Press, 1988.

Morgenthau, Hans J. *Human Rights and Foreign Policy.* New York: Council on Religion and International Affairs, 1979.

Mower, A. Glenn, Jr. *Human Rights and American Foreign Policy: The Carter and Reagan Experiences.* Westport, CT: Greenwood Press, 1987.

Newsom, David D. *The Diplomacy of Human Rights.* Lanham, MD: University Press of America, 1986.

Samet, Andre J. *Human Rights Law and the Reagan Administration 1981–1983.* Washington, DC: International Law Institute, 1984.

Schoultz, Lars. *Human Rights and United States Policy toward Latin America.* Princeton, NJ: Princeton University Press, 1981.

Vincent, R. J. *Human Rights and International Relations.* Cambridge: Cambridge University Press, 1986.

V. HUMAN RIGHTS, TRADE, AND AID

Addo, M. K. "Some Issues in European Community Aid Policy and Human Rights." *Legal Issues in European Integration* 1 (1988): 55–85.

Alston, Philip. "Linking Trade and Human Rights." *German Yearbook of International Law* 23 (1980): 126–58.

Baehr, Peter. "Concern for Development Aid and Fundamental Human Rights: The Dilemma as Faced by The Netherlands." *Human Rights Quarterly* 4 (February 1982): 39–52.

Brysk, Alyson, ed. *Globalization and Human Rights.* Berkeley: University of California Press, 2002.

Dommen, Caroline. "Raising Human Rights Concerns in the World Trade Organization Actors, Processes and Possible Strategies." *Human Rights Quarterly* 24: 1 (February 2002): 1–50.

Douglas, William A., John-Paul Ferguson, and Erin Klett. "An Effective Confluence of Forces in Support of Workers' Rights: ILO Standards, US Trade Laws, Unions and NGOs." *Human Rights Quarterly* 26: 2 (May 2004): 273–99.

Kamara, S., M. T. Dahniya, and P. Greene. *The Effect of Structural Adjustment Policies on Human Welfare in Africa South of the Sahara.* Freetown, Sierra Leone: UNICEF, April 1990.

Rehof, L. A., and C. Gelman, eds. *Human Rights in Domestic Law and Development Assistance Policies of the Nordic Countries.* Dordrecht, Netherlands: Martinus Nijhoff, 1989.

VI. HUMAN RIGHTS AND WOMEN AND CHILDREN

Agnelli, Susanna. *Street Children: A Growing Urban Tragedy.* London: Independent Commission on International Humanitarian Issues and Weidenfield and Nicolson, 1986.

Agosin, Marjorie, ed. *Women, Gender, and Human Rights: A Global Perspective*. New Brunswick, NJ: Rutgers University Press, 2001.

Beigbeder, Yves. *New Challenges for UNICEF: Children, Woman and Human Rights*. New York: Palgrave Macmillan, 2002.

Black, Maggie. *Children First: The Story of UNICEF, Past and Present*. Oxford: Oxford University Press, 1996.

Bonnet, Michel. "Child Slavery: The Kharkar Camps of Pakistan." *International Children's Rights Monitor* 5, nos. 2–3 (1988): 4–5.

Bouvard, Marguerite Guzman. *Women Reshaping Human Rights: How Extraordinary Activists Are Changing the World*. Lanham, MD: SR Books, 1996.

Cook, Helena. *The War against Children: South Africa's Younger Victims*. New York: Lawyers Committee for Human Rights, 1986.

Cook, Rebecca J., ed. *Human Rights of Women: National and International Perspectives*. Philadelphia: University of Pennsylvania Press, 1994.

Dodge, Cole P., and Magne Raundalen. *Reaching Children in War: Sudan, Uganda and Mozambique*. Uppsala, Sweden: Scandinavian Institute of African Studies and Sigma Forlag, 1991.

Edelman, M. W., and J. D. Weill. "Status of Children in the 1980s." *Columbia Human Rights Law Review* 17, no. 2 (Spring-Summer 1986): 139–58.

Elahi, Maryam. "The Rights of the Child under Islamic Law: Prohibition of the Child Soldier." *Columbia Human Rights Law Review* 19, no. 2 (Spring 1988): 259–79.

Ennew, Judith. "Child Soldiers: Serving or Working?" *International Children's Rights Monitor* 2, no. 2 (1985): 18–19.

Farr, Kathryn. *Sex Trafficking: The Global Market in Women and Children*. London: Worth Publishing, 2004.

Hewlett, Sylvia Ann. *Child Neglect in Rich Nations*. New York: UNICEF, 1993.

Howland, Courtney W., ed. *Religious Fundamentalisms and the Human Rights of Women*. New York: Palgrave Macmillan, 2001.

LeBlanc, Lawrence J. *The Convention on the Rights of the Child: United Nations Lawmaking on Human Rights*. Lincoln: University of Nebraska Press, 1995.

Macksoud, Mona. *Helping Children Cope with the Stresses of War: A Manual for Parents and Teachers*. New York: UNICEF, 1993.

Myers, William E., ed. *Protecting Working Children*. London: Zed Books and UNICEF, 1991.

Peters, Julia Stone, and Andrea Wolper, eds. *Women's Rights, Human Rights: International Feminist Perspectives*. London: Routledge, 1995.

Rädda, Barnen, and Swedish Save the Children. *A Humanitarian Appeal for Children in Armed Conflicts*. Stockholm: 1987.

Ressler, Everett M., Joanne M. Tortorici, and Alex Marcelino. *Children of War: A Guide to the Provision of Services*. New York: UNICEF, 1993.

UNICEF. *State of the World's Children 2005: Childhood under Threat*. New York: UNICEF, 2004.

VII. CIVIL AND POLITICAL RIGHTS

Amnesty International. *Administrative Detention*. London: 1988.
——. *Conscientious Objection to Military Service*. London: 1988.
——. *Getting Away with Murder: Political Killings and "Disappearance" in the 1990s*. London: 1993.
——. *The Imprisonment of Persons Seeking to Leave a Country or to Return to Their Own Country*. London: 1986.
——. *States of Emergency: Torture and Violations of the Right to Life under States of Emergency*. London: 1988.
Centre for Social Development and Humanitarian Affairs. *Women in Politics and Decision-Making in the Late Twentieth Century: A United Nations Study*. Dordrecht, Netherlands: Martinus Nijhoff with UN Publications, 1991.
Conboy, Kevin. "Detention without Trial in Kenya." *Georgia Journal of International and Comparative Law* 8, no. 2 (1987): 441–61.
Gastil, Raymond D. *Freedom in the World: Political Rights and Civil Liberties* Westport, CT: Greenwood Press, annual publication.
Grant, James P. *The State of the World's Children, 1988*. New York: UNICEF, 1989.
Heginbotham, Chris. *The Rights of Mentally Ill People*. London: Minority Rights Group, 1987.
Hull, Elizabeth. *Without Justice for All: The Constitutional Rights of Aliens*. Westport, CT: Greenwood Press, 1985.
Human Rights Watch. *Global Report on Prisons*. New York: Human Rights Watch, 1993.
Lobsack-Fullgraf, Lilli. "State of Emergency and Human Rights." *Alternative* 2, no. 1 (1987): 8–13.
Otto, Diane. "Nongovernmental Organizations in the United Nations System: The Emerging Role of International Civil Society." *Human Rights Quarterly* 18, no. 1 (February 1996): 107–41.
Ramcharan, B. G. *The Right to Life in International Law*. Dordrecht, Netherlands: Martinus Nijhoff, 1985.
Rodley, Nigel S. "The International Legal Consequences of Torture, Extra-Legal Execution, and Disappearance." In *New Directions in Human Rights*, ed. Ellen L. Lutz, Hurst Hannum, and Kathryn J. Burke. Philadelphia: University of Pennsylvania Press, 1989.

——. "UN Action Procedures against "Disappearances," Summary or Arbitrary Executions, and Torture." *Human Rights Quarterly* 8, no. 4 (November 1986): 700–30.

Scoble, H. M., and L. S. Wiseberg. *Freedom of Association for Human Rights Organizations.* Washington, DC: Human Rights Internet, 1981.

Steiner, H. J. "Political Participation as a Human Right." *Harvard Human Rights Yearbook* 1 (1988): 77–134.

Veenhoven, Willem A., ed. *Case Studies on Human Rights and Fundamental Freedoms: A World Survey.* 5 vols. The Hague: Martinus Nijhoff, 1975–1976.

Witte, John, Jr., and Johan van der Vyver, eds. *Religious Human Rights in Global Perspective.* The Hague, Netherlands: Kluwer Law International, 1996.

VIII. ECONOMIC, SOCIAL, AND CULTURAL RIGHTS

Alston, Philip. "Making Space for New Human Rights: The Case of the Right to Development." *Harvard Human Rights Yearbook* 1 (Spring 1988): 3–40.

——. "Out of the Abyss: The Challenges Confronting the New UN Committee on Economic, Social, and Cultural Rights." *Human Rights Quarterly* 9, no. 3 (August 1987): 332–81.

——. "The Shortcomings of a 'Garfield the Cat' Approach to the Right to Development." *California Western International Law Journal* 15 (Summer 1986): 510–18.

Brietske, Paul H. "Consorting with the Chameleon, or Realizing the Right to Development." *California Western International Law Journal* 145 (Summer 1985): 560–606.

Brownlie, Ian. *The Human Right to Food.* London: Commonwealth Secretariat, 1987.

Center for Human Rights. *Right to Adequate Food as a Human Right.* New York: United Nations, 1989.

Cortese, Michele. "Property Rights and Human Values: A Right of Access to Private Property for Tenant Organizers." *Columbia Human Rights Law Review* 17, no. 2 (Spring-Summer 1986): 257–82.

Donnelly, Jack. "In Search of the Unicorn: The Jurisprudence of the Right to Development." *California Western International Law Journal* 15 (Summer 1985): 473–509.

——. "The Theology of the Right to Development: A Reply to Alston." *California Western International Law Journal* 15 (Summer 1985): 519–23.

Drinan, Robert F., ed. *The Right to be Educated.* Washington, DC: Corpus, 1968.

Dunning, Harold. "The Origins of Convention No. 87 on Freedom of Association and the Right to Organize," *International Labour Review* 137, no. 2 (1998): 149–68.

Eide, Asbjorn. "Food Security and the Right to Food in International Law and Development." *Transnational Law and Contemporary Problems* 1 (Fall 1991): 415.

———. *Right to Adequate Food as a Human Right.* Human Rights Study Series 1. Geneva: UN Centre for Human Rights, 1989.

Felice, William F. *The Global New Deal: Economic and Social Human Rights in World Politics.* Landover, MD: Rowman & Littlefield, 2002.

———. "The UN Committee on the Elimination of All Forms of Racial Discrimination: Race and Economic and Social Rights," *Human Rights Quarterly* 24, no. 1 (February 2002): 205–36.

Forsythe, David P., ed. *Human Rights and Development: International Views.* New York: St. Martin's Press, 1989.

François, Louis. *The Right to Education; From Proclamation to Achievement, 1948–1968.* Paris: UNESCO, 1968.

Goldstein, Joan. *Demanding Clean Food and Water: The Fight for a Basic Human Right.* New York: Plenum Press, 1990.

Independent Commission on International Humanitarian Issues. *Famine: A Man-Made Disaster?* New York: Vintage, 1985.

International Commission of Health Professions. *Health and Human Rights.* Geneva, Switzerland: Author, 1986.

Joyce, James A. *World Labour Rights and Their Protection.* London: Croom Helm, 1980.

Pontifical Commission *"Justicia et Pax."* What Have You Done to Your Homeless Brother? The Church and the Housing Problem. Vatican City: Pontifical Commission, 1985.

Roth, Kenneth. "Defending Economic, Social and Cultural Rights: Practical Issues Faced by an International Human Rights Organization." *Human Rights Quarterly* 26, no. 1 (February 2004): 63–73.

Tarrow, Norma Bernstein. *Human Rights and Education.* New York: Pergamon Press, 1987.

United Nations Educational, Scientific and Cultural Organization. *Education for All: Roundtable Themes, World Conference on Education for All.* Paris: UNESCO, 1992.

IX. ETHNIC CONFLICT AND SELF-DETERMINATION

Ambrosio, Thomas. *Irredentism: Ethnic Conflict and International Politics.* Westport, CT: Praeger, 2001.

Connor, Walker. "Nation-building or Nation-destroying?" *World Politics* 24 (1972): 319–55.

Esman, Milton J., and Shibley Telhami, eds. *International Organizations and Ethnic Conflict*. Ithaca, NY: Cornell University Press, 1995.

Fischel, Jack. *Historical Dictionary of the Holocaust*. Lanham, MD: Scarecrow Press, 1999.

Gottlieb, Gidon. *Nation against State: A New Approach to Ethnic Conflicts and the Decline of Sovereignty*. New York: Council on Foreign Relations Press, 1993.

Gurr, Ted Robert, and Barbara Harff. *Ethnic Conflict in World Politics*. Boulder, CO: Westview Press, 1994.

Moynihan, Daniel Patrick. *Pandaemonium: Ethnicity in International Politics*. Oxford: Oxford University Press, 1993.

Ryan, Stephen. *Ethnic Conflict and International Relations*. Aldershot, UK: Dartmouth, 1990.

Smith, Anthony D. *National Identity*. Reno: University of Nevada Press, 1991.

X. HUMANITARIAN ASSISTANCE, ASYLUM, AND REFUGEES

Adelman, Howard, ed. *Refugee Policy: Canada and the United States*. Toronto, ON: York Lanes Press, 1991.

Carlin, James L. *The Refugee Connection: A Lifetime of Running a Lifeline*. London: Macmillan, 1989.

Chandler, Edgar H. S. *The High Tower of Refuge: The Inspiring Story of Refugee Relief throughout the World*. New York: Praeger, 1959.

Cuny, Frederick. *Disasters and Development*. New York: Oxford University Press, 1983.

Ferris, Elizabeth. *Beyond Borders: Refugees, Migrants and Human Rights in the Post–Cold War Era*. Geneva: World Council of Churches, 1993.

——. *Central American Refugees and the Politics of Protection*. New York: Praeger, 1987.

——, ed. *Refugees and World Politics*. New York: Praeger, 1987.

Forsythe, David P. *Humanitarian Politics: The International Committee of the Red Cross*. Baltimore, MD: Johns Hopkins University Press, 1977.

Gallagher, Dennis, and Janelle Diller. *CIREFCA: At the Crossroads between Uprooted People and Development in Central America*. Washington, DC: Commission for the Study of International Migration and Cooperative Economic Development, 1990.

Gibney, Mark, ed. *Open Borders? Closed Societies?* New York: Greenwood Press, 1988.

Goodwin-Gill, Guy S. *The Refugee in International Law*. Oxford: Clarendon Press, 1983.

Gordenker, Leon. *Refugees in International Relations*. New York: Columbia University Press, 1987.

Gorman, Robert F. *Historical Dictionary of Refugee and Disaster Relief Organizations*. 2nd ed. Metuchen, NJ: Scarecrow Press, 2000.

———. *Mitigating Misery: An Inquiry into the Political and Humanitarian Aspects of U.S. and Global Refugee Policy*. Lanham, MD: University Press of America, 1993.

———, ed. *Refugee Aid and Development: Theory and Practice*. Westport, CT: Greenwood Press, 1993.

Grahl-Madsen, Atle. *The Status of Refugees in International Law: Refugee Character*. Vol. I. Leyden, Netherlands: A. W. Sijthoff, 1966.

———. *The Status of Refugees in International Law: Asylum, Entry and Sojourn*. Vol. II. Leyden, Netherlands: A. W. Sijthoff, 1972.

Guest, Iain. *The UNHCR at 40: Refugee Protection at the Crossroads*. New York: Lawyers Committee for Human Rights, 1991.

Hathaway, James. *The Law of Refugee Status*. Toronto, ON: Butterworths, 1991.

Helton, Arthur. *The Price of Indifference: Refugees and Humanitarian Action in the New Century*. Oxford: Oxford University Press, 2002.

Holborn, Louise. *The International Refugee Organization: A Specialized Agency of the United Nations: Its History and Work, 1946–1952*. London: Oxford University Press, 1956.

———. *Refugees, A Problem of Our Time: The Work of the United Nations High Commissioner for Refugees, 1952–1972*. 2 vols. Metuchen, NJ: Scarecrow Press, 1975.

Jones, Mervyn. *In Famine's Shadow: A Private War on Hunger*. Boston: Beacon Press, 1965.

Keller, Stephen. *Uprooting and Social Change: The Role of Refugees in Development*. Delhi, India: Manohar Book Service, 1975.

Kent, Randolph. *Anatomy of Disaster Relief: The International Network in Action*. London: Pinter, 1987.

Loescher, Gil. *Beyond Charity: International Cooperation and the Global Refugee Crisis*. Oxford: Oxford University Press, 1993.

———. *The UNHCR and World Politics: A Perilous Path*. Oxford: Oxford University Press, 2001.

Miserez, Diana, ed. *Refugees—The Trauma of Exile: The Humanitarian Role of Red Cross and Red Crescent*. Dordrecht, Netherlands: Martinus Nijhoff, 1988.

Ogata, Sadako. *The Turbulent Decade: Confronting the Refugee Crisis of the 1990s*. New York: W. W. Norton, 2005.

Plender, Richard, ed. *International Migration Law*. 2nd ed. Dordrecht, Netherlands: Martinus Nijhoff, 1988.

Smyser, William R. *Refugees: Extended Exile*. New York: Praeger, 1987.

Steiner, Nicholas, et al. *Problems of Protection: The UNHCR, Refugees and Human Rights*. London: Routledge, 2003.

Tanner, Fred, and Stephen Jon Stedman, eds. *Refugee Manipulation: War, Politics, and the Abuse of Human Suffering*. Washington, DC: Brookings Institution Press, 2003.

UNHCR. *The State of the World's Refugees 1993: The Challenge of Protection*. Geneva: UNHCR, 1993.

Vernant, Jacques. *The Refugee in the Post-War World*. London: George Allen and Unwin, 1953.

Zarjevski, Yéfime. *A Future Preserved: International Assistance to Refugees*. Oxford: Pergamon Press, 1988.

Zolberg, Aristide, Astri Suhrke, and Sergio Aguayo. *Escape from Violence: Conflict and the Refugee Crisis of the Developing World*. New York: Oxford University Press, 1989.

XI. HUMANITARIAN LAW AND POLICIES IN ARMED CONFLICTS

Anderson, Sean K., and Stephen Sloan. *Historical Dictionary of Terrorism*. Lanham, MD: Scarecrow Press, 2002.

Bassiouni, Cherif. "Nuremberg Forty Years After: An Introduction." *Case Western Reserve Journal of International Law* 18, no. 2 (Spring 1986): 261–66.

Baxter, R. "Human Rights and Humanitarian Law: Confluence or Conflict." *Australian Yearbook of International Law* 9 (1985): 94–105.

Boczek, Boleslaw A. *Historical Dictionary of International Tribunals*. Lanham, MD: Scarecrow Press, 1994.

Cahill, Kevin M., ed. *A Framework for Survival: Health, Human Rights, and Humanitarian Assistance in Conflicts and Disasters*. New York: Basic Books and Council on Foreign Relations, 1993.

Chesterton, Simon. *Intervention and International Law*. Oxford: Oxford University Press, 2003.

Chopra, Jarat, and Thomas G. Weiss. "Sovereignty Is No Longer Sacrosanct: Codifying Humanitarian Intervention." *Ethics and International Affairs* 6 (1992): 95–117.

Dörmann, Knut. *Elements of War Crimes under the Rome Statute of the International Criminal Court: Sources and Commentary*. Cambridge: Cambridge University Press, 2003.

Doswald-Beck, Louise, ed. *Blinding Weapons*. Geneva: International Committee for the Red Cross, 1993.

Doswald-Beck, Louise, and Jean-Marie Henckaerts, eds. *Customary International Humanitarian Law*. Cambridge: Cambridge University Press, 2005.

Erlich, Thomas, and Mary Ellen O'Connell. *International Law and the Use of Force*. Boston: Little, Brown, 1993.

Friedlander, Robert A. "The Enforcement of International Criminal Law: Fact or Fiction." *Case Western Reserve Journal of International Law* 17, no. 1 (Winter 1985): 79–90.

Hannum, Hurst. "International Law and Cambodian Genocide: The Sounds of Silence." *Human Rights Quarterly* 11, no. 1 (February 1989): 82–138.

Harff, Barbara. "Bosnia and Somalia: Strategic, Legal, and Moral Dimensions of Humanitarian Intervention." *Report from the Institute for Philosophy and Public Policy* (University of Maryland, College Park) 12, no. 3 (Summer/Fall 1992): 1–7.

Henri Dunant Institute. *International Dimensions of Humanitarian Law*. Dordrecht, Netherlands: Martinus Nijhoff and UNESCO, 1988.

Hoffmann, Paul. "Human Rights and Terrorism." *Human Rights Quarterly* 26, no. 4 (November 2004): 932–55.

International Committee of the Red Cross. *Mines: A Perverse Use of Technology*. Geneva: ICRC, 1992.

Jean, François, ed. *Life, Death and Aid: The Médecins Sans Frontières Report on World Crisis Intervention*. London: Routledge, 1993.

Lemkin, Raphaël. *Axis Rule in Occupied Europe*. New York: H. Fertig, 1973, reprinted with permission from the Carnegie Institute for International Peace.

Lifton, Robert J. *The Nazi Doctors: Medical Killing and the Psychology of Genocide*. New York: Basic Books, 1986.

MacAlister-Smith, Peter. *International Humanitarian Assistance: Disaster Relief Organizations in International Law and Organization*. Dordrecht, Netherlands: Martinus Nijhoff, 1985.

Meron, Theodor. *War Crimes Law Comes of Age*. Oxford: Oxford University Press, 1998.

Niarchos, Catherine N. "Women, War and Rape: Challenges Facing the International Tribunal for the Former Yugoslavia." *Human Rights Quarterly* 17, no. 4 (November 1995): 649–90.

Patrnogic, J., and Z. Meriboute. *Terrorism and International Law*. San Remo, Italy: International Institute of Humanitarian Law, 1987.

Paust, Jordan J. "Aggression against Authority: The Crime of Oppression, Politicide and Other Crimes against Human Rights." *Case Western Reserve Journal of International Law* 18, no. 2 (Spring 1986): 283–306.

Provost, René. *International Human Rights and Humanitarian Law*. Cambridge: Cambridge University Press, 2002.

Ratner, Steven R., and Jason S. Abrams. *Accountability for Human Rights Atrocities in International Law: Beyond the Nuremberg Legacy*. Oxford: Clarendon Press, 1997.

Riemer, Neal, ed. *Protection against Genocide: Mission Impossible?* Westport, CT: Praeger, 2000.

Rudolph, Christopher. "Constructing an Atrocities Regime: The Politics of War Crimes Tribunals." *International Organization* 55, no. 3 (Summer 2001): 655–91.

van Sliedregt, E. *The Criminal Responsibility of Individuals for Violations of International Humanitarian Law.* Cambridge: Cambridge University Press, 2003.

Weiss, Thomas G., and Larry Minear, eds. *Humanitarianism across Borders: Sustaining Civilians in Times of War.* Boulder, CO: Lynne Rienner, 1993.

XII. INTERNATIONAL LAW, HUMAN RIGHTS, AND STATE RESPONSIBILITY

Bernhardt, R. "Domestic Jurisdiction of States and International Human Rights Organs." *Human Rights Law Journal* 7 (1986): 205–16.

Boczek, Boleslaw A. *International Law: A Dictionary.* Lanham, MD: Scarecrow Press, 2005.

Brownlie, Ian, ed. *Basic Documents in International Law.* Oxford: Oxford University Press, 1967.

Brownlie, Ian, and Guy Goodwin-Gill, eds. *Basic Documents in Human Rights.* 4th ed. Oxford: Oxford University Press, 2002.

Buergenthal, Thomas. *International Human Rights: In A Nutshell.* 3rd ed. St. Paul, MN: West, 2002.

Crawford, James. *The International Law Commission's Articles on State Responsibility.* Cambridge: Cambridge University Press, 2002.

Eide, Asbjörn, and August Schou. *International Protection of Human Rights.* Stockholm: Alinqvist and Wiksell, 1968.

Ezejiofor, Gaius. *Protection of Human Rights under the Law.* London: Butterworths, 1964.

Hannum, Hurst. *Guide to International Human Rights Practice.* London: Macmillan, 1984.

Jessup, Philip C. "Responsibility of States for Injuries to Individuals." *Columbia Law Review* 46 (1946): 903–28.

Kamminga, Menno T. "Human Rights and the Lomé Conventions." *Netherlands Quarterly of Human Rights* 7 (1989): 28-35.

——. *Inter-State Accountability for Violations of Human Rights.* Philadelphia: University of Pennsylvania Press, 1992.

Lauterpacht, Hersch. "The International Protection of Human Rights." *Recueil des cours de l'Academie de droit international* (1947): 5–105.

Lillich, Richard B. "Forcible Self-Help by States to Protect Human Rights." *Iowa Law Review* 53 (October 1967): 325–51.

——. *The Human Rights of Aliens in Contemporary International Law*. Manchester: Manchester University Press, 1984.

——. *U.S. Ratification of the Human Rights Treaties: With or without Reservations?* Charlottesville: University Press of Virginia, 1981.

McDougal, Myres S., Harold D. Lasswell, and Lung-chu Chen. *Human Rights and World Public Order*. New Haven, CT: Yale, 1980.

Meron, Theodor, ed. *Human Rights and Humanitarian Norms as Customary Law*. New York: Oxford University Press, 1989.

——. *Human Rights in International Law: Legal and Policy Issues*. Oxford: Clarendon Press, 1984.

Moskowitz, Moses. *International Concern with Human Rights*. Dobbs Ferry, NY: Oceana, 1974.

Oraá, Jaime. *Human Rights in States of Emergency in International Law*. Oxford: Clarendon Press, 1992.

Pease, Kelly-Kate, and David P. Forsythe. "Humanitarian Intervention and Contemporary Law." *Austrian Journal of Public and International Law* 45 (1993): 1–20.

——. "Human Rights, Humanitarian Intervention, and World Politics." *Human Rights Quarterly* 15: 2 (May 1993): 290–314.

Robertson, Arthur H. *Human Rights in National and International Law*. Manchester: Manchester University Press, 1968.

——. *Human Rights in the World*. Manchester: Manchester University Press, 1982.

Said, Abdul Aziz. *Human Rights and World Order*. New York: Praeger, 1978.

Schwartz, Bernard. *The Great Rights of Mankind: A History of the American Bill of Rights*. New York: Oxford University Press, 1977.

Skalnes, Tor, and Jan Egeland, eds. *Human Rights in Developing Countries, 1986*. Oslo: Norwegian University Press, 1986.

Shaw, Malcolm. *International Law*. Cambridge: Cambridge University Press, 2003.

Sieghart, Paul. *The International Law of Human Rights*. Oxford: Clarendon Press, 1983.

Sohn, Louis B., and Thomas Buergenthal, eds. *Basic Documents on International Protection of Human Rights*. Indianapolis, IN: Bobbs-Merrill, 1973.

Steiner, Henry, and Philip Alston. *International Human Rights in Context: Law, Politics and Morals*. Oxford: Oxford University Press, 2000.

van Boven, Theodoor D. "Survey of the Positive International Law of Human Rights." In *The International Dimensions of Human Rights*, ed. Karel Vasak. Westport, CT: Greenwood Press, 1982.

von Glahn, Gerhard. *Law among Nations: An Introduction to Public International Law.* New York: Macmillan, 1995.

XIII. MINORITIES AND INDIGENOUS RIGHTS

Anaya, S. James. *Indigenous Peoples in International Law.* 2nd ed. Oxford: Oxford University Press, 2004.

Barsh, Russel L. "Indigenous Peoples: An Emergency Object of International Law." *American Journal of International Law* 80 (1980): 369–85.

———. "Indigenous Peoples and the UN Commission on Human Rights: A Case of the Immovable Object and the Irresistible Force." *Human Rights Quarterly* 18, no. 4 (November 1996): 782–813.

Bennett, Gordon. *Aboriginal Rights in International Law.* London: Royal Anthropological Institute, 1978.

Berger, Thomas R. "Native Rights Movements." *Cultural Survival Quarterly* 11, no. 1 (1987): 13–15.

Bizot, Jack. *The Forgotten Cause: East Timor's Right to Self-Determination.* London: Parliamentary Human Rights Group, 1988.

Boldt, Menno, and J. Anthony Long, eds. *The Quest for Justice: Aboriginal Peoples and Aboriginal Rights.* Toronto, ON: University of Toronto Press, 1985.

Claude, Inis L. *National Minorities: An International Problem.* Cambridge, MA: Harvard University Press, 1955.

Crawford, James, ed. *The Rights of Peoples.* New York: Oxford University Press, 1990.

Davis, Shelton. *Land Rights and Indigenous Peoples: The Role of the Inter-American Commission on Human Rights.* Cambridge, MA: Cultural Survival, 1988.

Fein, Helen. "Accounting for Genocide after 1945: Theories and Some Findings." *International Journal on Group Rights* 1 (1993): 79–106.

Field, Alison. "The Indigenous Peoples' Network." *Cultural Survival Quarterly* 8, no. 4 (1984): 66–67.

Gilbert, Geoff. "The Burgeoning Minority Rights Jurisprudence of the European Court of Human Rights." *Human Rights Quarterly* 24, no. 3 (August 2002): 736–80.

Gurr, Ted Robert. *Minorities at Risk: A Global View of Ethnopolitical Conflicts.* Washington, DC: U.S. Institute of Peace, 1993.

Gurr, Ted Robert, and J. T. Scarritt. "Minorities at Risk: A Global Survey." *Human Rights Quarterly* 11 (1989): 375–405.

Heraclides, Alexis. *The Self-Determination of Minorities in International Politics.* London: Frank Cass, 1991.

Human Rights Watch. *Playing the "Communal Card": Communal Violence and Human Rights*. New York: Human Rights Watch, 1995.

Independent Commission on International Humanitarian Affairs. *Indigenous Peoples: A Global Quest for Justice*. London: Zed, 1987.

Kiss, Alexandre. "The Peoples' Right to Self-Determination." *Human Rights Law Journal* 7, nos. 2–4 (1986): 165–75.

Lerner, Natan. *Group Rights and Discrimination in International Law*. Dordrecht, Netherlands: Martinus Nijhoff, 1991.

Minority Rights Group. *World Directory of Minorities*. Chicago: St. James Press, 1990.

Musgrave, Thomas D. *Self-Determination and National Minorities*. Oxford: Oxford University Press, 2000.

Watson, Michael, ed. *Contemporary Minority Nationalism*. New York: Routledge, 1990.

Wilmer, Franke. *The Indigenous Voice in World Politics: Since Time Immemorial*. Newbury Park, CA: Sage, 1993.

Wright, Jane. The OSCE and the Protection of Minority Rights." *Human Rights Quarterly* 18, no. 1 (February 1996): 190–205.

XIV. UNITED NATIONS AND HUMAN RIGHTS

Bailey, Sidney D. *The UN Security Council and Human Rights*. New York: St. Martin's 1994.

Borefijn, Ineke. "Towards a Strong System of Supervision: The Human Rights Committee's Role in Reforming the Reporting Procedure under Article 40 of the Covenant on Civil and Political Rights." *Human Rights Quarterly* 17, no. 4 (November 1995): 766–93.

Bossuyt, M. "The Development of Special Procedures of the United Nations Commission on Human Rights." *Human Rights Law Journal* 6 (1985): 179–210.

Burgers, J. Herman, and Hans Danelius. *The UN Convention against Torture*. Dordrecht, Netherlands: Martinus Nijhoff, 1988.

Esman, Milton J., and Shibley Telhami, eds. *International Organizations and Ethnic Conflict*. Ithaca, NY: Cornell University Press, 1995.

Fischer, Dana D. "Reporting under the Covenant on Civil and Political Rights: The First Five Years of the Human Rights Committee." *American Journal of International Law* 76 (January 1982): 142–53.

Green, James T. *The United Nations and Human Rights*. Washington, DC: Brookings Institution, 1956.

Heffernan, Liz. "A Comparative View of Individual Petition Procedures under the European Convention on Human Rights and the International Covenant on Civil and Political Rights." *Human Rights Quarterly* 19, no. 1 (February 1997): 78–112.

Howland, Todd. "Mirage, Magic or Mixed Bag? The United Nations High Commissioner for Human Rights' Field Operation in Rwanda." *Human Rights Quarterly* 21, no. 1 (February 1999): 1–55.

Humphrey, John P. *Human Rights and the United Nations: A Great Adventure.* Dobbs Ferry, NY: Transnational, 1984.

LeBlanc, Lawrence J. *The Convention on the Rights of the Child: United Nations Lawmaking on Human Rights.* Lincoln: University of Nebraska Press, 1995.

McGoldrick, Dominic. *The Human Rights Committee: Its Role in the Development of the International Covenant on Civil and Political Rights.* Oxford: Clarendon, 1991.

Mégret, Frédéric, and Florian Hoffmann. "The UN as a Human Rights Violator? Some Reflections on the United Nations Changing Human Rights Responsibilities." *Human Rights Quarterly* 25, no. 2 (May 2003): 314–42.

Rodley, Nigel S. "UN Action Procedures against 'Disappearances,' Summary or Arbitrary Executions, and Torture." *Human Rights Quarterly* 8, no. 4 (November 1986): 700–730.

———. "The United Nations Human Rights Treaty Bodies and Special Procedures of the Commission on Human Rights—Complementarity or Competition?" *Human Rights Quarterly* 25, no. 3 (November 2003): 882–908.

Tolley, Howard, Jr. *The United Nations Commission on Human Rights.* Boulder, CO: Westview Press, 1987.

Weiss, Thomas G., David P. Forsythe, and Roger A. Coate. *United Nations and Changing World Politics.* Boulder, CO: Westview Press, 2004.

Zuijdwijk, Ton J. *Petitioning the United Nations: A Study in Human Rights.* Aldershot, Hampshire, UK: Gower, 1982.

XV. NONGOVERNMENTAL ORGANIZATIONS AND HUMAN RIGHTS

Blaser, Arthur W. "How to Advance Human Rights without Really Trying: An Analysis of Nongovernmental Tribunals." *Human Rights Quarterly* 14 (August 1992): 339.

Cernea, Michael M. *Nongovernmental Organizations and Local Development.* Washington, DC: World Bank, 1988.

Drzemczewski, Andrew. "The Role of NGOs in Human Rights Matters in the Council of Europe." *Human Rights Law Journal* 8, nos. 2–4 (1987): 273–82.

Ferris, Elizabeth. *Beyond Borders: Refugees, Migrants and Human Rights in the Post–Cold War Era.* Geneva: World Council of Churches, 1993.

Forsythe, David P. "Human Rights and the International Committee of the Red Cross." *Human Rights Quarterly* 12 (1990): 265–89.

Korey, William. *NGO's and the Universal Declaration of Human Rights: 'A Curious Grapevine.'* New York: Palgrave Macmillan, 2001.

Livezey, Lowell W. *Nongovernmental Organizations and the Ideas of Human Rights.* World Order Studies Program Occasional Paper No. 15. Princeton, NJ: Center for International Studies, 1988.

Martens, Kerstin. "An Appraisal of Amnesty International's Work at the United Nations: Established Areas of Activities and Shifting Priorities since the 1990s." *Human Rights Quarterly* 26, no. 4 (November 2004): 1050–70.

Miserez, Diana, ed. *Refugees—The Trauma of Exile: The Humanitarian Role of Red Cross and Red Crescent.* Dordrecht, Netherlands: Martinus Nijhoff, 1988.

Nichols, J. Bruce. *The Uneasy Alliance: Religion, Refugee Work, and U.S. Foreign Policy.* Oxford: Oxford University Press, 1988.

Otto, Diane. "Nongovernmental Organizations in the United Nations System: The Emerging Role of International Civil Society." *Human Rights Quarterly* 18, no. 1 (February 1996): 107–41.

Smith, Jackie, Ron Pagnucco, and George A. Lopez. "Globalizing Human Rights: The World of Transnational Human Rights NGOs in the 1990s." *Human Rights Quarterly* 20, no. 2 (May 1998): 397–412.

Staples, Lee. *Roots to Power: A Manual for Grassroots Organizing.* New York: Praeger, 1984.

van Boven, Theo. "The Role of Nongovernmental Organizations in International Human Rights Standard-Setting: A Prerequisite of Democracy." *California Western International Law Journal* 20, no. 2 (1989): 207.

Welch, Claude Emerson. "Mobilizing Morality: The World Council of Churches and Its Programme to Combat Racism, 1969–1994." *Human Rights Quarterly* 23, no. 4 (November 2001): 863–910.

——. *NGOs and Human Rights: Promise and Performance.* Philadelphia: University of Pennsylvania Press, 2000.

Weiss, Thomas, and Leon Gordenker, eds. *NGOs, the UN, and Global Human Rights.* Boulder, CO: Lynne Rienner, 1996.

Wiseberg, Laurie S. "Protecting Human Rights Activists and NGOs." *Human Rights Quarterly* 13 (1991): 525–44.

XVI. REGIONAL HUMAN RIGHTS ISSUES

A. Africa

Abdullahi, Ahmed an-Na'im, and Francis Deng, eds. *Human Rights in Africa: Cross-Cultural Perspectives.* Washington, DC: Brookings 1990.

Adepoju, Aderanti. "Illegals and Expulsion in Africa: The Nigerian Experience." *International Migration Review* 18, no. 3 (Fall 1984): 426–36.

Asante, S. K. B. "Nation Building and Human Rights in Emergent Africa." *Cornell International Law Journal* 2 (Spring 1969): 72–107.

Bindman, Geoffrey, ed. *South Africa: Human Rights and the Rule of Law.* London: Pinter for the International Commission of Jurists, 1989.

Cobbah, Josiah A. M. "African Values and the Human Rights Debate: An African Perspective." *Human Rights Quarterly* 9 (August 1987): 309–31.

Cohen, Ronald, Goran Hyden, and Winston P. Nagan, eds. *Human Rights and Governance in Africa.* Gainesville: University Press of Florida, 1993.

Conboy, Kevin. "Detention without Trial in Kenya." *Georgia Journal of International and Comparative Law* 8, no. 2 (1987): 441–61.

DeMars, William. "Tactics of Protection: International Human Rights Organizations in the Ethiopian Conflict, 1980–1986." In *Africa, Human Rights, and the Global System: The Political Economy of Human Rights in a Changing World,* ed. Eileen McCarthy-Arnolds, David R. Penna, and Debra Joy Cruz Sobrepeña, 81–106. Westport, CT: Greenwood, 1994.

Dodge, Cole P., and Magne Raundalen. *Reaching Children in War: Sudan, Uganda and Mozambique.* Uppsala, Sweden: Scandinavian Institute of African Studies and Sigma Forlag, 1991.

Eades, Lindsay Michie. *The End of Apartheid in South Africa.* Westport, CT: Greenwood Press, 1999.

Graybill, Lyn S. *Truth and Reconciliation in South Africa: Miracle or Model?* Boulder, CO: Lynne Rienner, 2002.

Howard, Rhoda. "Evaluating Human Rights in Africa: Some Problems of Implicit Comparisons." *Human Rights Quarterly* 6 (May 1984): 160–79.

———. *Human Rights in Commonwealth Africa.* Totowa, NJ: Rowman and Littlefield, 1986.

Human Rights Watch/Africa. *Easy Prey: Child Soldiers in Liberia.* New York: Human Rights Watch, 1994.

Khushalani, Yougindra. "Human Rights in Asia and Africa." *Human Rights Law Journal* 4 (1983): 403–42.

Magnarella, Paul. "Promoting Peace, Human Rights and National Security: Focus on Sub-Saharan Africa." *Human Peace* 8, no. 2 (Summer 1990): 3–8.

Makinda, Samuel M. *Seeking Peace from Chaos: Humanitarian Intervention in Somalia.* Boulder, CO: Lynne Rienner, 1993.

Mays, Terry M., and Mark W. DeLancey, *Historical Dictionary of International Organizations in Sub-Saharan Africa.* Lanham, MD: Scarecrow Press, 2002.

McCarthy-Arnolds, Eileen, David R. Penna, and Debra Joy Cruz Sobrepeña, eds. *Africa, Human Rights and the Global System: The Political Economy of Human Rights in a Changing World.* Westport, CT: Greenwood Press, 1994.

Mercer, John. *Slavery in Mauritania Today.* Edinburgh, Scotland: Human Rights Group, 1982.

Minear, Larry. *Humanitarianism under Siege: A Critical Review of Operation Lifeline Sudan.* Washington, DC: Bread for the World Institute on Hunger and Development, 1991.

Motala, Ziyad. "Human Rights in Africa: A Cultural, Ideological and Legal Examination." *Hastings International and Comparative Law Review* 12 (1989): 801–17.

Murray, Rachel. *Human Rights in Africa: From the OAU to the African Union.* Cambridge: Cambridge University Press, 2004.

Mutua, Makau wa. "The African Human Rights Court: A Two-Legged Stool?" *Human Rights Quarterly* 21, no. 2 (May 1999): 342–63.

Odinkalu, Anselm Chidi, and Camilla Christensen. "The African Commission on Human and Peoples' Rights: The Development of its Non-State Communication Procedures." *Human Rights Quarterly* 20, no. 2 (May 1998): 235–80.

Ojo, Olusola, and Amadou Sessay. "The O.A.U. and Human Rights: Prospects for the 1980s and Beyond." *Human Rights Quarterly* 8 (February 1986): 89–103.

Peter, Chris Maina. *Human Rights in Africa: A Comparative Study of the African Human and Peoples' Rights Charter and the New Tanzanian Bill of Rights.* Westport, CT: Greenwood Press, 1990.

Rotberg, Robert, and Dennis Thompson, eds. *Truth v. Justice.* Princeton, NJ: Princeton University Press, 2000.

Wai, Dunstan. "Human Rights in Sub-Saharan Africa." In *Human Rights: Cultural and Ideological Perspectives*, ed. Adamantia Pollis and Peter Schwab. New York: Praeger, 1979.

Welch, Claude E., and Ronald I. Meltzer. *Human Rights and Development in Africa.* Albany: State University of New York Press, 1984.

Zartman, I. William. *Ripe for Resolution: Conflict and Intervention in Africa.* New Haven, CT: Yale University Press, 1989.

B. Asia

Adamec, Ludwig W. *Historical Dictionary of Afghan Wars, Revolutions and Insurgencies.* Lanham, MD: Scarecrow Press, 2005.

Amnesty International. *India: A Review of Human Rights Violations.* London: Amnesty International, 1988.

Anderson, Michael R., and Sumit Guha, eds. *Changing Concepts of Rights and Justice in South Asia.* Oxford: Oxford University Press, 2000.

Asia Watch. *Human Rights in Tibet: An Asia Watch Report.* Washington, DC: Asia Watch, 1988.

——. *A Stern, Steady Crackdown: Legal Process and Human Rights in South Korea.* New York: 1987.

Bauer, Joanne A., and Daniel A. Bell, eds. *The East Asian Challenge for Human Rights.* Cambridge: Cambridge University Press, 1999.

Bizot, Jack. *The Forgotten Cause: East Timor's Right to Self-Determination.* London: Parliamentary Human Rights Group, 1988.

Foot, Rosemary. *Rights beyond Borders: The Global Community and the Struggle over Human Rights in China.* Oxford: Oxford University Press, 2000.

Human Rights Watch/Asia. *Cambodia at War.* New York: Human Rights Watch, 1993.

——. *Prison Conditions in Japan.* New York: Human Rights Watch, 1995.

Khushalani, Yougindra. "Human Rights in Asia and Africa." *Human Rights Law Journal* 4 (1983): 403–42.

Koshy, Ninan. "The Erosion of the Rule of Law in Asia." *Human Rights Forum* (March 1988): 1–8.

Luce, D., and R. Rumpf. *Martial Law in Taiwan.* Washington, DC: Asia Resource Center and Formosan Association for Human Rights, 1985.

Mitra, Kana. "Human Rights in Hinduism." *Journal of Ecumenical Studies* 19 (Summer 1982): 77–84.

Nirmal, C. J. *Human Rights in India: Historical, Social, and Political Perspectives.* Oxford: Oxford University Press, 2000.

Regional Council on Human Rights in Asia. *The Law and Practice of Preventive Detention in the ASEAN Region.* Manila, Philippines: Human Rights in Asia, 1988.

Shawcross, William. *The Quality of Mercy: Cambodia, Holocaust, and Modern Conscience.* New York: Simon and Schuster, 1984.

Taswell, Ruth, ed. *Southeast Asian Tribal Groups and Ethnic Minorities.* Cambridge, MA: Cultural Survival, 1987.

U.S. Committee for Refugees. *From Isolation to Exile: Refugees from the Chittagong Hill Tracts of Bangladesh.* Washington, DC: U.S. Committee for Refugees, 1988.

Vije, Mayan. *Where Serfdom Thrives: The Plantation Tamils of Sri Lanka.* Madras, India: Tamil Information and Research Unit, 1987.

Whitfield, Susan, ed. *After the Event: Human Rights and Their Future in China.* London: Wellsweep, 1993.

C. Europe

Amnesty International. *Bulgaria: Continuing Human Rights Abuses against Ethnic Turks.* London: 1987.

Bloed, Arie, and Pieter Van Dijk. *Essays on Human Rights in the Helsinki Process.* Dordrecht, Netherlands: Martinus Nijhoff, 1985.

Buergenthal, Thomas. "The Effect of the European Convention on Human Rights on the Internal Law of the Member States." *International and Comparative Law Quarterly* no. 11 (1965): 79.

Buergenthal, Thomas, ed. *Human Rights, International Law and the Helsinki Accord.* Montclair, NJ: Allenheld, Osman, 1977.

Dinan, Desmond. *Historical Dictionary of the European Community.* Lanham, MD: Scarecrow Press, 1993.

Drzemczewski, Andrew. "The Role of NGOs in Human Rights Matters in the Council of Europe." *Human Rights Law Journal* 8, nos. 2–4 (1987): 273–82.

Fawcett, James E. *The Application of the European Convention on Human Rights.* Oxford: Clarendon, 1969.

Forsythe, David P., ed. *Human Rights in the New Europe: Problems and Progress.* Lincoln: University of Nebraska Press, 1994.

Gearty, Conor A. *Principles of Human Rights Adjudication.* Oxford: Oxford University Press, 2004.

Gilbert, Geoff. "The Council of Europe and Minority Rights." *Human Rights Quarterly* 18, no. 1 (February 1996): 160–89.

Gubin, Sandra L. "Between Regimes and Realism— Transnational Agenda Setting: Soviet Compliance with CSCE Human Rights Norms." *Human Rights Quarterly* 17, no. 2 (May 1995): 278–302.

Heraclides, Alexis. *The Helsinki-II and Its Aftermath.* New York: Pinter, 1993.

McGoldrick, Dominic. "Human Rights Developments in the Helsinki Process." *International and Comparative Law Quarterly* 39, no. 3 (October 1990): 923–40.

Moravcsik, Andrew. "The Origin of Human Rights Regimes: Democratic Delegation in Postwar Europe." *International Organization* 54, no. 2 (Spring 2000): 217–52.

Morrisson, Clovis C. *The Developing European Law of Human Rights.* Leyden, Netherlands: A. W. Sijthoff, 1967.

Mowgee, Tasneem. "The European Community Humanitarian Office, 1992–1999 and Beyond." *Disasters* 22, no. 3 (September 1998): 250–67.

Muggeridge, Malcolm. *Something Beautiful for God.* San Francisco: Harper and Row, 1977.

Nowlin, Christopher J. "The Protection of Morals under the European Convention for the Protection of Human Rights and Fundamental Freedoms." *Human Rights Quarterly* 24, no. 1 (February 2002): 264–86.

Power, Jonathan, with Anna Hardman. *Western Europe's Migrant Workers.* Minority Rights Group Report no. 28. London: Minority Rights Group, 1984.

Robertson, Arthur H. *Human Rights in Europe.* Manchester: Manchester University Press, 1977.

Robertson, Arthur H., and J. G. Merrills. *Human Rights: A Study of the European Convention on Human Rights.* Manchester: Manchester University Press, 1993.

Sieghart, Paul, ed. *Human Rights in the United Kingdom*. London: Human Rights Network, 1988.

Solomos, John, and John Wrench, eds. *Racism and Migration in Contemporary Europe*. Oxford: Berg, 1993.

Spink, Kathryn. *Mother Teresa: A Complete Authorized Biography*. San Francisco: Harper San Francisco, 1997.

Stark, Christian. "Europe's Fundamental Rights in Their Newest Garb." *Human Rights Law Journal* 3 (1982): 103–40.

Thomas, Daniel. *The Helsinki Effect: International Norms, Human Rights, and the Demise of Communism*. Princeton, NJ: Princeton University Press, 2001.

Williams, Andrew. *EU Human Rights Policies: A Study in Irony*. Oxford: Oxford University Press, 2004.

Wright, Jane. The OSCE and the Protection of Minority Rights." *Human Rights Quarterly* 18, no. 1 (February 1996): 190–205.

D. Latin America

Americas Watch Committee. *Human Rights in Panama*. New York: 1988.

Amnesty International. *Haiti: Deaths in Detention, Torture, and Inhuman Prison Conditions*. London: 1987.

——. *Human Rights Violations in Paraguay*. London: 1985.

Ball, M. M. "Issue for the Americas: Non-Intervention v. Human Rights and the Preservation of Democratic Institutions." *International Organization* 15 (1961): 21–37.

Cabranes, J. A. "The Protection of Human Rights by the Organization of American States." *American Journal of International Law* 62 (1968): 889–908.

Colonnese, Louis M., ed. *Human Rights and the Liberation of Man in the America's*. Notre Dame, IN: University of Notre Dame Press, 1970.

Crahan, Margaret E., ed. *Human Rights and Basic Needs in the Americas*. Washington, DC: Georgetown University Press, 1982.

Farer, Thomas J. "Intervention and Human Rights: The Latin American Context." *California Western International Law Journal* 12 (1982): 503–7.

——. "The Rise of the Inter-American Human Rights Regime: No Longer a Unicorn, Not Yet an Ox." *Human Rights Quarterly* 19, no. 3 (August 1997): 510–46.

Garro, A. M., and H. Dahl. "Legal Accountability for Human Rights Violations in Argentina: One Step Forward and Two Steps Back." *Human Rights Law Journal* 8, nos. 2–4 (1987): 283–44.

Harris, David J., and Stephen Livingstone, eds. *The Inter-American System of Human Rights* Oxford: Oxford University Press, 1998.

Human Rights Watch/Americas. *Generation under Fire: Children and Violence in Colombia*. New York: Human Rights Watch, 1994.

Human Rights Watch/Americas. *Honduras, the Facts Speak for Themselves: The Preliminary Report of the National Commissioner for the Protection of Human Rights in Honduras.* New York: Human Rights Watch, 1994.

Human Rights Watch/Americas and the Physician's for Human Rights. *Mexico: Waiting for Justice in Chiapas.* New York: Human Rights Watch, 1994.

LaFeber, Walter. *Inevitable Revolutions: The United States in Central America.* New York: W. W. Norton, 1993.

Lutz, Ellen, and Kathryn Sikkink. "International Human Rights Law and Practice in Latin America," *International Organization* 54, no. 3 (Summer 2000): 633–59.

Manz, Beatriz. *Refugees of a Hidden War: The Aftermath of Counterinsurgency in Guatemala.* Albany: State University of New York Press, 1986.

Moir, Lindsay. "Decommissioned? International Humanitarian Law and the Inter-American Rights System." *Human Rights Quarterly* 25, no. 1 (February 2003): 182–212.

Ortiz, R. D. *Indians of the Americas: Human Rights and Self-Determination.* London: Zed Books, 1984.

———. *The Miskito Indians of Nicaragua.* London: Minority Rights Group, 1988.

Pion-Berlin, David. *The Ideology of State Terror: Economic Doctrine and Political Repression in Argentina and Peru.* Boulder, CO: Lynne Rienner, 1989.

Quiroga, Cecelia Medina. *The Battle of Human Rights: Gross, Systematic Violations and the Inter-American System.* Dordrecht, Netherlands: Martinus Nijhoff, 1988.

Seider, Rachel. *Multiculturalism in Latin America: Indigenous Rights, Diversity and Democracy.* New York: Palgrave Macmillan, 2002.

Schreiber, Anna. *The Inter-American Commission on Human Rights.* Leyden, Netherlands: A. W. Sijthoff, 1970.

Yundt, Keith W. *Latin American States and Political Refugees.* New York: Praeger, 1989.

E. Middle East

Buehrig, Edward. *The UN and the Palestinian Refugees: A Study in Non-Territorial Administration.* Bloomington: Indiana University Press, 1971.

Human Rights Watch/Middle East. *Iraq's Crime of Genocide: The Anfal Campaign against the Kurds.* New York: Human Rights Watch, 1994.

Ishaque, Khalid M. "Human Rights in Islamic Law." *Review of the International Commission of Jurists* 12 (June 1974): 30–39.

Makiya, Kanan. "The Anfal: Uncovering an Iraqi Campaign to Exterminate the Kurds." *Harper's Magazine* 284, no. 1704 (May 1992): 53–61.

Mawdudi, Abul A'la. *Human Rights in Islam.* Leicester, England: Islamic Foundation, 1976.

Middle East Watch. *Human Rights in Iraq.* New Haven, CT: Yale University Press, 1990.

Ungor, Beraet Z. "Women in the Middle East and North Africa and Universal Suffrage." *Annals* 375 (January 1968): 72–81.

United Nations Department of Public Information. *For the Rights of the Palestinians: The Work of the Committee on the Exercise of the Inalienable Rights of the Palestinian People.* New York: United Nations, 1992.

XVII. REFERENCE WORKS ON INTERNATIONAL ORGANIZATIONS AND HUMAN RIGHTS

Center for Human Rights. *United Nations Reference Guide in the Field of Human Rights.* New York: Author, 1993.

Everyman's United Nations. New York: United Nations, various editions.

Everyone's United Nations. New York: United Nations, 1986.

Finley, Blanche. *The Structure of the United Nations General Assembly: An Organizational Approach to Its Work, 1974–1980s.* 2 vols. White Plains, NY: UNIPUB/Kraus International, 1988.

Gibson, John S. *Dictionary of International Human Rights Law.* Lanham, MD: Scarecrow Press, 1996.

Greenfield, Stanley R., ed. *Who's Who in the United Nations and Related Agencies.* 2nd ed. Detroit, MI: Omnigraphics, 1992.

Hovet, Thomas Jr., Erika Hovet, and Waldo Chamberlain. *Chronology and Factbook of the United Nations.* Dobbs Ferry, NY: Oceana, 1979.

Hunt, Kimberley N., ed. *Encyclopedia of Associations: International Organizations.* 39th ed. Detroit, MI: Gale Group, 2002.

Lawson, Edward, and Mary Lou Bertucci. *Encyclopedia of Human Rights.* New York: Taylor and Francis, 1996.

Matsuura, Kumiko, Joachim Müller, and Karl Sauvant, eds. *Annual Review of United Nations Affairs.* 2 vols. Dobbs Ferry, NY: Oceana, 1993.

———. *Chronology and Factbook of the United Nations.* Dobbs Ferry, NY: Oceana, 1992.

Merritt, John G. *Historical Dictionary of the Salvation Army.* Lanham, MD: Scarecrow Press, 2006.

Osmañczyk, Edmund J. *Encyclopedia of the United Nations and International Agreements.* New York: Taylor and Francis, 1990.

Schiavone, Giuseppe. *International Organizations: A Dictionary and Directory.* 3rd ed. New York: Palgrave Macmillan, 1993.

The Europa Directory of International Organizations. 7th ed. New York: Taylor and Francis, 2005.

Union of International Associations. *Yearbook of International Organizations.* 36th ed. 3 vols. Munich: K. G. Saur, 1999.

United Nations Yearbooks. Vols. 1–48. New York: United Nations, 1946–1994. Annual publication.

van Ginnekan, A. H. M. *Historical Dictionary of the League of Nations.* Lanham, MD: Scarecrow Press, 2006.

XVIII. OTHER SOURCES

Abraham, Henry J., and Barbara A. Perry. *Freedom and the Court.* New York: Oxford University Press, 2003.

Aldrige, Alfred O. *Man of Reason: The Life of Thomas Paine.* Philadelphia: Lippincott, 1959.

Aristotle. *Nicomachean Ethics.* Oxford: Oxford University Press, 1992.

Aristotle. *The Politics.* Trans. Lord Carnes. Chicago: Chicago University Press, 1984.

Augustine. *Commentary on the Sermon on the Mount.* In *Nicene and Post-Nicene Fathers.* Vol. 6. First Series. Ed. Phillip Schaff, 1 63. Peabody, MA: Hendrickson, 1995.

Augustine. *The Political Writings.* Comp. Henry Paolucci. Washington, DC: Regnery, 1996.

Babyonysher, Alexander, ed. *On Sakharov.* New York: Knopf, 1982.

Bacon, Margaret Hope. *Valiant Friend: The Life of Lucretia Mott.* New York: Walker, 1980.

Bailyn, Bernard. *The Ideological Origins of the American Revolution.* Cambridge, MA: Belknap Press of Harvard University Press, 1967.

Barry, Kathleen. *Susan B. Anthony: A Biography of a Singular Feminist.* New York: New York University Press, 1988.

Battle, Michael. *Reconciliation: The Ubuntu Theology of Desmond Tutu.* Cleveland, OH: Pilgrim Press, 1997.

Becker, Carl. *The Declaration of Independence.* New York: Harcourt Brace and Co., 1922.

Branch, Taylor. *Parting the Waters.* New York: Simon and Schuster, 1988.

Brockman, James R. *The Word Remains: A Life of Oscar Romero.* Maryknoll, NY: Orbis Books, 1982.

Budziszewski, J. *What We Can't Not Know.* Dallas, TX: Spence, 2003.

Clinton, Catherine. *Harriet Tubman: The Road to Freedom.* New York: Little, Brown, 2004.

Cromwell, Otelia. *Lucretia Mott.* 2nd ed. New York: Russell and Russell, 1971.

Dalton, Dennis. *Mahatma Gandhi: Nonviolent Power in Action.* New York: Columbia University Press, 1993.

Davis, Allen F. *American Heroine: The Life and Legend of Jane Addams.* New York: Oxford University, 1973.

Dorr, Rheta Childe. *Susan B. Anthony.* New York: Frederick A. Stokes, 1928.

du Boulay, Shirley. *Tutu: Voice of the Voiceless.* Grand Rapids, MI: Eerdman's, 1988.

Eringer, Robert. *Strike for Freedom! The Story of Lech Walesa and Polish Solidarity.* New York: Dodd, Mead, 1982.

Fatton, Robert, Jr. *Black Consciousness in South Africa: The Dialectics of Ideological Resistance to White Supremacy.* New York: State University of New York Press, 1986.

Frederick, Howard H. *Global Communication and International Relations.* Belmont, CA: Wadsworth, 1993.

Fruchtman, Jack. *Thomas Paine: Apostle of Freedom.* New York: Four Walls, Eight Windows, 1994.

Garrow, David J. *Bearing the Cross.* New York: W. Morrow, 1986.

Green, Martin. *Gandhi: Voice of a New Age Revolution.* New York: Continuum, 1993.

Griffith, Elisabeth. *In Her Own Right: The Life of Elizabeth Cady Stanton.* New York: Oxford University Press, 1984.

Hart, Ellen. *Man Born to Live.* London: Gollancz, 1953.

Hatch, Alden. *A Man Named John.* New York: Hawthorn Books, 1963.

Hirsch, John, and Robert Oakley. *Operation Restore Hope.* Washington, DC: U.S. Institute for Peace, 1995.

Hittinger, Russell. *The First Grace: Rediscovering the Natural Law in a Post-Christian World.* Wilmington, DE: ISI Books, 2003.

Hobbes, Thomas. *The Leviathan.* New York: Penguin, 1982.

Hoyer, Liv Nansen. *Nansen: A Family Portrait by His Daughter.* London: Longmans, Green, 1957.

Humez, Jean. *Harriet Tubman: The Life and the Life Stories.* Madison: University of Wisconsin Press, 2003.

King, Martin Luther. *Strength to Love.* New York: Harper and Row, 1963.

———. *Stride toward Freedom.* New York: Harper and Row, 1958.

———. *Where Do We Go from Here: Chaos or Community?* New York: Harper and Row, 1967.

———. *Why We Can't Wait.* New York: Harper and Row, 1964.

Krasner, Stephen. *Sovereignty: Organized Hypocrisy.* Princeton, NJ: Princeton University Press, 1999.

Lash, Joseph. *Eleanor: The Years Alone.* New York: W. W. Norton, 1972.

————. *Eleanor and Franklin.* New York: W. W. Norton, 1971.

Levine, Daniel. *Jane Addams and the Liberal Tradition.* Madison: State Historical Society of Wisconsin, 1971.

Locke, John. *The Second Treatise on Government.* Amhurst, NY: Prometheus, 1986.

Luthuli, Albert. *Let My People Go.* New York: Harper Collins, 1987.

Lutz, Donald. *The Origin of American Constitutionalism.* Baton Rouge: Louisiana State University Press, 1988.

Maathai, Wangari. *The Canopy of Hope: My Life Campaigning for Africa, Women, and the Environment.* New York: Lantern Books, 2002.

————. *The Green Belt Movement: Sharing the Approach and the Experience.* New York: Lantern Books, 2003.

Mahoney, Daniel J. *Aleksandr Solzhenitsyn: The Ascent from Ideology.* Lanham, MD: Rowman and Littlefield, 2001.

Malone, Dumas. *Jefferson and His Times.* Boston: Little Brown, 1981.

Mandela, Nelson. *Long Walk to Freedom: The Autobiography of Nelson Mandela.* Boston: Little, Brown, 1994.

McFeely, William S. *Frederick Douglass.* New York: W. W. Norton, 1991.

Narasimhan, C. V. *History of the United Nations University: A Personal Perspective.* Tokyo: United Nations University Press, 1994.

Nye, Russel B. *William Lloyd Garrison and the Humanitarian Reformers.* Boston: Little, Brown, 1955.

Paine, Thomas. *Rights of Man.* New York: Prometheus Books, 1987.

Peterson, Merrill D. *Thomas Jefferson and the New Nation.* Oxford: Oxford University Press, 1970.

Pinckaers, Servais. *The Sources of Christian Ethics.* Washington, DC: Catholic University of America Press, 1995.

Plato. *The Republic.* Trans. Allan Bloom. New York: Basic Books, 1991.

Plato. *Five Dialogues: The Euthyphro, Apology and Crito. Meno, Phaedo.* Trans. G. M. A. Grube. Indianapolis, IN: Hackett, 1981.

Reynolds, E. E. *Nansen.* Harmonsworth, Middlesex, England: Penguin Books, 1932.

Romero, Oscar. *Voice of the Voiceless.* Maryknoll, NY: Orbis Books, 1985.

Sampson, Anthony. *Mandela: The Authorized Biography.* New York: Knopf, 1999.

Sandoz, Ellis. *A Government of Laws.* Baton Rouge: Louisiana State University Press, 1990.

Schuman, Michael. *Elie Wiesel: Voice form the Holocaust.* Berkeley Heights, NJ: Enslow, 1994.

Stein, Ellen Norman. *Elie Wiesel: Witness for Life.* New York: KTAU, 1982.

Stewart, James Brewer. *Wendell Phillips: Liberty's Hero.* Baton Rouge: Louisiana State University Press, 1986.

Thomas, D. M. *Alexander Solzhenitsyn: A Century in His Life*. New York: St. Martin's Press, 1998.

Tutu, Desmond. *The Rainbow People of God*. New York: Image, 1996.

Tutu, Naomi. *The Words of Desmond Tutu*. New York: Newmarket Press, 1989.

UN Chronicle, various issues.

Wallace, Aubrey. *Eco Heroes: Twelve Tales of Environmental Victory*. San Francisco: Mercury House, 1993.

Weigel, George. *The Final Revolution*. New York: Oxford University Press, 1992.

———. *Witness to Hope: The Biography of Pope John Paul II*. New York: Harper Collins, 1999.

Weigel, George, and Robert Royal, eds. *Building the Free Society*. Grand Rapids, MI: Eerdmans, 1993.

Williams, George. *The Mind of John Paul II*. New York: Seabury Press, 1981.

Wiwa, Ken. *In the Shadow of a Saint: A Son's Journey to Understand His Father's Legacy*. Hanover, NH: Steerforth, 2001.

Woods, Donald. *Biko*. New York: Henry Holt, 1991.

About the Authors

Robert F. Gorman holds a PhD in political science from the University of Oregon and teaches international relations at Texas State University. He served as a Council on Foreign Relations Fellow in the U.S. Department of State's Bureau for Refugee Programs in 1983–1984. He spent the following year as a visiting scholar at Africare, an American private voluntary organization, and subsequently traveled throughout Southeast Asia doing research on the refugee problem there. He is author of numerous books and articles on refugee affairs, African politics, foreign affairs, and international relations. His most recent books include a second edition of the award-winning *Historical Dictionary on Refugee and Disaster Relief Organizations* (Scarecrow, 2002) and *Great Debates at the United Nations: An Encyclopedia of Key Issues, 1945–2000* (2000).

Edward S. Mihalkanin is associate professor of political science at Texas State University. He holds a PhD in international relations from the American University in Washington, DC. His specialties include international relations, Latin American politics, and international political economy. He is the editor of *American Statesmen* (2005) and numerous articles on topics related to his fields of expertise.